THE
FINAL
CRUCIBLE

ALSO BY LEE BALLENGER

The Outpost War: U.S. Marines in Korea,
Vol. I: 1952

THE
FINAL
CRUCIBLE

U.S. Marines in Korea
Vol. II: 1953

BY LEE BALLENGER

BRASSEY'S
WASHINGTON, D.C.

Library of Congress Cataloging-in-Publication Data

Ballenger, Lee.
    The final crucible : U.S. Marines in Korea, Vol. II, 1953 / Lee Ballenger.
        p. cm.
    Sequel to: The outpost war: U.S. Marines in Korea, Vol. I, 1952
    Includes bibliographical references (p.) and index.
    ISBN 1-57488-333-X
    1. Korean War, 1950–1953—Regimental histories—United States.
    2. United States. Marine Corps. Division, 2st—History   I. Ballenger, Lee.
    Outpost war.   II. Title.

DS919 .B281 2001
951.904'242—dc21

                                                        2001016521

ISBN 1-57488-333-X (alk. paper)

Printed in the United States of America on acid-free paper that meets the American National Standards Institute Z39-48 Standard.

Brassey's, Inc.
22841 Quicksilver Drive
Dulles, Virginia 20166

First Edition

10 9 8 7 6 5 4 3 2 1

This Book is dedicated to the memory of

Maj. Gen. James L. Day,
USMC (Ret.) 1925–1998

The late Maj. Gen. James L. Day,
USMC (Ret.), in 1998. THE DAY FAMILY

From Stripes to Stars, Forty-Three Years a Marine,

Medal of Honor
Distinguished Service Medal
Three Silver Stars
Defense Superior Service medal
Legion of Merit, with Combat "V"
Bronze Star, with Combat "V"
Two Navy Commendation Medals with Combat "V"
Seven Purple Hearts

"The name Jim Day belongs on the roll of the Corps'
greatest heroes, alongside of Dan Daly, Smedly Butler,
Joe Foss, and John Basilone."

[Clinton]
President of the United States,
20 January 1998

"cru–ci–ble /'krü–sa–bal/ n . . . 2: a severe test 3: a place or situation in which concentrated forces interact to cause or influence change or development."

—*Merriam-Webster's Collegiate Dictionary,*
Tenth Edition

CONTENTS

LIST OF MAPS

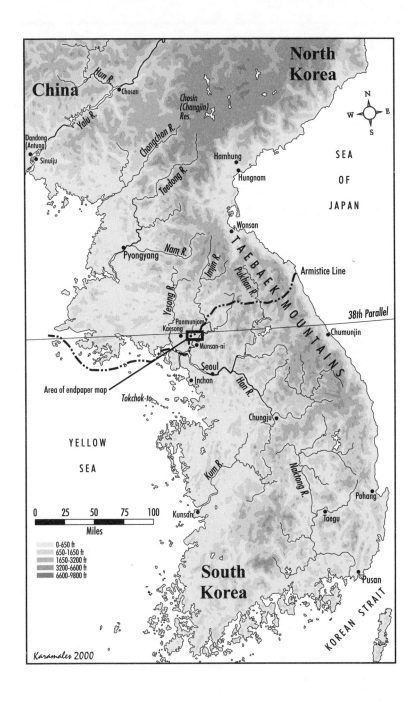

PREFACE

This volume is a sequel to *The Outpost War, U.S. Marines In Korea, Vol. I: 1952*. It is my expectation that its readers have read *The Outpost War*, or another detailed account of the Korean War to bring them historically to the place where this volume begins.

I dedicate this work to the memory of Maj. Gen. James L. ("Jim") Day, USMC. In 1952–53, Jim Day was a second lieutenant, a platoon leader with the 1st Division in Korea. He served with Charlie Company, 1st Battalion, 7th Marines, and the 1st Reconnaissance Company. One of his three Silver Stars was earned, on the morning of 28 February 1953, when he repeatedly led his men into the face of heavy enemy mortar and machine-gun fire to seek three Marines missing in a firefight. The author was present that morning and was personally aware of Day's valor, as were other members of the Reconnaissance Company. Lieutenant Day's conduct gained lasting admiration and respect from those men. What none of us knew at the time was just how courageous the lieutenant had been years ago, on another hill, in another war. That action belatedly earned Jim Day the Medal of Honor, our nation's highest military award.

During the World War II island fighting in the Pacific, Jim Day found himself on Okinawa. In 1945, after two years in the Corps, Day was a veteran, a corporal, and a squad leader with George Company, 2d Battalion, 22d Marines, 6th Division. He attracted particular notice in mid-May during a battle for a key hill strangely resembling a large loaf of bread.

Among the fiercely defended Japanese strongholds was a group of three low hills, mutually supporting and honeycombed with deep tunnels, with the loaflike terrain called "Sugarloaf" in the center.

For almost a week, Marines fought across the valley and up the forward slope of Sugarloaf only to be repeatedly repulsed by the tenacious and skillful Japanese defense. Fire and counterattacks from the two adjacent hills rendered Sugarloaf nearly impossible to take and even more difficult to hold. Corporal Day and his squad became pinned down in a bomb crater, a terrain position forward of the Marine lines that was critical to the continued assault on the hill. The squad was ordered to hold the position until it could be reinforced, but the Japanese had other plans. They did not want the Marines on Sugarloaf, and they were determined to drive them off.

It was not long before barrages of enemy artillery killed every Marine in the crater except two, Jim Day and Pvt. Dale Bertoli, who was sick with dengue fever and so severely wounded that he was unable to lift a rifle or to throw a grenade. The fight was up to eighteen-year-old Corporal Day to retain the position and single-handedly hold off the Japanese infantry assaults. For the next four days and three nights, he was equal to the task.

Reinforcements were unable to reach the courageous young man so he survived on sheer adrenaline and, virtually alone, continued to fight. Hearing wounded Marines calling for help behind him, he left the crater and, one by one, dragged, carried, and pulled four men into the relative safety of his hole. Then he went back for their machine gun and ammunition. The machine gunner was soon killed while helping Day to fire the gun as the enemy attacked. The same round that killed the machine gunner disabled the gun and wounded Day in both hands. The three other wounded men also died, and Day was again fighting alone. A Marine historian later wrote:

> For four days and three nights he held the right flank of Sugarloaf alone, against infantry and artillery attacks, during which time he was wounded in both hands, the legs and groin. During the entire time, he had no artillery or air support, for he had no radio. Although Bertoli couldn't help in the fight, he refused to leave Day. Delirious from pain and fever, and incontinent Bert stayed by him till the end.
>
> When Sugarloaf was finally secured on 17 May, there were eight dead Marines—their bodies literally blown to pieces by artillery and mortar fire—and 12 dead Japanese in the crater with Jim and Bert. The bottom of the muddy crater was filled with blood, mixed with water from the intermittent cold rain; body parts floated in it. On the rim of the crater and stretching for 70 yards to the front were more than 100 dead Japanese. The air was heavy with the smells of death. . . . By the time it was secured, the Sugarloaf area was blasted into a lifeless, rocky moonscape. . . .
>
> In the closing days of the campaign, far south of Sugarloaf, Dale

Bertoli, back in the fight was shot dead; Jim Day was grievously wounded and medevac'd.[1]

Corporal Day was offered a battlefield commission on Okinawa but turned it down. Later, in 1952, he accepted a commission and served as a Marine officer in the Korean War and again in Vietnam. When he retired from the Marine Corps on 1 December 1986, General Day was believed to be the last active duty Marine officer to have fought in all three campaigns.

Twelve years after Day's retirement and nearly fifty-three years after the event, on 20 January 1998, President William Jefferson Clinton presented the Medal of Honor to General Day for his individual bravery on Sugarloaf. (The original paperwork had been lost, found, brought forward, and belatedly processed.) The following October, with three wars and seven Purple Hearts behind him, Jim Day died of a heart attack at his home.

On 3 November 1998, accompanied by a few men from the Reconnaissance Company in Korea, the author, amid several hundred other Marines, attended a memorial service for General Day at the Marine Corps Recruit Depot, San Diego, California. The ceremony was reported in *Chevron,* the base newspaper:

> Under clear blue San Diego morning skies, eight Marines, resplendent in their dress blue uniforms, slowly carried the casket from Pendleton Hall between two platoons of Marines whose bodies were locked at attention. . . .[2]

The article went on to describe how the ceremony honored General Day with testimonials, music, salutes, and all the fanfare due a solemn and dignified general officer. To those of us from the Recon Company and others who had known him in battle, he was not a general but a comrade. A courageous NCO and an officer who always put his men before his own comfort, he was a Marine.

Humble to the end, General Day was buried in Rosecrans Military Cemetery. He was in a simple pine casket and wearing utilities, neither of which was adorned or embellished.

Forty-eight years before, 2d Lt. Jim Day was a platoon leader fighting in the final crucible of the outpost war—Korea, 1953. For Americans, the war in Korea was not a uniting event as World War II had been, but neither was it divisive as the Vietnam War would be. The final two years of the Korean War were bland, strategically boring, and nearly ignored. As a consequence, much that occurred there has been only superficially examined. Volumes I and II of this series attempt to correct that omission, at least in regard to the U.S. Marine Corps.

Volume I of the series described the U.S. Marine 1st Division moving from East-Central Korea in 1952 and establishing the Jamestown Line, a powerful defensive line against opposing Chinese forces across a 35-mile front. North of the meandering Imjin and Han rivers, the line protected the primary invasion route to Seoul, capital city of the Republic of Korea.

For the United Nations (UN) armies, the war had turned defensive. There would be no more forward movement. UN policy prohibited the Eighth U.S. Army, which included the Marines, from advancing. The war was to be settled around the conference table in Panmunjom. The fact that the talks had dragged on for more than a year with no solution in sight did not seem to matter, at least to the policy makers. To the soldiers and Marines in the trenches, however, it mattered a lot. They were still fighting and bleeding.

The Jamestown Line was drawn on an acetate overlay covering the army topographical map of Korea. It was called the main line of resistance (MLR). On the ground, however, the MLR consisted of trenches, bunkers, fighting holes, and tank slots. In front of the MLR were strong points called Combat Outposts (COPs). The fighting occurred at the COPs. Here, and in the no-man's-land surrounding the COP's, the outpost war claimed more than 7,800 Marine casualties in 1952 and 5,246 in 1953. And, when considering use of the armored vest, the thermal boot and improvements in helicopter evacuation introduced at this time, one can only imagine what casualties might have been without them.

U.S. Marines have been variously known as "elite troops," "assault troops," "light infantry," and, in the words of President Harry S Truman, "the Navy's police force." They had never been known as a defense force. They were not trained in defense tactics and were not equipped for defensive operations, yet they were considered the best unit available to defend the Jamestown Line and Korea's capital city.

In 1952, however, Marines learned how to defend the line and fight on the outposts. They learned which hills were valuable and which were not and how to avoid mines, to patrol, to ambush, and to raid enemy positions from selected combat outposts. In the process, men and outposts were lost. The period of trial and error continued until the end of the year when defenses became firmly established and stable. As noted by the casualty figures, however, there was no less fighting in 1953. If one were to extrapolate the figures, an argument might be made that the casualty rate was higher for 1953 than for 1952. Despite peace talks in Panmunjom, the war was far from over.

The Chinese People's Volunteer Army was a strong, motivated force. It was filled with seemingly fearless soldiers who attacked at night, some without weapons hoping to gather them from the enemy or dead comrades as the fighting progressed. Fighting close, they used hand grenades, bayonets and submachine guns (called "burp guns") when they had them. They attacked in human waves as they crawled over downed comrades and barbed wire to get at the Marines holding an outpost. Like the Marines, the Chinese patrolled and set up ambushes in no-man's-land in the hope of catching the enemy unaware during a careless moment.

The fighting, bloody and intense, continued into 1953, but it would end that year. The last six months of the war constituted a severe test, "a place or situation in which concentrated forces interacted to cause or influence change or development." It was the "Final Crucible."

INTRODUCTION

War is cruelty and you cannot refine it.
—W. T. Sherman: Letter to
the Mayor of Atlanta,
12 September 1864

The waning months of 1952 saw the 1st Marine Division in Korea settle in to fight a number of bloody and terrible battles as the outpost war continued. Experimentation was over, as were opportunities for surprise and maneuver. Digging in, the opposing forces simply slugged it out. Like prizefighters with their shoes nailed to the floor, each side prepared to fight until one or the other became too exhausted to continue.

After the fighting at the Hook in late October 1952, (see *The Outpost War,* Vol. I of this series) the MLR could have been built of poured concrete. There was no movement. Outposts in front of the MLR, like protective sentinels, were also stabilized. Both sides knew which positions they would fight for—everything in between was a killing field, a no-man's-land.

The area between combatants was zeroed in, every trail and path mined or targeted with mortar and artillery. Each approach to an outpost or the MLR was a field of fire. All that prevented complete annihilation of one side or the other was its lack of sufficient manpower and ordnance.

The war might be compared to an enormous medieval siege—the outposts were the ramparts, and the MLR was the keep. In place of boiling oil, there were "box-me-in" patterns of mortars and artillery, mines, overhead air bursts of artillery, and napalm bombs dropped from aircraft. This was the Jamestown Line in Korea.

The MLR was intended to hold against the enemy, and it did. Never in the history of the outpost war was the Jamestown Line breached to any significant degree. There were occasional breaks, the worst of which was the Hook in October 1952, but the line was resilient and bounced back. The enemy could not exploit the situation.

After October 1952, the Marine line shortened to the left as the British Commonwealth Division assumed responsibility for the area around the Hook. Simultaneously, the number and location of outposts stabilized. The few that were retained, approximately sixteen, were garrisoned full time and built for strong defense. There, the Marines stayed and took full advantage of their usually superior fire power.

In 1953, the war changed from a mere stalemate to marked stagnation. The trial-and-error phase passed, and the Marines began to mark time and hold what they had. Generals became superfluous, largely a communication conduit for a long chain of command. There were few strategic decisions to make; tactical decisions occurred at the regimental, battalion, or even company level. Strategically and tactically, the war became predictable, a continuous repetition of small unit raids, incoming fire, patrols, and ambushes over the same terrain. As soon as one skirmish was finished, another followed—like a parade marching around in a circle.

Yet, the people changed, and in the eyes of an individual Marine or soldier, a battle, a wound, or the death of a friend was a significant event. It would become a small piece of history in which he had personally participated, and he could relate the details to his grandchildren or write books about them.

Politics also changed. In November 1952, Americans had elected a new president, Dwight D. Eisenhower. Expectations about U.S. policies worldwide were confused. More important for men fighting the war, the peace talks in Panmunjom were suspended on October 8. After months of struggling to seek a common ground for discussion, the delegation from the United Nations Command (UNC) walked out and announced for the record:

> . . . The UNC did not intend to come to Panmunjom merely to listen to the abuse and false propaganda issued by the Communist delegation. Therefore [Lt. Gen. William K. Harrison continued], the UNC was declaring a recess until the Communists were willing to accept one of the UNC plans or submit in writing a constructive proposal of its own. With that, Harrison and the rest of the UNC delegation rose and left the conference tent.[1]

Political decisions affect strategy, which, in turn, affect tactics. After the walkout, diplomats began to argue over who had caused the suspension and how to get the talks resumed on a favorable note. In Washington and Tokyo, the UNC adopted a wait-and-see attitude. The war continued its deadly slugfest on the ground, while diplomats and politicians bickered across a table or in the press.

Neither side was able to advance its ground force. The Communists could not, and the UNC would not. This was America's first limited war, one in which military victory is prohibited. Statesmanship was the prevailing goal, and armies were restricted from gaining ground. A military victory, as defined by one side decisively defeating the other, was neither sought nor achieved.

The bulk of the American press and many military historians tended to ignore the continuous small-unit battles that occurred on a daily basis as not newsworthy. The cumulative effect of this small but tediously regular fighting made little impression on reporters. Disasters and triumphs came piecemeal, in miniature doses too small for headlines. The big news in Korea related to politics, truce talks, and prisoners but rarely a battle, whether large or small. In his book, *Pork Chop Hill,* S. L. A. Marshall commented on the lack of press coverage for that particular action. He called it a Won-Lost battle: "It was won by the troops and lost to the people who had sent them forth."[2] General Marshall's words apply to most of the fighting in Korea at that time. For a lack of reporting by the military and civilians alike, the conduct and outcome of most battles were lost to history.

Boulder City, for example, a place unheard of by most Americans, was the location of a decisive battle that, but for the determination and heroism of a small company of Marines, could have changed the entire course of the war. The enemy lost, the Marines won, and history evolved as though nothing had happened—it was a won-lost battle.

During their time on the Jamestown Line (March 1952 through July 1953), the Marines fought four major battles: Bunker Hill and the Hook in 1952 and the Nevada Cities and Berlin Outposts/Boulder City in 1953. Casualties for those months were 13,087 Marines killed, captured, missing, or wounded.[3]

By January 1953, the system of outposts was permanently established in front of the MLR, which functioned primarily to support the outposts rather than as a line of military resistance and, more accurately, might have been named a Main Line of Support. Most of the fighting was then taking place at the COPs. To defend an outpost, the Marines used their superior firepower to advantage. On the MLR, they had rifle companies, light and heavy machine guns, recoilless rifles, mortars, and tanks.

Behind the MLR, Marines placed large 4.2-inch mortars, artillery, and rockets. On call from an outpost, artillery and mortars fired "box-me-in" patterns of shells that fell on all enemy approaches, thus surrounding a hill with a protective curtain of death. Artillery also used variable time (VT) fused concentrations that exploded over the heads of troops in the open and cut them to pieces with a rainstorm of shrapnel. Frequently, when a COP was overrun, the Marines sought cover and called for VT over their own position, a desperate step barely short of suicide but usually effective.

In addition, the Marines had their ace in the hole, close air support (CAS). Marine Corsairs dove so low during air strikes that riflemen swore they could see the pilots grinning. Many a Marine on an outpost felt the heat of burning napalm as bombs landed almost close enough to light his cigarette.

Not content to let the enemy come to them, Marines on the Jamestown Line maintained an aggressive defense by bringing the war to the enemy. Terrain in front of the MLR and surrounding an outpost was known as no-man's-land or, less formally, "goonie land," that consisted of hills, abandoned rice paddies, bunkers, and fighting holes from previous battles. Here, too, were small hills, draws, trails, and roads, most of which were mined. No-man's-land was also a battlefield. Nightly, patrols set out from the outpost or the MLR to locate and ambush enemy patrols that had set out from the other side with the same objectives.

The Marines struck at enemy patrols and raided positions to kill troops and to disrupt defenses. Territory was not desired, captured, or held. Their sole aim was to kill the enemy.

CHAPTER 1

PREPARATION FOR WAR

*A government is the murderer of its citizens which
sends them to the field uninformed and untaught. . . .*
—Henry ("Light Horse Harry") Lee,
1756–1818

Who were these young men in faded green dungarees and camouflaged helmet covers? Who voluntarily risked death and maiming in the trenches, hills, and valleys of Korea? Who seemingly enjoyed war? And why were they so damned gung ho?

These men, mostly boys really, came from the same neighborhoods, schools, and families that produced American soldiers, sailors, and airmen, but they were different. They were volunteers;[1] many even chose to serve in Korea; and, more important, they were trained—well trained.

At the beginning of the Korean war in 1950, there were fewer than 75,000 officers and men in the entire active duty U.S. Marine Corps. Three years later when the war ended, there were nearly 250,000, a massive expansion of personnel. The total number of Marines who served during the Korean War era was 424,000.

When the war began, the Marine Corps shook every limb in its organizational tree to find a sufficient number of men to build a brigade. Every shore station and embassy was drained; guard units and ships' detachments were stripped. Fleet Marine Forces (FMF) from every base in the world were directed to give up personnel to form a brigade of Marines for Korea.

After the 1st Marine Brigade was formed and sent to Korea on 2 August 1950, the tree was shaken again and enough men were found to bring the Brigade up to division strength in time for the landing at Inchon a month later. Reserves were uprooted from their homes and jobs to respond, and they did, some perhaps more willing than others. A full-strength Marine division numbers approximately 25,000 officers and men; the contingent in Korea at that time totaled one-third of the entire regular Marine Corps as it had existed two months previously. If the Marines were to remain in Korea, more men would have to be recruited, trained, and shipped eastward to reinforce and replace the men already there. As a consequence, the Marine Corps underwent a massive buildup and reorganization over a very brief period of time.

By January 1953, where this volume begins, the Marine Corps had been at war in Korea for two and one-half years. Organizational buildup pains had been solved and routines developed to supply, support, and maintain the 1st Division in Korea. Despite the fact that truce talks were ongoing in Panmunjom, a cessation of fighting and peace were not foreseeable options in the near future. A personnel replacement organization was in place and functioning. Called the Staging Regiment, it was located at Camp Pendleton, California. The training was effective and the routine efficient.

TENT CAMP TWO

In 1953, Camp San Onofre, a subarea of the vast Camp Pendleton Marine Base in Southern California, consisted of several hundred eight-man pyramidal tents, dirt roads, and Quonset huts. At the time, called simply Tent Camp Two, it was home to the Staging Regiment, Marine Barracks, Camp Pendleton. The job of the Staging Regiment was to provide the administrative processing, physical training, and combat conditioning of troops prior to their embarkation to Korea. With few exceptions, all Marines passed through Staging Regiment en route to Korea.

Marines with more than six months' experience in a Military Occupational Specialty (MOS) were considered sufficiently well trained to proceed directly to the Staging Regiment. Others, at the rank of sergeant and below who had not had the requisite six months, were sent to the Infantry Training Regiment (ITR),[2] also at Tent Camp Two, for four weeks of infantry training. Marines fresh from boot camp who were designated for any of the supporting arms groups, such as tanks or artillery, were sent to the Supporting Arms Regiment for an additional four weeks of training. Thus, a Marine could have as much as two months' training, not counting specialized schools, before he ever reached the Staging Regiment.

The Staging Regiment consisted of three replacement battalions and a headquarters cadre. It was faced with the multitudinous task of putting each outgoing group of replacements through its final phase of preparation before the men joined combat units in the Far East. The battalions operated on a hectic, merry-go-round-like schedule. Simultaneously, one battalion was en route to Korea, another was in training and processing, and a third was being formed.

It took about ten days to form a battalion, but processing began as soon as a company was formed. Each month, the Staging Regiment received about seven companies of men from the ITR; the others came from FMF units and various posts and stations around the world. Some specialized units consisted of naval corpsmen, officers, and staff noncommissioned officers (SNCOs) who required only the readying stage and cold-weather training to prepare them for Korea. The entire staging phase lasted approximately three weeks, including a week of intensive cold-weather training, high in the California Sierras.

The first step of processing was the issuance of the Marine's "782 gear." This was government-owned equipment issued to an individual: web gear, helmet, rifle and bayonet, mess kit and canteen, field pack, and other items that the Marine would take to the combat zone. Processing included lectures by the personal affairs officer, the chaplain, and representatives of various benefit organizations. The young Marines were treated to the always important lectures on venereal disease, complete with photos and movies of scabbed, deformed, and oozing genitalia, horrible examples of the consequences of a dissolute life. Few young men believed that it could happen to them, and the lectures fell largely on deaf ears.

Clothing issues were checked and brought up to date. In winter, each Marine received a complete issue of cold-weather clothing. With it came the inevitable lecture on proper use, care, and cleaning. Little was left to chance.

Sandwiched among lectures, field training, and combat conditioning, the men received physical examinations and dental work. Examinations were thorough; no one went to Korea unless he was physically capable. Glasses were fitted and teeth filled or pulled. Naturally, a full set of shots was in order. The men grew accustomed to standing in line; they had needles in both arms, chest X-rays, and blood testing and typing. Then, they had to stand up and strip, bend over, and smile. Nothing was left to chance, no body part left unexamined.

The men found barely a single spare minute in the schedule. They participated in conditioning marches; obstacle courses; classes for squad and platoon tactics; and, in their spare time, personnel inspections and close order drill. A myriad of administrative details had to be covered. It was necessary to update pay records, allotments, dog tags, and insurance papers and ensure that wills were legally prepared and on file and that information on each man's emergency data form was complete and correct. Then it was back to more physical training.

The terrain in Camp Pendleton's backcountry was ideal for training. The hills, similar to those in Korea, acquired such names as "Old Smoky," "Discipline Hill," and "Nellie's Tit." It was up one hill and down another, sometimes with a full field pack and sometimes without it, then off to the rifle range to zero in on targets. Each man would take his rifle into combat; it had to be accurate. There were more lectures; including classes on laying and removing land mines, booby traps, and demolitions. The men practiced with live hand grenades and increased their familiarity with carbine, pistol, and Browning automatic rifles (BARs). There were demonstrations of supporting arms, tanks, artillery, and mortars, along with refresher courses on machine guns and other crew-served weapons. In reality, these were the fun things. Young men enjoy shooting and blowing up things.

For a breather, the men attended lectures on how to live in the field and life onboard ship, as well as inspiring discussions on the Uniform Code of Military Justice, "Don't steal, don't rape, don't get drunk, don't, don't, don't; and, if you do, you'll end up in Portsmouth Naval Prison for many years or worse."

At the end of each day, there was liberty call, but no one cared. The men were either too tired, too sore, or too broke. Oceanside was too far away to walk, and no one on his way to Korea had a car. Even those who managed to take a bus found that the town tended toward greater boredom than staying in camp and cost more, too. The evenings, most often, the men spent in their tents recovering from the day's activities, working on gear, at the free movies or in the slop chute drinking 10-cent beer and lying to one another about their love lives. The Marine Corps in those days did not pay very well. A private first class received about $80 per month; NCOs' pay was commensurably higher. It was a great experience and served to prepare a young man of eighteen or nineteen for life on the MLR—except for the killing.

Officers had it no better, especially second lieutenants. The leaders of patrols and platoons on the MLR and in the outposts soon learned that they were quite expendable. The very nature of their work did not allow lieutenants the luxury of a static foxhole or gun position. To do the job right, they had to move, to check each man, to organize a defense, to lead a patrol, to be first behind the point man. They had to be out in front and exposed. Consequently, a great many lieutenants never made captain. Others learned their job quickly and, in combat, did well and survived. Some of the lieutenants were "mustangs," men commissioned from the ranks, usually former staff NCOs. These men were older, more experienced, and many had seen combat in World War II or during a previous tour in Korea.

Recruitment efforts for Marine lieutenants became frenzied. College campuses were scoured and many young men recruited. Pushed through boot camp at one of the recruit depots, the fledgling lieutenants were soon graduated and transferred to Quantico, Virginia, and The Basic School. (TBS). There, special basic classes (SBCs) were formed and the training continued.

Upon their completion of The Basic School, these young men, now around twenty-one or twenty-two years of age, received their shiny gold bars and their new assignments. The orders for most of them read: "Infantry Training Command, Camp Pendleton, California, for further assignment overseas," or, simply translated into one word, "Korea."

Most of the new lieutenants went through additional training and processing with enlisted men in the Staging Regiment before leaving for Korea. More often than not, they were flown overseas. The need for lieutenants was too urgent to waste time on a two-week sea voyage. Thus, within weeks, these young leaders, schooled and trained but completely lacking in experience, found themselves being shot at on a combat outpost or patrol. Fortunately, many of them learned how to survive.[3]

PICKEL MEADOWS

Sometime during a Marine's tour in the Staging Regiment, he passed through a week of cold-weather training. In 1952 alone, twenty thousand men were trained at the Marine Corps Cold Weather Training Camp, Pickel Meadows, California. Named for an early settler in the region, this training facility is located in the Sierra Nevada high country near Sonora Pass, elevation 9,624 feet. It has snow nearly year round, and the winters are frigid. Temperatures of minus forty-eight degrees have been recorded, though the norm is usually ten to twenty degrees above during the day and perhaps twenty degrees below at night. It is an ideal setting to simulate combat during a Korean winter.

At Tent Camp Two in sunny Southern California, Marines from the Staging Regiment were scheduled for cold-weather training a few companies at a time. Again, the men attended lectures and movies depicting more do's and don'ts and emphasizing the horrible things that will happen if one fails to pay attention, along with sickening scenes of black, frostbitten toes being pulled off with a sock. (One wonders how the cameraman arranged to be there at the opportune moment that a toe fell off.) Regardless, the message came through—cold can be an enemy. Following the lectures were demonstrations of the use and care of the newest in government issue cold-weather fashion. Men were issued their long underwear, fur parkas, vests, wool gloves, socks, and hats, all of which had to be tested and tried on for fit in the plus eighty-degree temperatures of Camp Pendleton.

Of special interest were the new rubber thermal boots first issued in late 1952. These marvelous inventions were waterproof, airtight boots that sealed body heat in the boot. The more one walked, the warmer his feet became regardless of the outside temperature—no more frostbitten toes to fall off. Because of their black, bulbous look, the boots were immediately dubbed, "Mickey Mouse boots." Who cared what they looked like? They worked and were wonderful, a far cry from the old, ineffective shoe pac of 1950.

At the appointed hour, Marines from Tent Camp Two boarded chartered Greyhound buses for the twelve-hour ride to Pickel Meadows. For six days and nights, excluding travel time, they would live out of the packs on their backs in snow knee deep or worse. They would sleep in winter sleeping bags, under shelter halves pitched in the snow or in hollowed out igloo-like caves, only to be awakened at midnight by an attack. Hiking for miles in thin air, they would break trail, stop to cook lunch on little mountain stoves, and again be attacked by the aggressor. Pickel Meadows lent new meaning to the term "roughing it."

The Marines spent the first two days at the camp in relative comfort as they learned the basic fundamentals of cold-weather survival. Although they did not know it, their lungs were also acclimating to the rarefied air at 10,000 feet. Their training included care and cleaning of weapons, building of shelters, preparation of frozen rations, techniques of stream crossing, and making water from frozen snow. Most important, the men learned that just staying alive was not good enough. They had to be able to fight as well. A Marine is just as dead whether he freezes to death or the enemy kills him.

Early in the morning of the third day, each man in the company was issued a four-day supply of C ration before shoving off on a 15-mile, four-day trek through the mountain snow. The march was slow and tactical. Each night, the men bivouacked in a new location. Emphasis was on the individual, his movement, and care for his body, equipment, and clothing. They were trained to move slowly and deliberately, to conserve energy, and to avoid perspiring. This last was a particularly difficult feat considering that each man was carrying a heavy field pack and a 10-pound rifle and was hiking up the side of a mountain through 4 feet of snow.

Although the Sierra Nevada scenery is breathtaking, the training was no nature hike. During the next four days, trainees were harassed by aggressor forces. The aggressors were Marines; permanent personnel assigned to Pickel Meadows, whose job was to simulate Chinese troops and make life as miserable as possible for the visiting trainees.

Realism was of prime importance, and night attacks were regular occurrences. Equipped with skis and snowshoes and with white suits over their uniforms, the aggressors swooped down on the column of Marines as they moved during the day. At night, they employed typical Chinese tactics. The men were routed out of their sleeping bags in the middle of their sleep. Attacks were accompanied by bugles, whistles, and fanatic yells. Sentries were taunted into giving away their positions so the aggressors could infiltrate their lines and steal a trigger housing or foul a weapon. If a man were unlucky enough to be captured, he was interrogated all night in sign language and short Chinese terms.

Finally, on the last day of training, the weary men returned to their starting point. They were physically exhausted, but they had endured some of the roughest training that the Marine Corps had to offer.

Pickel Meadows was one of the great equalizers of the era. Every man, including chaplains, doctors, officers, and corpsmen, going to Korea went through the training. Even pilots had to pass through a modified but equally strenuous course. They were dropped off with the infantry and left there for two and a half days to survive, to "live with the elements," as a downed pilot might be expected to do.[4]

SHIPPING OUT

On their return to Tent Camp Two from Pickel Meadows, the men rejoined the processing schedule of their replacement draft. Last-minute details were attended to, perhaps winter gear was damaged or needed replacement, maybe a rifle needed a final ordnance check, or a man required completion of dental work or eyeglasses. Whatever the problem, it was fixed. The replacement draft was on a schedule, dates were set, and the clock was ticking.

The men took part in a final battalion parade on the grass-covered parade deck. Then, it was off for a weekend liberty, their last one Stateside for a while and, for some, their last liberty ever. They were going to war.

Field packs contained all that the men would need from now on. Early in the morning, they boarded Marine Corps buses or "cattle cars," semitrailers with wooden benches along each side and down the middle. Each trailer held approximately forty-five men with packs and rifles. The men were quiet and sober, their bravado subdued a little. They were leaving.

South on Highway 101 from Camp Pendleton, a convoy of green Marine trucks pulled the semitrailers loaded with men in full combat gear. After a 35-mile trip to Navy Pier at the foot of Broadway in downtown San Diego, the convoy stopped and the Marines unloaded. At the pier was a ship, maybe the USNS *Walker* or *Pope* or *Meig* or any of the Military Sea Transportation Service (MSTS) troopships under contract to the Navy that plied the Far East shuttle between San Diego and Japan and Korea. The ships brought tired, worn, and wounded Marines home and returned to the Far East with fresh batches of young enthusiastic Marines.

As the men unloaded from the trailers and formed up, a small crowd gathered. A Marine Band was there, of course, and also a few wives and girlfriends, mostly those of officers and senior NCOs. Given the order to board, the men filed off in columns and boarded the ship. Most of them went directly below to their assigned bunks to stow their gear and then returned topside to wave and yell at the small group of people on the pier. A pair of Women Marines in uniform waved and yelled something. Who could hear above the din of people and machines? A mother lifted her child to wave an unknowing good-bye to a face in the crowd. With more than three thousand Marines and sailors at the rail, everyone dressed alike, how could anyone pick out a single individual?

Sailors cast off the lines, horns blasted, and a band played "The Marines' Hymn" as the ship slowly backed away from the pier into the basin, turned, and made for the harbor entrance. Now under way, she passed North Island Naval Air Station on the port side as she entered the channel. With the sun still high off the horizon, the loaded troopship passed the Naval Submarine Base and Point Loma Lighthouse to starboard. Leaving San Diego Harbor, she entered the open sea.

On deck, troops watched the United States slowly disappear, seemingly sinking into the Pacific Ocean at the stern. What awaited them in Korea?

THE TROOPSHIP

A typical troopship drew about 17,500 tons and was crewed by civilian merchant seamen with a small complement of U.S. Navy personnel, mostly medical staff. Designed for six thousand troops, a ship usually carried about half that number, along with tons of military supplies for bases in Japan and Korea.

Life on a troopship could be accurately described in three words— boring and crowded. There were people everywhere, overhead, underfoot, and in the way. No one did anything that used more space than a single body could occupy. Reading was a favorite pastime or letter writing. For some it was cards, but most of them spent their time alone in a crowd as they stared at an unchanging ocean.

One young corporal from the 28th replacement draft described his introduction to life at sea on board one of Uncle Sam's cruise ships:

Our ship was an old WW II transport. In the troop compartments below decks, bunks were stacked five deep, floor to ceiling, about eighteen inches apart. Aisles between the stacked bunks were narrow, maybe two feet, but filled with piles of seabags, field packs and rifles. You could say that we were close. We lived out of our packs as there were no lockers or storage facilities for the troops. At specified times we took salt water showers with special soap that was supposed to lather but didn't. Despite the crowding, the ship was reasonably clean and well maintained so the two or three week voyage wasn't too uncomfortable.

At eighteen years old I just became eligible for combat and was looking forward to joining the war. For me it was an adventure, hell, I didn't know any better.

Aboard ship there was little to do. Many men read, played cards, wrote letters or just sat around exchanging lies. Some of us pulled mess or guard duty. I chose guard duty thinking that the smells of food preparation might contribute to sea sickness. Somehow, I managed to retain most of my meals, most of the time, even during rough weather when the ship would pitch and roll. When the swells were really high, the ship's propeller would leave the water causing the entire ship to shudder and groan.

Meals aboard ship were served in one of several mess halls called compartments. We went in shifts and stood in line for an hour or more in narrow passageways. The tables were long narrow affairs, maybe 12 inches in width, covered with stainless steel. There were no chairs or stools. Troops were required to stand while eating. No seconds, just stand in line, grab a tray of food, stand at the table, wolf it down, and get the hell out to make room for the next guy. It was hardly luxurious but as there was nothing better to do, chow became the high point of the day.[5]

Each month, the scene was repeated as new replacement drafts were sent to Korea. Somewhere in the bowels of bureaucracy, the drafts acquired numbers, 10th Draft, the 17th, the 29th, and so forth. Every Marine in Korea knew his draft number and compared it with his buddy's. The lower the number, the more seniority a man had in the country. It became a status symbol implying experience in combat, like time in the Corps, or a low service number—the old salt is defined.

Most of the troopships docked in Kobe or Yokohama, Japan, for a day a two before sailing on to Korea. There, they off-loaded cargo and men destined for units in Japan, mostly U.S. Army and Air Force personnel, and took on supplies for Korea. While in port, the troops on board were given a few hours of liberty to explore those exotic foreign cities. One or two might have actually gone sightseeing, though they never would have admitted it. The corporal continued, as he recalled his visit to Japan in January:

> During the week of New Year 1953, our ship docked in Yokohama. We were allowed a few hours ashore. Because of the holidays most of the Japanese ladies dressed in traditional Kimonos with wooden Geta on their feet. Geta were the old wooden sandals with a thong between the great and first toe. The men had suits but often they too wore Geta. The sights, sounds and smells all felt very foreign to an eighteen year old Marine corporal from Los Angeles. Like most of the men on board, I spent my brief evening liberty enjoying a meaningful cultural exchange among the young ladies of Yokohama's numerous saloons.[6]

Eventually, the ship was under way again and, within a few hours, was pulling in to Inchon Harbor. Here, the niceties of Japan and San Diego vanished. Korea was a country devastated by war, broken buildings, and torn-up roads.

LAND OF THE MORNING CALM

Probably the first thing that every American remembers of his intro-duction to Korea was the smell—an indescribable mixture of charcoal, garlic, smoke, human waste, unknown food, and the lingering scent of war. It was not pleasant, but, like everything else, one became accus-

tomed to the odor and it was soon forgotten. In his unpublished memoir, the corporal related:

> In early January we tied up in Inchon Harbor, Korea. It was cold,
> very cold. So cold the troop compartment doors were frozen shut.
> Sailors had to chip away the ice to swing the hatch open and release
> us out on deck. We disembarked over the side climbing down rope
> nets with all our gear, full field pack, rifle, helmet, etc. Just like an
> invasion force, except no one was shooting at us. Into the LCM's
> [landing craft mechanized] we crawled and fell, pushing against one
> another like sardines in a can. The LCM's, those flat bottomed, all
> purpose, naval boats used for just about everything, wallowed to the
> dock at Inchon. At least we didn't have to climb over the sea wall
> under fire as our counterparts did two years ago.
>
> . . . Upon disembarking the boats we were trucked to Ascom City
> to await assignment and transportation to our respective units. Ascom
> City was a massive Marine supply base that linked shipping from the
> harbor to the railroad tracks where supplies and people were trans-
> ported north to the Main Line of Resistance (MLR).
>
> While at Ascom City, we were assigned to a Casual Company
> housed in squad tents. Snow was on the ground, and with no grass nor
> pavement, there was mud everywhere. The cold was a shock but we
> had adequate cold weather clothing, and the tents were equipped with
> kerosene heaters. I spent one night on guard duty with live ammuni-
> tion, having first been warned to watch out for enemy infiltrators (I'm
> probably fortunate I didn't shoot myself in the foot). There was another
> day or two of waiting around with no place to go and nothing to see.
> We weren't permitted to leave the personnel compound. It was as bor-
> ing there as it was at sea.
>
> At Ascom City our seabags were stowed for the duration of our
> tour in Korea. From now on we would live out of our field pack and
> a "Willie Peter" bag. The Willie Peter bag, military jargon for "WP,"
> waterproof, was a short, thin nylon bag used for carrying anything
> you had, or ever wanted. At this point none of us had any personal
> gear except clothing, toilet articles and weapons. Uncle Sam furnished
> everything we'd need in Korea.[7]

Ascom City was also the port of debarkation from Korea. A seabag,
the sum total of a Marine's personal property, was stored there while the
man went forward to fight. If he failed to return, his seabag remained.
Eventually, the seabags of dead, missing and evacuated Marines were
collected for return to the United States without their owners.

Sgt. Robert A. Gannon, newly arrived at Inchon, was queued up to await transportation when he noticed a large stack of seabags set apart for stevedores to load into an outgoing ship. These seabags would be traveling without owners. It was dusk, the day dreary and overcast. Clouds rolled in, and with darkness came rain. The image of those seabags and what they represented seared deep into the memory of that young sergeant. The image remained, dormant but not forgotten.

Years later, far from Korea, on another cloudy and rainy day, the image of those stacked seabags suddenly returned to Gannon. With it came the words of this poem:

SEABAGS IN THE RAIN
When clouds are gray and lowering
And fog obscures the plain
I sometimes think I catch a sight
Of seabags in the rain
I know it is a vision
Too ethereal to last
But it brings a wisp of sadness
And a haunting from the past
We had come ashore at Inchon
In Nineteen-Fifty Two
An Administrative landing
Just a unit passing through
We were mustered at the railhead
Lining up to board a train
When through the stormy darkness
I saw seabags in the rain
There was no need to question
Why they were lying there
Looking lonely and abandoned
In the damp Korean air
Their owners had gone northward
And would not return again
From where hills of bitter battle
Took the lives of fighting men
Now, when fog and darkness gather
I rarely can restrain
My saddened thoughts of Inchon
And seabags in the rain[8]

MOVING FORWARD

After a day or two of getting organized at Ascom City, the men were herded to an old, rickety Japanese passenger train. Wooden four-man benches in sets of two faced each other, with windows on the sides of the car and an aisle down the middle. The train was reminiscent of the Old West; all that was lacking were hordes of Indians, or the Dalton gang. Each man had his rifle and a single clip of ammunition with orders not to load it except on command. The men were warned that Communist infiltrators might be anywhere. To a young man fresh from combat training who was now entering a war zone, the admonishment was canonical. Every tree, every hut, every oriental man between four and one hundred and four years of age became a threat, a potential ambush. Miraculously, it seemed, the train arrived at division headquarters without anyone getting shot or shooting.

Cpl. John (Jack) Orth summarized his ride on the train headed north from Ascom City to where he was to join the 7th Marines:

> We went ashore at Inchon and quickly boarded a train for the front. Christ, it was right out of World War I. The only difference was that there were no cheering people waving flags as we boarded, just a few pathetic looking kids in rags, trying to sell us chewing gum and booze. One of them was yelling, "Sheba, Sheba," which we later found out meant broads. How he figured we were going to work it while we were on the troop train I never did find out.
>
> The train was a real relic. It made that one from Yemassee to Port Royal in South Carolina look like the *20th Century Limited*.
>
> And cold, good God it was cold! Remember this was the dead of winter. We froze our asses off. There was no head on the train. This meant that we'd have periodic stops on the way to relieve ourselves. It was so bad we were actually glad to reach the front, even though we could hear gunfire.[9]

Off-loading from the train, the Marines formed into their respective units for further transportation by truck to their assignments. Most of the men went to rifle companies.

Another man, Cpl. Robert A. Hall from the 29th Replacement Draft, wrote of arrival at his unit of assignment:

> . . . It was dark by the time we arrived at 5th Marines [regimental headquarters]. We had no idea where this was. We had eaten C Rations on the train. The regimental replacements were assembled for a talk by Col. Lewis Walt, the 5th Marines CO[commanding officer]. He

introduced Maj. Gen. Edwin Pollock CO of the 1st Marine Division. . . . I recall that Gen. Pollock said how proud he was of the division and of Col. Walt. . . .The assignments were read off, and about 135 of us rode trucks to the 2nd Bn HQ's. . . . It was very cold and very late when we crossed the Imjin [River] and got to 2/5.

Several days were spent at Bn HQ's. [Replacements typically remained at the battalion command post (CP) for five days of orientation before being moved forward to the line.] The units were mostly in heavily protected bunkers located in a draw by the main road back to the Imjin. The mess tent was across the road near an open paddy area. The replacements were in 16 man squad tents with sandbagged sides, not in bunkers. We were issued equipment, heard lectures about the Korean War in general, were told about the Chinese unit opposing us in particular, and made practice patrols at night in the paddies. There were a few incoming rounds in the area, but only on one occasion were they close, and even then up the draw behind the bunkers. It seemed like a movie about war with noise from the "front" barely audible. One day a Marine plane, a Corsair, was hit while flying over the MLR. Even over the tops of the hills, it could be seen that he was in trouble. Activity stopped and the troops came running out to watch as the plane went down and a parachute opened. We watched him drift below our ridgeline and hoped he was safe.

. . . After four days or so we were assigned to companies within the battalion. I was assigned to the 3rd section, Heavy Machine Gun Platoon of Weapons Company. Weapons Co. platoons included heavy (water cooled) .30 cal machine guns, 81-mm mortars and assault/demolition personnel. These platoons were each broken into three sections and assigned to the three rifle companies in a battalion. The 3rd sections were attached to Fox Company, the third letter company in the 2nd Bn. . . . I was put into the crew of a HMG [Heavy Machine Gun] in a bunker about 15 yards to the right of the gate of OP Berlin.[10]

Each month, more Marines came to Korea. Every replacement draft went through the same approximate routine. Ultimately, most of the replacements found themselves on the MLR and outposts because that was where they were needed and where other men had been lost.

Was the training effective? Most men think that it was. On reaching the MLR, the Marines received the graduate course—actual combat. Every man had his "first night," whether it was on a patrol or standing watch in a fighting hole. On a Marine's first night, every bush was an enemy, each sound a threat.

A typical first night on line was experienced by Pfc. Richard Champagne, who joined George Company, 3/1 (3d Battalion, 1st Marines), in January 1953. Describing his feelings on watch a few hours after midnight, Champagne related:

> I heard something hit the wire ahead of me and slightly to my left. The night was totally black. I took off my hood, "Mongolian Pisscutter" and helmet in order to hear better. I remained frozen for at least 30 minutes, then relaxed and half turned to the right and ran into Lt. Kingsbury. This scared the hell out of me. He asked if I had heard anything, and I explained the bang on the wire, but suggested it might only have been the cold in the wire.
>
> We talked for a minute, and he started to leave when a burp gun opened up about 30 feet in front of us. I dropped to my knees without ever seeing the flash of the 30 round magazine. As I tried to see who was firing, Lt. Kingsbury crawled back into the hole and asked if I were OK. There had been rounds hitting all around, and we obviously were the target. I explained to the lieutenant that I was OK and added, "Sir, I think those silly sons of bitches were shooting this way."
>
> Lt. Kingsbury then put his hand on my head to see if I had on my helmet. When he realized I had nothing on my head, he shook his head back and forth, but said nothing. I could just make out his white face in the dark. After that he had me as point whenever he went on patrol with my squad. Either he figured I was the coolest rookie he had ever seen, or I was completely expendable. I'll never know which it was.[11]

T/Sgt. Jack Little, a former drill instructor from Marine Corps Recruit Depot Parris Island, South Carolina, was newly arrived in Korea and assigned as platoon sergeant of the machine-gun platoon for Charlie Company, 1/5. Barely days after getting off the ship at Inchon, Little learned that an acquaintance in the same draft had been killed. A few days later, he ran across the body of another man in his draft who had died on Bunker Hill when an incoming mortar round exploded in front of him. The experience was sobering. Days later, Little lost more friends and paused to reflect. He later wrote of his thoughts:

> One day, two of the young Marines in my bunker were assigned a daylight patrol. The patrol left the gate and when the men got a few hundred yards forward of the MLR, the Chinese dropped mortar rounds in their midst. They were all either KIA [killed in action] or WIA [wounded in action]. Another patrol quickly went out and brought them back. Both of my young bunkmates were dead.

Later, I sat on my bunk and thought. I felt saddened and angered at the losses close to me in the short time I had been in Korea. But this was my first combat experience and I recognized that this was happening every day all along the MLR. You simply had to put the emotion somewhere-not to be forgotten, and get on with what had to be done. You learned from the experience so you could support other Marines with the mission. As I look back, the experience certainly prepared me for what was ahead.[12]

CHAPTER 2

BEGINNING OF ANOTHER YEAR

They say that Americans are good at long shot but cannot stand the cold iron. I call upon you to give a lie to the slander. Charge!
—Winfield Scott, at the battle of Chippewa, July 5, 1814

By God, these are regulars!
—Maj. General Riall, British Army opposing Winfield Scott July 5, 1814

As 1953 opened, the 1st and 7th Marine Regiments were on line and the 5th Regiment in reserve. The 1st Marines, on the division's far right, manned the MLR and six combat outposts with its 2d and 3d Battalions and retained the 1st Battalion in reserve. The 7th Marines had the center sector, east of Panmunjom. Its 3d Battalion was in reserve while the 1st and 2d Battalions managed the defenses on the MLR with eleven outposts.

The Division Command Diary for January reported, "Marine casualties for the month amounted to forty-two killed, six died of wounds, three hundred fourteen wounded (evacuated), two hundred nine wounded (not evacuated), and five missing. There were four deaths from other causes."[1] Compared with other months, January had been slow.

On 20 January, General Eisenhower had moved into the white house on Pennsylvania Avenue to replace Truman, the former artillery captain from Missouri. Eisenhower had promised to end the war in Korea and, because of his military background, was generally well received by the troops. When and how they would leave Korea, however, was altogether another matter.

The rumor mill was rife with "hot scoop"—the 1st Marine Division soon would be relieved by the 3d Marine Division, or the Marines were slated to go to the aid of the French now fighting in Indochina. There was speculation that UN forces would intervene in other parts of the world, but scuttlebutt remained just that and there was no change. January 1953 began to look remarkably similar to December 1952. There was really no reason why it shouldn't. In Korea, nothing had changed except a page on the calendar.

RAID ON HILL 134

Looking down from Combat Outpost Two (COP-2), the Marines saw that Hill 134 was a mess—dirty, barren, and rocky. Months of bombardment had turned the low hill into a dusty sandbox unfit for habitation above ground. The Marines did not want to occupy it. They wanted only to make it uncomfortable for the enemy to remain there. It was a place to kill—an arena where modern gladiators clashed for no discernible purpose, not even to amuse the Caesar.

On 8 January, with a stated objective, "to kill or capture enemy encountered and to destroy fortifications," the Marines raided Hill 134. Tanks, artillery, aircraft, and men from Item Company, 2/7, engaged the enemy.

A great deal of preparation had gone into this raid. The Marines were determined to inflict damage on the Chinese. The general plan called for a frontal assault by a reinforced platoon consisting of three groups: (1) a shock group armed with automatic weapons, demolition charges, and flamethrowers would advance on the hilltop and create confusion; (2) the main assault group, following the shock group, would complete destruction of the position while killing or capturing enemy personnel; and (3) the cleanup detail would travel by armored personnel carrier to pick up casualties, prisoners, and materiel.

On the night of 7 January, engineers swept the approach routes for mines. Once cleared, the area was kept under constant surveillance by infantry patrols. Predesignated tank-firing positions in no-man's-land were cleared and protected by layout patrols for the remainder of the night.

Thursday, 8 January, turned out to be a beautifully clear day. Patches of light snow remained in sheltered hollows and draws. Beginning with a low of 4°F in the early morning, the temperature warmed eventually to 36°F. At 0630, ten tanks from the 2d and 3d Platoons of Capt. Gene M.

("Jinx") McCain's Charlie Company, 1st Tank Battalion, crossed the MLR. They were accompanied by four tanks from the 7th Marines Antitank (AT) Platoon,[2] two flamethrower tanks, three armored personnel carriers (APCs), and a tank retriever, twenty vehicles in all. As the tanks approached their firing positions, four of them received rocket fire from Hill 134, but the rockets were ineffective because of distance and poor marksmanship. Return fire from the tank guns was more useful, and it silenced the rockets.

Without further incident, the tanks positioned themselves as planned. The previous night's precautions had paid off, and they encountered no mines. Two 2d Platoon tanks took positions backed up to the peace corridor, which rendered them safe from return fire, while the others drove out to Gray Rock Ridge, a spit of land jutting east from COP-2. Tanks from the 3d Platoon were located on Outpost Marilyn and Hill 90 and faced 134, while the 7th AT's tanks fired from the MLR. Hidden from Hill 134 the flame tanks, APCs, and a retriever moved directly to their respective assembly areas.

Tank and infantry company commanders established a command post on COP-2 where they could observe and direct the conduct of their forces by radio. A secondary CP was created on COP-1 (Nan) with similar radio equipment. Both CPs communicated with each other via land line.

As each tank arrived in position, gunners began firing adjustment rounds at previously selected targets. The objective was to make range cards for each target from each position while the targets were plainly visible. Later, during the battle, when vision was obscured by smoke, dust, and other contributors to the fog of war, accurate supporting fire could be delivered on specific targets as called for by infantry commanders. Tank gunners would not actually have to see the target. They could simply fire at coordinates listed on their range cards.

After range cards were made, the tanks fired on various targets of opportunity while waiting for the infantry assault to commence. At 0800, air support arrived to bomb and strafe Hill 134. In the rear, artillery began its preparatory fire that added to the tumult created by the tanks and dive bombers. Ten minutes later, 4.2-inch mortars laid smoke on the objective. With no wind, the white smoke hung low and hugged the terrain. Five minutes later, at 0815, the infantry assault began.

Advancing into the smoke and chaos, A Platoon from Item Company moved out. The small hit-and-run shock group swiftly reached its objective and deployed flamethrowers and satchel charges. Then, just as quickly, the shock group withdrew to enable the main assault force, led by 2d Lt. Donald F. Lambert, to advance. Charging the hill in a skirmish line, the assault force drove through enemy fire and attained the first trench line near the top of the hill. Despite the preassault preparations, the platoon encountered more than eighty-five effective enemy soldiers dug in and fighting back. Outnumbered two to one, the Marines took cover in the trenches. The defenders had stopped them with a fusillade of hand grenades, automatic weapons, and mortar fire.

Two flame tanks, led by platoon leader 1st Lt. Michael McAdams, moved out with the main assault. The tanks crossed a wide expanse of frozen rice paddies and went up the hill with the infantry. When the assault bogged down, the tanks continued advancing into a hail of ineffective bullets and hand grenades. Lieutenant McAdams led his tanks through the stalled infantry. Five mortar rounds found their targets but exploded harmlessly against the armored vehicles. Machine-gun bullets and hand grenades ricocheted off the armor.

Relentlessly, the tanks crawled forward and soon reached the enemy trenches. Spraying burning napalm on bunkers, fighting positions, and trench lines on both the forward and reverse slopes, McAdams's tanks wreaked havoc on the enemy. Surviving Chinese soldiers continued to fight, however, and showered the tanks with more grenades and small-arms fire. On several occasions, concussions from exploding ordnance extinguished the ignition fire burning at the end of a tank's flame tube, but they were merely temporary setbacks. Like pilot lights, the flames were relit and more jellied gasoline spewed on enemy troops and positions.

Meanwhile, held up in the trenches on the forward slope, Lieutenant Lambert found that he was unable to observe or lead his men. He needed a vantage point from which to direct the assault, so he scrambled to the top of the hill where he was able to rally the men to him. Fully exposed, he was cut down by an enemy machine gun. Although gravely wounded and unable to rise or move, Lambert continued to direct his troops in returning fire to the enemy.

On the right flank of the assault line, Sgt. Thomas P. McGuire's squad also reached the Chinese trenches. Leaping into a hole, the Marines found it occupied by enemy troops and the fight continued at close quarters. McGuire states:

> I remember standing on the lip of the trench firing down at them [Chinese] as they ran toward a large hole at the end of the forward trench. On my left was Pfc. McGee firing his BAR. I threw two WP [white phosphorus] grenades into the cave. One Chinese came out running and I fired my Thompson at him. He dropped.

Returning to the forward slope I found that the remainder of my group had been held up by an automatic weapon firing from the saddle of the hill. The gun was a major threat to the advance into the trenches. The demolition man had been wounded, as were most of the others, from grenades being rolled down the hill while the machine gun kept them from moving.[3]

To extricate his squad from annihilation, Sergeant McGuire took the demolition charge from the wounded Marine and rolled away from the group. Crouching and running, he successfully reached the lip of the enemy trench near the enemy machine gun. When he was within throwing distance of the gun pit, McGuire extracted the five-second delay pull pin, pitched the charge into the enemy machine-gun position, and hit the ground. The ensuing detonation destroyed the gun, the men using it, and the entire top of the trench.

Survivors of his squad, now free from the machine gun's threat, were able to proceed into the remainder of the trench line and search out enemy soldiers. As they attained the crest of the hill, they learned that Lambert was severely wounded. McGuire reorganized his squad and led his men down the opposite side of the hill to the left flank where he assumed command of the remaining men.

The infantry, with Sergeant McGuire and Lieutenant Lambert leading, had broken the stalemate. The Marines overran the hill and destroyed what was left of the enemy, but Hill 134 was not a place to hold. At 0850, the Item Company commander ordered the assault group to withdraw.

Remaining under fire from nearby hills, albeit lighter fire than previously experienced, the APCs and a clean-up detail raced up the hill to recover dead and wounded Marines. Then, more smoke was directed to the hill to cover their withdrawal.

Inside the tanks deployed around the periphery of the action, the prepared range card technique proved most useful. The cards allowed the gunners to continue firing effectively at obscured targets during all phases of the operation.

At 0923, the infantry platoon returned to COP-2. It had sustained one Marine killed, twenty-four wounded, and two men missing in action. (One of the missing men was Private McGee.) Sergeant McGuire was later awarded a Navy Cross for his actions that morning. Lieutenant Lambert succumbed to his wounds while being carried back to the MLR. He was the only Marine killed in the raid and was posthumously awarded a Navy Cross.[4]

The survivors were victors in a raid that appeared to have little lasting purpose. Yet, if the Marines did not remain aggressive and take the
war to the enemy, the enemy would surely bring it to them. One way or
another, the war was destined to continue.

FAILED AMBUSH

The Division's Reconnaissance Company remained active in January,
occasionally with missions that bordered on the bizarre. One of its milder
tasks was an effort to capture an enemy prisoner in the Korean Marine
Corps (KMC) sector near the Sachon River on 12 January. The operation
came close to becoming a disaster. Sgt. Arthur Lipper III described the
action in a letter home:

> The second platoon left outpost Nan (OP-1) at 1930 Monday [12
> Jan] and walked about 3000 yards out to a reservoir where it set up.
> Our platoon followed along the same route, passed through them
> and set up on the bank of the Sachon River. Our mission was to cross
> the river and continue on for about 1000 yards where we expected to
> come upon a tank trap, bunker and 76-mm gun set up. We were to
> knock out one of the guards and drag him back to our lines.
> The original plan called for eight of us to cross the river in
> advance of the platoon to check for an ambush. But, because of the
> strong current, I changed it at the last minute to just two of us. The
> river was covered with one half to one inch of ice as it was 10 degrees
> below this morning. I couldn't see the point of every one in the team
> getting wet so I had them cover from the bank. Sgt. John Detering,
> the platoon guide, and I made the plunge.
> Thank God the water was only crotch deep (on me that is, it hit
> Detering about mid thigh). We checked the far bank walking back to
> back. I had my grease gun and he carried a Thompson. In going up
> stream I walked backwards, coming down stream we switched and I
> faced forward. The bottom was firm and we pushed the ice out of our
> way with our legs.
> We crossed the fifteen to twenty yard span of ice, slush and water.
> Attaining the other side, we heard machine gun bolts being cocked
> and saw movement. They were waiting for the platoon to cross behind
> us. Noisily, we re-crossed the river, hoping they would follow.
> What the Chinks had done was set up an ambush. If the river had
> been frozen as anticipated, we would have all crossed and been cut
> down. There was no cover at all. Steep banks on one side and sandy
> beach on the other. One of their listening posts must have alerted
> them by radio, phone or bird calls.

Setting up on the opposing bank, we quietly waited for them to come to us—a counter ambush. We lay in position for three and a half hours, just waiting, waiting and freezing. My trousers were literally stiff as a board, so were the greens and the long johns I had on underneath. I could bend my legs but not the trousers. My thermal boots were full of water. At first the water felt good as it was warmer than the air, but that didn't last and they soon got as cold as my legs. I thought my feet would drop off.

We started back about 0500. My feet were numb but as the water in my boots warmed to body temperature, they began to tingle. We had been out for about seven hours about five of which with soaked feet. Thank the Lord for Navy brandy, I think it saved Detering and me.

This time the Chinks were too smart for us. They stayed about 500 yards away, following us all the way, just out of effective range making tocsan noise. ["Toksan" is Japanese for big, great, or large amount.]

Two of our men in the first squad detonated a booby trap. Both got it in the legs. We had to carry them back, a distance of two or three miles. At 0605 we arrived back at the outpost. My feet improved from the walking but the toes were still dead. Davis, the corpsman, says he thinks they'll be all right in a week or so.

I truthfully believe that Detering and I saved the platoon from being hit—hard. We didn't snatch a prisoner, but when you are 5,000 yards away from help, it doesn't pay to take chances. Not with a platoon of men, that is.[5]

A TANK IS LOST

Outpost Hedy, the near end of the Bunker-Hedy ridgeline, had continued to be a problem since Bunker Hill was first occupied in July 1952. Whoever occupied the hill could count on continuing enemy probes and harassment. Outpost Hedy, like Bunker Hill, was configured in such a manner that a squad of Marines held the crest, while Chinese held the bottom. The reverse slope was no problem as it could be protected by guns from the MLR. The forward slope, however, was concealed from the MLR by the hill itself. Due to terrain features, defenders atop the hill could neither see nor effectively fire into enemy positions below them. Moreover, the forward slope was protected by enemy positions on Yoke, Taedok-san, and Hills 123 and 120.

Outpost Hedy was a classic standoff. Neither side could budge the other. But each tried—the Chinese with manpower, the Marines with firepower. Neither were successful. Even tanks, traveling out to Hedy, tried but could not depress their guns low enough to threaten targets on the slope below them until Captain McCain, commanding officer of

Charlie Company, 1st Tank Battalion, thought of a way. In a modern version of dumping boiling oil from the wall of a castle, he suggested driving a flame tank out to Hedy and shooting a load of burning napalm over the edge. Gravity would do the rest, as the napalm fell onto the Chinese positions. The concept was accepted, but closer examination indicated that the road to Hedy would first require some improvement. It was necessary to cut a depression at the end of the road to enable the tank to depress its guns sufficiently to deliver flame on enemy personnel.

At 0830 on the morning of 18 January, tank A-42, a dozer tank[6] from Able Company, rolled out to Hedy to begin road construction. It immediately came under fire, but the crew continued to work. For an hour and a half, they drove the tank back and forth to smooth and form the road and to dig the required depression at the end. Occasionally, they stopped work long enough to return fire. Between 0830 and 1000, A-42 expended nine rounds of 90-mm and five hundred rounds of .30-caliber machine-gun ammunition. In return, the tank received fourteen rounds of 76-mm artillery and twenty rounds of 82-mm and 120-mm mortar. Two direct hits destroyed a periscope and one road wheel. When incoming fire finally drove the tank off the hill, the crew had completed much of the work.

A lone flame tank followed the freshly cut road to Hedy at 1015 and fired a load of flame over the side. The operation was unsuccessful because of mechanical failure. The carbon dioxide (CO_2) cylinders that pressurized the napalm were too cold. Cylinder pressure should have been 1,200 pounds per square inch (psi) but registered only 400 psi. It was another consequence of winter's cold. (Thereafter, the tank crew stored the cylinders in their living quarters until they were ready to use them.) This effort, though ineffective, was not a complete loss. The flame crew was able to check out the dozer effort and to make recommendations for further improvements. For the next three days, A-42 again worked on the road.

An alteration of the plan, requested by the 7th Marines, was a protected means to supply the outpost. Consequently, while the tank road was being built during the day, a deep trench was being dug at night. Marines and Korean work parties used picks and shovels to dig a trench 8 feet deep to the outpost. The new trench paralleled the tank road and enabled the infantry to be supplied and reinforced in far greater safety. Despite intensive cover fire from other tanks on the MLR, A-42 was limited to about one hour per day of dozing operations. Then, on 21 January, enemy antitank teams found their way within range and fired off four rounds of 3.5-inch rockets. The dozer blade was damaged, a periscope destroyed, and four crewmen wounded. When the vehicle returned to the MLR, each of the wounded tankers required evacuation to an aid station.

The timing of the Chinese antitank teams was poor. Although they had chased the dozer off the hill, the road and trench were complete. Consequently, the 7th Marines developed plans for a tank-supported infantry raid on enemy positions at the forward base of Hedy. Using the new road, a flame tank would drive to the edge of the hill and drop flame over the enemy trenches. It would then back off the hill to clear the way for an infantry assault. During the operation, air and artillery would saturate the Chinese stronghold on Yoke while gun tanks on the MLR picked off other targets. Under this umbrella of protective fire, Marine infantry would travel to Hedy via the new personnel trench, attack down the hill, and mop up enemy survivors in the trenches.

It was a simple enough plan that gave every indication of being workable, but success was dependent on two factors: (1) the flame tank's capacity to shock, burn, and otherwise disable enemy troops at the base of Hedy long enough for the Marine infantry to reach and overpower them and (2) the ability of air, tanks, and artillery to neutralize enemy support fire from Yoke and other nearby hills.

S/Sgt. Kenneth Miller, the flame platoon sergeant, led the tank assault from Hedy. His flame tank, F-22, was an M-4 Sherman with a four-man crew. Miller left Hedy Gate at 0700 on 1 February and traveled the few hundred yards to Outpost Hedy. Reaching the end of the road, the tank rumbled slightly over the crest, tipped forward a little, and prepared to unload a full load of napalm, approximately 400 gallons, into the trenches below. Simultaneously, infantry from the 7th Marine Regiment moved out to Hedy via the trench that paralleled the road.

The tank had almost stopped and was getting into position to unload its napalm. The road was very narrow and precarious. Sergeant Miller was looking to the rear with his head partially exposed through the hatch as he told the driver to turn first one way and then the other. As the tank was positioning, it began receiving incoming mortar and artillery fire from Yoke. Two rounds struck the turret and broke the viewing prisms on the tank commander's cupola, inches from Miller's face. Other rounds struck elsewhere on the tank. As the tank continued to back up, one track slipped off the road and the vehicle began sliding to the right. Slowly, as if it had a mind of its own but in less time than it takes to tell, the flame tank slid gently down the hill and slowly rolled over onto its side. It skidding a few more feet before it came to rest on the slope of the hill. Quite obviously, it was out of action.

To the troops on the MLR, it appeared that the tank had been hit. In an effort to protect the crew and enable their escape, observers called for air and artillery strikes around the disabled tank. As bombs and shells struck around them, the men squirmed out of the tank and scrambled the 100 yards back to the MLR. Although it was close, with enemy fire from Yoke and large ordnance falling behind them, they escaped unhurt. Seeing that his three crew members were safely evacuated, Sergeant Miller was relieved that no one was injured. He disabled the radios and guns and evacuated the tank. As he tried to run for the MLR, Miller found that he had injured his knee during the rollover and could only limp. With excellent covering fire, however, he made it to the Marine lines without being hit.

Without the disabling shock value of a flame tank, an infantry assault on the base of Hedy would be suicidal. Wisely, the 7th Marines called off the operation and retired to the MLR.

The next day, Lt. Col. John I. Williamson, commanding officer of the tank battalion, visited the MLR to assess prospects for recovering the damaged tank. After making his decision, he described the scene in a letter home:

> . . . One of them went out the rather tortuous road we've built out to Hedy with a tank dozer. It got to the end of the road and went up and over a little rise in order to better bring the tank to bear against the enemy. As it went over this rise, the ground caved away under it and it rolled over on its side. The crew disabled the gun and radio and got out of it without getting hurt.
>
> The tank lay out there all day today, and the goonies didn't fire a round at it, which amazed us until we figured they were just waiting till we made a move to retrieve it and then would let us have the kitchen sink plus. I went up to the front today to look at it. . . . Inspection of the tank led me to believe that its recovery would be too risky to attempt. It is in such a position that we would probably lose personnel and other tanks in trying to retrieve it. Thus far I have decided not to attempt to get it, unless the General directs that I do otherwise. The distance between us and the enemy at that point is measured in tens of yards.[7]

The abandoned tank was destroyed by gunfire and allowed to lie on the slope of Outpost Hedy for the remainder of the war. It became a landmark, and figured quite often in subsequent patrols, raids, and ambushes for both sides, becoming a favored sniper position for the Chinese. Many Marines and soldiers observing the now burnt-out tank from their fighting holes and bunkers on the MLR might have wondered how it came to be where it was and what had happened to it. Martin Russ, in *The Last Parallel,* mentions this old hulk several times.[8] It is still there, just as it was on 1 February 1953, a machine left rusting in the Demilitarized Zone of peacetime Korea, another piece of war's detritus.

RAIDING HILDA

The 1st Marines, on line east of the 7th Marines, also managed to keep the Chinese on their toes. The 1st and 2d Battalions manned the MLR. The 3d Battalion was in regimental reserve. Each night, 3/1 furnished a reinforced platoon to the Dog Company 2/1 area, where the men spent the night in front of the MLR on Hill 47, more commonly known as "Reno Block."

Early in the morning of 13 January, two platoons from George Company 3/1 moved forward and were passed to operational control of the 1st Battalion. The George Company platoons were to conduct a raid on an enemy-held position in the vicinity of Hilda, the former Marine outpost lost on 11 August, 1952. The raiding party arrived at the MLR at 0100, quickly filed out the Frisco Gate, and walked toward Hilda. The weather was clear, dry, and cold, about 35°F. Moving quietly but with speed, the platoon arrived at the base of the hill, set up, and quickly commenced its assault at 0330.

The attacking Marines engaged an estimated twenty-five enemy troops well dug in on the hill. The Chinese response was heavy. Burp guns, hand grenades, and machine-gun bullets rained down from the top of the hill. Mortars and more machine guns opened up from adjacent hills. Then came the artillery. One of the first casualties was the platoon leader, 2d Lt. Ray Wilson, wounded by machine-gun fire. T/Sgt. Walter C. Borawski immediately assumed command, but then he was hit. Mortally wounded but conscious, the sergeant remained in command long enough to encourage his men to continue the attack.

A squad leader, Sgt. Howard C. Hensley Jr., took over from Borawski and continued the attack. Still in the face of incoming fire, Hensley directed flamethrower teams into enemy forward trenches. The napalm burned trenches and all that was nearby and caused a large secondary explosion, presumably from a cache of ammunition.

Achieving their objective on Hilda, Sergeant Hensley collected the wounded, accounted for all personnel, and organized a withdrawal. The platoon broke off the fighting at 0415 and began its trek to the MLR. Carrying the wounded and fighting their way through pursuing

Chinese, the men took more than an hour and a half to travel 750 yards to the MLR and safety. Cpl. Jess E. Meado, a fire team leader, remembers the attack on Hilda:

> Machine guns from a distant hill and burp guns from the hill in front of us opened up. I heard a thud on the back of the man in front of me. He hollered and went rolling away from me. I didn't know until later that it had been a gook grenade that landed on his back but didn't explode.
>
> We went up the hill and ran off the gooks, who really liked throwing grenades at us. There was a lot of shooting and grenade throwing. There were also many wounded, and I started helping the wounded get off the hill.
>
> When I got to the bottom, I asked if everyone had gotten off the hill. Someone said that he thought the Gunny Sergeant ["Gunny" is Marine Corps jargon for a gunnery sergeant, which, in turn was commonly used to denote the official rank of technical sergeant], the corpsman and Lt. [Ray] Wilson were still up there. I took off up the hill, yelling for some men to help me. At first they didn't come, but I went on and crawled around and called out until someone answered me.
>
> It was the Gunny Sergeant. He had been hit real hard. He told me to leave him and go on to find the others. By this time other Marines had joined me and they carried him and the corpsman down the hill. That left only the lieutenant who was farther on up the hill.
>
> I continued on alone looking for him. I finally found him. He had been hit in the legs. I tried to pick him up, but couldn't. I asked if his arms and hands were okay. He said yes. I told him to hang on to his carbine, and I started dragging him down the hill. I happened to think about how I was dragging him—I had the barrel, he had the stock. I told him to make sure it was on safety so he wouldn't accidentally shoot me.
>
> A gook must have heard us talking because a grenade was thrown. The lieutenant was hit again, but not bad. We finally got to the bottom of the hill and placed all of the wounded together to wait to be carried back to our line.
>
> . . . We finally got our wounded on stretchers and headed for our lines. We went across the rice paddy to the first hill. I was the last man out. We heard voices from across the paddy at the bottom of the hill that had been raided. As we were about to fire, I cautioned the men to listen again because I thought I could understand what they were saying. I'm glad we listened again because it was one of our stretcher teams that had gotten turned around and was going the wrong way. We let them know what the situation was and gave them cover while they crossed the paddy. We got back to our lines about 0500.[9]

Sergeant Borawski was posthumously awarded a Navy Cross for his actions on Hilda. Sergeant Hensley, who was also wounded, survived to receive a Navy Cross as well. When the battle ended, twenty-three Marines had been wounded. Stricken with grief over the death of his friend Gunny Borawski, 2d Lt. Richard Guidera wrote the following epitaph to his fallen comrade:

> When I returned to the Company CP, I saw the stretcher covered with a poncho, and I really did not need to be told, "the Gunny is dead." After all, not many minutes earlier I had helped to carry him and that stretcher up the forward slope of the MLR on Hill 111 across from Frisco.
>
> Tech Sergeant Walter Borawski was the Gunny on the stretcher. He was my friend and had said to me very softly and very quietly as we carried him, "Lieutenant, I am getting very cold." It was the stretcher bearers that night in January of 1953 who had told me that Sergeant "Ski" had a potato masher go off between his legs while he was in a squat position out in front of Frisco.
>
> It was those same bearers who had told me that the Gunny would not allow himself to be evacuated from the raid until the end. He was a great guy and on that night was Lt. Ray Wilson's assistant combat patrol commander. A little more than a month earlier, when I was a replacement draft company commander, he had been my Gunny.
>
> We became good friends while organizing that replacement draft. We trained physically together; we would often race each other to the top of the steep hills surrounding our training area at Camp Pendleton.
>
> And one day after we had raced each other to a hilltop carrying backpacks loaded with sand, and while we lay down at the top to catch our breath, he asked me if he could call me Dick. He went on to tell me about his having been in Recon during World War II and that he had never received a scratch. Then he told me his premonition, that he had bad feelings about Korea and that he hoped he would not be hit too badly—after all, he had a family.[10]

For Gunny Borawski, the raid had taken place ten days too soon. On 23 January, after two months on line, with 24 men killed, 19 missing and 366 wounded, the 1st Marine Regiment was relieved. The 5th Marines now assumed responsibility for the division's right sector of the Jamestown Line. Unfortunately, during the following two months, some of the bloodiest and most destructive fighting of the war would occur. The 5th Marines were destined to be involved—up to their heroic eyeballs and then some.

CHAPTER 3

A YEAR ON THE JAMESTOWN LINE

War sank into the lowest depths of beastliness
and degeneration. . . For years the armies had to
eat, drink, sleep amidst their own putrefaction.
—Sir Ian Hamilton: *The Soul and Body*
of an Army, 1921, vii

Positional warfare fought from the same places month after month began to tell. A man occasionally might be tired or depressed with the progress of the war or the lack of it, but he had something to look forward to—eventual rotation. Sooner or later, with or without war's end, every man would ship out of Korea for discharge or for another duty station.

In the meantime, Korean real estate began to wear out. There was a visible similarity to World War I. Fixed positions on the hills, battered by constant shell fire and endless digging, lost cohesion and turned to dust. More digging was required to get deeper. Trenches and fighting holes eroded. Bunkers and other temporary shelters collapsed from the weight of water-soaked sandbags or landslides. During spring thaw and summer rains, dust turned to mud and, after drying, was blown into dust again. It was 1917 France all over again but mountainous rather than flat.

On seeing the MLR for the first time, one new replacement described it as ". . . a rambling messy ditch or series of ditches five to seven feet deep. Bunkers were marked by trash: ration cans, paper, canvas and stovepipes. No doubt the Chinese knew where nearly every position was located."[1]

Trails, paths, and roads became static as well. With the Korean valleys covered in rice paddies, flooded calf deep in water, and fertilized with human waste, patrol routes were confined mostly to trails. Soon, the trails were worn and marked, beckoning targets for mortar fire. Communication wire, the umbilical cord of repeated patrols, was strewn in great quantities on every path. Secreted under mats of discarded wire, land mines and trip wires awaited a careless footstep.

On the MLR, toilet facilities usually consisted of a pit, dug on the reverse slope of the hill, that was surmounted by a wooden ammunition box for comfort (except for slivers). Despite being surrounded by sandbags shoulder high to a sitting man, no one tended to loiter on the head. Some locations had "piss tubes," urinals located at strategic defilade locations about the area. Though out of direct enemy observation, these conveniences were well within range of mortar and artillery. Rather than travel through a shallow portion of trench or otherwise be exposed to observation, the men often chose the quick relief afforded by a nearby but sheltered rock, a ration can, or an empty ammunition box.

The farther behind the lines one traveled, the more elaborate (and clean) were the facilities. By way of contrast, a Marine recalled facilities provided for the men in reserve south of the Imjin River, well beyond the range of enemy guns:

> In reserve one of our daily work details involved burning out the heads. This was a ritual practiced each morning for cleanliness. Our toilets were simple pits in the ground over which a structure was built to protect the occupant from the elements. Privacy was never a consideration as evidenced by the "piss tubes" near every tent. A piss tube was a urinal, consisting of a four inch pipe placed in a hole in the ground and conveniently angled to enhance the aim of the user. As male urination is rarely a lengthy process, no shelters were provided around the tube. Thus, every couple of tents had a tube or two stuck in the ground in plain sight of everyone. The user simply approached the tube, possibly while engaged in friendly conversation with a buddy, unbuttoned his fly and urinated in the tube, getting most of it inside.
>
> During the winter piss tubes created some unique problems that apparently hadn't been considered by their creators. With temperatures in the low teens and worse, and the men wearing multiple layers of heavy clothing, it was often difficult to even find one's equipment, much less to drag it out through buttons, zippers, flaps and assorted openings of underwear, long johns, utility trousers, cold weather trousers and parkas. And then, when finally ready, to accurately direct an entire stream into a four inch pipe without spilling any on yourself and nearby terrain. It became quite a challenge. The result was often a

considerable amount of over spray and other evidences of misalignment. As a consequence, towers of frozen urine began to form on the ground around the tube. And, as the yellow stalagmites melted and re-froze from multiple use, a frozen pool of ice formed at the base extending out from the tube, like a miniature lemon colored glacier. Consequently, the ever spreading pool of ice caused the user to stand farther away to avoid slipping and falling on the mess. Quite naturally increasing the range caused further inaccuracy and the cycle grew worse. By spring thaw it was time to sink new tubes somewhere else.

For some reason piss tubes were rarely burned, only pit toilets. Cleaning the heads involved washing off the seats, restocking them with toilet paper and splashing a quantity of gasoline or fuel oil into the pit, followed by a match. Ordinarily this would start a flame burning in the hole that theoretically killed the germs. I wonder about that now, but at the time it was the way of things. Done right the gasoline burned briefly and then died. As a matter of fact, a gas can was kept at the ready outside the head and was often used by occupants to warm up the place in the winter. It took off the chill and modified the odor somewhat.

Our platoon was blessed with a particularly elegant head. It was a four holer, constructed over a wood floor with a two by four frame. It was covered with chicken wire and had roofing paper on the walls and roof. It even had a swinging screen door, with a spring. The frame supporting the seats was painted a deep, contemplative Marine green. It had a nice view as it was situated on the side of a hill overlooking our company area in the draw below.

One particular morning, another Marine and I had the head cleaning detail. Everything went fine until we got to our own head. After cleaning the seats, sweeping the floor and replenishing the paper, it was time for the gasoline. I threw in a canteen cup full, lit a match and nothing happened. I threw in another cupful, followed by another match, still nothing. After a third try with the same results my companion became impatient and sloshed in more gas directly from the can, to hell with measuring. He tried one more match and still nothing. I was now beginning to think that someone had replaced the gasoline with less volatile kerosene or stove oil. Taking a break, we sat outside and smoked a cigarette, watching the company assemble for morning formation at the bottom of the hill and figuring our next move. Deciding to give it one more try, my buddy opened the door and tossed a match into the hole from outside. WOOOSH! The subsequent explosion blew my partner ten feet down the hill, singeing his eyebrows and hair. The blast went right over the top of me.

Men standing the morning formation two hundred yards below turned at the sound of the blast. I was told that the building shot five feet straight up, fully intact. Then, while airborne, the roof and walls separated and began to fall in pieces, amid fluttering bits of toilet paper and debris. It all happened so fast that there wasn't even a fire, just pieces of wood held together with bits of roofing paper and chicken wire.[2]

If one considers the MLR lacking in creature comforts, outposts were worse. The smaller the outpost, the more primitive were the facilities. Spending nights on alert and hiding in holes during the days, the men had few places to go when nature called. Frequently, they simply used empty C-ration cans and threw the contents over the slope, preferably on the side fronting the enemy.

Without question, life on the outposts was rough. Outposts were supplied daily with food, water, ammunition, and replacement personnel. Everything that was needed to live, fight, and survive went out to the outposts on the backs of Marines and Korean Service Corps (KSC) laborers. The KSC was a collection of Korean men too old to be conscripted into the army. They worked in various capacities throughout the war zone. They dug trench lines and bunkers, filled sandbags, strung barbed wire, and carried stretchers and supplies.

What did not happen with equal regularity or thoroughness on an outpost was disposal of trash. C rations came in cans and paper boxes, plus there were ammunition crates, fired brass, worn-out clothing, and supply containers. The older and larger the outpost, the greater was the accumulation of rubbish.

When exposing one's limbs or head brought down the wrath of incoming mortars or the instant response of a sniper, orderly disposal of trash did not assume a high priority. In some cases, trash dumps were established but only when safe and practical. Often as not, rubbish was simply thrown down the hill. When possible, a returning supply train carried out rubbish on its return to the MLR, but wounded and sick Marines had a higher priority, followed by an occasional prisoner or empty water and fuel cans.

The Marines themselves were in no better condition. People, it seems, get grimier faster than their surroundings. Hollywood does not portray the filth and smells of war to their movie audiences. Movies do not show the ground-in layers of dirt, blood, food, sweat, and worse that remained on the clothing and skin of men living on an outpost. Or the smell! Without water for bathing, shaving, or washing and without clean clothes, the men became walking rubbish heaps. On an outpost, water was a precious commodity. Every drop was carried across no-man's-land to the hill. It was not unusual for men to boil coffee, drink some of it, wash their faces with the residue, and use what was left to brush their teeth. Sgt. John J. O'Hagan with Able Company 1/7 wrote:

> Water was so precious that taking a bath was out of the question. When you live in a hole in the ground, you look like it and you smell like it. If you did clean up, it wouldn't last long, especially when you go out at night and lay in a dirty stinking rice paddy. Water was not to be wasted.
>
> Being Irish I was raised on tea instead of coffee. Tea was ideal for trench and outpost duty. A hot can of water and a tea bag. My folks sent me a box of Lipton tea bags about every month. I was able to get eight cans of tea out of one teabag. After each use I wrung the hell out of it and hung it up to dry. Sometimes I had five or six tea bags hanging to dry.[3]

Men on patrol spoke of smelling the garlic and sweat of nearby Chinese. Perhaps they did not consider what an American Marine smelled like? 2d Lt. William (Bill) Watson of George Company 3/7 wrote of smelling the men whom his platoon was relieving well before he ever saw them. Like the outpost on which they lived, the men smelled horrible.

Of Outpost Carson, Pfc. Patrick Luminello of Dog Company 2/1 wrote, "I recall the misery of living in that cave during the winter of 1952. The craziness that would ensue when a shipment of fruit or other food arrived. It wasn't handed out but simply thrown into the cave for us to catch and grab as best we could. It wasn't a pleasant sight, I assure you. It was amazing how fast we reverted to the law of the jungle there."[4]

In that "jungle," Marines coped with a different variety of native wildlife. Attracted by the food and rubbish, rats were everywhere. Sergeant O'Hagan continued:

> I've seen rats on top of the trenchline and also running in front of me down the trench. They were so common that no one made an issue of them. It was not at all unusual to hear a gun shot and find that someone had shot one of them. I remember seeing a rat swimming in the water in the bottom of a trench just ahead of me. I was faster and got him.
>
> On OP [Outpost] Dagmar, my buddy from New York, while sleeping in his bunker, was awakened by a rat chewing on the cuff

sleeve of his long handles. It had dried food on it and the rat chewed a hole in the sleeve. I can still hear his ranting and raving.[5]

Some men never became accustomed to the thought and sight of living among the squirrel-sized rats of Korea, especially those sharing their sleeping bunkers with the rats. 2d Lt. Howard Matthias of Dog Company 2/5 wrote of one such person:

> . . . One of the men, an officer, became nearly petrified with fear at the sight of a rat. This would set off his screams to others nearby to "get down here and kill this son of a bitch." In most cases the screams frightened the rodent off by the time help would arrive.
>
> On one fateful day one of the men was nearby when this officer sighted a huge rat in his bunker. The would-be hunter broke into the bunker with his Colt 45 ready to fire. The rat was poised just above the screamer's bed. Two shots were fired and a good part of the rat (the bloodiest part) fell onto the sleeping bag and the remainder was blown into a shallow opening behind the wall.
>
> The roar of the 45 in the small confine of the bunker deafened both of the men for a couple of days.
>
> The shooter nodded approvingly and hurriedly left to a hero's welcome from the rest of the men.
>
> It was only then that the officer with the overpowering phobia against rats realized that he had a horrible mess on his hands. His hearing was temporarily disabled and a rotting carcass was inaccessible in his bunker.
>
> The shooter was honored as "Sharpshooter of the year" by the rest of the men.[6]

Author S. L. A. Marshall describes living in the trenches of France in 1917:

> The forward battalions, living in dugouts, sloshed through trenches knee deep in mire. Red slugs crawled the walls of these ditches; frogs splashed in the muck of the floor; rats and roaches plagued the sleeping quarters. At intervals the front-line companies would be run through delousing stations on the regimental rear. Men bathed while their clothing was put through a steam chamber. Then back to the dugouts, and within twenty-four hours they were again lice-infested.[7]

Thirty-six years later and half a world away, little had changed. In Korea, the static nature of the war had enabled defenses, particularly on the MLR, to evolve into semipermanent installations. Trenches were deeper and, in some places, reinforced. Bunker roofs and walls were thicker. Loose, unstable dirt was replaced with tons of sandbags. Timbers, hewn and milled in Japan, were installed to reinforce bunkers, CP's, and machine-gun positions.

Typically, trenches were dug into the forward slope of the ridges a few yards down from the skyline, a place known as the "military crest." Located every few yards was a dugout position, a firing or fighting hole that faced the enemy, where a man could stand to fire his rifle and expose only his head and shoulders. Across from the firing hole was a hole, tunneled into the side of the ridge, variously called a bunny hole, a crab hole, a cubby hole. Here, a man could remain during the artillery barrage preceding an attack. When the barrage lifted, he could immediately move to his fighting hole, which often had a built-in shelf for keeping hand grenades and ammunition at the ready.

Along the trench line were living bunkers, covered fighting bunkers, and storage bunkers for ammunition. The roof of each structure was built of the thickest available timbers and covered with roofing paper and tiers of sandbags. Doorways were covered with panchos, shelter halves, or blankets. In the winter, there might be several layers for more warmth. Some of the entrances were so low that men had to enter on their hands and knees.

If the bunker was large enough, bunks kept the men off the floor. Often, a bottom bunk was a standard folding cot. For a second tier, barbed-wire stakes were driven into the walls leaving a couple of feet exposed. A stretcher might be suspended across the stakes, or if one lived in the poor section of town, communication wire was strung between the stakes to create a surface on which to throw an air mattress and a sleeping bag. There were few rules. Over the months, each bunker took on an individual character as various occupants came and went.

Candles provided light. Issue candles were 4-inch affairs drawn from company supply when they were available, which was rare. Usually, they were on the bottom of the list and seldom made it as far as the line. On rare occasions, a Red Cross worker appeared in the vicinity and passed out candles, but candles often came from home. They were not as good as cookies, but they lasted a lot longer.

During daylight hours, stoves were turned down very low, regardless of the temperature. When they burned high, the smoke offered a tempting target to the enemy. Another advantage was that a low-burning stove used less fuel and required fewer trips to the supply bunker. Hiking uphill with 5 gallons of fuel oil on a packboard made for heavy going.

Cooking or, more accurately, warming up was also done in the living bunkers on the oil stove or, if one was fortunate, a Coleman stove that someone had acquired from home and passed on when he left. Sergeant O'Hagan shared some recollections of cooking on the MLR:

> I can't remember where I picked up my Coleman cooking stove. It burnt white or red gas and the Company had plenty of it. I can't begin to tell you how precious that stove was to me. It would heat up a bunker in fifteen minutes to a half hour. Not to mention heating up C rations. I remember being offered one hundred dollars in script for my Coleman stove.
>
> When it comes to C rations, it was quicker to heat a can of heavies [an entree, such as hamburger, beef stew, etc.] by throwing the can on the fire unopened, than to use your P-38 can opener [a small folding can opener contained in each box of C ration] and hold the can over the flame by its folded back lid. When you throw the unopened can directly on the flames you must be able to see the ends of the can. When the ends pop out you remove the can from the fire and shake it like hell till the ends pop back in.
>
> No one liked corn beef hash. It was packed too tight and wouldn't heat all the way through. Most of us pitched it. You could heat it by spreading it out in your mess gear and frying, but there was no way to clean up. Water was too precious to use for washing dishes.
>
> For obvious reasons prunes were not too popular either. They were usually thrown away with the corn beef. The most valuable can in C-rats was fruit cocktail. You could trade a can of fruit cocktail for anything. I remember on various outposts we would combine this can of heavies with that can. Some of the better combinations were ham and lima beans with sausage, or beans and pecker heads [small wieners] with hamburger and gravy. It was amazing what good combinations we could come up with.[8]

Like all fine dining, no discussion of food is complete without the wine. Beer and liquor were not permitted on the MLR or outposts, but the resourcefulness of the average Marine should never be underrated. If prostitutes could be smuggled north past the Military police (MP) checkpoints at the Imjin River (which occurred more often than anyone cared to admit), concealing a few bottles of liquor or a case of beer was no trouble at all. The contraband could be purchased or stolen from staff NCOs or officers in the rear, bought on the black market from Korean nationals, or liberally traded during neighborly visits with troops of the British Commonwealth Division.

Another source of libation was home brew. The brewer had only to obtain a few common ingredients, mix them up, let the concoction ferment, and soon produce a very potent drink. Applejack seemed to be the mixture of choice, but the men soon learned that any fruit would do.

Most of the drinking occurred immediately behind the line among cooks, clerks, forward supply personnel, and others living in the combat zone but not in the trenches. It was not that combat troops were too righteous to play, but they just did not have the time. Sleeping during the day and standing watch all night left little energy for partying.

Hot showers were a refreshing aspect of life on the MLR. Shower points were located behind the lines, within a long walking distance of the trenches. Often, they were near the battalion CP where the mess hall was located and supplies stockpiled. Each day, small groups of men were relieved from the line, one group at a time, to walk to a shower point. The men looked forward to a shower run. It was an opportunity to socialize, clean up, and grab a hot meal at the mess hall. While at the CP, the men might stop at the supply bunker and try to argue the supply clerk out of a few extra candles, a pair of new socks, or a bottle of Tabasco. Cpl. Robert A. Hall, a machine gunner from Weapons Company 2/5, described his typical trip to the showers:

> A common pastime was to walk back to battalion for a hot meal and a shower. This could be done every few days dependent on schedules worked out with bunkmates. . . . The mess personnel at battalion treated men from the line very well, allowing us to straggle in and feed us. Hot showers were at what everyone called the "changie-changie." This was two or three squad tents joined together with a hot water unit. It was very pleasant and steamy inside in sharp contrast to the outside. Walk in, remove weapons, helmets, flak-jackets and clothes, hot shower, then get fresh clean socks, skivvies, long johns and utilities and go on your way.
>
> A source of amusement was making "shower rates." One might be given a clean utility jacket with staff sergeant's or gunnery sergeant's chevrons inked on the sleeve. This was before the Marine Corps adopted the small metal interchangeable collar chevrons for rank identification. Unless you knew a person you couldn't be sure what his rank was.
>
> The walk back and forth to the battalion meant passing through a portion of the road called "76 Alley." This was about a mile of valley floor open to direct Chinese observation from their hills in the Vegas area. The Chinese usually wouldn't waste rounds on a couple of isolated infantrymen, or perhaps even a single jeep, but occasionally they'd prove why it wasn't smart to relax or take too much for granted in Korea.[9]

SNIPERS

Snipers were prevalent in Korea. Both UN troops and the Chinese became effective at this technique of war. Sharpshooters in the trench line of an outpost or the MLR patiently trained their scoped rifles on enemy positions and fired when an imprudent head or body appeared.

Lt. Col. Norman Hicks, in his thesis on outpost warfare, provides an interesting anecdote on the subject of snipers:

> The old tried and true employment of sniper teams is another effective outpost technique. During the summer of 1952 the enemy made the existence of Marines manning outposts veritably a "living hell," for any movement above the trenchline might bring death in the form of a swift bullet.
>
> This problem was solved by the battalion commander of 3/1, after a CCF [Chinese communist forces] sniper shot his binoculars from his hands one afternoon. Colonel [Gerard T.] Armitage organized about three dozen sniper teams whose members were specially trained to be better snipers than the enemy. These Marines practiced for three weeks, and then went to work in earnest from the outposts. Within a few days' time, enemy sniping was reduced to practically nothing, and Marines on outposts could breathe a little easier. The newly-trained snipers were using either sniper rifles or scope-sighted .50 caliber machine guns, and these larger guns proved to be effective at distances greater than 1,000 yards. They were in fact invaluable.
>
> What was once a hotbed of snipers soon became an area safe enough for the division commander to walk the entire length of a company outpost without drawing enemy fire. About a week after the Marine snipers went into action, Maj. Gen. John T. Seldon visited 3/1's Company I on BUNKER HILL. Jauntily carrying his walking stick, the general paced the whole length of the company parapet, at all times in full view of the enemy. Finishing his stroll, he jumped down and exclaimed to the company commander, "By God, Spike, it works! what we need are more snipers on this front."[10]

Deployment of Marine sniper teams noticeably lowered the Marine mortality rate in the trenches. Battalion Command Diaries of the period appear to reflect a reduction of friendly casualties from enemy sniper activity that was accompanied by an increase in reported enemy KIAs from Marine sniper action.

As Command Diaries report only unit activity and/or numbers of killed and wounded, it is rare to find anyone named and credited with a given action. It is therefore notable to find the following entries in the 5th Marine Regimental Command Diary:

July 14—In mid-afternoon Sgt. Boitnott, on outpost "Bruce," expended one round in killing one enemy.

July 15—S/Sgt. Boitnott on outpost "Bruce" expended eight rounds of rifle ammunition in killing four enemy.

July 17—This morning S/Sgt. Boitnott, on outpost "Bruce" killed one enemy at long range with a rifle and four hours later, killed another.

July 18—S/Sgt. Boitnott, of "I" Company, killed one enemy with one round of rifle fire.[11]

Within Marine Corps archives, Sergeant Boitnott appears to have disappeared. No further mention of his sharpshooting activity is found. Many references to Marine sniping, which continued throughout the war, are in the records but, regrettably, no other names are recorded.

On at least one occasion there was a Chinese sniper that remained anonymous and deservedly so because he was a very poor shot. 2d Lt. Stan Rauh tells about making one of his position checks on the MLR and spotting a young Marine, fully exposed to enemy observation, who was sitting on an ammunition box atop the trench line. He wore no flak jacket or helmet. As the lieutenant approached, he saw a puff of dirt hit a few yards from the Marine and it was followed by the distant crack of a rifle. When Rauh began to chew him out, the lad replied, "Don't sweat it, lieutenant—he's a lousy shot—that's his eighth round and he can't hit shit."[12]

Probably the ultimate sniper weapon, more deadly even than the Chinese 76-mm artillery piece, was the 90-mm gun on a Marine tank. Sitting on the ridgeline of the MLR and perching over a trench line, the tank gunner had a full sweep of enemy positions. All he had to do was to see a target. The gun had a flat trajectory like an M-1 rifle. With a maximum range of more than 8 miles and sighted with a range finder and the gunner's twenty-power scope, it was extremely accurate and far reaching. Although he preferred to fire at troops in the open or at vehicles and tanks, it was not above the dignity of a tank gunner to fire at a single Chinese soldier who was careless enough to show himself. It was simply a matter of priorities, and the business of war is to kill. In the 5th Marines Command Diary cited above, for example, there is mention of a tank killing four enemy soldiers casually swimming in a river.

The .50-caliber machine gun was also useful for sniping. Some of these guns had scopes that enabled a skilled gunner to "tap" the butterfly trigger and accurately fire a single round more than 1,000 yards. More frequently, however, the standard .50 in a bunker was zeroed in on a specific area while the gunner waited for a spotter to call for fire. Corporal Hall describes his experience with this technique:

> Sometimes during the day, machine gunners would go over to the ".50 bunker." This was a position toward the right flank of the Fox Company trench line with a .50 cal machine gun in place. This gun was used to mark targets for artillery and tank fire. I think it was the only one on the company front. It was also useful for sniping. Up the slope behind the .50 was the Arty FO bunker [artillery forward observer]. The FO's had a powerful set of permanently mounted binoculars that were referred to as a "BC scope." Using this, FO's would pick out areas where Chinese were likely to appear—a curve in their trench, stairs, a bunker. These potential targets were all at extreme ranges, perhaps 1,000 or 2,000 yards. The gun would be set on such a target using one or two rounds of tracer and then "locked in" and left pointing at its target for hours if necessary.
>
> . . . The .50 bunker was a casual gathering place—kind of like a coffee shop, or a corner tavern with no booze. You'd see people from other squads; two or three might stop in to "shoot the shit," or bring a guitar and just sit and listen. Most days nothing would happen relating to the machine gun. It was just sitting there locked in on some target pointing way up north while we socialized. But, once in a while the sound power would alert us with a call from the FO behind us. He'd spot something on his BC scope, "Gook on the stairs" or just "Stand by." One of us in the bunker, usually the closest to the gun, would grab the handles, and when the FO said. "Let 'er go" a long burst of ten or so rounds were fired. The FO would then report the results. While an occasional success didn't set the Chinese Army back much, it made us feel a lot better.[13]

PICK UP YOUR BRASS

In March 1952, when the Division was packing for the move to the west coast, an unidentified Marine was overheard grousing to his buddies. His words went something like this: "This is some fucking war. You go out on a fucking patrol. You get in a fucking firefight. You knock off a few fucking Chinks. A coupla' our guys get hit and word comes to move out. What does the fucking lieutenant say? Pick up your fucking brass."

"Pick up your brass and fall back." Every Marine who has ever fired the rifle range, and that means all of them, knows the meaning of that phrase. Literally, it is a range command directing shooters to police up their spent cartridges and fall back to the next firing line. Metaphorically, it indicates that the job at that place is finished and everyone will be moving out. They will go elsewhere to do the same thing under different conditions.

Little did the complaining Marine know that he was a prophet. A year later, the Marines were actually picking up their brass and salvaging the spent metal of war. The salvage procedure had worked well on Stateside target ranges, where was no distraction of a shooting war. Severe ammunition rationing in October 1952 resulted in a move to recover and recycle brass, especially that produced by tank and artillery units. The problem did not result from a parsimonious supply operation in Korea. It could be traced 5,000 miles east to the United States, where the manufacture of artillery ammunition had lagged behind the war. Most people, members of Congress included, wanted to believe (and acted as though) the war soon would be over. Money was not being allocated for ammunition and manufacturers were not producing sufficient quantities.

Gen. Mark W. Clark, Commander, UN Far East Command, deplored the shortage and wrote to Secretary of Defense Robert A. Lovett. Clark noted that the current ninety-day level of supply was adequate but that "many of the items were below the ninety-day level and that shipments scheduled for the remainder of the year [late 1952] would not make up the deficits. Since a high rate of artillery fire resulted in lower friendly casualties, he deplored the need to reduce the allocations of 155-mm howitzer ammunition from 15 to 9.4 rounds per day"[14] Lovett replied that one way the troops could help to alleviate the shortage would be to return brass cartridge cases from expended artillery and tank rounds because they represented a choke point in production.[15] In the military, suggestions from cabinet secretaries equal commands, and a massive effort to salvage brass began in Korea.

Picking up brass was no hardship for artillery units. Their positions behind the MLR were static and semipermanent. The process simply amounted to piling the spent brass somewhere and arranging to ship it out of the country. Tankers had a different problem. They had no room inside the tank for storing empty brass; there was barely space to store live ammunition. Normally firing in the open, a tank was exposed to enemy observation and fire. Tankers disposed of brass by simply throwing it outside through either an open hatch or the pistol port (a small round, porthole-like window in the left side of the turret). During a mission, the port is customarily left open to facilitate the exhaust of powder fumes, to obtain fresh air, and to dispose of brass. Consequently, collection of brass from a tank fire mission presented a problem. It would be suicidal for men to expose themselves on a skyline and walk around to collect empty shells.

Early efforts involved returning the expended brass to the space provided for live ammunition. Because of space limitations, this solution proved awkward and reduced accessibility to ammunition ready racks. Then, in February 1953, Marines with the 1st Tank Battalion fabricated baskets from barbed wire stakes and welded them to the outside of tank turrets. Although unsightly, they were functional, and much of the brass was returned to the United States for recycling.

A serendipitous consequence of the external brass basket was added protection to the turret. On a number of occasions, an incoming round striking the basket detonated before it struck the tank, and the explosive force of the shell was ineffectively expended in the open air. This phenomenon was a particularly useful defense against antitank rounds, which depended on the force of a shaped charge to burn a hole through a tank's armor-plated hull. Subsequently, during a follow-on experiment, entire turrets were encircled with chain-link fencing attached to 1-foot standoffs. The result proved to be too awkward, however, and the project was abandoned.

With the war static across the front, reserve areas also had time to stabilize, which yielded a few well-deserved "perks" to the men as they rotated off line. Many of the Command Diaries record beer busts, barbecues, sports, USO (United Service Organization) shows, and other forms of recreation for the men before they resumed the serious business of training.

Regarding the outpost war, Colonel Hicks summarized the Marine's progress: ". . . They met its problems as they had met other problems before—head on. And although they may not have been able to impose their will on the tenacious and resourceful Chinese communists, at least they prevented the enemy from completely realizing his announced goals."[16]

A MATTER OF ATTITUDE

In January 1953, despite peace talks, press speculation, President Eisenhower's promise to "Go to Korea," and optimistic scuttlebutt about the war ending soon, the Marines saw no end in sight. Negotiations in Panmunjom had little meaning. They seemed remote and abstract—much bickering with nothing to show for it. The peace talks were largely political posturing. The troops wanted to fight the "damn war" instead of sitting around and getting shot at while others discussed nuances of perceived offenses and the effects of world opinion.

In an article appearing in *Leatherneck* magazine, R. R. Keene quotes Cpl. John [Jack] Orth, How Company 3/7:

> "There was talk of the ending but, after a while nobody in the whole Division took anything serious or paid any attention to it. We heard talks of peace, but it was business as usual," recalled Orth. "The veterans had heard how the war was soon going to be over lots of times."
>
> Another veteran Marine recalled an officer visiting them the year before (1952) saying, "You'll be home by Christmas." Christmas had come and gone and so had the Marine officer, but the Marines he'd addressed were, like Orth, standing guard in the muddy, spring rainwater of Korea.[17]

All that the men knew about progress toward peace was what they heard from scuttlebutt or read in rarely acquired and usually outdated newspapers or in letters from home. A nineteen-year-old sergeant William Janzen with Charlie Company 1/5, in a letter home, expressed his view of the peace talks:

> Where we are you can see the Panmunjom peace light every night and in the daytime the barrage balloons above it. We're pretty close, and everyday men are dying around it. It kind of gets to you at times. Everybody over here is thoroughly disgusted with those peace talks. It makes you wonder sometimes just what the hell you're fighting for anyway.
>
> . . . We are doing nothing but holding on to what we already have and fighting to get back what we lose. Then, after getting it back we sit down and wait for them to try and take it away again. We should be pushing on and getting this war over and done with. We really hate those peace talks. If they'd do some good it would be all right, but they're not.[18]

The attitude of this Marine was typical of the young enlisted men. They were aggressive, full of bravado, and blessed with youth's immortality. In a perverse way, they enjoyed the war about them. It was an adventure, a summer camp with real guns, which is why they fought so well. As they bled, they learned and aged, but, as a group, they never lost their spirit.

For other Marines, perhaps the more mature, war created such problems as homesickness and longing for loved ones. Although equally brave, they saw the killing and destruction through different eyes. Married men, in particular, were susceptible to the sense of distance and perhaps the reality of their own mortality. What follows is a different point of view.

THOUGHTS OF HOME

On a spring night in Korea, a young Marine lieutenant, absorbed in thought, was sitting at a field desk in his tent. He had duty that night and was waiting for midnight so that he could check posts with the Sergeant of the Guard. The other officers sharing his tent had gone to bed when the lights went out at 2230. He felt very alone.

The evening was warm. Through the open doorway, off to the north, he could hear the muffled impact of artillery. The horizon sometimes lit up and silhouetted the steep hills behind the company CP. "Someone is catching it," he thought, glad that he was no longer on line. Recently, he had been a platoon leader, but he was now the company executive officer, the XO, a job that was safer but somewhat boring.

The minutes passed much too slowly, but, sitting there alone, he was not thinking about time. He was thinking of home and of his future. The man was homesick, terribly homesick. He had been in Korea for six months and did not like it one bit. He yearned to be home with his wife and child. In his early twenties, he had been married for three years. At home, there was a small baby boy growing up without a father and a young wife, barely a woman, struggling to be a mother by herself. The young couple wrote often, nearly once a day, but it was not the same as being there. He ached to be with his wife and baby.

The lieutenant had joined the Marine Corps right out of college, at about the same time that he had married. He joined for all the right reasons—patriotism, esprit de corps, service, security—many of the same reasons that prompted him to marry. He had been satisfied with both situations. Then, came the war and Korea.

As a Marine, he knew he could be deployed to many parts of the world and that his career would involve separation from his family, but he had not foreseen how painful it would be. He had not been prepared—youth often have difficulty visualizing consequences. Now, here he was in Asia, thousands of miles from everyone whom he loved and stagnating in a war that made no sense while his young family grew up without him.

It was not that he disliked what he was doing, that was the ambiguity of it. He actually enjoyed many of his duties. On line, he led men in war and was successful. Off line, he was a good and capable staff officer. He was proud to be a Marine and, until very recently, was planning his life around a career in the Corps. Now, he was not so sure.

Alone in the tent that night as he waited for time to pass, he was absorbed with doubt and self-pity. Lately, things had piled up. The job of XO, while occasionally interesting, was not a busy one, and he had too much time on his hands. Recently, through no fault of his own, he had missed being promoted. The captain's list had cut off just above his name. That was depressing. Letters from his wife indicated small troubles at home, minor conflicts, little things that might have been prevented had he been there, but, more than anything, he wanted to hold his son.

Agonizingly, he weighed the choices—a career in the Marines with the consequent sacrifices or a life at home with his family. If he chose the latter, how would he provide for them? His struggle was discouraging and his thoughts melancholy. He labored to break the anguish of a depression that had no cure, at least not tonight.

To change his mood, the lieutenant picked up a pen and began writing a letter to his wife. He told of his love for her and a little of the struggle that he was having with himself. That night, by the light of a flickering candle, he found that he had a need to communicate with her. The act of writing was a catharsis, a therapy that allowed his thoughts to flow uninhibited from his heart to the paper. He was speaking directly to his wife and revealing thoughts that were private, formerly unshared. Now, the sharing gave him strength.

He recalled a radio program from the States that he had heard the night before. The announcer had spoken of an essay contest titled, "What America Means to Me." The lieutenant, in his conflict, chose to answer that challenge and write of what his country meant to him. The letter to his wife included the following words:

WHAT AMERICA MEANS TO ME

It means a wife who wants me home, but who understands why
   I'm not;
It means a son who was only a month old when I left;
It means a mother who has never forgotten me in her prayers;
It means a home with a family and a dog;
It means good food, green tossed salad, milk, cold beer;
It means a warm bed with clean sheets, and a mattress;

It means a new car with no payments due;
Driving slowly on a smooth highway on a Sunday afternoon;
It means hunting with my father on a clear, crisp November
   morning;
It means clean hills with clean smells;
It means big cities, nice towns and pretty buildings;
It means happy people, free from poverty, suffering and filth;
It means clean clothes and comfortable furniture, electric lights;
It means a refrigerator with ice, hot coffee when I want it;
It means a hamburger stand on the corner, an expensive restaurant;
It means a night club with an orchestra;
It means dancing with my wife, coming home late;
It means bright lights and pleasant sounds;
It means green fields with cattle and sheep;
It means a bath tub with hot water;
It means the companionship of friends, the love of a woman, the
   wonder of a child;
To me, America means everything I so completely took for granted
   before I left.[19]

Putting his pen aside, the lieutenant sealed the letter in an envelope and addressed it to his wife, writing "Free" where the stamp would have gone. He blew out the candle, went out to check his guard posts, and returned later to his tent. Crawling into his sleeping bag on the narrow cot, he felt much better, and slept. Somewhere else the war continued on.

In his anguish, his homesickness, and his youth, this young man had put to paper what many of his contemporaries felt in Korea at that time. He had captured the essence of things left behind and of things desired, the dream of a perfect America. Though unattainable in the whole, it was something worth struggling for to achieve, if only in part.

CHAPTER 4

RAID ON UNGOK

War is the realm of the unexpected.
—B. H. Liddell Hart,
Defense of the West, 1950

OPERATION CLAMBAKE

On January 23, 1953, after a period of winter inactivity in reserve, the 5th Marine Regiment, commanded by Col. Lewis W. ("Lew") Walt, reoccupied the divisional right on the Jamestown Line. While in the rear, Colonel Walt had required his staff to plan a number of raids. The first was to be against two hills, 31 and 31A, in the Ungok hill mass. Code-named Operation Clambake, it was scheduled for early February.

Ungok is a hill remembered by many Marines for its little Korean cemetery on the tip of a long finger of land visible from the MLR. It was an observation and listening post overlooking trails and rice paddies, a favorite place for Chinese snipers to plink at unwary Marines who poked their heads above the trench line. Ungok and its sister hill, Kumgok, were located approximately 1,000 yards north of the MLR between Outposts Carson and Stromboli. These Chinese-held hills represented a constant source of danger to the MLR.

On Tuesday, 3 February, Ungok was to be assaulted by two reinforced platoons from Able Company 1/5, then in regimental reserve. From the MLR, direct fire support would come from heavy machine guns, gun tanks, and 75-mm recoilless rifles. Behind the line, regimental 4.2-inch mortars and a battery of 105-mm howitzers from the 11th Marines would fire overhead support to supplement battalion- and company-level mortars. Operating in front of the line would be sixteen gun and four flame tanks. Close air support from Marine air would also be on station with napalm and high-explosive bombs.

Execution of Clambake was based on two age-old military principles, feint and surprise. The feint would involve a tank attack on the Kumgok Hills, west of Ungok, the infantry objective. The tank attack would be preceded by two days of pounding by artillery and air strikes. The 5th Marines anticipated that a massive air-tank-artillery feint would lead the Chinese to believe that a major UN breakthrough was under way on Kumgok and cause them to reposition their defenses away from Ungok. The 5th Marines would thereby gain an element of surprise as its Able Company platoons stormed objectives on the eastern slope of Ungok. Assault troops would be armed with four flamethrowers, four rocket launchers, and six light machine guns, as well as hand grenades, bangalore torpedoes, and automatic weapons.

PREPARATION

Planning for Clambake was a complex task that required weeks of preparation. Battalion staffs and supporting arms representatives met several times during a six-week period to create detailed plans that coordinated all resources to be used.

Capt. Clyde Hunter, commander of Able Company, 1st Tank Battalion, was assigned operational control of all thirty-four tanks to be deployed in the operation. When told of the plan, Hunter immediately objected to having tanks assault the Chinese positions without protection of accompanying infantry. He was overruled by Colonel Walt, with the concurrence of Colonel Williamson, the Tank Battalion commander. As a consequence, Hunter fell back on his second-best alternative. He made preparations to provide artillery protection for the exposed armored vehicles.

In cooperation with the artillery commander, Captain Hunter developed a multitude of pre-positioned registration points around the feint area that would give tank commanders the option of calling in high-explosive, VT fuse artillery detonations over their buttoned-up tanks should the Chinese infantry get too close. The planners estimated that one hour's worth of tank and artillery preparation would convince enemy troops of the feint's authenticity and motivate them to redeploy away from the true objective. Consequently, they planned to keep tanks on the hill and subject them to the accumulation of enemy defenses for the full hour.

Pilots slated to conduct air strikes were briefed on the plan of maneuver and afforded the opportunity to walk the MLR where they noted actual targets from the ground. Attending this briefing was Capt. Ted

Williams, professional baseball player turned Marine aviator. He later wrote: "The raid was a big one. We were told that there could be as many as 10,000 Chinese encamped behind their lines. As always, they'd be camouflaged damn well. Those bastards could hide in a bath tub. This meant we'd be dropping 'daisy cutters', a very potent antipersonnel bomb."[1] At the briefing, one of the tank commanders S/Sgt. Ken Miller recalls, Captain Williams remarked that the commander would be advised to lower the radio antenna on his tank if he didn't want it severed by a low-flying Corsair.[2]

For infantry preparation, a suitable rear area was selected where rehearsals could be conducted to fine-tune the plan. During the ensuing weeks, the Marines conducted six full rehearsals and gained valuable time and space information. They became comfortable with details of the scheme of maneuver and the timing and acquired confidence in the plan. Treating the raid like an amphibious landing, the Marines developed it to a fine art, with comprehensive plans, a scripted scenario, and follow-up critiques of the multiple rehearsals. When the time arrived, the men were ready.

An example of that type of preparation is in *The Last Parallel* by Martin Russ, a private first class with the 1st Marines, who wrote of activity that he and his companions underwent for a similar raid elsewhere. Though times, days, and people differed, the preparation and effect were typical:

> . . . We gathered in an outdoor classroom, several miles behind the lines. We sat on the ground and listened attentively to a Major from division headquarters. There were fifty of us gathered around him. I glanced around once or twice and thought: This is a fine collection of soldiers, probably more capable than any in the world. . . .
>
> The major unfolded a large map of the target area, not a regulation military map, but a simplified one, done in water colors. Two peons held it up against the wind for all to see. The schooling lasted two hours. . . .
>
> Before noon chow, the Major led us out to an open area which resembles the objective. Nearby was a smaller duplicate of Saugech'on ridge, with a paddy in between. We rehearsed the entire operation in slow motion. After chow we went back and continued the dry runs until late in the afternoon. Several weak spots were detected and ironed out during a critique. Although the tank crews were present, the tanks themselves were not used during the rehearsal.
>
> The flanking movement of the second wave—our squad—appeared to be the bottleneck of the assault. It required great coordination for

thirteen men to shift from an echelon formation into a single skirmish line. It sounds easy, but the terrain made it difficult and we re-
worked it many times.

. . . After the final run-through we regrouped and hiked to another
area, where we were given ammunition. There each man test-fired his
weapon, firing into a deep ravine. . . .

Returning to the area and our tents, we set about cleaning our
weapons. Later we picked up our unit of fire—the ammunition for
the raid from the supply people. Each man received four grenades and
as many rounds (bullets) as he wanted. Sgt. Barefield, a trusting soul,
said "Thank you" when given his. . . .

At 7 P.M., the night before the raid, a chaplain came and held special services for the raiders. . .

The conversations in the tents that evening were morbid as hell;
some clumsy puns referring to our forthcoming rest in a grave or a
hospital. . . .[3]

RECONNAISSANCE

Because the terrain around the maneuver area was known to be heavily
mined, intensive clearance work was necessary. During the week preceding the raid, nightly patrols searched for and removed mines. As it
turned out, mines were not the most dangerous threat with which the
patrols would have to contend.

Very early in the preparations for Clambake, Captain Hunter arranged
for the Tank Battalion's Reconnaissance Section to map and prepare tank
assault routes to Kumgok. At this time, the recon unit consisted of at
least three men (records do not reveal much about this unit), a Sergeant
Kelly, and M/Sgt. Charles J. ("Tiny") Rhoades led the section.

Sergeant Rhoades was briefed on details of the plan. Under cover of
darkness, his group, accompanied by mine detection teams from the 1st
Engineer Battalion, was to reconnoiter the area in front of the MLR
over which the tanks were expected to operate. The approach lanes were
to be cleared of mines and defensive barbed wire removed.

Rhoades took his detail out nearly every night. The men removed
mines and some of the wire. To remove all of the wire would have
revealed the plan, however, so it was decided that the tanks would blow
the remaining wire with gunfire during the initial assault. To avoid mis-
takes with people on the line, Captain Hunter and Sergeant Rhoades
contacted the infantry company commanders and other personnel defending the involved sections of MLR. Infantry units were provided a
schedule of times and dates that the recon unit would be operating in
front of their positions.

On one of the last nights before the attack, the recon men passed through the MLR to make last-minute checks of the assault route. Rhoades had to ensure that the mines had not been reset, and to determine if there were other indications of the Chinese being aware of Marines' intentions.

About midnight, Captain Hunter heard that the recon section had been engaged in a firefight and casualties were being carried in. He went immediately to the MLR and learned that Rhoades and his men had been seriously shot. After he was loaded into the side basket of a waiting evacuation helicopter, Rhoades told Hunter that, while returning to its own lines, the patrol had been ambushed by a group of Chinese. Hunter later learned that on the MLR, a machine gunner, who was unaware of Tiny's recon patrol in front of him, had brought his gun into action. Caught in the crossfire, one man was killed, Sergeant Kelly was seriously wounded, and Tiny was hit in the chest. On the morning of 29 January 1953, Rhoades also died, another victim of someone's failure to pass the word.

The following day, Colonel Williamson wrote to his wife:

> My Reconnaissance Chief, MSgt. "Tiny" Rhoades, was killed in action last night. He was out on patrol reconnoitering for some operations we are planning when our patrol ran into an enemy ambush. Our men were trying to disengage when he caught two slugs in the back, which pierced his lungs. They got him back to the lines and evacuated him by helicopter, but he was dead on arrival at the Medical Company.
>
> As you can gather from his nickname, he was a mammoth of a man. He had a pug nosed boyish face, always wreathed in good natured smiles. He had an awkward, lumbering gait, because of his size and chronic carbuncles which often pained him. He was very active nonetheless.
>
> He was out here in the Battalion once before and volunteered to come back again—a usually fateful decision. We tried him out as 1st Sgt. of a Company, but the little administration he had to do was too much for him, and he longed to be in a more active combat billet. When the Recon job opened up, he accepted it eagerly. He must have made upwards of fifty patrols before he finally got it. He was unscathed on all the others. Tiny was the type that is the mainstay of the Corps, or any other fighting unit for that matter—a courageous and active man who seemingly enjoys combat. He was a simple, pleasant, and thoroughly likable guy, exceptionally proficient in the work he was doing. He had a wife, but no children. A guy who pushes his luck seems to run smack into the law of averages a lot quicker than most.[4]

Tiny Rhoades was mourned for days. His widow received the Silver Star, awarded to him posthumously, and all who knew him felt that they had lost a friend. The circumstances of his death made it all the more tragic. One of his closest friends in Korea, M/Sgt. Henry Bookhardt, recorded the date of Tiny's death in his family Bible and, years later, named a son after Tiny, a tribute of his respect and lasting admiration.

A day later, Colonel Williamson mentioned Tiny in another letter that proved to be doubly prophetic:

> Last night Lieutenant McAdams came in and told me what a grand job "Tiny" had been doing prior to his death. He told me stories of what great presence of mind he had shown under fire—getting several Lieutenants out of holes when their patrols were being clobbered. He also said that Tiny had told him a few nights before that he wanted to be transferred out of Reconnaissance, as he felt that his luck had run out—another instance of a warrior's fateful premonition of death that we usually view with such suspicion in fiction.[5]

Lieutenant McAdams, former leader of the Tank Battalion's Recon Section, was a short-timer and anticipating rotation home. He had been transferred to a "safer" job with the flame platoon where he would not be required to go out in front of the MLR. During Clambake, however, McAdams chose to lead his men. He, too, had a premonition of death.

THE FEINT

At first light on 3 February, with snow on the ground and the temperature a chilly minus 2°F, the operation began. Preceding the infantry attack by fifty minutes, tanks led off on their feint. Crossing the MLR, 1st Lt. Albert R. Bowman's 1st Platoon encountered double-apron barbed wire across its approach to Red Hill (Hill 33B). In the lead tank, Bowman breached the wire with four rounds of high explosive, and the other tanks trailed him through the gap.

Five tanks leaving the MLR at sunrise and blowing their way through barbed wire hardly could be described as a discreet operation. Chinese mortars and artillery were immediately aroused, and incoming fire began to search out the armored vehicles. As tank A-15 commenced its approach to Red Hill, a direct hit exploded on the rear of the turret and flames erupted from the engine compartment. The fire was immediately suppressed by the tank's extinguisher system, and the tank proceeded with the others to its predesignated position.

As yet, the Marines had observed no enemy activity on Kumgok, and visibility to Ungok was obscured by smoke and dust from the artillery preparation. It was necessary for the tanks to switch to their secondary target. When the tankers observed enemy troops in the trench lines above them, they engaged the Chinese with machine guns and 90-mm fire and called for artillery on the enemy trenches.

The 2nd Platoon, led by 1st Lt. James B. McMath Jr., moved out from the MLR and found wire across its path as well. Blowing the wire with gunfire, the tanks crossed through the gap and took up their preplanned positions to cover the flame tanks that followed.

Able Company's 3d Platoon had the mission of making a feint against Hill 104, west of Kumgok, and providing covering fire for the flame tanks. Leaving the MLR, the tanks passed the wire without difficulty, formed into a forward echelon line, and, buttoned up and nearly blind, charged across the frozen rice paddies.

Climbing over an unseen paddy dike and coming down the other side, each tank, one after the other, slammed its long 90-mm tube onto a parallel dike in front. The blows were so hard that the elevation mechanism of each tank was severely damaged. Neither the main gun nor its coaxial machine gun could be elevated or sighted. As a consequence, the firepower of the platoon was immediately reduced from five 90-mm cannons and five .30-caliber machine guns to a single .30-caliber machine gun each, a critical reduction in capability. Learning of the situation, Captain Hunter ordered the tanks to remain where they were and stand by to assist as needed. The 1st Platoon—five toothless tigers waiting to be summoned—formed into an irregular skirmish line and remained idle throughout the action.

The four flame tanks deployed to burn out infantry trenches on Kumgok had been traveling behind the 3d Platoon and using the gun tanks for cover. Seeing the 3rd Platoon's difficulty, Lieutenant McAdams directed his tank commanders to dismount and carefully pick a new route on foot across the paddies but to avoid the fateful dikes.

Two flame tanks, McAdams in F-31 and F-12, commanded by Cpl. Elmer Betts, began their assault on Kumgok. As both tanks entered the dense cloud of smoke and dust on the hillside, visibility of their 2d platoon support was lost. Without the support of the 3d platoon, which was supposed to have provided covering fire, the flame tanks were vulnerable to enemy tank-killer teams. S/Sgt. Don C. Paules, 2d Platoon sergeant, moved his tank section forward until visibility with the flame tanks was somewhat restored. (A section of tanks is a portion of a five-tank platoon. Two tanks are a light section, and three are a heavy section.)

With the absence of the 3d Platoon's five tanks and the lack of visibility for three of the 2d Platoon's tanks, the tank support for the flame assault was reduced from ten to two. This was a major contribution to the near disaster that began to unfold. From the MLR, Captain Hunter watched in escalating frustration and sheer helplessness as his carefully laid plans unraveled before him.

The first section of flame tanks, F-31 and F-12, commenced to climb up the left finger of Kumgok. The second section, led by S/Sgt. Kenneth Miller, the platoon sergeant in tank F-32, was followed by F-21, commanded by Cpl. Thomas E. Clawson. They trailed Lieutenant McAdams's section by 50 yards.

Leading the attack, McAdams found that his radio was not working and then discovered that his hatch would not close. With hand signals, he informed his platoon sergeant, and Miller's group passed McAdams to assume the lead. As the tanks closed with the enemy, a Chinese antitank gunner leaped from a hole and ricocheted a round off the front slope plate of Miller's tank. Before the gunner could reload and fire again, Miller backed off and called for another tank to cover him. A tanker in Sergeant Paules's section heard the broadcast and destroyed the Chinese gunner with a single round of 90-mm fire.

During the interval that the Chinese antitank gun was being sought out and destroyed, McAdams's section continued forward and resumed the platoon lead. Arriving on top of the hill, F-31 unloaded burning napalm on enemy positions while tank F-12 fired its machine guns. In a 20-foot trench the tankers found troops streaming to reinforce Ungok, now under attack by the 5th Marines. The tanks exhausted the remainder of their napalm on the enemy and began backing off the hill. As they reversed, enemy infantry on the ground surrounded them and attacked with grenades, small arms, and rocket launchers.

Miller followed McAdams's tank up the hill with his section. Passing McAdams, he arrived on top of the hill and saw that the lieutenant's tank was stopped. It had taken a bazooka round in the turret that had penetrated the armor and instantly killed McAdams. The loader, Cpl. Marvin Dennis, was standing upright in his hatch, his left arm nearly shot off, and firing a pistol at Chinese soldiers climbing up the front of the tank. The driver, Cpl. Charles Craig, had a wound in his head that was pouring blood and blinding him.

Simultaneously, Miller saw a Chinese soldier pointing a rocket launcher at his tank. The soldier was close enough for Miller to read the words "US Army" stenciled in white lettering on the side of the tube.

Miller flamed the bazooka that threatened his tank. As the loaded launcher became engulfed in flames, it exploded and took the soldier with it.

Tank F-21 drew up on the right side of McAdams, and the crew saw Dennis wounded and exposed through his hatch. Simultaneously, the men spied another Chinese rocket man approaching for the coup de grace, and they took him out with machine-gun fire.

Meanwhile, Miller's assistant driver, Sgt. Charles Foley, left his vehicle to exchange places with the wounded Craig in McAdams's tank and drive McAdams's tank off the hill. (Normally, Foley was tank commander for F-31, but Miller had displaced him for this operation. Preferring to stay with his tank, Foley bumped the regular assistant driver.) Foley was no sooner out of his compartment than he was struck in the face by shrapnel from an exploding hand grenade. Simultaneously, another bazooka round penetrated the turret of F-31, and Corporal Dennis was hit again, this time in the leg.

The crew in tank F-12 spotted McAdams's stationary vehicle in a small ravine behind them, and Corporal Betts moved the vehicle closer until it was stopped by a ditch. Observing the exposed and wounded Marines on foot beside their tank, Betts maneuvered to rescue them and dismounted from his tank into Chinese small-arms and mortar fire. With hand signals, Betts guided his driver out of the ditch and into a ravine near the disabled tank. Accompanied by Clawson of F-21, Betts ran to the disabled tank and led Craig and Foley to Betts's vehicle where they were temporarily out of danger.

After seeing to the safety of the wounded Marines, Betts and Clawson returned through enemy fire to McAdams's tank. Climbing aboard, Betts began to drive it back to the MLR while the Chinese continued to fire at him. As the tanks backed off of Kumgok, Clawson leaped onto the rear of McAdams's tank to seek cover from enemy small-arms fire. Remaining exposed on the rear of the tank, he was subsequently wounded several times.

Meanwhile, it appeared to Captain Hunter from his command post on the MLR that confusion had erupted all over the field of battle. Through his binoculars, he watched Chinese infantry swarming around the tanks, firing small arms, and throwing hand grenades; others carried bazookas. His men began frantically calling on the radio for cover fire, but it was impossible to use the predesignated artillery registrations because of dust, smoke, confusion, and general disorientation. With no friendly infantry or artillery, the tankers were on their own and in trouble.

Holding small bushes in front of them, several enemy antitank teams ran down the trench line. They boldly advanced to within 15 yards of a tank before opening fire with their rockets. When Captain Hunter heard that McAdams had been killed, he radioed Miller to assume command of the platoon and to withdraw his tanks to the cover of the 2d Platoon. Miller acknowledged and advised Hunter that his crews were still on the ground and he could not move until they remounted.

Colonel Williamson, on the MLR with Captain Hunter, watched the battle. In another of his letters home, he wrote:

> . . . We began hearing alarming transmissions over the radio: "My tank is on fire!"—"One of the flame tanks is burning!"—"Tank F-31 has been hit! The hatch is open and all I can see is a bloody head sticking out of the turret, but there is at least one man left alive in the tank!"—"The enemy is closing in and is within three yards of tank F-31!"—"Have them close the hatch and we'll bring VT fire down on them!"
>
> As the information ebbed and flowed around us, our hopes were alternately plunged and raised.[6]

The activity on the ground among flame tanks prevented the remainder of Lieutenant McMath's 2d Platoon from firing support or calling in VT. The only covering fire available to protect the injured flame crews came from the machine guns of other flame tanks or from Sergeant Paules's light section that had managed to maneuver into a position of support.

Adding to the confusion was more smoke called in by infantry units on Ungok. The tank maneuver area was covered with dust, gun smoke, and drifting smoke. Visibility was severely restricted, and tank drivers were nearly blind. By necessity, the tanks had to remain unbuttoned to move, which required crew members to expose themselves to danger. The smoke and dust permitted enemy gunners to venture even closer. Guided by engine noise, the Chinese troops effectively utilized small arms and bazookas against the armored vehicles and their exposed crews.

Amid the smoke, fire, and shrapnel, the crews of F-31 and F-21, McAdams's section, were able to remount the damaged tanks and head for the MLR with their wounded. As they withdrew, Miller's section remained on the hill, a position uncertain at best. It was very likely to be overrun by the same enemy soldiers who had taken out McAdams's tank.

Miller called for help and requested permission to withdraw. His request denied, he was ordered to remain in position to draw Chinese artillery away from the 5th Marines still attacking Ungok. Via radio, Captain Hunter advised Miller to button up his hatches and call in VT on his position. When the VT arrived, it successfully kept enemy soldiers at bay and enabled the tanks to remain there until they were finally permitted to withdraw.

As Miller's tank came off the hill, he heard a voice break over his radio that ordered him to stop where he was. (Unknown to Miller, the order was not issued by the command post; the voice belonged to a Chinese soldier with a captured Marine radio who was setting up an ambush.) When he stopped as directed, Miller's tank was immediately hit in the gas tank with a round from an armor-piercing 57-mm anti-tank rifle. The gasoline ignited, and flames engulfed the engine compartment. The crew discovered that the fire extinguisher system was inoperative. They would have to abandon the tank before it blew up. With the guns of Sergeant Paules's 2d Platoon covering them, Miller and his crew evacuated their burning vehicle and ran through enemy fire to board another tank.

They returned to the MLR and left tank F-32 burning on the slope of Kumgok. On orders from Captain Hunter, the flaming tank was destroyed with gunfire from 2d Platoon tanks. Ironically, this was the second tank that Miller lost in front of the MLR. He had been commander of a tank that rolled over and was abandoned on Outpost Hedy the month before.

During withdrawal of the flame platoon, Lieutenant McMath's platoon was having mechanical difficulties. While covering the flame tanks, one of the vehicles developed an electrical problem. It stalled and would not restart. Stationary in the midst of battle, the tank presented a perfect target for enemy artillery. Another tank, continually under fire, pulled alongside and two crew members left its safety to exchange batteries with the disabled tank and get it restarted. Reassembled, the 2d Platoon withdrew toward the MLR amid a torrent of enemy artillery shells. Many of them exploded at the very spot where the disabled tank had stalled.

Meanwhile, Able Company's 1st Platoon also had its hands full. Following the original plan, Lieutenant Bowman's tanks moved to their position on the right flank of the 2d Platoon. There, they were confronted by fortifications and a large concentration of Chinese infantry armed with bazookas. When the tanks met with heavy fire and were in danger of being overrun, Bowman circled them back to back at one of the preregistered artillery points. In this position, he was able to fire at the enemy while calling for a protective umbrella of VT over his tanks. Using all of the preplanned fire support from the MLR, support tanks, and artillery, the 1st Platoon gunners began to stack up enemy dead. Under continuous attack, they held their ground, fought off numerous Chinese, and withdrew on order. Badly scarred, they were the last tanks to leave the battlefield. Antennas and all exposed equipment on the tank exteriors had been cleaned off by the series of VT bursts over their position.

The entire operation lasted about two hours, and nearly every tank, including those in MLR positions, had expended their basic ammunition allotment, approximately 75 rounds. Many of the tanks required replacement or major repair. 1st Tank Battalion casualties were two killed and six wounded. In addition to the casualties of the flame platoon, two men from Able Company also sustained serious wounds and were evacuated to a hospital ship for treatment.

A few days later, Colonel Williamson wrote that he visited with men of the flame platoon at their command post behind the lines:

> Talked to the Platoon Sergeant of my flame platoon, and he allowed as how they were hot to go to get revenge on the goonies for the pasting they took. I am recommending one of those lads for the Navy Cross [Bettsl, two for the Silver Star [Dennis and Clawson] and the Platoon Sergeant [Miller] for at least a Bronze Star. Five lads in this outfit put in to extend their tour in Korea. All of them are draftees, too—they just want to stay out here and fight with the outfit as long as they have to be in any way. Magnificent Marines.[7]

The Marine Corps accepted the Colonel's recommendations and each of the men was later awarded the decorations mentioned. Of McAdams, Williamson wrote on February 3:

> I brood about Lt. McAdams, the lad who was killed, for he had three sons who were the apples of his eye, just as I do, one a six month old baby whom he'd never seen. He too seems to have suspected that his number was up from the meticulous arrangements about his personal affairs he made just prior to going out. Ironically enough it was he who was telling me of the premonition of disaster "Tiny" Rhoades had, and that was not a week ago. He was a fine lad. I had just recently moved him from the Recon job to take over the flame platoon.[8]

This was the feint, the armored diversion on Kumgok, created to draw enemy troops from the infantry's objective on Ungok. Success was obvious; the feint drew more enemy than it could handle. The infantry, too, found more Chinese than they wanted. Their casualties were much greater than the tankers.[9]

THE INFANTRY ATTACK

Having rehearsed the operation for the past week, Able Company 1/5 was ready. The two-platoon assault force was divided into two maneuver units—northern and southern. Each consisted of an assault element and a support element of approximately two squads each. Both groups would attack the east slope of Ungok at a side most distant from the feint area. The objective of the northern group was Hill 31, and the southern group would attack Hill 31A, two low peaks on the same ridgeline.

Under cover of darkness, before the tanks began to move, Able Company platoons worked their way forward of the MLR and halted to wait for the feint to begin. When the tanks became engaged on Kumgok, assault troops moved on Ungok. The time was 0810.

The men raced across the valley over previously cleared mine trails and frozen paddies, while supporting arms from the MLR fired to prepare the way. Two platoons of tanks, a section of 75-mm recoilless rifles, and a battery of heavy machine guns delivered direct fire to Ungok. Simultaneously, enemy observation posts on nearby high ground were smoked with artillery and 4.2-inch mortars. (This was the smoke that had drifted west into the tank maneuver area on Kumgok.)

The assaulting infantry experienced little difficulty in crossing the valley. As the Marines neared their objective, artillery fire was lifted but mortars continued, The southern attack force reached its objective first and easily swept into enemy trenches. The northern group experienced a little more difficulty as a result of enemy artillery and mortars, which the enemy fired on its own positions. The Marines took some casualties but attained the enemy trench lines with relative ease. It was apparent that the feint had been effective. Most of the Chinese troops were on Kumgok to battle the tanks, but, as the assault continued, enemy troops returned to reinforce Ungok. Soon, there were an estimated one hundred Chinese, divided equally between Hills 31 and 31A, and more were coming. Enemy soldiers employed their normal complement of weapons, burp guns, rifles, and grenades. Defensive support came largely from 57-mm recoilless rifles, mortars, and artillery.

Countering Chinese reinforcements on Ungok was the Marines' ace in the hole—close air support. Just how close is illustrated in Capt. Ted Williams's account of how his Corsair was hit while he was flying in support of the ground-pounders that day:

> It didn't take us long to reach our target. As we were going down, I was startled to see the guy ahead of me starting to jinx (zigzag). You

weren't supposed to do that until you were coming out of your dive. I'm going straight for the target so naturally I'm closing in on him.

So I have to start jinxing while I'm looking for a feasible target. We were told to drop our bombs from 2,000 feet, but we never did. We'd usually go lower than that, and this time I'd gone a lot lower.

I released my bombs, and as I did, it seemed that every gook in Korea opened up on me. Machine guns, burp guns, even rifles, you name it, they were all zeroing in on me and they all didn't miss.

. . . My stick is shaking, my fire warning light, my dual warning light, my hydraulic lighting, every goddamn light in my cockpit is lit. My stick is shaking like hell, which tells me I've got a hydraulic leak.

So I began to climb. My plane is starting to smoke. Another pilot, Lieutenant Larry Hawkins, pulls up near me. I get on the radio, but it isn't working. I'd been hit in the accessory section. I was lucky the engine was working.

Anyway, he followed me up and we started for home. Thank God his radio was working. He alerted the fields that I was in real trouble.

We quickly got behind our lines and Larry is trying to talk to me with motions. I later found out he was telling me to bail out, but that was one thing I always dreaded. I am just a fraction under the height limit for a pilot, and I was always afraid I might not make it out of the small cockpit.

So, it took us about fifteen minutes to spot one of our fields. I think it was K-13. Now it's time for me to land. The fire is getting worse. I tried to put my wheels down when—boom!—an explosion occurs. It blows off one of my wheels and it was only by the grace of God it didn't blow off one of the wings.

Then I went in. I could see two fire engines waiting for me. I hit the ground flush and started to skid. I must have skidded close to a mile. There were a group of Marines standing on the other end of the runway. They sure as hell scattered.

I kept pumping the brakes, but of course they weren't working. I'm yelling out loud, "When is this plane going to stop? Stop, you bastard, stop."

It finally did stop, right near the end of the runway. Two Marines appeared out of nowhere to help me out of the cockpit. The plane is burning just about every where but the cockpit. When I touched ground, I threw my flight helmet down. Was I mad. I'd been scared, but now I was just mad, mad at the whole world. . . .[10]

Meanwhile, the assault groups on Ungok clashed with the enemy as barrages of mortar and artillery tried to knock them off the hill. The defenders were well entrenched in deep trenches, caves, bunkers, and spider holes. Later, Marines discovered that Hills 31 and 31A were connected by a trench that varied in depth from 12 to 3 feet, the shallow points being cave-ins from air and artillery strikes. According to T/Sgt. James F. Coleman, "One Marine, manning a flame thrower, caught three unlucky Chinese coming up a trench line. . . Hand to hand fighting was heavy."[11]

The Marines found that the caves on Ungok were large and very deep, with personnel shelters built into walls near the entrances. On several occasions, the enemy continued to throw grenades from the caves even after satchel charges had been thrown into the entrances. Flamethrowers were found to be the most effective means of neutralizing caves.

The spider-hole defense was well planned and coordinated. Holes were dug into the slope of the hill in such a manner that, when the rifleman was in position to fire, he was not silhouetted against the skyline. During the attack, the Chinese coordinated their sniper fire from these holes. When one sniper pinned down a Marine, another sniper in a different hole opened fire. White phosphorus grenades thrown in a spider hole often created smoke in another, which indicated that the positions were connected by tunnels.

One of the attacking fire teams advanced to within a few yards of an enemy trench when it became pinned down by fire from a nearby bunker. Unable to move forward or back, the team was in trouble. Quickly, Pfc. John Elwell rose from the dirt and charged the bunker. Firing his carbine and simultaneously throwing hand grenades, he routed the enemy soldiers so that the rest of his team could advance. Later, while leading his fire team into more trenches, Elwell was hit with fragments from an exploding mortar and mortally wounded. He was posthumously awarded a Navy Cross.[12]

An Able Company officer also distinguished himself that day, not only by surviving but by actions that would earn him a Medal of Honor. 2d Lt. Raymond Murphy commanded the 3d Platoon of Able Company, which was designated a reserve and evacuation element. His platoon did not stay long in reserve. When the assault stalled at the enemy trenches, the 3d Platoon went into action. In his book, *Korean War Heroes,* Edward Murphy (no relation) wrote extensively about Lieutenant Murphy's exploits. Following is the relevant excerpt for 3 February:

> . . . Murphy decided to go forward and find out for himself what was going on.

What he found was chaos. The Chinese resistance had proven to be much stronger than anticipated. As a result, the attack had stalled. Almost all the officers and senior NCOs were killed or wounded. The surviving Marines sought shelter. Murphy saw immediately that the attack had fallen apart. He had to act now to save what was left of the company.

He led his platoon in an attack on a key enemy strong point. At the front of his men, Murphy maneuvered them with words of encouragement and praise. Bounding from one position to the next, he brought his platoon to the rescue of the others.

. . . The gallant lieutenant was hit and painfully wounded when an enemy mortar exploded near him while going to the aid of one casualty. Blood poured from the numerous holes that dotted his left side but Murphy hardly felt the enemy metal; he was intent only on getting the Marine to safety.

While several of his men provided covering fire, Murphy made uncounted trips across open ground to save the wounded. One of the sergeants who witnessed Murphy's heroics said "it would be impossible to know how many trips Murphy made under enemy fire to pull guys to safety."

As the wounded picked their way downhill through the rocky ground, Murphy noticed an enemy detachment pouring a deadly stream of fire at them. Determined to protect the casualties to the fullest extent possible, he stalked the enemy soldiers. He cornered them and, in a lightning-fast duel, killed them.

Through his radioman Murphy had kept the battalion commander apprised of the situation. Based on his reports it was decided to break off the attack. Murphy moved across the bullet-swept hillside, passing the word to withdraw. As the others pulled back, the young lieutenant covered their movement with deadly accurate fire from his carbine. At one point he picked up a discarded BAR and used it with telling effect to repulse a vicious enemy attack.

At the base of Ungok Murphy quickly started the casualties on their way to the MLR. Then he organized a search party to sweep the battleground for any overlooked Marines. He located and helped carry down the hill the bodies of a machine-gun crew. Only when he was convinced all the Marines had been accounted for did Murphy leave the battlefield.

On the way back to the MLR Murphy helped carry the stretcher of one badly wounded Marine. As he did so, the Chinese dropped harassing artillery fire on the retreating Marines. A piece of shrapnel from one round tore into Murphy's right hand but he maintained his grip on the stretcher, preventing further injury to the man.

Once back in the friendly confines of the MLR, Murphy stead-fastly refused treatment for his wounds until he was assured all the other casualties had been treated. Only then did he allow the corps-man to treat him.[13]

After being treated for wounds in the United States, Murphy was released from the Marine Corps in April. On 27 October 1953, President Eisenhower awarded him a Medal of Honor.

WITHDRAWAL

Before retiring from Ungok, the Marines destroyed Chinese defenses and fought off three separate counterattacks. The first, in estimated platoon strength, advanced through a deep trench line from positions to the north of Hill 31. The Marines stopped this attack with mortar fire. In a second attempt, two Chinese squads attacked the flank of the northern assault group from the east. The Marines stopped this effort with small arms and machine guns. A third and final counterattack was actually a reoccupation of the hills that occurred as the raiders began their withdrawal. As soon as the Marines were clear of the hill, friendly VT rounds saturated the air above the Chinese troops, cut them to pieces, and halted any attempts at pursuit.

The withdrawal was slow because of enemy artillery and mortar concentrations falling along the return routes. It became apparent that the enemy had preregistered all possible approach routes to Ungok and was now able to saturate them at will. The surprise that had been achieved with the assault did not carry over to the withdrawal. The enemy had time to reorganize and concentrate on punishing the raiders as they attempted to return to their own lines. Chinese incoming fire along the withdrawal route was brutal. The longer the men were exposed to hostile fire, the greater was the number of casualties.

To expedite removal of casualties, the tank battalion provided four armored personnel carriers. Clambake again demonstrated the versatility of these swift armored vehicles. To clear the way for the APCs early in the assault, demolition teams from the southern assault group had breached a high roadblock with bangalore torpedoes and satchel charges. The APCs also made numerous trips to the forward aid station behind the MLR and evacuation points on Ungok. On return trips the vehicles carried ammunition, napalm, water, and medical supplies to the Marines still fighting off the Chinese. On a curious humanitarian note, APC crews reported "that sniper fire lifted while they were placing stretchers on the vehicles and began once the vehicles started moving."[14]

On the MLR, other units and men had been watching the infantry attack with interest. It was obvious to many of them that the assault appeared to have been conducted satisfactorily but the withdrawal had run into difficulty. One of the observers was Sgt. William ("Bill") Janzen from Charlie Company 1/5, whose platoon had been placed on standby to evacuate wounded. A few days after the operation, he wrote home to his family and described his observations:

> . . . They sent our platoon out with stretchers as evacuation teams. Our guys had to go almost a mile and a half out to where the others were fighting. The lieutenant left me behind on the MLR to count our own men as they came in and find out which were casualties and stuff like that. It was a nice soft job. I tried to talk the lieutenant into letting me go out but he wouldn't.
>
> Able company had thirteen dead and over sixty wounded that morning. Our platoon had two slightly wounded. I swear I've never seen anything like it. . . . When they started bringing in those dead and wounded, they were so shot up and blown apart that it seemed like a miracle that some were still alive. Almost all the wounded were stretcher cases with very few walking wounded. They had so many casualties that they not only used our platoon and Able Company men, but George Company and chiggie bears [KSC laborers] as well. The last people got in around 1:30 in the afternoon. They had to stay out there long enough to get all the casualties, and the longer they stayed the more casualties they took.
>
> It was a pretty bloody mess, but the Marine Corps has paid a lot higher prices before, and they'll do it again.[15]

The raid cost the 5th Marines fifteen men killed and seventy-three wounded. Enemy casualties were higher, approximately seventy men killed by Marine infantry and a conservative estimate of 320 deaths from supporting arms. Numbers of wounded were unknown but no doubt greater. No prisoners were taken.

Colonel Walt reported that he considered Operation Clambake a success because enemy casualties were high and most of the Chinese positions on Ungok had been obliterated.

February had begun with a gusto, and more raids were scheduled for that month. As the offensive pace picked up, the Marines were in the thick of the fighting.

CHAPTER 5

FEBRUARY, A MONTH OF RAIDS

There is no better way of defending a long line
than by moving into the enemy's territory.
—Robert E. Lee: Letter to
Brig. Gen. John R. Jones, CSA,
21 March 1863

During the winter, Communist forces had built their strength by stock-piling ammunition and rations at the front. They had replaced three Chinese armies and one North Korean corps with fully equipped, combat-trained units. Remaining divisions had been increased from reserve elements so that, by 1 February 1953, there were an estimated 1,071,080 North Korean and Chinese troops in Korea.[1]

By contrast, all U.N. forces in Korea, including the Republic of Korea (ROK) army, numbered 932,539.[2] This number included air and naval personnel, who were virtually nonexistent on the Communist side, and a huge UN rear-echelon support unduplicated in the north. At the point of the spear, UN combat troops were vastly outnumbered.

North Korea, devastated by bombing and famine, survived only on the largesse of China and the Soviet Union. South Korea was almost totally dependent on the United States for sustenance. Both Koreas, while still game to fight, had been weakened to the point of near deple-tion. If denied their continuing sources of foreign aid, both factions would have collapsed from a state of exhaustion, but that was not to be. Momentum to continue the war was too great.

OUTPOST HEDY

The month of February was a mere fifteen minutes old when fighting began for the 7th Marines. At 2400, a platoon from George Company 3/7 left Outpost Hedy on a combat patrol. Fifteen minutes later, the support group, which had left first, was ambushed by an enemy squad on the forward base of the hill. The enemy squad apparently was the vanguard of two companies advancing toward Hedy. Decisively outnumbered, the Marine patrol quickly withdrew to the OP and prepared for the onslaught that was sure to follow.

Thirty minutes later, 150 Chinese troops, supported by a mortar preparation, assaulted Hedy. After a fierce thirty-minute firefight, they withdrew but only temporarily. Taking advantage of the respite, the outpost commander called for and received reinforcements. A squad from Able Company's 2d Platoon joined the men on Hedy.

The second assault came at 0330 and was also repulsed after a brief firefight, but mortar fire continued to pound the defenders for three hours. During the second attack, enemy attempts to get reinforcements from the vicinity of Hill 118 were beaten back by machine-gun fire, mortars, and artillery from the MLR. George Company lost six men killed and thirty-one wounded on Hedy that night. The company commander, Capt. Stanley D. Curyea, was among the dead. Considering that the outpost had been originally defended by less than a platoon of Marines, thirty-six casualties represented a substantial percentage of men.

The Command Diary entry for this action attributes the successful defense of Hedy to several factors, among which ". . . were the friendly employment of a combat patrol to force the untimely commitment of enemy reserves, utilization of a prearranged supporting fire plan intended for the patrol, and excellent coordination with supporting, adjacent, and reserve units."[3]

Later in the month in a dedication ceremony, the 3d Battalion command post area was named in memory of Captain Curyea, who had lost his life while directing the defense of Outpost Hedy.

BRINGING BACK THE CASUALTIES

In February, the 7th Marine sector stretched between COP-2 and Outpost Corrine. The 1st Battalion, on the left, and the 3d Battalion, on the right, abutted the 5th Marines. Item Company 3/7 was responsible for Outposts Dagmar, Corrine, and a portion of the MLR.

Lying between the small, squad-sized outposts of Samoa and Corrine, Dagmar was garrisoned by nearly a platoon, maybe thirty-five men (exact numbers often varied). It was situated on a low hill and commanded valleys on either side and the approach to the MLR behind it. Seven hundred yards in front of the MLR, it was not much to look at, but there were few choices. Seven hundred yards north of Dagmar was Hill 144, now owned by the Chinese. Ironically, Hill 144 was formerly Marine COP-4, which had been abandoned in May 1952 but now menaced Dagmar.

On 22 February, twenty-eight Marines from Item Company's 2d Platoon, commanded by 2d Lt. James G. Severns, departed Dagmar to raid Hill 144. They did not get there. The 3/7 Command Diary, in a single paragraph, tried to describe what happened that night:

> Approximately 300 yards from COP Dagmar the point heard noises. The patrol observed three Chinese on the skyline. Immediately the point employed a base of fire, while the rear element moved to the right in an attempt to envelop the enemy. At this time the assault group moved up and killed the three enemy. This was the initial contact which occurred at 0050 and was followed by a ten minute fire fight. The enemy consisted of one platoon which suffered 12 known KIA and 6 estimated KIA. The Chinese broke contact at 0105 leaving the friendlies with 5 WIA. Immediately after, an intense mortar barrage was received by the patrol forcing them back to CT 034052 where they were pinned down.[4]

Unfortunately, the event was a little more complex. Cpl. Jack Scholten later wrote of his experience:

> I was second radioman, number thirteen in line, which excited the hell out of me. We left the MLR at dusk and headed for Dagmar. About halfway there we left the trail and circled to the east out and around the outpost, about halfway across goonie land an enemy patrol walked up to us, at my position which was halfway in the column. We immediately hit the deck. About ten men in front of me kept going in spite of my warnings. I immediately radioed the first radioman that we were in close contact with "GOLD," the enemy, he acknowledged my signal and we waited for the patrol to return.
>
> I was lying down behind a bush and the gook point man was on the other side of the same bush, he kept swatting at the twig in his face which was my antenna. There was a sergeant lying next to me,

and I kept asking for permission to shoot. The gook could hear me and kept going back to the officer in charge, then returning to my bush; he could hear my radio but didn't know where I was.

I know now that I should have fired, that would have forced the first part of the patrol to hit the deck, instead they circled around and walked into the middle of the enemy patrol. Our point man challenged the gooks and got a burst of burp gun fire in return. We opened fire and I finally got that little shit looking for me. They pulled back and we moved forward to rejoin the patrol, the point had a chest wound and Lieutenant Severns a broken leg, we formed a perimeter around them and waited for stretcher bearers. I later found out that we had walked into a gook assault patrol preparing to attack Dagmar.

When the gooks heard the shooting, they lobbed mortars on Dagmar and wiped out our relief party, so nobody knew where we were. Then they hit us with mortars and we took more casualties. By now someone decided we were in deep shit and ordered a withdrawal. I and Shanneyfelt were helping another Marine up when I got hit in the stomach with a burst from a burp gun. A round penetrated my flak jacket and I went down. They laid another mortar barrage on us and I was hit again, it was then that Shanneyfelt was killed along with the Marine we were helping.

We caught hell all night but managed to hold off the gooks. About 5 AM a relief column found us, and we started back to the MLR. I remember the stretcher bearers that picked me up; one of them was going to shit can his parka, but from the cold and loss of blood I was frozen, so he gave it to me. I threw it over my head and with me on the stretcher, they loaded all the weapons they could find. Then we started for the MLR. Silverstein, bless his heart, was someplace ahead of me and he kept cussing the gooks; they zeroed in on the sound and I was hit twice more. Three sets of bearers were hit before they got me to the MLR.

I got hit four separate times that night and a bayonet through my thigh from a dead Chinaman. Those damn carbines had no muzzle velocity, fifteen rounds and he still fell on me. The carbine belonged to one of our Corpsman; the point was carrying my 12 gauge. Our Corpsman was one of the first to die; he was kneeling up during the initial mortar barrage helping a wounded Marine.

I will never forget how careful those Marines were with me getting me back to the lines; the ground was frozen and they were having a hell of a time. One would slide off the trail and before my stretcher hit the ground, another was there keeping it upright, reassuring me all the time.[5]

Hospitalman 3d Class (HM3) Charles Pope, the corpsman whom Scholten referred to in his letter, was wounded while tending to injured Marines. He had refused evacuation so that he could continue administering aid to them. Kneeling beside a wounded Marine amid falling Chinese mortar rounds, Pope was hit and died on the battlefield with his comrades.

In the meantime, Dagmar was in chaos. Incoming fire was raining on the hill, communication with the pinned-down raiding party was poor, and the extent of damage was unknown, as was the exact location of the wounded men. A thirteen-man rescue group with stretchers was hastily assembled to find the assault force and assist with casualty retrieval. Led by 1st Lt. Robert Farrell of Item Company, the rescue group picked its way down the forward slope of Dagmar. Incoming artillery was so severe, however, that Farrell and all but three of the other members of the rescue party became casualties.

Nevertheless, the rescue party continued forward and managed to make contact with Lieutenant Severns's 2d Platoon. Between both groups, the wounded and dead numbered almost thirty. Severns's foot had been shot nearly off, and Farrell sustained a severe concussion. The situation quickly worsened as the men, unable to withdraw, were being pummeled by Chinese artillery and expecting a counterattack at any moment. Sgt. Joseph U. ("Joe") Ogden was part of Farrell's group. In a statement of facts prepared immediately on his return to Dagmar, he wrote:

> It was approximately two hours before a [our] rescue party found the patrol. I was squad leader of a thirteen man rescue party and only had four men left with me when we found the patrol. I was dismayed to find every member of the patrol except two were stretcher cases. We had only six stretchers.[6]

On the radio in the CP bunker, 1st Lt. Vincent Walsh heard Farrell's predicament. Intuitively, he knew that another effort to rescue the trapped platoon must be made. He immediately organized twenty volunteers into a second recovery group. Walsh had no trouble in finding help. Every man on Dagmar was willing to go. Gathering his men and fifteen stretchers, the second rescue group left the outpost. The men encountered artillery, mortar, and small-arms fire but moved fast through it. Fortunately, they sustained only minor injuries and reached Farrell's position. Sergeant Ogden's statement continues:

Just when it seemed impossible to get our dead and wounded out, Lt. Walsh arrived with a second rescue party and sufficient stretchers to remove all our wounded except three dead Marines. Lt. Walsh's calmness and cool courage was a constant inspiration to all of us and, even though we were receiving constant heavy mortar and artillery fire, Lt. Walsh kept urging our men to keep going until we had all our wounded on the way into our outpost. And, after all the wounded were on the way, he searched the area for our automatic weapons, machine guns and bazooka, and damaged them to prevent enemy use. . . . Then he insisted on staying with our dead until we could get them in.[7]

A corpsman, HM3 John Rogers, was one of the volunteers traveling with Walsh. On reaching the injured, he immediately started to treat them and then accompanied them to the outpost. In a letter home, written the following day, he described the walk back:

I made a trip about 200 yards in front of our trench line and got twelve walking injured and got them back here. Then I went out to the same spot with four men and two stretchers to where the raiding party wounded were, out in open territory. Found our lieutenant [Severns] with a leg broken by a slug. We loaded him and another fellow [Cpl. Jack Scholten] on stretchers and got them back to the outpost. . . . Just as we got the lieutenant near a bunker and were going inside, mortars started landing all around us. We all hit the deck and stayed there till the barrage lifted. Someone counted thirty-seven rounds in one minute, so it was no picnic. A piece of shrapnel flew by and cut my left fore finger. [The finger was laid open to the bone, but Rogers chose not to disclose all the details to his parents.] I've got a field dressing on it and can still do anything I did before.

We all worked like the devil taking care of the wounded and getting them evacuated. The corpsman I came here with was killed.[8]

With the wounded safely on their way to Dagmar, there remained the bodies of the three Marines who had been killed. Lieutenant Walsh described that phase of the operation in a letter to Lieutenant Farrell:

Recovery of the wounded required the use of all available stretchers. Remaining in the area were the bodies of three dead. [Sgt.] Joe Ogden, [Cpl.] Jim West and I carried the dead men on our backs from the base of the enemy position, across the rice paddies and up the forward slope of Dagmar. Continuous artillery and mortar fire swept our avenue of withdrawal. At times, when we had to rest due to sheer exhaustion from the weight of the dead, we shielded ourselves under their bodies. Luckily Ogden, West and I sustained only superficial wounds primarily from flying rock and debris thrown by exploding shells.

The uncommon discipline and dedication exemplified by Ogden and West was a continuing inspiration to me. Enemy flak was so intense that visibility, at times was non-existent. Relying on verbal contact, I constantly questioned whether West and Ogden were alive and ambulatory. Every communication was met with, "We are here Lt.," or "We're with you. Keep going."

We succeeded in moving the three dead men to within 300 yards of the friendly trench lines on Dagmar. Daylight was quickly setting in, which forced us to leave the dead in a shallow ravine which we hoped would not be under enemy observation. Once the sun came up we would have been sitting ducks under direct observation of enemy small arms and machine guns. Unencumbered by the bodies, Ogden, West and I scrambled the remaining distance to Dagmar.[9]

The bodies were left in the ravine for the remainder of the day. It would have been suicide to attempt a recovery during daylight. By 0830 on that morning of 22 February, the raid had cost thirty-four wounded and three dead Americans. Records indicate that five hundred rounds of incoming fire fell on Dagmar during the seven hours between 0100 and 0800.[10]

On Dagmar, the rest of the day was spent in licking wounds, repairing damage, attending to medical needs, recapping the previous night's action, and planning another effort to recover the bodies. A plan was formulated whereby Lieutenant Walsh would lead a recovery group of nine Marines with three stretchers to the place where the bodies had been left that morning. Carrying only personal weapons and hand grenades, the men would travel light. Their return trip with the bodies would be burdensome enough. Walsh continued his narrative:

The evening of 22 February was lit with a full moon which we thought would assist us in locating the shallow ravine and quickly remove the dead.

At sunset we jumped off as planned. The group reached the objective within minutes and established a base of fire above the shallow ravine. The stretcher bearers and I moved into the ravine and commenced loading the bodies. Within seconds enemy small arms fire erupted from the surrounding area. We had been ambushed!

Our men returned fire immediately and in the ensuing firefight

Pfc.'s George Robinson and Elpide Rodriguez were mortally wounded. Two other Marines sustained severe gunshot wounds but were able to evacuate without assistance.

With our return fire and several well placed fragmentation grenades thrown among the enemy, their fire momentarily ceased. This afforded us an opportunity to regroup on higher ground. Subsequently, more Chinese fire erupted from the lower ridge overlooking the ravine. With that coverage it would have been impossible to retrieve the dead without sacrificing the lives of the remaining Marines. It also appeared that enemy units were maneuvering into positions to flank us. I decided to take the men out of "no-man's-land" and back up the hill, covering our withdrawal with our remaining ammunition, which was running low.[11]

Thus Item Company lost two more killed. Of the mission, the Command Diary entry records simply: " 'I' Company made contact with twelve enemy at approximately 1930. A ten minute firefight commenced, resulting in eight enemy counted KIA and undetermined amount of enemy KIA and WIA. The friendlies suffered three wounded and two killed, not recovered."[12]

Item Company now had five bodies left on the slope of Dagmar. Then, on 2 March, a forward observer reported movement in front of Dagmar. It was surmised that the enemy might be setting up an ambush around the bodies lost on 22 February. A barrage of VT was called on their position, after which it was noted that the "bodies disappeared after the barrage."[13] Then, without further information, the 3/7 Diary entry of 0155, 6 March, reports: " 'I' Company special patrol recovered five KIA bodies at CT34051.[14]

RAIDING THE ENEMY

The incessant arguments across the truce table did little to shorten the war and more likely prolonged it. Since the beginning of the "peace talks," the war in Korea had gradually evolved into one of simple attrition. Which side could outlast the other? A military solution to the problem had been long rejected, which could lead one to ask, "What was the mission of the military?" Despite remote goings-on in the truce tent, the Marines on line knew their purpose. It was to kill enemy soldiers. Why else were they there?

Probably, the most frequently used tactic by Marines for killing the enemy was the raid. If February were to be characterized by a title, it could accurately be named "The Month of Raids."

A raid might be described as a unit attack on an enemy position, well supported by firepower, for the sole purpose of killing the enemy and destroying defenses. If initiated by friendly forces, it was called a raid or sometimes a combat patrol. When conducted by enemy forces, it was more often called a probe or simply an attack. Another way of looking at a raid might be derived from a description by a Marine corporal in a letter to a friend. He wrote that the purpose of a raid was, "to destroy and kill the enemy, which meant kick over their stoves and steal anything not nailed down."[15]

On 23 February, a tank-infantry raid was initiated by the first battalion, 7th Marines. Its target was Hill 70A, a Chinese position commonly called the Boot because of its distinctive shape on the map. Earlier, the 5th Marines' raid on Ungok, Operation Clambake, had been an arguable success. Three weeks later, the 3/7 raid on Hill 144 might be called unsuccessful because the raiding party never reached its objective.

Another raid, Operation Dog, would likewise fail to reach its objective. Nonetheless, for those involved it was "one helluva fight" and demonstrated the necessity of being able to switch objectives quickly to fight the unplanned battle.

Whether any of the raids should be called a failure is debatable. Strategies of the outpost war rendered most difficult the assessment of operational success and failure. As no effort was made to win territory, how was victory to be measured? Killing more of the enemy than they killed? And who was to count? This was a major problem of the Korean War that began with the "stalemate" and exists today. Who won the war? Perhaps President Truman was right when he called it a "police action." If so, it is a shame that so many cops had to suffer. Definitions often become a problems.

Operation Dog was planned to be a nighttime frontal assault on the Boot, located 2,100 yards in front of the MLR. Nearby Marine outposts were Marilyn (Hill 92), Ingrid (Hill 64A), and the bastion on COP-2. Enemy hills in position to support the Boot were Hill 80 (Three Fingers), Hill 88 (the former OP Blue), and Hill 70 (the Claw).

The Marine plan was to position forces on each of the friendly outposts to counter threats that might come from either of the enemy support hills. According to the Special Action Reports, "Provisions were made to provide a reserve force prepared to counter enemy reaction at any point."[16] The objective would be surrounded on three sides but at some distance away.

Two squads from Easy Company 2/7 were designated as the assault force. The plan called for supporting tanks and infantry to set up a base of fire and begin the attack. When the Boot was sufficiently softened, Easy Company would attack. Men from Baker Company 1/7 would support the tanks, reinforce the assault, and aid with evacuation if needed.

The key to the assault was Hill 90 (former Marine Outpost White). Hill 90 controlled the assault approach to the Boot, as well as the corresponding withdrawal route. The 1/7 "Special Action Report" emphasizes that ". . . Hill 90 had to be held in order to use the stream bed as a reinforcing and evacuation route for the raid."[17] Subsequently, four tanks would be positioned atop Hill 90 for direct fire support on the Boot. Accompanying the tanks would be a platoon of infantry from Baker Company 1/7. A reserve of three tanks, also with protective infantry, would be on OP Marilyn to fire on various enemy hills as called for. Two more tanks were sited on high ground slightly forward of the MLR to provide additional support.

Armored personnel carriers were stationed west of Marilyn with another platoon of infantry from Baker Company 1/7. This mobile group could quickly reinforce the assault group if required. A platoon from the Division Reconnaissance Company was deployed to the forward slope of COP-2 should help be needed from that direction. Three standby tanks, on alert behind the MLR at Hill 229, were prepared to roll out as the battle progressed. Armored support for Operation Dog, numbering fourteen tanks in all, was from Charlie Company, 1st Tank Battalion.

One would think that all bases were covered, and they were—until Murphy once again chose to exercise his law. As it happened, the Easy Company assault squads scheduled to hit the Boot never left the MLR.

At 2020, on 23 February, the Baker Company platoon and four Charlie Company tanks left the MLR for Hill 90. During their approach, artillery VT blasted the top of the hill while the tanks paused periodically to fire at targets of opportunity. Arriving on Hill 90, the infantry quickly established a perimeter defense and tanks moved into position. As the last tank (C-35) moved into its slot, it struck an antitank mine that damaged the suspension and disabled the tank.[18] The position immediately came under enemy fire, and Chinese troops were seen moving down the trench line from Three Fingers.

The entire area erupted in exchanges of fire. Small-arms fire from the Horseshoe, directed at Hill 90, was followed by incoming artillery fire.

Outpost Ingrid began receiving mortar fire, and machine guns from Three Fingers fired on Outpost Marilyn. A report of Tank-Infantry Action on Hill 90 relates:

> Two tanks equipped with fighting lights illuminated the area and friendly forces returned fire. The enemy suffered heavy casualties crossing the open area between Hill 80 [Three Fingers] and 90. The tank and infantry platoon leaders and several of the tank commanders manned the turret mounted fifty caliber machine guns at this time to increase the volume of fire. In spite of the intensity of friendly fire, the enemy reached the forward slope of Hill 90 and the area known as the "Horseshoe." From these positions the enemy closed with the friendly forces and tried to overrun their position.[19]

The enemy attack on Hill 90 was supported by fire from Hills 88 (Blue), 70 (Claw), and 64. Rockets were fired at the Marine tanks from the Horseshoe. One of the tank lights was put out of action and another suffered electrical failure. Mortar flares were brought in to illuminate the area as mixed mortar and artillery fire fell. During the intervening darkness, Chinese forces established themselves between Hill 90 and Outpost Marilyn which precluded effective fire from the latter. Incoming fire at Hill 90 caused three casualties among the infantry and tankers.

All other Marine units assigned to the operation were ordered to stand fast and await further orders. Operation Dog had become the Battle for Hill 90. The Special Action Report continues:

> Heavy fighting continued on Hill 90. The enemy made repeated assaults on friendly positions and once succeeded in penetrating the perimeter defense and fighting their way to the tanks. This force was immediately destroyed by friendly units and six (6) enemy dead were counted within the defensive perimeter. Friendly troops stood their ground and engaged in hand-to-hand fighting with bayonets. The enemy was able to penetrate the position only after one complete fire team had become casualties. Friendly illumination provided artificial light in order to inflict heavy casualties on attacking and reinforcing enemy units. The enemy attempted to police the battlefield, but was immediately interdicted by friendly infantry, tank, mortar and artillery VT fire. Illumination was almost continuous.[20]

At 2200, Hill 90 began receiving mortar fire again. (The first episode had ceased when Chinese infantry attacked.) The enemy also began walking 81-mm mortar rounds up the forward slope of Marilyn. Tanks on Marilyn were hit, but the crews reported only superficial damage. Outpost Kate also received enemy mortar fire. At 2203, the enemy began walking 120-mm mortar fire up the slope of Outpost Marilyn to search for the tanks positioned there. Enemy dead were observed around friendly positions on Hill 90.

The enemy launched another assault on Hill 90 with ten to fifteen burp guns and ten other automatic weapons. The attack was repulsed with heavy enemy losses. By 2245, Baker Company's infantry platoon reported casualties of two killed, four wounded, and one missing. A search squad successfully recovered the missing man. The enemy next employed white phosphorus (WP) mortars on Hill 90. At 2246, small-arms fire on Hill 90 became sporadic, but, at 2256, the Chinese launched another assault. This attack was also repulsed with heavy losses to the enemy.

The Chinese soldier was an aggressive and tenacious enemy, and the fighting was not over. If the Chinese couldn't take the hill, they would, at least, hit the Marines as they left, and they set up an ambush on the return route. A tank evacuating wounded Marines from Hill 90 to the streambed had to fight its way back as Chinese troops ambushed the tank with hand grenades and small arms, which were ineffective against steel but dangerous to men exposed on the outside the tank. Six wounded Marines were riding on the tank. The assistant driver, also exposed while holding one of the wounded, was hit. The tank commander took a BAR from a wounded man and accounted for five enemy casualties. Illumination flares, exploding overhead, were most useful. The enemy ambush was quite visible, and tanks on Marilyn and Hill 90 accounted for fifteen more enemy casualties.

Meanwhile on Hill 90, morale among the Marines remained high; they were doing the job for which they had trained. When they received a radio message asking if reinforcements were needed, they replied, "We can hold out for six days if you send us rations, and hot coffee."[21] At 2400, another group of Chinese closed to within 20 yards of the tanks. Four of this group were killed by infantry and point-blank tank fire.

Forty minutes later, the enemy reinforced its ranks and tried again to attack the hill. More illumination was provided, and tanks and infantry had a field day with 90-mm tank fire, .50-caliber machine guns, 30-caliber machine guns, and infantry weapons. Enemy dead were strewn all over the hill and adjoining rice paddies. No estimate could be made at the time, but one tank crew counted eighteen dead Chinese in front of their position and eleven in the rear.

The Chinese ceased fire at 0139. The Marines attempted to retrieve tank C-35 that had hit the mine at the onset of the battle, but they were unsuccessful. They pulled it a short way off the crest of the hill, stripped it, and left it for a later recovery attempt. The infantry destroyed emplacements on Hill 90 with satchel charges and made ready to leave. Withdrawal was ordered at 0155.

During the fighting, the Marines had discovered that Chinese forces were using radio frequencies identical to theirs. While withdrawing, they entertained the Chinese by singing "The Marines' Hymn" on the frequency.

No prisoners were taken, so five Chinese bodies were loaded on the back of a tank and transported to the MLR for intelligence purposes. Unfortunately, the Marines neglected to relieve the bodies of ammunition. En route, one of the bodies lying near a hot muffler caught fire and ignited the soldier's supply of hand grenades and ammunition. This, in turn, lit off the other bodies, and they all began to burn and explode. On reaching the MLR, the tankers stopped and unceremoniously dumped the grizzly mess on the ground. So much for intelligence efforts.

During the remaining darkness of 24 February, two tanks were left in position on Marilyn with fighting lights focused on the disabled C-35. Periodically, they raked the area around the tank with machine-gun fire in order to prevent the enemy from further damaging the tank or setting booby traps. At first light, mechanics took a retriever to Hill 90 and towed C-35 back to the MLR.

Colonel Williamson was very pleased with the conduct of his tankers. On the evening of 24 February, he wrote in a letter home:

> . . . The enemy got so close to the tanks that Lieutenant Norton, the tank platoon leader, shot one with a pistol. His radio went out and while running from one tank to another he was hit by a mortar shell and wounded in the hand and legs. He was bandaged and placed into a tank. The battle continued with SSgt. Naze, the platoon sergeant, running the show in a cool and competent manner. The infantry didn't lie in their holes and wait for the enemy either. They aggressively pursued the Chinese, chasing them all over the hill.
>
> . . . Another one of my men was wounded by a grenade when the tank hauling the wounded back was ambushed. The infantry casualties weren't too severe, and we figured we killed upwards of seventy five of the enemy and wounded a hundred more. That will teach the bastards to try to ambush us. . . .
>
> I went by A Med this morning to see Lieutenant Norton. He was

on the operating table when I got there. . . . . The other man that was wounded went directly to the hospital ship so I didn't get to see him.[22]

Operation Dog was officially secured at 2350 when it was determined that the fighting on Hill 90 would preclude any effort to attack the Boot. It was nevertheless a good fight, the wrong objective perhaps, but in battle one has to expect the unexpected. According to the record, the enemy lost 96 killed and 123 wounded, a total of 219 casualties. Marine casualties were 5 killed and 22 wounded.

OPERATION CHARLIE

The 5th Marines were on line to the right of the 7th Marines. The order of battle was 2/5 on the far right, with Easy Company anchoring the east, Fox Company in the center, and Dog Company on the west. Three outposts were maintained by 2/5, Berlin, East Berlin, and an unnamed position. At the beginning of February, 3/5 occupied the regimental left and held four outposts, Ava, Reno, Carson, and Vegas.

Following the Clambake raid in early February, activity in the 5th Marine sector had been somewhat subdued. Incoming was light to moderate and consisted mainly of harassing fire to the outposts and the MLR. Nightly patrols prowling the terrain in front of the MLR found little to report. Each day, however, someone died or was injured—perhaps because of a sniper or a mortar, or from stepping on a mine or tripping a booby trap, or by participating in a patrol engagement. Even in the absence of large battles, war took its toll.

On the morning of 22 February, a How Company 3/5 platoon, reinforced with four flamethrowers, raided Kumgok. Hitting the hill at daybreak, the Marines attacked two platoons of Chinese troops. The engagement was indecisive, and the Marines withdrew with fourteen casualties but no fatalities. Enemy KIAs were estimated at twenty-one.

Not content with earlier successes, Col. Lew Walt's 5th Marines planned yet another raid. This operation would be an early-morning infantry assault using two reinforced platoons. Named "Operation Charlie," the objective for this raid was Hill 15, better known as Detroit, the Marine outpost lost in October 1952. The assaulting platoons were drawn from Fox Company 2/5. As with Clambake, Able Company tanks would support the raid, only this time from prepared tank slots on the MLR. No tanks would venture into no-man's-land, a prudent decision because the tank battalion no longer had a functioning reconnaissance section or flame platoon.

Detroit was a tough hill. When the Chinese took it in October 1952, they had paid a heavy price in blood. Now the shoe was on the other foot, and the Marines would make the assault. The difference was that the Marines had no intention of keeping the hill. They just wanted to get there, kill a few people, capture some if possible, "kick over a stove or two," and leave.

Detroit was 600 yards in front of the MLR. The Chinese had spent a good deal of time and energy in improving the hill since it had been abandoned by the Marines. Using the gift of hindsight provided by an after action report, one can see just how good the defenses were:

> From all indications the raiding party encountered approximately one (1) company of enemy troops, well entrenched in a deep circular trench, caves, bunkers and spider holes. The trench lines on the objective were connected by a large deep trench leading towards hill 125 and another leading to hill 13A. The main trench line on the top of the objective was from 6 feet to 7 feet wide at the top, narrowing to about 4 feet at the bottom and from 6 feet to eight feet deep. From this trench a network of passageways extended downward to caves with other outlets giving the enemy a covered entrance to other portions of the main trench. Rabbit holes and deep bunkers, both living and fighting, were found to have held up under constant artillery and mortar bombardment and air strikes.

> The defense of the hill was organized in such a manner that all bunkers and fighting holes were mutually supporting. The enemy would withdraw to caves and rabbit holes to fight when their positions were overrun. He would issue forth again to pour out fire as the assault echelon withdrew.[23]

Like other 5th Marine raids, Operation Charlie was marked with intensive and meticulous planning. Staff conferences were held with attendance by supporting arms. Pilots designated to fly the air strikes were brought forward and briefed. Targets were pointed out from the MLR and the infantry scheme of maneuver described. Reconnaissance patrols and mine clearance teams went out on successive nights prior to the raid. Five infantry rehearsals were held.

The approach to Detroit was across 300 yards of open rice paddies, thus rendering it dangerous to negotiate during the light of day. Consequently, the infantry attack was planned to commence during BMNT (beginning–morning–nautical–twilight, that period before sunrise when visibility is limited to approximately 300 yards). In this case, BMNT was 0615.

On 25 February, Operation Charlie began as scheduled with concentrations of artillery and mortar fire on the objective. Using high explosives and smoke, the Marines bombarded Detroit for eight minutes. At H-hour, two reinforced platoons from Fox Company crossed the line of departure and began their assault. As the troops moved out, preparatory artillery fire shifted to nearby hills. Fire to the objective was assumed by tanks and machine guns from the MLR and mortars.

For twenty-six minutes, the Fox Company platoons advanced on the objective. At first, they received little in the way of incoming fire from the defenders, but that soon changed. Still, they had apparently achieved surprise. Reports note that Chinese attempts at radio jamming were annoying but unsuccessful. By 0648, the Marines had fought their way into the trenches and were employing demolitions, flamethrowers, grenades, and small arms. The platoon on the right flank of the assault became pinned down briefly with enemy grenades and automatic weapons. The other platoon, already in the trenches, shifted to drive the Chinese off the men who were pinned down. Eventually, the men were able to break through and move to a more advantageous position but not soon enough.

Pfc. Donald Johnson was in Fox Company 2/5 and remembers the raid that morning:

. . . As we approached the wire on the top, the Chinese started throwing potato-masher grenades down at us. Our platoon was supposed to enter the Chinese trenchline from the point and then meet up with the first platoon, which would sweep in from the left.

But only four of us made it to the trenchline: A. P. Goff, who had taken over from Kelly as squad leader; Houseman; Jones; and me. Our platoon leader, Lieutenant Russell, was killed as he stepped into the trench. Goff's left arm was shattered by a burp-gun blast, Houseman was hit in the leg, and I somehow got a piece of tin embedded in my chin.

We cleaned out a lot of Chinese, and we didn't worry about taking prisoners. Goff, who refused even to look at his arm, spotted a lot of Chinese massing on the reverse slope of the hill, so he ordered us out. We were four, who should have been forty.

We fought our way back out, carrying Lieutenant Russell's body with us. On the way down the hill, Jones went into shock, and we lost him for a week or ten days.

Goff was taken to an aid station, and I never did see him again until we met a long time later in Oakland, California. He never did regain the use of his arm, but he was awarded a Silver Star for bravery.[24]

The entire raid had taken sixty-eight minutes and, at 0720, both platoons were ordered to withdraw. After reaching the MLR, the men determined that the two platoons had lost a total of four killed and fifty-eight wounded. One man was missing. Enemy losses were estimated at sixty-two killed. According to the Special Action Report, "No estimation was given as to WIA's."[25] Unfortunately, no record was made of efforts to recover the missing Marine.

Supporting fire during Operation Charlie was intense; it was a wonderment that Chinese defenses remained sufficiently strong to enable the damage they did. One report states, "In nearly three hours of firing, the 11th Marines and its attached units, including the first Royal Canadian Horse Artillery, expended 11,881 rounds."[26] Another indication of the firepower placed on Detroit can inferred from Lt. Col. Andrew Geer's book about the exploits of Reckless, the 5th Marines' ammunition-carrying mare. During Operation Charlie, Reckless made twenty-four trips between the ammunition supply point and 75-mm recoilless rifle positions on the MLR and packed six rounds per trip. It was estimated that the little horse traveled 20 miles and carried a total of 3,500 pounds.[27] From positions on the MLR, tanks fired more than seven hundred rounds of 90-mm. ammunition. Cpl. Robert A. Hall, one of the machine gunners with Fox Company, reported that his gun alone used thirty boxes of ammunition that morning.[28]

For no reason that can be identified, February had been a busy month for Marines on the outposts and on the MLR. The Division Reconnaissance Company was also busy and, as the month drew to a close, suffered its worst casualty event of the Korean War—an ambush on a small finger of land called Gray Rock Ridge.

CHAPTER 6

AMBUSH ON GRAY ROCK RIDGE

*Major, tell my father
I died with my face to the enemy.*
—Col. I. E. Avery, CSA:
At Gettysburg, 2 July 1863

The Division Reconnaissance Company was part of Headquarters Battalion. It was a small company with fewer than two hundred officers and men divided among three platoons. Many of the men had been trained at the Army's Intelligence School, Fort Riley, Kansas, and carried an MOS (military occupational specialty) of 0211, reconnaissance. The company specialized in patrolling no-man's-land to gather intelligence and to capture prisoners. Rarely did recon Marines fight prolonged battles or defend fixed positions as did the regular infantry.

Recon Marines, when not at work in front of the MLR, were relatively well situated in their company CP behind the lines. By outpost standards, their home might have been considered luxurious. Rarely were they required to cope with incoming artillery, and snipers did not exist. Before going on a patrol, a man could eat a hot meal, take a shower, slip into clean clothes, and sometimes catch a movie. If one were going to die, it was probably better to go clean and with a full stomach. Recon men, however, could also move quieter, go farther, see more, and report better than most line company recon units. Their specialty was combat intelligence.

For these specialists, February began as a quiet month, marked largely by rear area patrols to seek out enemy agents and line crossers. It ended with their bloodiest action of the war, which virtually decimated the company. As in most disasters, small, identifiable circumstances slowly came into play and led to a climatic event. This incident began no differently than others; it was routine.

Midmonth in February, major personnel changes took place in the company. The 1st Platoon was broken up and the men redistributed among the other two platoons in order better to equalize expertise and experience throughout the entire company. Rotations, transfers, and evacuations during previous months had tended to affect the 2d and 3d Platoons more than the 1st Platoon. Consequently, the more experienced men had accumulated in the 1st Platoon. Because of the shuffle, men in each platoon were not acquainted with one another and had never worked together. That intangible bond of trust and instinct, so essential for success in combat, would take time to rebuild. Time, however, was a luxury that the Reconnaissance Company did not have.

About that time, a new platoon leader, 2d Lt. William Livingston, joined the company and was well received by the men of the 1st Platoon. Livingston wanted to be there; he had asked for the assignment. One of his first acts was to convince the company commander, Maj. Dermott MacDonnell, that his platoon should spend more time patrolling in front of the MLR rather than behind it. If the men were going to develop into an effective fighting unit, they needed to fight.

The 1st Platoon also had a new platoon sergeant, T/Sgt. Joseph R. Errgang. Gunny Errgang, however, was anything but new. He had joined the Marine Corps in 1942 and was fighting in World War II while most of the men in the 1st Platoon were still riding tricycles. His last assignment before coming to Korea was at The Basic School, where he had been a drill instructor for new officers. Errgang, coincidentally, had been Livingston's senior drill instructor in the 10th Special Basic Class at Quantico, Virginia.

Adding to the confusion of a new platoon leader, a new platoon sergeant, and the internal reshuffling of personnel was yet another dimension—new men to train. On the afternoon of 20 February, the tank battalion sent a squad of men, most of whom were fresh off the troopship, to Reconnaissance Company for training in reconnaissance techniques. The tank battalion's reconnaissance section was being reconstituted after Sergeant Rhoades had been killed and his group destroyed in January. These new men (one of whom was the author) were equally distributed among platoons and then integrated into squads and fire teams, which further ensured that everyone was a stranger to the others. Strangers or not, two patrols were scheduled to leave the following night—so much for preliminary introductions.

Reconnaissance Company Patrol 146 was an early-morning, two-platoon patrol in the Korean Marine Corps sector. Its purpose was to investigate recent enemy activity around a bowl-shaped terrain feature known as the Stadium.

The 2d and 3d Platoons departed Combat Outpost One (COP-1) at 0120 on 22 February. En route to the objective, the patrol encountered a Korean civilian. (Try as they might, the Marines were never totally able to rid the battle area of civilians.) Through an interpreter, the civilian indicated that the area had been free of Chinese "since the tanks were here." Two hours later, the patrol arrived at the Stadium and made a futile search for evidence of enemy presence. The old man had been correct. Expanding their search in both directions, the men still found no evidence of Chinese activity. According to battalion records, "Absolutely no enemy could be found in the area searched. . ."[1] The patrol returned to COP-1 at 0625.

Another patrol that night, Patrol 145, conducted by Livingston's 1st Platoon, investigated a terrain feature east of COP-2 called the Island. The patrol discovered no evidence of enemy activity except for a few propaganda leaflets. It was an uneventful night. Five days later, these men would return to this area with a far different outcome. For many, it would be their last visit.

In the meantime, the men of each platoon struggled to train new men, cope with the strengths and weaknesses of each other, and strive to learn and share the experiences that were so vital to their work. At least one group went out each night to patrol or to set an ambush.

Reconnaissance Company ambushes were usually set up in two segments, an ambush group and a support group. The ambush group went out first and set up in the target area, a trail or position believed to be frequented by the enemy. The support group left a bit later and set up within range to assist the ambush group as might be needed.

Sitting most of the night on an ambush could be a trial. Cpl. Bev (Scotty) Bruce stated it well:

> In warm weather it just got boring but in cold weather it got miserable very quickly. The first two hours you hoped nothing would happen. During the second two hours you wished they would come so you could shoot them and go home. In the third two hours you didn't want them to show up because you were too cold to shoot, and during the last two hours you wanted them to come and shoot you. (Bless the corpsman and his magic cough syrup—180 proof alcohol and wintergreen.)[2]

Another view of the ambush experience comes from one of the tank battalion trainees sitting on a hillside with the 1st Platoon:

> Sitting out an all night ambush I had trouble avoiding sleep, often I would nod off and suddenly awake to what appeared to be thousands of advancing Chinese, which fortunately turned out to be nothing more than bushes. I also had trouble with coughing. I was a smoker and had a chronic smoker's hack. I tried everything to muffle it, gloves in my mouth, a scarf, the crook of an arm, anything.
>
> On one occasion a hoarse whisper said, "Who in the hell is doing that damn coughing?" There was a whispered reply, "It's one of the tankers." Lt. Livingston quietly made his way forward and gave me a well deserved chewing out. Then he told me to chew a little cigarette tobacco. It didn't taste great but gave a scratchy sensation to the back of the throat and relieved the need to cough. It worked.[3]

For much of Wednesday, 25 February, the men took the day off. They relaxed, cleaned their weapons, did laundry, wrote letters, and tended to other creature comforts. The movie that night was *Iron Maiden* with Alan Ladd. Many of the men attended out of sheer boredom. After the movie, two platoons went out. No contact was made, but the patrol received six to eight rounds of mortar fire en route back to the MLR. Battalion records indicate, "The patrol returned to the MLR at 0400, 26 Feb."[4]

That same night, a single-platoon, rear-area patrol (Patrol 153) near the Han River was sweeping for infiltraters. The only things swept up were three civilians, a drunken schoolteacher, a firewatch, and the latter's assistant. The patrol turned them over to the ROK National Police for questioning.

At 2400 on 26 February, a patrol investigated an area north of Outpost Carson. The men made no contact but heard unidentified noises around Ungok. They received nine rounds of incoming mortar, which missed them by 75 yards, before they returned to the MLR at 0445.

The day was Friday, 27 February.

That night, a two-platoon ambush was set up near the Island. Tactically, it was a carbon copy of Patrol 145 completed five days previously. The ambush group, thirty-six men from the 2d Platoon, was led by 1st Lt. Herbert R. Oxnam Jr. The Marines departed COP-2 at 1835 and proceeded immediately to the Island. By 1920, they were in position.

An hour later, the support group, consisting of Lieutenant Livingston and thirty men from the 1st Platoon, were leaving the outpost for their backup position. As they were leaving, they learned that a group of Chinese troops had been seen in the valley below. Intent on intercepting the enemy before they could attack the ambush group, the 1st Platoon proceeded rapidly down the finger of land known as Gray Rock Ridge, extending northeast from COP-2. (Some reports refer to this land feature as No Name Ridge.) Here, the platoon ran into a bit of difficulty.

In a letter home, Sergeant Arthur Lipper, with the 1st Platoon, described what happened:

> I pray this letter will reach you before the form telegram from the Navy Dept. I am well and unhurt. I caught a tiny piece of lead in the right side of my head just above my ear. It did not hurt much then and still does not bother me. It's such a small piece that they won't bother taking it out. In time it will work itself out.
>
> I'll start from the beginning, leaving out nothing. Above all, do not disseminate any of this information. No one must know how badly Recon was hit.
>
> We left here Friday afternoon at 1645. Two platoons, the 1st and 2nd. The first platoon had only two squads going out. My squad (at my suggestion) was split into the 1st and 3rd because it was so under strength (6 men) I was acting as platoon guide. (The guide is the 3rd in command, he assists the Platoon. Sgt.) The 2nd platoon was up to strength.
>
> We were to act as one of the jaws of a trap which had been set at the base of one of our outposts (near Panmunjom). There was a full moon and not a cloud in the sky. It was just like day when we left the outpost gate. I, as guide, was last in the column (this was a switch for me).
>
> As we were nearing our set-up point, the 2nd platoon, which was already set up on a piece of high ground about 400 yards away got hit. All hell broke loose.
>
> Machine guns, burp guns and mortars seemed to hit us simultaneously. The first round hit the headquarters section which was in the middle of the column between the two squads. Lt. Livingston was severely wounded, both legs, his throat and jaw. The platoon radioman, Corporal [Robert] Bush, was hit from the rear and saturated with lead (he later died as we got him finally to the forward aid station on OP-2). The platoon runner, [Frank] Benenati, must have been killed on the spot.
>
> By the time I found the lieutenant we were pretty badly cut up. Sgt. Bob [Robert] Kosmeder, the 1st squad leader, took a burp gun slug through the chest and a few in the arms. All three of the radio men were badly hit. Cliff Davis, the Corpsman, had been hit in the

arm thus making his left arm useless. Despite his wounds he did a great job of treating, as best he could, the wounded we could get to him. All three BAR men were badly hit. Snuffy found, picked up and fired all the ammo for every weapon he could find. All this time the mortars never ceased, and we could hear the Chinese moving in around us. Platoon sergeant, Gunny Errgang was nowhere to be found. The Lt. told me to take over, he was in a semistate of shock. He did a wonderful job out there and I hope he gets written up for something.

We gathered the wounded as best we could and made a search for others. I started the wounded and walking wounded up a draw and on the way back.

Snuffy and two other men stayed with me to hold the rear. We could hear Chinese just over the top of the ridge, moving in. It was then that a mortar landed right between Snuffy, another man and myself. Snuffy got a scratch on the leg and was lifted clear off the deck; the other man was out for a few minutes, and I took this small piece of lead. If the round had been further away by a few yards— finis. The proximity of the burst is what saved us. We moved back, pursued by fire and mortars all the way and finally got back to OP-2. It was rough going. Almost all of us were out of ammo, only a few were not hit. We had three or four stretcher cases and only two stretchers. . . .[5]

FIREFIGHT

The record shows that the 2d Platoon, after setting up its ambush, began receiving 82-mm mortar fire at 1940. Immediately following the mortars, it received machine-gun fire from Hills 134 and 80. Men of the 2d Platoon returned fire to both positions. Obviously, there would be no ambush that night.

Meanwhile, as related in Lipper's letter, the 1st Platoon got into trouble crossing over Gray Rock Ridge. Later inquiry determined that the lead and middle squads virtually collided into a thirty-five man platoon of enemy soldiers preparing to occupy their own ambush position. The two groups apparently surprised one another. Recovering quickly, each side began throwing grenades and firing their weapons. All of the action was at the point of the column that was over the ridge from COP-2. The remainder of the column, trailing behind the lead squads, was uninvolved except for incoming mortar fire. Close-in fighting continued for about ten minutes until 2000, when the Chinese troops slowly began to give ground.

As the Marine column disengaged, it fell back on itself, carrying the wounded. Enemy mortar and machine-gun fire began to increase in intensity. After a few rounds, the Chinese had the range, and the platoon took more casualties. The men were surrounded by the "crump" of incoming mortars and the strike of long-range machine guns. The mortar barrage resulted in eleven wounded.

Lieutenant Livingston and his radioman, Corporal Bush, were among those wounded early in the fighting. Livingston recovered the radio and was able to call in mortar counterfire to protect the withdrawal of his platoon. He ordered an evacuation of the wounded to a casualty collection point in a fairly well defiladed draw on the slope of Gray Rock. Enemy fire continued while Chinese troops attempted an envelopment of the flanks. As casualties were moved to the collection point, Livingston was hit again but continued to help evacuate the wounded and carry stretchers.

As the withdrawal continued, an orange flare burst in the vicinity of Hill 134. Enemy fire increased and covered the ridge with mortar rounds. Several more Marines were wounded, and the movement of casualties became extremely difficult. At 2020, Livingston called for aid in evacuating his wounded. Ten minutes, later a reinforced squad from Able Company 1/7 arrived to help the badly hurt platoon move its wounded to COP-2.

Sgt. John J. O'Hagan, a squad leader with Able Company 1/7, had patrolled Gray Rock countless times and knew the terrain well. He was one of the first to go out to reinforce and help the Recon men:

> I remember the heavy mortar and artillery fire we caught. . . . I ran out to help Lt. Livingston make it back. Coincidentally, we knew each other from Camp Lejeune when we were in Able 1/6 together. He remembered me. After we were in a safe place, we had a few words until someone hollered for help. I ran out again to help with more wounded. I found one guy and tried to help him up an incline. I grabbed him by the ass to boost him and one or both cheeks were missing. I stuck my hand in that mess and then grabbed for his waist. I never heard how he made out. He did holler that he couldn't use his legs, I don't wonder.
>
> . . . When I got back to the spot where I last saw Lt. Livingston, everyone was gone.[6]

While the 1st Platoon, trying to withdraw, was being shelled and shot at, the 2nd Platoon was on the Island. Enemy long-range machine-gun and mortar fire made movement extremely precarious. The platoon sustained five casualties and was likely to have more if it remained. Major MacDonnell, on COP-2, ordered its immediate withdrawal by the most direct route possible. Twenty minutes later, the 2d Platoon arrived on the outpost.

Around 2110, still under heavy fire from the Chinese, Livingston requested more help with his evacuation. Elements of the 2nd Platoon, standing by after their return from the Island, went out and, along with men from Able 1/7, helped to return the wounded and set up a rear guard to cover the final withdrawal of the 1st Platoon. Sgt. John L. Camara, a tank Recon man attached to the 2d Platoon, kept a personal diary. The following day, he recorded:

> . . . Never in my life seen anything like it. Goonies all over the place, walking through their own mortar barrage to hit us. Our 81's [mortars] from Weapons Company 1/7 saved us for sure as they did before when we were at the Island.
>
> They boxed us in for two hours to keep gooks from wiping us all out completely. I never prayed so much in my life as I did during that night. I said the Act of Contrition about 100 times at least. God must have heard me to save me as he did.
>
> . . . Pvt. Witron [probably Pfc. John Whitson, another tanker] caught an HE [High Explosive] grenade in the face after standing up and firing a rifle grenade at a platoon of goonies moving in on us. He died like a Marine. His last words were, "I'm having more fun than a barrel of monkeys!" Finkle lost his right arm and right leg.
>
> I forgot how many stretchers I helped carry in. Every corpsman attached to our company was hit. Pete, the corpsman for the 2nd platoon, got hit twice and still took care of the wounded while we held off the goonies. . . .[7]

Returning to COP-2 at 2041, the men of the 1st Platoon men took time to count noses, assess their losses, and reorganize. A quick head count revealed that three men were unaccounted for: T/Sgt. Joseph R. Errgang, Pfc. Frank Benenati, and Pfc. John Whitson. Of the thirty Marines who had left COP-2 with the support group at 1940, twenty were casualties: one killed, sixteen wounded, and three missing. The first platoon had been reduced to less than a squad (among whom was the author).

The firefight had lasted two hours. Enemy casualties were an estimated twenty-nine killed and thirty wounded. The tragedy at Gray Rock, however, was only beginning to unfold.

THE SEARCH

The Marines immediately began to organize an operation to find the missing men. At 2315, they initiated the first search. Deploying thirty-five men, the 2d Platoon conducted a search of Gray Rock Ridge as far north as the initial point of contact. The Marines retrieved weapons and other gear, but did not find the missing men. Throughout the search, they received sporadic mortar rounds accompanied by machine-gun and small-arms fire from Hill 134. At 2240, two men were wounded and evacuated to the outpost.

Sergeant Lipper was with the search party. He described the action:

> Six of us went out with the second platoon to act as guides. On the way out the Chinese hit us with mortars again. Two of the second platoon people were badly hit (one will die most likely). Two of my people had to help the wounded in.
>
> I was with Lt. Oxnam helping direct the search. We found my man's weapon and that was all, except his gloves and scarf. Most of the time mortar rounds were coming in but they were well off target this time.
>
> We returned to the OP. Out of thirty men who went out on patrol with us, I brought thirteen down to the truck. The second platoon lost eight, six the first time and two while going out on the search. Sgt. [Norm] Haney, my first team leader, got hit in the legs and shoulder. Corporal Allen, my radio man, led the point back on guts alone; he was hit in both legs and in the neck. (He wouldn't give up his radio till I pulled it out of his hands.) He was also out of ammo. Haney and Allen will go Stateside.
>
> . . . I'll close with this thought. I don't know why I was just scratched or why the rounds landed where they did, or why the piece of shrapnel wasn't larger, or why I can still write. I do know that I am mighty thankful. Maybe St. Jude is responsible, maybe not. If he is the patron Saint of "Close ones," then he must have been on top that night, that I do know. Thanks for soliciting his aid.[8]

In his own way, Lipper expressed thoughts shared by nearly every survivor of combat. "Why me?" Some people harbor a lifetime of guilt because they survived; others are grateful to their God. None, however, has forgotten the experience. The late Ernie Pyle, a famous combat correspondent killed in the Pacific, is credited with saying, "There are no atheists in foxholes." His words were as accurate in Korea as they had been during World War II.

While the 2d Platoon was conducting its search, Reconnaissance Company's 3d Platoon, led by 2d Lt. James L. Day, moved north from the company CP to help in the search. (Jim Day, a mustang officer, is the Marine to whom this book is dedicated.) When the 3d Platoon arrived on COP-2 about 2345, it was immediately placed on alert to support the 2d Platoon should it get into trouble. The entire Reconnaissance Company was now committed to the action.

By 0030, the 2d Platoon search was complete and the men returned. It was decided, as a result of this effort, to secure the search until daylight. For the remainder of the night, the men developed plans for a second attempt that would commence at first light. The 3d Platoon stood down to await daybreak.

Shortly after midnight, now 28 February, the company commander on COP-2 had requested a concentration of artillery over a group of fifteen Chinese troops, seen in the moonlight, who were moving between the Island and Hill 134. The fire was delivered with excellent results and dropped all of the enemy soldiers.

At 0630, a smoke screen was placed across Gray Rock Ridge in preparation for another search effort. Tank fire commenced from positions on Outposts Marilyn and Kate, and artillery and mortar concentrations were delivered to various Chinese positions. Ten minutes later, Lieutenant Day's 3d Platoon, with thirty-six men, deployed in a skirmish line covering the width of the entire ridge. The platoon moved out northeast toward enemy lines. Twenty minutes into the operation, it began to receive machine-gun fire from Hill 134 and the Island. This was followed by more fire from Hill 80 and then followed by a mortar barrage that wounded six Marines. Enemy fire slackened as more smoke was brought into the area to obscure the target.

The platoon was crossing Gray Rock in a skirmish line when the center squad discovered the bodies of two Marines. The first one was lying on his back on a slight slope, the body partially stripped. His trousers, utility jacket, and field jacket were gone. His feet were bare, but a pair of thermal boots had been placed neatly beside them. The body, thought to be that of Benenati, showed evidence of mutilation; the chest had been cut several times with a knife or bayonet. The second body was found about 25 feet southeast of the first one. It had not been stripped, but the utility jacket was badly torn in front. This body was thought to be that of Whitson, the tanker. Gunny Errgang was not found.

As the Marines approached the second body, they noticed three more bodies lying on a nearby road. Positioned oddly, they were lying end to end in the center of the road. Each was covered with a blanket or a similar material and had a large, well-made cross, about 6 feet long, lying perpendicular across it. The heads of two of the bodies were visible. One had red hair, and the other was dark blond. The feet of the third body were not covered with a blanket, and the Marines noted that he was wearing what appeared to be thermal boots.

The men moved down the slope to investigate but were stopped by machine-gun fire from Hill 134, which forced them to seek cover. One of the men located Lieutenant Day and reported the discovery. Because of the intensity of enemy fire, no attempts were made to investigate further. The machine gunners were searching and the bullets traversing all of Gray Rock Ridge. The platoon suffered two more casualties, and the squads were subsequently ordered to return to COP-2 under cover of a thickened smoke screen. By 0815, the entire platoon had returned to the outpost.

Pfc. Charles ("Chuck") Burrill had been with the 1st Platoon of Reconnaissance Company since May 1952. Because of his experience, however, he had been reassigned to Lieutenant Day's 3d Platoon. Some of Burrill's best friends, including Bush, Benenati, and Howard Davenport (later evacuated with wounds in December 1952), had remained in the 1st Platoon. In a letter, Burrill wrote of his experiences during the early morning of 27 February when word came down that the 1st Platoon had been hit badly and had suffered extensive casualties:

> My squad had been out on an ambush that night. Lt. Day wanted to check out the activity in an area called the "Cathedral" and to capture a prisoner, so our squad went out there and set up. We waited and waited but no luck. The lieutenant decided that this wasn't our night so we started back.
>
> It was then that we got the word to return to the company CP because the first platoon was in trouble. They were at OP-2 and had three MIA [missing in action]'s. When I heard this, I felt a terrible pain in my gut, as if someone just kicked me as hard as he could. I cried out to myself, "Oh no—not Benenati—please God, not Benenati!" I prayed all the way back for this not to be Ben.
>
> Returning to the CP, we were informed that the first platoon had really been clobbered, and the second platoon had been hit while going to aid them. Our platoon loaded up and headed for OP-2. We

arrived there just before daylight and were briefed by Lt. Day. I asked about the three MIA's and my worst fears were realized—Ben was among the missing.

I was stunned—I just couldn't believe it. The only thread of hope I had now was that he might still be alive.

It was now February 28th and we were going to thoroughly search Gray Rock for the missing men. As I recall, the plan was for the line to comb the area and then start across no-man's-land and head toward the enemy lines. We were to stop about a third of the way there and the line would pivot 180 degrees around the center and return. In this way the left and right sides of the line would exchange places for return to OP-2. The area would be searched twice by different people, once going out and again coming in. Naturally we would come under fire by the Chinese while executing the maneuver.

At daybreak, with the support of tank fire, artillery and mortars we began the search. There was a thick layer of smoke covering the search area. I was on the left end of the skirmish line as we started down the ridge. The smoke was doing a great job of concealing our sweep and we received no enemy fire. My thoughts were that if Ben wasn't a prisoner, then he was probably dead. My heart was heavy with grief and pain as I was accepting that I would probably never again see Ben alive. I fought back my emotions as I combed every inch of ground before me—looking, hoping and praying for some sign of Ben.

The smoke was still providing good cover so I went on ahead, just a little farther. Then the smoke lifted and enemy fire began to hit all around me. From the Island, from Hill 134, and from Hill 80, mortar rounds began to fall all over the place. I began shooting, returning fire toward the Island and looking behind me toward the others. Then I heard the command, "Pull back, Pull back."

I saw everyone pulling back and followed. I zigzagged back, turned and fired, hit the deck and fired again. This happened about three times before I landed and rolled next to another Marine. I didn't have the time to look at him because a gook machine gunner was zeroing in on me, slugs and dirt were following my every move. As I rolled up next to the downed Marine, the machine gun followed and gave me no place to escape. It plowed up the dirt behind and headed right at me. Before I could move again I took a slug in my left leg, a flesh wound. The other guy wasn't so lucky. The machine gun hit him about six inches above his knee, blowing a large hole in the leg. I could see that the large bone was broken with the jagged end sticking out. I never learned this guy's name, but he seemed to be about six feet tall and weighed a ton. He screamed as I tore off a section of his shirt and tied it tightly above the wound. I told him to push with his good leg while I began dragging him toward our lines. I was surprised that we weren't both killed. All the way back we took mortar and machine gun fire. It was intense.

Reaching the foot of Gray Rock, a Corpsman helped me with the wounded Marine and paused to bandage my leg. Someone from the first platoon ran up and told me that he had seen Benenati. My response was, "Where? Is he alive?" "No," he answered, "But he's up this road and to the right a little." I followed him for what seemed to be a long time but was actually only about three minutes. There in front of us on the road, were the bodies of three Marines. They were positioned oddly—lined up end to end with a cross over each body—very strange.

I had to find out for sure if it was Ben. We started for the bodies but were stopped by machine gun fire. We pulled back and soon other men joined us. I waited a few minutes and started moving forward again—I had to find out if it was Ben. I reached the same place as before and again was stopped by the same machine gun. Pulling back to the others I waited briefly and tried a third time with the same result. I couldn't get there.

Telling the others to remain where they were, I made my way back to Lt. Day. Hearing the situation he ordered us to secure and return to the outpost. They would try again later. I returned to the men waiting by the bodies, and we all made our way back up the hill to the safety of OP-2.[9]

Pfc. Herbert Pinkston was one of the tankers attached to the 3d Platoon. As the search commenced, he, like Burrill, was positioned on the left of the skirmish line. Suddenly, the call went out, "There they are." Just as suddenly, a Chinese machine gun began firing. Pinkston hit the dirt and rolled over next to a Marine known as "Chicken." The machine gun continued, and Pinkston saw branches and twigs being shot away as the bullets came closer. He hugged the ground and prayed. Then, looking ahead, he watched a man in front of him get hit, first in the calf and then in the knee. Dust puffed out from his trousers as the bullets struck.

Pinkston's squad leader, Sgt. John Crabtree, also saw the wounded man and yelled at Pinkston, "Take him back." Grabbing the man's flak jacket by the armholes, Pinkston began dragging him up the hill. Another man came soon to assist, and the two of them managed to drag the wounded man up the hill and into the trenches of the outpost.

Sgt. Robert Finn, another tanker in the 3d Platoon, recalls being separated and lost in the confusion:

Several of us became separated from the platoon, laying flat on the ground as machine gun bullets trimmed the shrubbery over our heads. I heard, "Fall back to OP-2." I could only see "Chicken" and "Chief," so I fell in with them. The three of us managed to crawl a long way around the hill to an abandoned trenchline and bunker. Entering the bunker we were out of harms way, temporarily. Taking stock, we thought over our situation and decided to try to return to the OP, we knew we couldn't stay there.

As we left the bunker a stray mortar round landed close, so close in fact, that the concussion pushed the three of us back into the doorway. Miraculously no one was hurt. Exiting again we cautiously made our way to a small draw and worked our way up the hill, through the shrubbery. Finally we entered the trenchline, arriving near the .50 cal. machine gun bunker around 1100. The situation was so confused and hectic we hadn't even been missed.[10]

Returning to the outpost, the 3d Platoon discovered that four men were unaccounted for—S/Sgt. Stanley W. Boyko, the platoon sergeant; HM3 Louie James ("Luigi") Rightmire, the corpsman; Sgt. Donald J. MacDonald, platoon guide; and Pfc. Val H. David. They had not been seen since Lieutenant Day ordered them to move to the right side of the skirmish line shortly after the platoon set out from OP-2. The 3d Platoon's morning search had lasted for one hour and thirty-five minutes. Its cost was eight men wounded, three of them seriously, and four men missing.

At 0850, the 3d Platoon regrouped, and twenty-four men prepared to conduct a search for the new MIAs. When they left OP-2, the smoke screen thickened and concentrations of VT were placed on Hills 82, 134, and 80. The Marines spread out and retraced the ground to the area where they had last seen the four men. The search proved negative, and renewed enemy fire forced them to return to the outpost. No casualties were sustained.

Another attempt to locate the missing Marines was initiated at 1035, this time with a squad of fifteen men from the 3d Platoon. The squad moved out onto Gray Rock Ridge with orders to take observation positions around high points, study the terrain in detail, and investigate any likely area. Four such areas were searched in detail, but results were again negative. Every move of the squad or an individual brought renewed incoming mortar and automatic weapons fire, which became especially intense as the smoke screen diminished with the wind. No casualties resulted, however, and the squad returned to the outpost empty-handed at 1115.

Fifteen minutes later, a third effort was made to find the MIAs by another squad of fifteen men. This patrol searched three more places with negative results. Enemy fire was quite meager, and the group returned at 1215 with no casualties.

A fourth attempt was launched at 1245 with elements of two platoons making a last, desperate sweep of the ridge. They were supported by artillery support fired on all known enemy positions. The men were ordered to carry the search as far as enemy fire would allow. As the sweep moved out, a VT artillery mission directed at Hills 134 and 80 and at the rice paddy north of the Island was fired. One of the rounds was short and detonated over the Marines. Burrill's letter continues:

As we started down the hill, we were met by fierce mortar and machine gun fire. I hit the deck for a few seconds and started moving to my left. Suddenly, a short round from our own artillery burst overhead. I hit the deck and felt a sting in my left arm. Looking to my right I saw the body of a Marine that was in the same hole I had left just seconds before. I went to him but he was dead. It was Corporal [Gerald J.] Day, the platoon radio man, his body was covered with holes—he never knew what hit him. I thought, "A few seconds earlier and it would have been me."

Looking to my right I saw another Marine sitting on the ground holding his leg—the foot was missing. Laying three to four feet in front of him was his foot, still in its boot and sock. Running over to help, I recognized that it was Sgt. Norm Haney. He had joined my squad while I was in the first platoon. I put a tourniquet above his wound and yelled for a corpsman. Being exposed, I dragged him a few feet to a small crater for protection. Then I noticed he was hit in the shoulder and as I tried to stop the bleeding we started receiving more incoming. I protected him with my body until the incoming stopped. I told him that he would be OK and not to worry. Two Marines came to help, one I think was Ed Tacchi [Pfc. Edward H. Tacchi], while the other was a corpsman.

. . . After the short rounds, the sweep was called off and we made our way back to OP-2 . At this time I learned that another buddy from the first platoon, Bush, had been hit during the initial fighting and died from loss of blood before they got him back to the outpost.

What a terrible day this had been, Benenati was dead, Bush was dead—the wounded men, Hess, Haney, myself, and all the others. I just prayed, "Oh Lord, help me make it through this day." It was all I could do to put one foot before the other. I sat there—frustrated, angry and feeling helpless, it was terrible. That was the worst day of my life.

I know that I did all I could that dreadful day. It haunted me then and does today. My best friend and buddy Frank Benenati gave his life, along with Robert Bush and the other Marines of Recon Company. I was sick with grief. That afternoon I sat down and cried. With my head in my hands, tears flooded down my cheeks. It was a long time before I could get myself together and gain some control over my emotions. Ben was my best friend and a great Marine—now he is gone. [Chuck Burrill was twenty years old at the time.][11]

The short round was the final straw. Major McDonnell concluded that further search efforts simply would be too costly. The operation was secured at 1300 hours, and all the men of Reconnaissance Company were trucked back to their company area. Officially, they had two killed (Bush and Day) and seven missing, in action, although two of the seven (Benenati and Whitson) had been seen and confirmed dead.

RESCUE

Late in the evening of 28 February, Reconnaissance Company was notified that the four men listed as missing from the 3d Platoon had been found and rescued by Marines from Able 1/7. It seems that the men became separated from the platoon around 0730 during their first sweep of Gray Rock. They were at the rear of the platoon. Around 0750, they lost sight of the platoon as it passed over the top of a small finger of land to the north. The four men started over the finger but were forced back by enemy mortar and machine-gun fire. They sought concealment on the northern, forward slope. Every time they tried to leave their position, enemy fire drove them back. They tried several times to get over the top of the finger to a safer position on the reverse slope. After one man was hit, they decided to wait out the situation until there was enough smoke to cover an attempt to go forward and rejoin the platoon.

About 0930, the smoke screen thickened sufficiently to afford some concealment. The men ran forward over the next finger of land and found a hole and a small trench where they took cover. By noon, the platoon was completely out of sight. As the four men contemplated their next move, a machine gun opened up on them with very accurate fire. They tried to move, but, with each try, the machine gun fired. Two more men were wounded. Realizing that they were effectively pinned down, the men decided to stay with what cover they had and simply wait till dark to go for help. Rightmire, with a serious abdominal wound, was weak from loss of blood and could not move. Boyko and MacDonald had minor wounds, and David was unharmed. Together, they tried to care for Rightmire, but they could do little. The men stayed hidden for the remainder of the day.

Finally, about 1845, as it was becoming dark, Boyko and David decided to go for help. They left Rightmire in care of MacDonald and made their way up the hill to COP-2. When Boyko offered to guide a squad from Able Company to rescue MacDonald and Rightmire, Sgt. O'Hagan volunteered to lead his squad to pick up the wounded men. Twenty-two years old, with six years in the Marine Corps, O'Hagan was on his second tour in the Korean battle zone. He wrote:

> Two of the wounded recon men made their way back to one of our listening posts. Escorted to the company CP, the men told of two others that were wounded and couldn't make it back. I was notified to make up a patrol with stretcher bearers. One of the recon Marines volunteered to go back out and show us where the wounded men were located.
>
> We crawled out beyond Gray Rock and held up the squad. I crawled farther out and hollered one of the names, "MacDonald." There was no answer so I crawled out a lot farther and hollered his name again. I heard a very faint, "Yo" in reply. It came from way out there.
>
> I returned to the patrol and told them approximately where the wounded men were. I told them to move fast in case the gooks had heard me. I hoped we could get in and get out before they could react.
>
> After moving a ways out I held up the patrol and crawled out again. I yelled and MacDonald hollered back again. I crawled out to where they were and looked down from a bluff of maybe fifteen feet. I started down the steep grade and lost my footing, falling the rest of the way. As I was sliding and falling I dislodged a dud 105-mm artillery shell which fell right along with me. I landed on my back with the shell resting on my elbow. I don't know why but I was laughing. It wasn't very funny.
>
> I hollered back to Corporal Paul E. Kelly, from Boston, Mass., my first fire team leader. This was his second tour in Korea also. Kelly dropped off the edge of the bluff and landed on top of me.
>
> We found the wounded corpsman lying on his back with an abdominal wound. Sgt. MacDonald had a machine gun bullet through his upper right arm and another through his helmet. The bullet had entered the front center and passed completely around and exited alongside the entry hole.
>
> Rightmire had a fist full of guts hanging out of the wound. He held his intestines while I rolled up my scarf in a tight ball and held it

over the wound. Then I zipped up his flak jacket and he told me it felt better. We loaded him on a stretcher and started back in. Our big problem was the slippery slope. We tried not to jar him on the stretcher and not to fall ourselves. MacDonald walked in. We made it back in safely thanks to excellent covering fire from our mortars and artillery.[12]

AFTERMATH

The survivors of Gray Rock Ridge were tired, beat up, and discouraged; they needed a rest. Corporal Bruce remembers that at the company formation the following morning, he was acting platoon sergeant of the 2d Platoon and reported seventeen men in ranks. The 1st Platoon had eleven men.

Lipper wrote a follow-up letter home on 1 March. As platoon guide, he now commanded the 1st Platoon or what was left of it:

> Sent you a wire this afternoon which I hope will reach you before the official one. I sent the same sort of wire for several other men also.
>
> I have just finished writing to Norm Haney's mother and girl. His leg is busted in three or four spots, both arms and his right shoulder. I only told them about his arms, and that only to explain why I was writing for him. He was a great guy. He got hit the first time by burp guns while returning fire and the second time by mortars while patching up a kid [Bush] who later died.
>
> I was at both Medical Companies (field hospitals) today and will go at least once a day as long as the first platoon has men there. A few men were sent out to the hospital ship before I could get to them. Allen, my radioman, Kosmeder, Ripple and several others.
>
> The really tough letter I have to write I am putting off for a few days. I know that this kid is dead, but I'll have to see how we are officially going to carry him. This was one of the men from the Tank Battalion, here for Recon training. He was Gung-ho and wanted to stay here. What am I going to write his mother? John [Whitson] was taking a course in map reading and the Chinese got him. He was nice kid.
>
> The platoon is putting the lieutenant and Doc Davis up for the Navy Cross and Silver Star. Everyone out there deserves something, but a choice has to be made somewhere. Val [David] is fine and Don MacDonald was just slightly hit.[13]

Lieutenant William Livingston received a Navy Cross for his actions on 27 February, and a number of other men received lesser awards,

Silver and Bronze Stars. Of Livingston, Major MacDonnell wrote: "The platoon returned through the lines with its dead and wounded—the platoon leader [Livingston] carrying a stretcher when, with six holes in him, should have been on one."[14]

At Tank Battalion headquarters in Munsan-ni, a few miles down the road from Reconnaissance Company, Lt. Col. John I. Williamson was also writing a letter home. He, too, referred to the Gray Rock battle:

> Four of my men were wounded and one was killed last night on a patrol. A very messy deal. I went up to see one of them today in the hospital. He was hit in the arm, leg, and had a chunk go through his butt into his stomach . . . two [others] weren't too bad off. One was wounded in the arm and the other in the shoulder. They were in good spirits, as were others from the Recon Co. who had been with my lads. They all showed great spirit, even one red-headed kid who had a foot missing. I left the hospital not feeling as dispirited as I had the day before, especially on learning that four lads who'd been missing in action had been recovered. One of them lay there with a machine gun slug through his middle, talking animatedly to his buddies.[15]

The battle at Gray Rock Ridge on 27–28 February severely hurt the Reconnaissance Company. Casualties were eventually listed as four killed, three missing, and thirty-four wounded. Twenty-five of the wounded required evacuation. Adding Tank Battalion personnel and corpsmen, total casualties increased by four more wounded and two killed. (Rightmire died of wounds on the hospital ship a few days later.) With six killed and twenty-nine evacuated, Gray Rock was the single deadliest engagement for the Reconnaissance Company recorded during the Korean War. At the time of the engagement, the company roster listed a total of 148 officers and men.

On orders from 1st Division Commander, Maj. Gen. Edwin A. Pollock, Reconnaissance Company operations were suspended for a period of two weeks. During the hiatus, personnel from line companies were transferred to the company, and, as strength built up, training of the new men commenced. On 15 March, operations resumed with a small patrol in the KMC sector. The following night, a ninety-man patrol (the entire company) separated into two groups, left OP-1 in the KMC sector. One group promptly became lost and had to be reoriented with marking fires on known locations. It would take time to rebuild the company to its former level of expertise.

LOOSE ENDS

Luigi Rightmire, the 3d Platoon corpsman, did not survive his wounds. He had remained on the hillside too long with his untreated abdominal wound. On board the hospital ship *Repose,* infection set in, and he died on 18 March 1953. He was twenty-one years old.

The presence of the crosses with the three bodies found on the road remains unexplained. Probably, there never will be a satisfactory explanation; however, research has disclosed facts that, though entirely circumstantial, are worthy of conjecture.

Earlier, on 8 January 1953, a tank/infantry raid had occurred in the vicinity of COP-2. The Marines had used that road and directed the raid against a Chinese hill north of Gray Rock. Marine tanks, accompanied by infantry from 1/7, had destroyed a number of enemy positions. When the Marines withdrew, they left approximately sixty Chinese dead and, regrettably, some of their own. That night, the Chinese hoisted three Marine bodies onto crosses and left them prominently displayed for the Marines on COP-2 to view. Were the Chinese challenging the Marines to recover the bodies, or were they just showing contempt? On orders, one of the Marine tanks destroyed the gruesome display with gunfire.

The author believes it reasonable to speculate that, a few weeks later in the same vicinity, the same Chinese officers were in command and were likely to favor the same tactics or to show the same bravado. It is probable that the bodies and crosses found on February 28 were from a previous engagement and were being prepared for display like those on 8 January. Only the coincidence of Reconnaissance Company's ambush prevented a recurrence.

It is unreasonable to believe that the bodies of the three men on the road were related to the Reconnaissance Company engagement of 27–28 February. With two bodies on the slope and three on the road, there were too many bodies. And where had the crosses come from? They must have been prepared in advance and brought to that location. The fighting in the area at the time was far too severe for carpenters to stop and construct "well-made crosses." If they had brought crosses, could they not have brought bodies as well? Further, as the Chinese Communist army was not noted for its Christian beliefs, it is also probable to assume that the crosses had been built for a purpose other than religious symbolism, perhaps to taunt the Marines as the Chinese had done before. Undoubtedly, the Chinese also took heavy casualties that night and possibly concluded that the effect of their showmanship was not worth the risk. For whatever their reason, they failed to complete the macabre task.

Sergeant Errgang was never seen again. It is the author's speculation that he was captured by the Chinese and removed from Gray Rock. It seems unlikely that the Chinese would bother to carry a severely wounded enemy while withdrawing from a firefight. Consequently, it would be logical to assume that Errgang was ambulatory. He might have died in captivity, of wounds or mistreatment, or conceivably been taken to the Soviet Union, the fate of an unknown number of prisoners of war (POWs). Whatever occurred, his body was never found.

To this day, some mystery surrounds recovery of the bodies of Benenati and Whitson. That they were recovered is not in doubt. They are both buried in the United States; however, no record of either recovery can be found. Casualty reports for both men reflect a change from "Body not recovered" to "Body recovered." The report for Benenati includes a pencil notation, "Body recovered 18 May." Other evidence appears to indicate a recovery date in late April. Two questions remain. Where had the bodies been since February 28? And what were the circumstances of their late recovery?

A search of Reconnaissance Company's patrol reports between March and June are negative. No mention is made of a body recovery, which likely would have been reported. Command Diaries generally crow about such occurrences.

For years, a rumor circulated among Marines at Reconnaissance Company reunions that, sometime in 1953, a Marine patrol had found Benenati's body in a cave guarded by a Chinese soldier. The soldier was shot dead and the body recovered. The story bordered on the bizarre and was never confirmed.

In researching material for this book, the author managed to stimulate a few obscure memories and found a man who thought that the Marine who had recovered Benenati's body was a sergeant from Reconnaissance Company named Barrett. When Sgt. Barney B. Barrett was located by the author, he confirmed the basic content of the rumor and said that he was on a patrol that recovered a body from a cave. Barrett recalled that around mid to late March 1953, Marines from COP-2 found a Marine's body in a cave near the tank road. They shot the soldier who was with the body but did not, or could not, recover it. On the Marine's jacket, someone read the letters "EN" of an incomplete name. The Marines assumed that the body was one of the men lost by Reconnaissance Company on 27-28 February. Reconnaissance Company was notified, and a two-squad patrol went out to recover the body. (It is curious that the Marine unit that found the body did not recover it. Nor is it known why the body was believed to be that of a Marine in the Reconnaissance Company.)

According to Barrett, the patrol might have been led by a lieutenant, but the point squad leader was Sgt. Allen E. ("Brownie") Brown. His task was to figure out how to get the body out of the cave without being blown up by booby traps, and he spent several days in devising a plan. The patrol that left COP-2 on the recovery mission included KSC stretcher bearers with the point squad. Barrett had the second squad, and his task was to set up a base of fire while Brownie's squad went forward to make the recovery.

The patrol encountered no problems. Brownie's squad entered the cave and returned with the dead Marine on a stretcher. A field jacket covered his face and most of his body. As the stretcher passed Barrett, he noticed the exposed bare feet. They were bloated and discolored, a blue-black, with Chinese propaganda leaflets attached to the feet.

The body was taken to COP-2 and left for pickup by the Graves Registration Unit. Barrett never saw it again. Talk around the company CP, at the time, was that Benenati's body had been recovered, but Barrett was unable to confirm that identification. Nor does he know anyone who did. Sergeant Brown was located, he but could not add any information. Other men in the company at that time do not recall hearing of the recovery.

Another piece of the puzzle is found in the 3/1 Command Diary entry of April 23, which states, "At 0530I, the 1st Marine Division Recon Company retrieved four (4) friendly bodies, previously reported as missing in action." Barrett has no recollection of four bodies and thought that his patrol recovered only one. The Reconnaissance Company diary does not report any body recoveries.

Owing to the passage of time, incomplete records of the period, and the frailties of human memory, the full story probably never will be known. Regarding Gunny Errgang, the author prays that he died swiftly and painlessly.

Another Marine, William Manchester, in his book, *Goodbye Darkness: A Memoir of the Pacific War,* wrote: "Any man in combat who lacks comrades who will die for him, or for whom he is willing to die, is not a man at all. He is damned." The men who fought their battle on Gray Rock Ridge reaffirmed that observation with their blood.

CHAPTER 7

SPRING THAW

*Everything depends on
the skill of our subordinate officers
and still more on the morale of our soldiers.*
—Clausewitz: *Principles of War,* 1812

The third winter of war in Korea drew to an end. Rising temperatures, melting snows, and rain turned roads into quagmires and abandoned rice paddies into swamps of brown, smelly stew. Trenches, bunkers, and fighting holes fared a little better because they were on high ground, which allowed for better drainage. Tanks and trucks, road bound once again, were frequently stuck in the slimy goo. Maximum speed on the better roads was limited to 5 miles per hour when they were open. Some troops on line could be supplied only by the age-old method of all armies, shoe leather and a strong back. For the Marines, it was back to basics.

North of the MLR, Chinese troops faced the same conditions, but, being less mechanized, they were not as severely affected. Early in March, enemy strategists concentrated their major attention on UN forces east of the Marines and left the leathernecks pretty much alone.

Army historian Walter Hermes relates that the Chinese sent out large forces in an effort to regain the initiative along the entire I Corps front. On 1 March, an enemy company had attacked French-held positions along the U.S. 2d Division front. Two days later, the Chinese overran the Hook, then held by elements of the U.S. Army's 38th Regiment. That same night, a patrol from the 31st Infantry Regiment of the U.S. 7th Division disrupted an attack on the outpost atop Pork Chop Hill. Chinese gunners dropped eight thousand rounds of artillery and mortar fire on the two-platoon hilltop position.[1] The U.S. Army was receiving renewed Chinese attention, which left the Marines alone to stir up their own action.

According to the 1st Marine Division Command Diary: "The daily activity of the units on line was characterized by the manning of outpost positions and the main line of resistance. Constant work was performed to improve and repair them. Day and night patrols, raids and ambushes were conducted forward of the main line of resistance."[2]

In an effort to maintain pressure on enemy defenses while keeping casualties down, the Marines conducted small unit hit-and-run tactics to gain intelligence in preparation for future raids. In some circles, the first two weeks of the month might have been considered quiet. Nightly patrols resulted in a few firefights, none of which could be classified as important to the war effort. To the man behind the trigger, in front of an enemy burp gun, or within range of a mortar round, the patrols were most important. The difference in perspective lay in who was there rather than the purpose of the operation.

At 0030 on 1 March, a patrol from George Company 3/7 engaged five enemy soldiers digging a length of trench near Bunker Hill. The Chinese did not return fire but ran off. The patrol advanced into the trench and blew up a bunker. On 3 March, an Easy Company 2/5 patrol engaged an enemy squad near Hill 98 in the vicinity of the former outpost Frisco. After a three-minute firefight, the Marines withdrew and returned to the MLR. Their casualties totaled one killed, one missing, and seventeen wounded.

On 7 March, a combat patrol from Able Company 1/5 left the MLR at 0210. West of Outpost Stromboli (Corrine), the patrol was confronted by two enemy squads. After a brief firefight, the Marines withdrew to the MLR with three casualties. Reaching friendly lines, the patrol leader discovered that one man was missing. A rescue squad left the MLR at 0330 to search the area where the man was last seen but to no avail. Worse, the search party suffered four more casualties from enemy mortars. Two hours later, the men returned empty-handed to the MLR. At first light, under cover of smoke, a second squad went out but it was also unsuccessful.

Two days later, during daylight on 9 March, the body of a Marine was spotted in the vicinity of the firefight on 7 March. An Able Company patrol retrieved the body that night but discovered that it was not the body of the missing Able Company Marine.

Infantrymen were not the only ones to encounter problems. An entry from the 1/5 Command Diary of 10 March describes an occasion when, at 1030, men on the MLR watched as an observation plane was hit by enemy fire. The plane caught fire, and two men bailed out. The Marines saw one flyer land safely and begin the trek through no-man's-land toward Outpost Reno.

A fire team from Reno, under cover of smoke, was dispatched to aid the downed man, but they could not reach him in time. Marines on the hill watched helplessly as four enemy soldiers captured the flyer. A little later, they saw the other man walking north on a road in the hands of two Chinese soldiers.

By some standards, the war progressed slowly, but, as March advanced, activity picked up. Battalions on the MLR reported fifty or more rounds of incoming fire per day. Certainly, this was no concentrated barrage but nonetheless sufficient to keep a man on his toes.

Sometimes, the enemy was lucky. On 10 March, Sgt. Jess E. Meado of George Company 3/1 was looking out of his CP bunker while a Marine tank fired its mission. He recalls:

> As I watched the tank fire, a Chinese 76-mm shell hit the front of the bunker, blowing up our mailbox. White envelopes flew skyward and must have been seen by the gook forward observer.
>
> A piece of that round had gone through the doorway of another bunker, hitting the last of four men who were sitting in a row. I ran over to see if I could help, and the corpsman asked me to get his first aid bag which was in the Command Post bunker. I barely got back to the wounded man when another 76-mm round went through the CP bunker, the one I had just left. Seven men had been inside. Five of them ran out. I ran to the bunker and pulled one man out. He was dead. I went back in and pulled the remaining man out. He, too, was dead. It was a terrible loss. Those two, Pfc. Donel Earnest and Pfc. James Kimball, would have gone home in the next draft out.[3]

Two of the men in the CP bunker were calling fire missions for the tank. Colonel Williamson wrote: "Two of my boys were wounded today—Lieutenant Westenberger and Sergeant Bergman. They were spotting tank fire and got a direct hit from an enemy shell. . . . Westenberger looked like he'd been sprayed with bird-shot, all full of little holes. I only saw Bergman's eye, which was being worked on at the time by an eye surgeon, the tear duct was severed but the eye was otherwise OK."[4]

During the first two weeks of March, the Chinese were markedly unaggressive on the Jamestown Line, which left the initiative to the Marines. Col. Lew Walt's 5th Marines were willing to accommodate.

RETURN TO UNGOK

It had been barely two weeks since Operation Clambake, Able 1/5's raid on the Chinese stronghold in the Ungok hills. Following that raid, Marine planners analyzed their actions and contemplated their next move—they were going to do it again.

Lt. Col. Jonas Platt, battalion commander of 1/5, reported to Regimental Headquarters with plans for a raid on Hill 31A. Conceptually, the raid would involve two rifle platoons reinforced with machine guns and flamethrowers and supported by artillery. This time, no flame tanks would close with the enemy, but elements of three platoons of gun tanks, eleven in all, would support the operation by fire from the MLR. A heavy aerial bombardment using 1,000-pound bombs with a 4/5-second delay fuse was proposed. The planners anticipated that the large craters resulting from bomb detonations would provide places of cover—instant foxholes—for advancing infantry. As with Clambake, there would be a feint on Kumgok, but it would consist only of an artillery bombardment.

Colonel Platt's plan was approved and named Operation Item. On 17 March, Baker Company 1/5 was relieved on line and moved back to the regimental reserve area to prepare and rehearse the raid. D-Day was designated as 19 March. How Company 3/5 moved forward from regimental reserve and assumed the Baker sector of the MLR. It would support the Baker Company raid.

Behind the lines, Baker Company's 2d and 3d Platoons participated in seven rehearsals for the attack, from an early walk-through to a full-blown early morning dress rehearsal, including use of smoke. The last afternoon included test-firing of weapons, final briefing, and church services.

Concurrent with infantry rehearsals, extensive tests were made with flamethrowers in an effort to increase their range. The objective was to throw flames beyond the hand-grenade range of the enemy. After a series of experiments with fuel mixture and pressure variations of the propellant (compressed air), the operators were able to shoot flames in excess of 40 yards uphill, which was a satisfactory range.

Reconnaissance of routes leading to the target area took place over a period of one week prior to the raid. Mine-clearing patrols by How Company continued into the night of 18 March, when the route was declared clear.

Two days before the raid, Marine Air was on station. Over a six-hour period, ten air strikes were conducted across the entire battalion front, plus eleven more strikes the following day. Between air raids, regimental 4.2-inch mortars saturated enemy positions. The approach area to Ungok was cratered.

Intelligence estimated that approximately thirty-two enemy soldiers would be waiting on Ungok. Moreover, the garrison could be readily stiffened via an intricate network of trenches from adjacent hills. Despite the preparatory bombardment, the Marines expected the objective to be reinforced. At 0330, 19 March, two reinforced platoons totaling 111 Marines from Baker Company 1/5 assembled to conduct the raid.

At 0518, they left the MLR. Support fire poured on nearby hills as the lead element reached its first checkpoint. Then, as the men crossed a tank road, the raid commander called for artillery fire to be shifted to enemy positions on Ungok itself. Like an amphibious landing, the raid was on. Marines stormed the hill under cover of their artillery.

Tanks on the MLR began firing at their primary mission, a connecting trench through which Chinese reinforcements were expected to flow. One 90-mm round every thirty seconds was placed on target while simultaneously raking it with .50 caliber machine gun fire.

Baker Company's 3d Platoon, leading the assault, moved forward under mortar and artillery fire. Enemy small-arms and machine-gun fire was received on the flank but quickly neutralized by more fire from the MLR. Six flamethrowers moved into position 40 yards from the enemy trench line and spewed their load of burning napalm into enemy defenses. Two squads from the assault platoon swiftly followed the flames into the trenches. Simultaneously, enemy rifle fire was received from concealed spider holes, and a machine gun opened up on the flank of the 2d Platoon and pinned down a third assault squad. Only a small portion of the 3d Platoon advanced far enough to get into the trenches.

About this time, Chinese mortars entered the fray as gunners walked rounds down the hill and back up to traverse the area. The raid commander called for smoke concentrations to mask enemy observation.

Squads reaching the trenches found few enemy soldiers, only a quantity of grenades, and light-small arms fire from retreating Chinese. It appeared that the enemy had withdrawn into a feeder trench and left only a small rear guard. The 3d Platoon made contact with the 2d Platoon at 0645 and both platoons received word to disengage. The raid was complete.

Cpl. Madison Crosby was wounded during the first assault. Years later, he wrote a description of the raid as it related to him:

. . . After the barrage lifted, two flamethrowers made it to the top and lit the place up. Then we were given the order to move out and the mortars started coming in. A machine gun on our right flank opened up about that time.

I figured the safest place to be was in the trenches with the gooks. I started running for the trenchline and yelling to my fire team, "Let's go." I could see tracers from the machine gun, and mortars exploding everywhere.

Somehow I made it to the trenchline and jumped right in front of a bunker. For me that is when all hell broke loose. I remember wiping the sweat from my brow and firing a couple of rounds into the bunker. Then there was an explosion, and I found myself face down in the trench. I don't know what happened to my rifle; it had disappeared.

There was another explosion above my head. I was hit bad and started crawling on my hands and knees. I heard the order to pull out. I found a spot where the trench was partially level on an incline and started crawling up. At that time there was a third explosion just to the left of me and I couldn't find my left arm.

I took my right hand and felt out in front of me where it felt like it should be, but it was not there. I recall thinking, "The bastards have blown my arm off."

I remembered back as a kid; we had an insurance man with his arm off at the shoulder, and he wore his suit coat sleeve in his left coat pocket. I didn't want to be like that!

I raised up on my right elbow and my left arm came sliding down off my back. I grabbed it and cradled it to me and decided I was going to die right there.

Flares lit up and I could see Marines heading down the hill. I could not crawl any further, so I settled down to die. I recall how peaceful, warm and pain free I was. I assumed I was dying.

About that time a Marine came up behind me and said, "Hey man, let's get out of here." He was hit in the leg and I told him to go on as I could not go anymore. He reached down and grabbed my cartridge belt and started dragging me and yelling for someone to come help him with me.

Two guys came back, one from my squad who asked me if l could hold on if he put me on his back? I told him no, because I was holding on to my left arm and was not about to turn it loose.

Somehow they got me on his back, with one guy behind holding me up.

Mortars were still coming in and when we hit the deck all the pain came back. After the second or third time of hitting the deck, I looked over to my left and saw a body all crumpled up like a discarded rag doll. I asked who it was? They told me it was Martinez. He was dead.

Up to that point I had been ready to die, but after seeing Martinez, all that changed. I told them [the assisting Marines] that if they put me on his back I thought I could hold on. This time I wedged my left arm between his back and my stomach and wrapped my right arm around his neck. I think I almost choked him to death because when he hit the deck again, I would not let go.

About that time some angels came up with a stretcher and told me not to worry, they would get me down, and they did.

I think the most afraid I was, was when they put me on top of a personnel carrier to transport me back. I could almost feel some gook putting a mortar round between my eyes.

At the aid station I became aware of a conversation between a doctor and a corpsman. There was one space available on the bubbletop chopper, and the doctor wanted to send someone else, even though I was the most seriously wounded. The corpsman argued that if he did not send me on the chopper, he was consigning me to death. He reminded the doctor that policy was to send the most seriously wounded first. The corpsman would not back down and stated that he would put it in his report. At that the doctor relented and told him that if he felt that strongly to, "Send the Nigger on the chopper!" Along with the three Marines on Ungok, I owe my life to that courageous Navy Corpsman.[5]

Crosby was among these first casualties who came off the hill. Unfortunately, arrival of the APCs scheduled for casualty evacuation had been held up. An earlier battle in the 1st Marines sector had delayed their arrival at Ungok. In the meantime, an evacuation platoon from How Company on the MLR responded to help return wounded and, according to the Special Action Report, "most evacuations were hand carried with little reliance on APC's."[6] When they did arrive, only a few of the casualties were evacuated by the armored vehicles.

The Chinese continued to drop mortars on the evacuation route, during the disengagement, which made removing casualties most difficult. To aid the withdrawal, additional smoke was employed. The Special Action Report reveals, "Smoke pots were employed to cover the route over which the APC's worked. The expedient of lighting smoke pots on the outgoing APC and pushing them off at intervals along the road seemed to work excellently."[7]

On the MLR, incoming fire was heavy as the Chinese tried to suppress the tanks, recoilless rifles, and machine guns pouring fire on their positions. Still, the exchange of fire remained lopsided in favor of the Marines. Tank reports indicate that, over a two-hour period between 0600 and 0800, the Marines fired 526 rounds of 90-mm on enemy targets. In return, the armored vehicles received 58 rounds of mixed 122-mm, 105-mm, and 76-mm incoming fire. Although a tank is designed to withstand hits, a well-placed round from any of these large artillery pieces can knock it out, as well as the people inside.

A tank crewman, sitting very much exposed on the MLR that morning, watched through his periscope as huge explosions from Chinese artillery sought them out. He wrote:

> We began to receive incoming, artillery and large mortars. As the incoming obtained our range we watched exploding shells methodically "walk" up the hill toward our position. Our tank commander, a corporal, was worried. A short timer, due for rotation next month, he wanted to go home in one piece. He got on the radio and requested permission to back the tank from the slot, out of sight of enemy observers.
>
> The conversation went something like this, "Lieutenant, request permission to back off, it's getting hotter than a cunt up here." "Sorry, keep a tight asshole and stay there, the infantry needs you."
>
> "Aye aye sir."
>
> As ordered we stayed in the slot and kept firing. Incoming rounds came close, scattering dirt, shrapnel and debris, but they all missed.
>
> Then they stopped.[8]

By 0656, all units disengaged and returned to the MLR. Marine casualties were six killed (one body not recovered) and sixty-two wounded, a casualty rate in excess of 60 percent. Chinese casualties were unknown. Chinese trenches and other fortifications on Ungok were reduced to rubble; however, they would be rebuilt. Ungok was stunned but not down for the count.

DIVERSIONS

Earlier in March, the 1st Marines returned to the line relieving the 7th Regiment on the division's center sector. Men of the 2d Battalion replaced 1/7 on the left, next to Panmunjom and the KMCs. The 3d Battalion moved into the right battalion sector next to the 5th Marines. Movement began on 8 March as designated squads exchanged places on the MLR and outposts. The relief took place over the next two days, and the tired 7th Marines were able to fall back and gain a respite from the war.

For some of the men, the rest would be only temporary. In a little more than two weeks, the 2/7 would be abruptly pulled from its reserve bivouac and thrown into one of the severest battles of the war. During a four-day period, 25 percent of the 2d Battalion, 7th Marines, would become casualties.

Not being prophets however, the troops enjoyed the amenities of time off line while they could. The beer was cold, the food hot, and the showers soapy. Accumulations of dirt ground into skin and clothing disappeared. Most important, they could stand upright without constantly watching for snipers or the occasional mortar round. And they could sleep at night.

In the meantime, men of the 1st Marines settled in for their turn on line. The 2d Battalion deployed Easy Company on COP-2 and borrowed Baker Company from reserve to complete the customary number of three companies on the MLR. Dog Company was on the left, Baker in the center, and Fox on the right. Each company was responsible for a single outpost in front of it, Marilyn, Kate and Ingrid.

Moving east, 3/1 was next in line on the MLR in the following order: How Company with outposts Hedy and Bunker; George Company, responsible for outposts Ginger and Esther; and Item Company with Dagmar and Corrine. The MLR east of Item Company was defended by the 5th Marines.[9]

Until mid-March, action in the 1st Marine sector was subdued. Men in the trenches reported one or two casualties each night from incoming mortars or a sniper. Patrols went out nightly, returned with one or two casualties, and reported the same number of enemy killed. No Marines died. A George Company patrol departed the MLR at 2000 on 18 March and made contact at 2110 near Outpost Ginger. The patrol observed eight Chinese soldiers in the process of setting up an ambush. The Chinese were on low ground, and the Marines moved unseen to a high bluff overlooking them. The patrol called in 60-mm mortars and attacked with hand grenades and small arms. The Chinese returned fire, but surprise was the deciding factor and the Marines killed or wounded all of them. The patrol returned to the MLR with no casualties or prisoners.

Outpost Esther

On the evening of 18 March, the weather was cool, clear, and dry. There was a first-quarter moonset at 0040, 19 March. Thirty-five minutes earlier, at 0005, a George Company patrol had left the MLR to cover an area west of Outpost Esther. After an hour, the Marines ran into elements of a Chinese company advancing toward the outpost. They immediately opened fire, which surprised the enemy point and slowed the Chinese enough to enable the Marines to withdraw to the protection of Esther. No sooner had they arrived when a company of Chinese attacked the eighteen-man outpost.

Bombardment preceding the attack had breached a section of barbed-wire entanglement sufficient to enable enemy troops access to the trenches. What followed was a violent exchange of small-arms, machine-gun, hand-grenade, and hand-to-hand fighting. Enemy troops swarmed up the hill to meet the outnumbered Marines. Despite the disparity in numbers, the hill would not be overrun and the Marines fought back with typical ferocity. According to the Special Action Report, "This penetration was short lived as once again deadly small arms fire repulsed the enemy and completely drove them from the outpost."[10]

Pfc. Gene Thomas of George Company remembers that night on Esther:

> Our trenchline nearest the Chinese trenches was very poor; the ground was just too rocky to dig adequate defenses. The very worst spot we called "deadman's corner" because it was closest to the Chinese and had the shallowest portion of the trenchline.
>
> After I had moved around placing men in positions, I returned to a part of the trenchline which was very close to the fighting hole of Pfc. James Devlin. It was not dark and so far pretty quiet.
>
> I was talking to Devlin when the first round fell on our position. It was a direct hit on Devlin. He never knew what hit him; the shell split him in two.
>
> The first shell was followed by so many more that all we could do was take cover. The massive bombardment allowed the Chinese to get into our trenches near "deadman's corner."
>
> Chinese mortar and artillery fire and our supporting arms continually raked the area. During any lull in the firing, we tried to make contact with each other and check out the trenchline between us to see if it was occupied by Chinese soldiers.
>
> Eventually, the Chinese called off the attack. The next morning we counted two or three dead Chinese in our trenches and few more in the barbed wire.[11]

Thomas was later awarded a Silver Star for his actions on Esther. Two Marines, Pfc. Richard Adams and Pfc. Frank Cross, earned the Navy Cross.

Outpost Esther was not going to be a walkover, and reinforcing elements were soon put into motion. The Special Action Report states: "When information of the enemy activities reached regimental headquarters, tanks of Dog Company, 1st Tank Battalion, were ordered to 3/1 to support defense of the outposts and the MLR, a reinforced platoon of the reserve battalion (1/1) was ordered to move to 3/1 CP, armored personnel carriers were moved to the forward aid station to assist in evacuation, and the regimental air officer requested a flare plane."[12]

During the attack on Esther, the enemy also shelled How Company positions on the MLR and Outpost Hedy. Then, at 0110, under its own artillery, a company of Chinese infantry stormed Hedy. Like Esther, this position was held by a reinforced squad of eighteen Marines, hardly a match for a full company. The difference here was the barbed-wire entanglement protecting the hill. Enemy incoming fire had not destroyed the wire, and it slowed the attack sufficiently to allow superior firepower to come into play. From the MLR, Fox Company 2/1 joined with How Company to place fire on Hedy. Small arms and machine guns from Able Company 1/5 directed at Hill 44, an enemy support position, reduced fire from that quarter. On Hedy, the Chinese were stopped at the wire.

By 0230, all enemy action broke off. During the pause, reinforcements were rushed to Esther from the MLR. A clutch platoon (a temporary platoon formed from a potpourri of men in normally noncombatant roles, such as clerks, cooks, supply people, and drivers) from Headquarters 3/1 was brought in to reinforce George Company, and the reserve platoon from 1/1 reinforced How Company. A squad patrol was dispatched to sweep the area around Esther in an effort to recover enemy casualties. Unsuccessful, it was recalled at 0500 so that aerial flares could be dropped over the area.

After dropping six flares, the plane had to be secured because the light was interfering with commencement of the Baker Company 1/5 raid on Ungok to the west. (The fighting on Outpost Esther was the cause of the delayed arrival of APCs to Baker Company that morning.)

At 0540, the enemy again commenced bombardment of Esther and the MLR. Under this covering fire, an unknown number of Chinese attempted to police the battleground for their dead, but the Marines would not permit it. Mortars and artillery drove the enemy back and forced abandonment of the effort. By 0700, all Chinese fire ceased, and four enemy bodies were left on Esther.

The Special Action Report recapped casualties for the engagement at 40 enemy counted killed and 115 estimated killed and wounded. The Marines suffered 7 killed and 20 wounded.

Vicinity of Ingrid

At 1933 on 20 March, a combat patrol of twenty-one men from Fox Company 2/1 left the MLR for Hill 64, a Chinese outpost opposing Outpost Ingrid. The evening was dark. Low hanging clouds masked the stars, and there was no moon. One might call it a perfect night for a patrol. The mission of this reinforced squad was to maintain the initiative, close with the enemy, and destroy what it could not capture.

At 2115, the patrol located and engaged a Chinese platoon west of Ingrid. As firefights go, it was not remarkable but almost routine. An exchange of small-arms fire and hand grenades was followed by the mutual application of mortars and artillery. Then, six minutes into the exchange, the patrol lost radio contact with Fox Company. Fearing the worst, reinforcements were dispatched to Ingrid. At 2144 the patrol sent a short radio transmission, but the message was garbled. The status and whereabouts of the patrol were unknown.

At 2210, three men from the patrol arrived at the Fox Company gate on the MLR. They reported that their companions were pinned down behind Ingrid. They had suffered casualties and needed help. A platoon immediately left the MLR with stretchers to help the patrol and return the men to safety. Fourteen members of the original patrol were returned to the MLR by 2320, but four men were unaccounted for. The rescue platoon was ordered to continue searching for the missing men. Investigating various possibilities, the men advanced into the area of the previous engagement but found nothing.

At 0255, two of the missing men were located. Both were dead, and their bodies were returned to the MLR. The platoon continued searching for the remaining men but was called back, empty handed, at first light. Overall, the patrol had cost the Marines two killed, two missing, and two wounded.

Nearly three weeks later, on 7 April, the two missing bodies were recovered by a Fox Company reconnaissance patrol. The bodies were found in a brush-covered area at the base of Hill 64 (near Ingrid). The 2/1 Special Intelligence Report states, "One body was clothed in underwear and boots and the other clothed in underwear, utility trousers and boots. Numerous pieces of equipment, both friendly and enemy, were scattered throughout the area from the point of patrol contact to location of bodies. Position of bodies and equipment indicated that they were hurriedly abandoned by the enemy after being carried several hundred yards from point of contact."[13]

Outpost Dagmar

In conjunction with the fighting on the Nevada Cities (Outposts Carson, Reno, and Vegas) on 26 March (see chapter 8), the Chinese launched a significant attack against Outpost Dagmar. At 2345, a reinforced platoon, supported by machine guns from nearby hills, attacked the outpost. At the time, twenty-seven Marines were defending Dagmar. The enemy breached the wire with bangalore torpedoes, and twenty-five Chinese gained the trenches. The Marines fought back hand to hand, using rifles and pistols when they could.

After twenty minutes of fighting, the Marines called for VT on their position and dived for cover. According to the 2/1 Special Intelligence Report, "Coordination between the outpost and the artillery forward observer was outstanding in that additional VT was used and the Marines on the outpost were given an 'on the way' by the forward observer and had time to get into their crab holes before the rounds hit the outpost."[14] The battle on Dagmar continued in a cycle, the infantry war alternating with artillery—into crab holes, explosions of VT overhead, then out of crab holes and return to the fighting. At 0100, a nine-man reinforcing patrol reported to Dagmar. One side of the artillery box was lifted so that the men could enter the outpost. Twenty minutes later, the enemy withdrew, and Dagmar held. Enemy casualties were estimated at sixty-five.

A summary of the actions occurring between 18 March and 26 March in the 1st Marines' sector is informative. The Special Action Report for that period states:

> a. It is believed that the five actions are closely related and comprise a portion of the enemy's plans as divulged by a POW who was captured on 11 February. The POW indicated that limited objective attacks would be attempted in the area of the above-described contacts and that the attacks would be in increasing strength. Documents removed from enemy dead on COP 52 [Dagmar] established the 3rd Battalion, 260th CCF Regiment as being involved in the attacks on the right. It is believed all attacks on the right were conducted by that unit. The heavy flare activity on YOKE, the patrol contact on hill 64A [Ingrid], and the direction of the attacks tend to indicate that the 1st Battalion, 360th, and the reserve battalion located behind them were

engaged in the attacks on COP 122A [Bunker], COP 124 [Hedy] and the MLR. These abortive attempts at dislodging us from our COP's resulted only in the decimation of one regiment of the 120th CCF Division.

i. For this ten day period the 1st Marines inflicted the following enemy casualties: 110 counted KIA, 127 estimated KIA, 4 counted WIA and 215 estimated WIA. The 1st Marines suffered 3 MIA, 14 KIA, 38 WIA and 8 WIANE [wounded in action not evacuated].

In defense of the outposts and MLR the 1st Marines expended 11,932 rounds of mixed mortars and 6,031 rounds of artillery. The enemy fired approximately 7,400 rounds of mixed mortars and artillery in his attacks.[15]

The end of March marked the relief of 3/1 on line. It was going to regimental reserve and would be replaced by 1/1. The 2d Battalion would remain in place.

On 24 March, Colonel Williamson wrote in a letter, "I'm sort of expecting all hell to break loose within the next two nights. Sort of a hunch."[16] The hunch proved prophetic. Two days later, the 5th Marines were so heavily engaged that reserves were brought forward and committed to the fight. This was the "Battle of the Cities."

CHAPTER 8

BATTLE OF THE CITIES

*No sane man is unafraid in battle, but discipline
produces in him a form of vicarious courage.*
—George S. Patton, Jr.:
War as I Knew It, 1947

The final days of March saw what were arguably the bloodiest four days of fighting during the Outpost War. Over the ensuing period, Marine and Chinese casualties climbed into the thousands. This was the "Battle of the Cities," when the Chinese army, in a David and Goliath scenario, threw battalions of troops against squads of Marines holding a few hilltop outposts. When the dust settled after four days of nearly continuous fighting, one outpost had been lost altogether, while another had been lost and regained several times.

BEGINNINGS

Recent enemy conduct had led Marine intelligence to conclude that a large offensive action was in the wind. An apparent reduction in incoming fire on the line had been noticed, along with fewer probes of Marine positions and an unusual lack of aggressiveness by enemy patrols. In addition, interrogation of prisoners in February indicated an ongoing buildup of enemy resources. Prudently, the Marines began preparing for an assault.

Reserves kept in readiness could be easily moved forward. Scheduled MARLEXs (Marine landing exercises, amphibious training) were canceled for the 7th Marines, then in Division reserve. During Operation Bullets, ostensibly undertaken to determine the capability of supplying ammunition by helicopter to the division supply point north of the Imjin River, nearly 600 tons of ordnance were moved forward.

In a 4 March estimate of Chinese forces opposing them, the Marines assumed fourteen infantry battalions on line, with eight more battalions in local reserve. These troops were supported by sixteen artillery battalions and forty-four tanks or self-propelled guns; total infantry strength was about 22,000.[1]

Although intelligence efforts had been utterly unsuccessful in pinpointing a specific time or place of attack, the Marines were preparing for what they considered to be inevitable. T/Sgt. Jack Little, machine-gun platoon sergeant with Charlie Company 1/5, describes preparations that he made to improve the company's defense:

> The western portion of Charlie Company's MLR had a Z shape to it and this was the first time I had seen the mortar platoon forward of the CP. They were tucked behind a hill at the top of the Z which gave them better range to Reno. The mortars were registered to box and support the OP's. Some of our trenches faced the Chinese positions directly and were deepened for better protection although one could still be seen when traversing the line. Everyone was on edge, alert for sounds of incoming.
>
> I set my machine guns with overlapping fields of fire where possible. We were able to register and log some oblong beaten zones across the top of Carson and Reno, to be used only in dire need. Two guns could reach the ridge north of Vegas and, with permission from How Company, beaten zones were established there too.
>
> I created a fire registration board to better enable fire control of the company's guns. Each gun position was numbered and comm wire strung to the CP from gun position phones. Gun registration numbers were entered on the main fire-control board at the CP. I could assist the CO by using a company CP phone when he called for guns or mortar coverage and registrations on or around Reno and Carson. This left other lines and the radio open for larger supporting arms fire.[2]

Gunny Little's attention to detail unquestionably paid off in lives saved. Marines on Carson and Reno would need all of the support they could get.

When battalions of Chinese struck at 1900 on 26 March, the "when" was certainly solved. But the "where" was still in doubt. Which was the concentration, and which was the diversion? 1st Marine Outposts Ava, Dagmar, Esther, Hedy, and Bunker were all attacked, as were 5th Marine Outposts Carson, Reno, Vegas, Berlin, and East Berlin. Within the hour, however, the enemy's objective was clear. It was the Nevada Cities.

THE SITUATION

Combat Outposts Carson, Reno, and Vegas (collectively known as the Nevada Cities) and Berlin and East Berlin were terrain features in front of the MLR. Each was manned by elements of the 5th Marines. The Nevada Cities, in particular, said to be named by Lt. Col. Anthony Caputo of 2/7 because "It's a gamble if we can hold them,"[3] had been a thorn in the enemy's side for some time, as evidenced by its frequent attacks on those hilltop positions commencing as early as the previous summer.

Outpost Carson was the farthest west of the Nevada Cities. Situated some 820 yards from the MLR, its purpose was to block two major Chinese strongpoints, Ungok on the left and Arrowhead in front. Its right approach was guarded by Outpost Reno. Both positions were manned by men from Charlie Company 1/5.

Reno, centered between Carson and Vegas, guarded approaches to both. It was the most distant from the MLR, approximately 1,600 yards. Reno was a poor position, but it had to be defended. Because of the adverse terrain, it had poor fields of fire and no protective bunkers. A cave, located amid the trenches, functioned as a CP, sleeping area, ammunition storage, and aid station for the forty-three Marines on the hill. Regrettably, this cave would become a tomb.

A major blocking position south of Reno was called Reno Block, which was manned only during hours of darkness. For its defense, Reno depended heavily on Carson and Vegas on its flanks and Reno Block in the rear.

The third and largest Nevada outpost was Vegas on Reno's right flank. Located more than 1,300 yards in front of the MLR, it was manned by one officer and forty men from How Company 3/5, which was under operational control of 1/5. The defense of Vegas depended heavily on Reno on its left and Outpost Berlin on its right. Its rear area was secured by fire from the MLR. To its front were enemy Hills 190, 153, and 150.

The location of the Nevada Cities was a problem. They were surrounded by higher ground held by the enemy, and each one depended on the others for flank defense. If one outpost fell, the others were as vulnerable as a stack of dominos in a hurricane.

As March waned, the winds began to blow.

THURSDAY, 26 MARCH

The day was clear and unseasonably warm. A man could strip down to a dungaree jacket or flack vest and still be comfortable. On the outposts and the MLR, hours passed slowly. Then, when the sun went down, the Chinese came without warning. They swarmed the outposts in over-whelming numbers like Tartar hordes from the steppes of Mongolia. Choreographed with artillery, mortars, and machine guns, two full bat-talions of Chinese troops attacked the handful of Marines defending three outposts. The Battle of the Cities had begun.

With diversionary attacks on Dagmar, Hedy, and Esther in the 1st Marine sector, the Chinese moved hardest against the 5th Marines' Nevada Cities outposts. Initially, incoming mortar and artillery fire fell at the gates and along trails leading to the outposts. On the outposts, incoming fire dropped at the rate of one to three rounds per second. An intercepted enemy radio message stated: "We are standing by for the signal."[4] Ten minutes later, at precisely 1910, a force of thirty-five hundred Chinese swarmed down from Ungok, Arrowhead, Hills 25A and 190 and launched a massive assault.[5] As the Chinese attacked all of the outposts simultaneously with overpowering strength, the Marines had little opportunity for mutual defense. Each outpost was kept busy defending itself, and each was a story.

Outpost Carson

As enemy troops began their assault, Carson received small-arms and automatic weapons fire. Entering under its own preparatory fire, an enemy company attacked and attempted to breach the wire. Carson, normally garrisoned with one officer and thirty-seven men, was fortu-itously augmented that night by an ambush patrol from Dog Company 2/5 that happened to be on the hill. Aided by boxed artillery fires, the entrenched Marines successfully repulsed the first assault and stopped the Chinese at the wire.

At 2000, the enemy tried again in the same strength and again failed. Thereafter, throughout the night, Carson received sporadic incoming fires, but no further assaults. The enemy had shifted its attention and forces elsewhere.

The successful defense of Outpost Carson could be attributed, in part, to preparations made earlier by the outpost commander, 1st Lt. John F. Ingalls of Charlie Company 1/5. As a young man in Canada, Ingalls had spent much of his time listening to World War I veterans dis-cussing details of trench warfare. He remembered graphic accounts of barbed wire, dugouts, artillery barrages, and trench construction, includ-ing fire steps, reserve trenches, and communication trenches. "When I arrived in Korea—all of those old lessons descended upon me with enormous impact."[6] Ingalls writes:

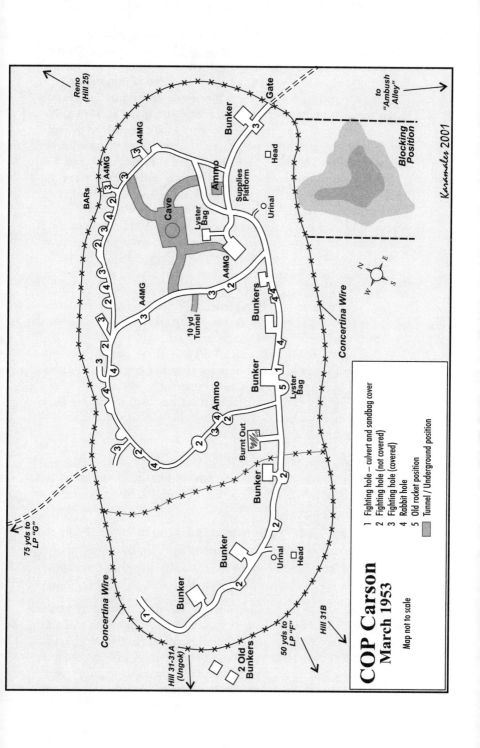

COP Carson
March 1953

Map not to scale

Fighting hole — culvert and sandbag cover
1

Fighting hole (not covered)
2

Fighting hole (covered)
3

Rabbit hole
4

Old rocket position
5

Tunnel / Underground position

Karamales 2001

Reno (Hill 25)

Gate

Bunker

A4MG

A4MG

A4MG

BARs

Cave

Lyster Bag

Ammo

Supplies Platform

Head

Urinal

A4MG

A4MG

10 yd Tunnel

Bunkers

Bunker

Lyster Bag

Ammo

Burnt Out

Bunker

Concertina Wire

Blocking Position

to "Ambush Alley"

Concertina Wire

75 yds to LP "G"

Bunker

Bunker

Urinal

Head

Hill 31B

50 yds to LP "F"

Hill 31-31A (Ungok)

2 Old Bunkers

. . . My personal plans for the defense of Carson against a heavy assault was to have the men withdraw into bunkers during the barrage, and on order, come out and defend the position. "Box-me-in" fires and VT would help us during the early phase of the defense.

Against lighter attacks such as probes or infiltration efforts, we relied upon listening posts for advance warning and then used the troops in the trenches to fire on the enemy. I must say, due to the limited fields of fire and poor visibility, rifles were not nearly as effective as hand grenades. We should have been called a "grenadier platoon."

Quite early in the evening of 26 March our landline with the MLR was knocked out. Our radio worked until about an hour or so after the attack started. I heard the radioman from Reno calling the company CP. (He was Pfc. James Moffitt, originally from my platoon.) What must have been only a few minutes later, I heard Chinese voices on the radio.

The initial barrage against us was bad, but it became much heavier. Some of our men were able to fire against what seemed to be the enemy using grenades and rifle grenades. As the bombardment intensified, the men withdrew into the bunkers. Ammunition shortage was a problem and I ordered them to fix bayonets.

As the action reached its crisis (we knew Reno was gone by this time), I signaled the company asking if they had any instructions for me. I was hoping to hear that our counter-attack was in progress, tanks were coming to reinforce us, or that something was taking place that would prolong our lives—at least for a while. The answer I received was, "Hold at all costs."[7]

The enemy's attempt to overrun Carson slackened at 2010, just as a relief force was leaving the MLR. An enemy message was intercepted at the 1/5 Battalion CP to the effect that "Charge Z has completely collapsed—searching field now."

Whether the Chinese forces found Carson too strong or simply abandoned their efforts in order to concentrate on Outposts Reno and Vegas is no known. Perhaps the assault on Carson was merely a diversion. In a letter to the author, Lieutenant Ingalls mentions:

Initially at least our collective attitude on Carson was rather aggressive. From time to time we would fire a quick volley of rifle grenades at the enemy position (reminiscent of "five rounds rapid," another WW I tactic). In the forward trench, during daylight, the men were instructed to thrust their bayonets into the air so that the enemy could see them. Lt. Seymour, who was later captured on Reno and then repatriated, told me that the Chinese were quite apprehensive about us.[8]

The defense of Carson, for whatever reason, was a most effective one, and the 5th Marines' Special Action Report took notice of that fact when it stated, "It is interesting to note here that the Marines on CARSON fought from covered fighting holes and used the cave there only to get the wounded under cover."[9]

Outpost Reno

At 1935, Reno and Vegas were also under attack. Within minutes, the men at Reno communicated that they were overrun and had enemy troops in the trenches. The Marines moved into the central cave for protection from friendly VT. Six minutes later, an identical message was sent from Vegas. The forty men on each outpost would not hold long against a battalion of enemy troops.

A message from Reno at 2030 requested reinforcements and indicated that the enemy had sealed entrances to the cave and men were passing out from lack of oxygen. The 3d Platoon from Charlie Company, led by 2d Lt. Warren C. Ruthazer, was immediately dispatched from the MLR to reinforce Reno.

The rescue platoon moved out quickly but was ambushed near Reno Block. Following a short firefight, the enemy withdrew, and the platoon moved on. On reaching a steep incline, called the "ladder," two squads of Chinese attacked and pinned down the platoon before it could reach Reno Block. Down to less than a squad of effectives, it could not move without reinforcements or rescue anyone.

Sgt. Bill Janzen describes the experience in greater detail:

> The Chinese were expecting and waiting for us. We went through two intense mortar barrages and two ambushes. . . . The Chinese had that trail zeroed in perfectly. Their mortars walked right down the center of it. As the mortars drew near, we would flop down along side of the trail. . . . After they had moved on past, we would jump up and move out again. It was terrifying! To keep my sanity while my face was buried in the dirt and mud, I would concentrate on repeating the Lord's Prayer, over and over. . . .
>
> At the base of the hill we received another mortar barrage. I saw an inviting hole up on the hillside and jumped in it. Immediately, I realized that it wasn't much shelter at all. . . . I had no sooner jumped out and flopped down below, when a mortar round landed right in that hole and threw dirt over me. We were lying head to foot, one behind the other. Pfc. Bobby G. Hatcher was right in front of me, my head at his feet. He survived that night unscathed and the next day told me that during that barrage he heard a thud, right in front of him. He

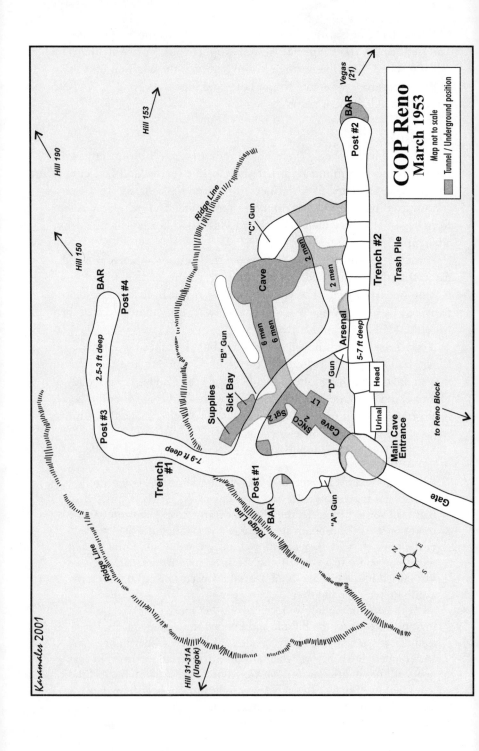

COP Reno
March 1953
Map not to scale
▓ Tunnel / Underground position

Kasumsler 2001

Hill 31-31A
(Ungok)

Hill 190

Hill 153

Hill 150

Ridge Line

Ridge Line

Ridge Line

Trench #1
7-9 ft deep
2.5-3 ft deep

Post #3

Post #4
BAR

"B" Gun
Supplies
Sick Bay

Cave

"C" Gun

6 men
6 men
2 men
2 men

Post #1
BAR

"A" Gun

SNCO
Cave
Sgt 2

LT

"D" Gun

Arsenal
5-7 ft deep

Head

Urinal

Trench #2
Trash Pile

Post #2

BAR

Vegas
(21)

Main Cave
Entrance

Gate

to Reno Block

N
W E
S

lifted up his face and there, right between the feet of the Marine in front of him, was a dud Chinese mortar round, half buried in the earth. He just buried his face back in the dirt.

The hill leading up to the Block was initially very steep and was known as the "ladder." Some Marines previously had tied a heavy hemp rope to a tree trunk farther up the hill. Each night the patrol going up to the Block would pull themselves up the hill, hand over hand, on that rope. When our lead elements got there, they found the rope cut in half by mortar fire. I remember seeing a big hunk of it laying there on the ground, so we climbed the hill without the benefit of a rope. We then moved into a very shallow connecting trench leading upwards toward the Block. If we sat down in that trench, our heads were still sticking out, so when incoming came we just had to hunker way down. By now the head of the column was heavily engaged with the Chinese at very close quarters. . . .

In the rear of the column, where I was, there was not much firing. All we could see were occasional muzzle flashes and we'd shoot at those. I only fired three rounds, and quickly discovered that my rifle wouldn't fire semi-automatic. I had to manually operate it. Upon cleaning it the next day, I discovered that I had split the barrel at the muzzle about an inch and a half. Evidently I'd gotten dirt in the muzzle while hitting the deck.

The fight up front was raging and our casualties were mounting. To one side of the trenchline was a draw. On the other side of the trench was open hillside. Our casualties were gathering there on the hillside. Walking wounded were being given the option of trying to make it back to our lines on their own. Because of the mine fields, we didn't believe any Chinese were behind us. Many did return. They all made it. One was Pfc. Henry A. Fifield. He and I joined C/1/5 together on October 5, 1952 when we arrived with the 25th Replacement Draft. Fifield was a BAR man. He was a skinny young Marine and he loved that weapon. He was wounded and knocked goofy by a mortar round that bent the barrel of his BAR. He didn't know if it would function or not, but said he'd take his chances with it and took off. That was his third wound in five and a half months.[10]

The reinforcements could not make it, but it would make no difference to the men on Reno. They were already gone. At 2144, a last message received from Reno stated that there were seven men still able to fight, and they were trying to dig out by hand in one direction while the enemy was trying to dig into their cave from another. Informed that reinforcements were on the way but held up at the Block, the radio operator made his last transmission, "Well, we'll give 'em hell anyway."[11]

Now retired M/Sgt. Bill Janzen, in a recent letter, sheds more light on this last battle for Outpost Reno. Sergeant Janzen's research confirmed that thirty-eight men were lost on the night of 26 March. His recent letter states:

> Five Marines and one Navy Hospital Corpsman were captured [on Reno]. Only Lt. Seymour and Pfc. Billie J. Morrow of Weapons Company were not wounded. Four Marines and "Doc" [Waddill] were repatriated. Pfc. Morrow was not and is officially presumed dead.
>
> Upon his repatriation on September 2, 1953, I and two other sergeants were able to visit with Lt. Seymour at Freedom Village for about five minutes. . . . He told us that the seven men alive in the cave knew we (3rd Platoon, reinforced, C/1/5) were coming, but that it was already too late as the Chinese were already digging their way into the cave. One of the seven Marines was also digging his way out. Upon succeeding, he crawled into the trench line and was promptly "burp gunned" from above by a Chinese soldier and killed.
>
> The remaining six played dead as the Chinese entered the cave. Doc Waddill was the first to move and a Chinese officer quickly shot him five times with a pistol, badly wounding him. Doc, Cpl. Jimmy E. Lacy and Pfc. George F. Hart were all repatriated on April 23, 1953 at Operation Little Switch. . . .[12]

Reno Block

Now stalled at Reno Block, the Charlie Company rescue platoon was in trouble and needed help. At 2230, a platoon from Fox Company 2/5, brought from regimental reserve, was dispatched with orders to reinforce the Charlie platoon and then move on to Reno to rescue the men there. That order was optimistic. The Fox Company platoon began taking casualties even before it arrived on the MLR. Pfc. Tom Kennedy writes:

> That night we were rousted from sleep in our reserve area. Fox/2/5 was going on the attack. We all climbed into trucks for the trip to the MLR. As we got close the trucks came under fire from mortars and artillery. [76 Alley, the supply road to the MLR, was under constant enemy observation. It was a dangerous run, but the men had to get there in a hurry.] The trucks stopped and we all baled out to run into a large rice paddy. I was on the ground hoping not to be blown away by all the incoming. The paddy was wet and stank of human manure. From the corner of my eye I could see the truck in reverse, getting to

hell out of there. I thought to myself, this is not a good way to begin my day—I was in deep shit with no prospects—if only I could live through this! After the incoming eased up we walked the rest of the way to the MLR bringing our wounded with us.

Reassembling at the MLR we ran like hell for Reno. Across open land it was like a civil war charge. We lost about sixty men to incoming and automatic weapons fire. I got about halfway up the hill. My BAR was glowing orange from firing, and I burned my hands picking it up and laying it down as I ran from place to place. The shells were falling all around us and finally I was unable to run anymore.

I was covered with dirt from all the explosions, and my flak jacket was peppered with rocks and debris. I noticed that the flash hider on my BAR was choked with dirt and I couldn't unscrew it because of the heat and the incoming. Now I worried that the weapon would blow up if I had to fire it again.

Then we began to withdraw from the hill; we couldn't advance any farther. We got only as far as the Reno Block. Pfc. Taylor and Pfc. Sweeny were all that were left of our squad. We were in a gully full of wounded and dead Marines. At the time I felt the Chinese were allowing the wounded and stragglers to fill up the Block with the intention of blowing us all to hell when they were ready....[13]

The Fox Company platoon had 70 percent casualties and was now pinned down with the platoon at Reno Block. Only seven men from the original Charlie Company platoon were still effective.

A second platoon from Fox Company was committed, reached the Block at 2340, but withering mortar fire rained on the men and they had to leave the position. They were ordered to make their way to the ladder and join the men already there.

Fox Company's commander, Capt. Ralph L. Walz, led his remaining platoon out to the ladder, but the men sustained numerous casualties en route. The entire company, or what was left of it, was now assembled at the base of Reno. Still, the enemy gave the men no respite as mortars ranged in on their location. Sergeant Janzen recalls the arrival of Captain Walz and his men:

. . . We were to hold what we had, "regardless of the cost" and that F/2/5 was on its way to reinforce us. Lt. Ruthazer had requested permission from company headquarters to disengage and withdraw. It was then that the hold order was issued. . . .

When F/2/5 arrived at around 2330, they moved up into the draw behind and to one side of us. Their Company Commander, Captain Ralph L. Walz, and his radio operator, seeking our Platoon Leader, Lt.

Ruthazer, crawled on their hands and knees over our bodies as we hunkered down in that shallow trench. . . . The Chinese threw in a devastating mortar barrage of HE and Willie Peter (WP—white phosphorous) right on them. It was horrible to behold! I will never forget the screams of the wounded and dying as that white phosphorous burned them. Then we heard someone yell, "Fix bayonets! Charge!!" and the men of F/2/5 went whooping and hollering up that draw and disappeared up the hill. It was magnificent, heroic and ghastly to observe.[14]

Privates Kennedy, Taylor and Sweeny were among the Fox Company men on that charge. Kennedy describes the experience in his letter:

Word came down that volunteers were needed to go back up on Reno to bring back dead, wounded and any weapons we could find. The three of us figured it would be a good way to get out of Reno Block before all hell broke loose. A Corpsman, Joe [Joseph F.] Keenan, was to go with us. We had a stretcher to carry and were told to leave our weapons behind.

With little to slow us down we ran up the hill as fast as we could; bullets were hitting all around us and the brush was burning. On top of Reno the trench had been blasted level and the bunkers caved in. There were shell holes everywhere. We needed water and found some canteens which we drank down along with our own. I picked up some M1 rifles that were lying around.

Then we located a Marine that had been hit in the leg. Lifting him on to the stretcher, we began our run back down the hill. As we came down, the Chinese started to use their mortars against us. We ran awhile then dropped to the ground. Try as we might, we couldn't keep the wounded man from occasionally falling off the stretcher. Several times he moaned, "No, not again! I don't want to be hit again." It was rough for him because we couldn't pause to help. Doc Keenan helped as much as he could, but the Marine had already been wounded at least twice and may have been hit a third time on our trip off the hill.

Approaching Reno Block, we were met by some KSC laborers who took the stretcher. We were exhausted and suffering from concussion. Despite his wounds, Doc Keenan went on to the MLR where he subsequently died of wounds.[15]

Outpost Reno had been lost, and the Marines at Reno Block were in trouble. Hampered by too many casualties, they were unable to move without help. The situation then became worse as 150 enemy soldiers were seen moving toward Reno Block in an effort to flank the Marines.

A tank marksman took care of the Chinese approaching the Block while an evacuation effort was hastily organized on the MLR. A provisional platoon (clutch platoon) from Headquarters & Service (H&S) Company 1/5, augmented by two squads from Dog Company 2/5, and a platoon from Easy Company 2/5, was organized. At 0250, this mixed assembly of Marines left to assist with evacuation of casualties from Reno Block.

Sergeant Janzen continues:

At about 0230, on March 27, 1953, we were ordered to disengage and return to the MLR. As we began to move down off of the hill, the first of the "Angel Teams" (casualty and evacuation) from D/2/5, E/2/5 and H&S/1/5 arrived with stretchers and medical supplies. Our two Corpsmen had just exhausted their supplies. Lt. [Bennet H.] Perry, from C/1/5, guided the last Angel Team out.

. . . The first man we put on a stretcher was Pfc. Albert H. Hughes. He was the biggest man in the platoon. He was on the point when a Chinese soldier threw a grenade at him. The grenade hit his chest, bounced off and exploded. The explosion knocked Hughes flat on his back in that shallow trench, still holding his rifle at high port. The Chinese soldier jumped in, stood on top of him, pulled his rifle out of his hands and shot him in the chest with it. Observing this, Pfc. Robert S. Durham, a BAR man better known as "Ma," killed the Chinese soldier. Just at that point in time, the lead element of the platoon was pulling back a few yards. Durham stood up with that BAR, directed other Marines to go and get Hughes and said he would cover them. With that, he began cutting down charging Chinese soldiers.

As we were assembling on the lower hillside and in the draw, we were trying to account for everyone. Some men informed me that Pfc. Mario Lombardi, a machine gunner, was missing. He was last seen, wounded, farther back up in the trench. I said I'd find him. I threw my worthless rifle in the previously mentioned hole that I had first jumped into hours before. I pulled out my .38 caliber Smith and Wesson Combat Masterpiece revolver, which I'd been carrying in the waistband of my trousers under my flak jacket, and took off up the hill and back into the trench.

I got farther up that trenchline than I had at any time all night. I first found three dead Marines from our platoon huddled together. The one in the center was our platoon radioman, Pfc. William B. Marshall. I verified that he was in fact dead. The other two I couldn't recognize because of massive head injuries. I tried to lift their bodies out of the trench, but was too weak and exhausted to do so. Another Marine came up behind me and started to give me a hand until he saw their injuries. He just made a guttural sound, like he was about to retch, and turned away. I cursed him and I think he went back down the hill. I never did know who he was.

I continued on up the trench until I came to a point where it jogged to the right and there was a small embankment. I saw two dark figures sitting against the embankment and didn't know if they were Marines or Chinese. Just then, they challenged me and I quickly answered "Sgt. Janzen, Charlie Company." With that, a voice between us started calling, "Sgt. Janzen, it's me, Lombardi, don't leave me. My legs are busted and I'm half buried in the trench." He was buried up to his chest. He knew those two Marines from F/2/5 were there, but thought they were Chinese and so was playing dead. I assured him that I would not leave him and started to dig him out. Just then Pfc. Joseph N. Levesque, another machine gunner arrived. Unbeknownst to me, he had quietly followed me up the hill. I couldn't have been happier to see him. About the time we got Lombardi dug out of that collapsed trench, two other Marines arrived, and with two rifles and two field jackets made a stretcher. We had to stand Lombardi on his broken legs in order to get him out of that trench. We couldn't carry him in the trench because of it being blocked by bodies. About this time, I noticed a shadowy figure about 35 yards away. Perhaps a Chinese soldier? I don't think he fired at us.

Just as we arrived back where everyone was assembling, the Chinese threw another mortar barrage on us. Pfc. Levesque took off his helmet and placed it over Lombardi's face and then lay down on top of him, shielding him with his own body. I ran back to where Hughes was and almost did the same thing, but he was so high off of the deck on that stretcher that I just didn't have the guts to do so and instead lay down on the ground and held his hand. At one point during the barrage, I heard Hughes grunt. I think he took a piece of shrapnel in the side. When the enemy fire lifted, before I could move or say a thing, Hughes said, "Are you O.K., Sarge?" To this day, my lack of courage in shielding him with my body has haunted me. Thankfully, he survived in spite of me.

As soon as I jumped up, I ran over to Lombardi and Levesque. Lombardi was O.K., but Levesque had been struck by shrapnel in the right ear and knocked unconscious. I put a battle dressing on his wound and we prepared to get out of there.

As we moved out for the MLR, I saw Doc [HM3 Paul N.] Polley walking behind SSgt. Hart with his good hand on Hart's shoulder. Polley should have been on a stretcher, but refused to be carried. With SSgt. Hart's guidance, Doc walked all the way back in, blind as a bat! I put my revolver away and retrieved my rifle. Initially four of us tried to carry Hughes, but on that rough, narrow trail and getting out of step with one another, we kept bouncing him right off of the stretcher onto the ground. He had a very rough trip. Once we switched to two men at a time, that solved the problem. Doc Hammond, restocked with medical supplies, refused to return to the MLR with us, but instead chose to remain out there assisting in caring for F/2/5's wounded. This devotion to duty would cost him his life. [16]

Twenty-one-year-old HM3 Francis C.(Doc) Hammond, a corpsman, was mortally wounded when a mortar round exploded at his feet while he ran to the aid of a wounded Marine lying in the open. He was posthumously awarded a Medal of Honor. Hospitalman Polley, the other corpsman, regained his eyesight and received a Navy Cross.

Berlin Outposts

Also on the evening of 26 March at 2045, the enemy launched attacks on Berlin and East Berlin, two small outpost hills in the 3/5 sector east of the Nevada Cities. Each position was garrisoned by a squad from George Company. A Chinese platoon probed Berlin while another platoon struck East Berlin. Within ten minutes, the George Company CP lost communication with both outposts; wires had been cut with preparatory mortar fire as the assault began. The Marines countered with boxing fire that drove the enemy from the wire, and neither outpost was penetrated. The assaults were apparent diversions, and the Berlin positions remained in Marine hands. (They, too, would have their day, but that would be later in the war.)

Outposts Hedy, Bunker, Esther, and Dagmar in the 1st Marines' sector were also struck that night, each attacked by an enemy company. The Chinese were making a tremendous effort to keep Marine defensives dispersed and to prevent them from being focused on Vegas. These attacks were readily beaten off, however, except on Dagmar, where approximately twenty-five Chinese soldiers managed to breach the barbed-wire perimeter and enter the trenches. They were killed, but it took a little longer.

Outpost Vegas

Pvt. James A. Larkin was possibly the last man to get off Vegas before it was overrun on 26 March. An artilleryman, Larkin was part of a forward observer team responsible for directing artillery support. Larkin writes:

> . . . Just getting around on Vegas was a nightmare. You had to keep low and move fast. The tangle of communication wires in the trenches made this damned hard to do, but we did it to stay alive.

My spot on Vegas was at Able gate, where the trench was deepest. I needed a deep place because the antenna on my 619 radio stuck up ten to twelve feet, making a perfect aiming point for the Chinese on Hills 150, 153, and 190 who could look straight down on Vegas. But Able gate was on the reverse slope of the Vegas hill, which provided some protection, even if not very much.

On the afternoon of the twenty-sixth the Chinese went all out. As intense as the shelling had been for the previous four and a half days, it suddenly got even worse. That afternoon three seriously wounded and one dead Marine had been carried down from the hilltop by Chiggie-Bears [KSC Laborers]. Most of the day everyone remaining had stayed in deep cover, pinned down by the constantly incoming artillery.

About 1740 on the twenty-sixth, Steve Drummond, my relief, arrived, having crawled all the way out from the MLR through the battered trenchline that was getting such a pounding.

Steve and I made with the small talk for a few minutes while I prepared myself for the running crawl back to the MLR. Steve was sure, and I agreed with him, that the Chinese were going to jump on us before dawn, and they were going to come in force. That was what intelligence thought, and they were usually pretty sharp in guessing what the goonies were going to do.

I helped Steve carry his FO gear to the bunker, where it would be relatively safe from the incoming. He also had to make up a watch schedule with another FO named Doyle, who belonged to another team. I never got to know Doyle. He was new, and seemed a good man. As it happened, he never got off the hill.

I shook hands with Steve and wished him good luck. I wasn't a bit sorry to be getting away from outpost Vegas and back to the relative safety of the MLR. I waited for an imaginary pause in the shelling and got my butt out of there fast. But going through the trenchline in the twilight, I was spotted by the Chinese on the hills, and they tried to bracket me with mortar shots. We had rabbit holes all along the trenchline to take care of situations like this, and the holes worked pretty well.

. . . As I humped along, I could tell that the tempo of the incoming was increasing. It sounded like a continuous roar, and the shells were lighting up the landscape and sending up huge spouts of water and mud.

When I reached the listening post fifty or so yards in front of the line, I didn't even bother to give a password. In fact, I wasn't challenged for one. Everyone was head down in the dirt to stay away from the fragments of artillery shell whistling through the air all around.

Once past the line I headed straight for the 1/5 area to make my report to the battalion FO. And while I had been humping across the open paddies, the Chinese had started attacking in force—attacking

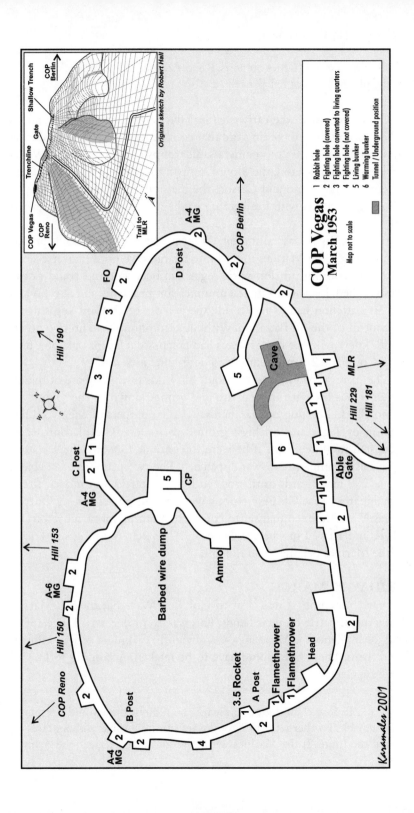

COP Vegas
March 1953

Map not to scale

1 Rabbit hole
2 Fighting hole (covered)
3 Fighting hole converted to living quarters
4 Fighting hole (not covered)
5 Living bunker
6 Warming bunker
Tunnel / Underground position

Original sketch by Robert Hall

COP Vegas
COP Reno
Trail to MLR
Trenchline
Gate
Shallow Trench
COP Berlin

Hill 190
Hill 153
Hill 150
COP Reno

A-4 MG
A-6 MG
A-4 MG
C Post
FO
D Post
A-4 MG
COP Berlin →

B Post
3.5 Rocket
A Post
Flamethrower
Flamethrower
Head

Barbed wire dump
Ammo
CP
Able Gate
Cave

Hill 229
Hill 181
MLR

Kosmider 2001

all of the Nevada Cities outposts. Reno, Carson, and of course, Vegas—the place I had just left.[17]

Concurrent with the early evening attacks on Carson, Reno, and the other outposts, the incoming fire that commenced at 1900 was followed by several companies of enemy assault troops charging Outpost Vegas. Severely outnumbered, the How Company platoon was quickly over-whelmed. Like Reno and Carson, the men on Vegas could not support adjoining outposts with fire because of the heavy fighting on their own hill.

By 1941, Vegas was calling for VT over its trenches. Seeking protec-tion from VT, the Marines moved into a large cave on the reverse slope. Battalion communication with Vegas had been cut and could not be reestablished. Because of the communication problems and also because the 1st Battalion had its hands full, the defense of Outpost Vegas passed to control of the 3d Battalion. Without communication, no one on the MLR knew whether or not Vegas had fallen, so, at 2205, a platoon from Dog Company 2/5 was sent out to determine its status.

The platoon had moved to about 400 yards from the base of the hill when it was hit with mortar fire and pinned down in the vicinity of Reno Block. Looking up, the men saw large numbers of enemy soldiers on top of Vegas and on high ground to its left. The platoon leader requested reinforcements if he were to continue forward, and a platoon from Easy Company 2/5 was dispatched. The two platoons were able to move 200 more yards until stopped by small-arms and mortar fire. It was apparent that Chinese troops were in full possession of Outpost Vegas. With the reconnaissance complete, both platoons retired to the MLR and arrived just before dawn on 27 March. Nothing was known of the Marines originally on the hill.

FRIDAY, 27 MARCH

By early morning, it was clear to Col. Lew Walt that the 5th Marines had a major battle on their hands. This was no ordinary raid. The enemy had taken Reno and Vegas and was obviously making a serious effort to hold them. These hills would have to be retaken. According to Lt. Col. Andrew Geer:

> . . . To lose these outposts meant the present line would become untenable. Further retraction southward was impossible without cross-ing the Imjin. If the Marines withdrew south of the river, the Army

units on the right would be forced to fall back across the Samichon River and, once again the gateway to the Korean capital would be open. With such a victory in view, the truce talks at Panmunjom would be delayed or broken off entirely.

. . . At 2:00 o'clock in the morning Walt was forced to a fateful decision. He requested permission to withdraw all troops to the rear of the MLR, to reorganize and launch a coordinated counterattack to retake Reno and Vegas during daylight. The remaining hours of darkness would be used to evacuate the wounded and dead.[18]

Permission was granted. Colonel Walt reorganized his regiment and prepared to counterattack both outposts. Reinforcement was provided by the 2d Battalion, 7th Marines, brought forward from division reserve. To retake the hills, Walt now had four infantry battalions at his disposal plus supporting arms from artillery, tanks, and air. Enemy strength, it was later determined, consisted of a reinforced regiment, about equal in number to the Marines.

Unlike the common small-unit actions of the past year, the counterattack would be a major operation. The Marines would attack the hills in columns of companies. If anything, the fighting would take on aspects of World War I, where companies and battalions of men, with bayonets fixed, had charged "over the top" yelling and screaming as they ran across no-man's-land to engage the Hun.

The retaking of Vegas had all the similarities of assaulting a hostile beach from the sea. At month's end, an unknown Marine officer was overheard describing the battle for Outpost Vegas, as the "highest damn beachhead in Korea." It was an accurate observation. The fight for Vegas was the most severe of the Nevada Cities battles. With no tactical way to flank the enemy, the Marines fought head on. Like an amphibious landing, wave after wave of Marines attacked the hill, were repulsed, and attacked again.

Bringing in the Reserves

During the outpost war, calling out battalions from division reserve did not often occur. The very act of assembling the men, issuing ammunition, and bringing them forward was an indication of a severe threat. By this time Chinese actions on the outposts and the MLR met that criterion, and a reserve battalion, 2/7, was moved forward where it could be swiftly deployed.

At the time, Dog Company 2/7 was comfortably situated at Camp Rose, a reserve area approximately 8 miles south of the MLR. Sgt.

Robert ("Bob") Kreid, a machine-gun section leader, remembers the move:

> That night we had just received our beer ration which we considered our duty to drink. Around 2000 I stepped outside of the tent with a buddy and saw that the whole north sky was lit with flares and our artillery was firing. Starting slow the firing swiftly turned into a roar. Asking my buddy what the hell was happening, he replied, "My God, the shit has really hit the fan." At that instant the Company Gunny yelled down the company street, "DOG COMPANY! OUTSIDE! WITH GEAR, MOVE!" All at once what had been a good time beer bust became a deadly serious, move your ass business.
>
> In less than five minutes the company fell out in the street. Squad leaders passed out hand grenades and bandoliers of ammo while some of the veterans stuffed extra battle dressings in their pockets. Battalion trucks warmed up in the motor pool and we climbed aboard. Soon we were heading north toward the sound of battle.
>
> In back of the trucks the Marines sat quietly in the dark facing each other; each with his own thoughts. Once in a while you could make out a face from the glow of a cigarette or a hand holding a rosary. Finally I was going to war, after two years in the Marines. Somehow I was not as gung-ho at twenty as I had been at eighteen. I was a boot sergeant now and knew weapons, tactics and was supposed to know how to lead men in combat. Would I do it right?
>
> I did not feel as big or confident as I did back at Camp Pendleton in the 3rd Marines three months before. I whispered, "Dear God my Father, please help me do my duty and not bring dishonor to myself and family." That night central Texas and home seemed awfully far away.[19]

In preparation for the assault, organizational lines of responsibility were redrawn. 1st Battalion 5th Marines, with 2/7 attached, would retain Reno and everything west. 3d Battalion 5th Marines, with 2/5 attached, would have Vegas and everything east.

Then, at 1100, a decision was made not to retake Reno, at least for the present. (Although the source of this decision could not be determined by the author, it seems reasonable to assume that it came from division level.) With Reno now out of the picture, all preparations could be directed toward retaking Vegas.

The defensive tables, however, had turned. Whereas, formerly, the three outposts could mutually support each other's flanks, Reno, in the middle, now became a problem rather than an asset. In enemy hands, it could be used against the flanks of both Carson and Vegas. Reno would be bombed into oblivion to destroy its usefulness to the Chinese.

The decision to eliminate Reno and concentrate on Vegas released 2/7, which originally had been scheduled for the Reno counterattack. In retrospect, this reassignment was a wise move because, in days to come, 2/7 would be well used on Vegas.

First Counterattacks on Vegas

At first light, on 27 March, tanks, airplanes, artillery, and mortars began neutralizing enemy positions on and around Reno with high explosives and smoke. Surrounding enemy hills were also taken under fire. Vegas was not bombed in hopes that its defenses could be spared for the Marines to use after they retook it, a decision that proved somewhat optimistic.

Along the Marine MLR, direct-fire weapons, heavy machine guns, tanks, and recoilless rifles were positioned where the gunners could view and fire on enemy hills in front of and beside Vegas. From the rear, batteries of artillery, mortars, and rockets registered on the hills and valleys while airplanes dived, strafed, and bombed. All available Marine firepower was brought to bear on targets of opportunity, machine-gun and mortar positions, forward observers, and especially troops in the open. On one occasion, a full enemy company, deployed south from Reno, was cut down by tank fire and VT rounds.[20]

The 5th Marines Recoilless Rifle Platoon's mare, Reckless, who been trained to carry ammunition for its 75-mm rifles (see chapter 5), would prove her worth on Vegas. She performed with distinction during the fighting. In his book about Reckless, Colonel Geer describes details of the Recoilless Rifle Platoon and its beloved ammunition carrier:

Behind the lines tanks growled into ridge-line tank wallows scooped out by bulldozers and, hull down, began to fire. Dubois and his section opened up in the Carson sector as did Reschke from behind Ava. High angling over all were the 4.2-inch (four deuces) mortars and behind all these were the batteries of artillery, medium and large, beginning to increase the tempo of fire.

Then came the sound that always made the most blasé veteran cock an ear. It was the frenzied tearing of air currents by a rocket ripple. One hundred forty-four rockets passed overhead in nearly solid flight. At the sound of them Marines all along the line looked northward. On the forward slopes of Hill 190 there was the clustered twinkle of dozens and dozens of orange lights and then the lights were lost in the Bikini blossom of yellow smoke and dust. Long seconds later came the roar of thunder. Even with that the Marines did not turn away, but waited for the second, smaller flight.

"Ah, The alibi round," meaning those rockets that had lain stillborn in their tubes on the initial firing had been rejuvenated and sent on their way of destruction. It was one sound of war that Reckless never understood or became accustomed to hearing.

At the beginning of the day the recoilless rifles had a small supply of shells in the vicinity of each firing position. Reckless began the day working against this backlog. Her efforts were augmented by members of the squad who were packing three rounds a trip. As the day wore on, time and terrain began to take their toll of Marine-packers and the little horse was making two trips for each of her friends.

The gun crews were following the established tactic of firing five rounds and shifting to an alternate site. The most distant position from the supply point was seven hundred yards, the nearest five hundred fifty. Despite the ruggedness of the terrain, Reckless was making the long haul in twenty minutes and the shorter one in twelve. During the early phase there was little or no counterfire from the Chinese. They were intent on waiting out the blistering Marine fire and saving ammunition for the infantry attack they knew they must face.[21]

Reckless made fifty-one trips from the ammunition supply point (ASP) to gun positions. She carried more than 9,000 pounds of explosives—386 rounds. 1st Lt. Eric Pederson estimated that the mare traveled more than 35 miles. While she was working, Reckless was wounded twice when flying shrapnel nicked her on the head and on the flank. She was subsequently awarded two Purple Hearts.

At 1120, after Vegas and the surrounding areas had been well blanketed with smoke, Dog Company 2/5 launched a frontal attack on the southern slope. Progress was slow, and the company began taking casualties immediately.

The enemy was lavish in its use of artillery. Company CPs and assembly areas behind the MLR were also hit, as was the 1/5 Battalion command post. The Able Tank Company CP recorded more than one hundred rounds of incoming fire. The situation did not improve when, later that afternoon, according to the 3/5 Command Diary, "a 4.2-inch mortar ammunition dump exploded as a result of an overheated mortar tube prematurely setting the increments afire."[22]

Chinese reinforcements streamed to Vegas from surrounding hills, and, despite accurate fire from Marine artillery and tanks, many of them got through. Between noon and 1300, four groups of varying sizes left Hill 153 for Vegas, and another company-sized group, with automatic weapons and mortars, followed them. The Marines observed a reinforced platoon making its way through a connecting trench from Reno, while another, larger unit attempted to reinforce Vegas from Hill 21B.

On the slope of Vegas, Dog Company's attack slowed to a near halt. By 1220, a provisional company, made up of 2/5's Weapons Company and H&S Company personnel, was thrown into the fray.

The 5th Marines now had three companies committed to the assault, all of which were pinned down on the south slope of Vegas. It was an artillery duel with the Marine infantry caught in the open. Smoke, air, tank, and counterbattery fire did little to slow the constant bombardment from enemy guns. Capt. John Melvin, commander of Dog Company, stated that incoming literally rained on the troops. He reported:

> It was so intense at times that you couldn't move forward or backward. The Chinese 60-mm. mortars began to bother us about as much as firecrackers. It was the 120-mm. mortars and the 122-mm. artillery that hurt the most. The noise was deafening. They would start walking the mortars toward us from every direction possible. You could only hope that the next round wouldn't be on target.[23]

By 1300, Dog Company and the provisional companies each had so many casualties that neither could advance. Consequently, at 1430, Easy Company was ordered to advance through the bogged-down Marines and continue the attack. It had gone no farther than the forward elements of Dog Company, approximately 150 yards short of the Vegas trenches, when it too was stopped.

Pfc. Luther Hudson of Fox 2/5 had been detailed to run a supply train between the MLR and Vegas to shuttle ammunition and medical supplies forward and wounded men back. He went only as far as the place where Dog Company and the provisional companies were pinned down. Hudson recalled:

> I'd gone back down a way and was directing the supply line out of a huge gully. The route was zeroed in by enemy mortars slowing everyone up. There was a bottleneck forming as the gully filled up with Marines. Bunched up as they were, it wouldn't take long for the Chinese to bring their mortars and artillery in on the group of wounded men.
>
> Realizing that we had to get out of there and back to the MLR, I scouted out a better route. One that was covered and concealed. The captain and his radio man arrived to take charge. I practically begged him to get the men out of there and moving, around the way I had found. When he refused, I figured that if he was going to fight a war

that way, I would dump my supplies and take my men and head down the supply line toward our lines. Well aware of what was about to happen to the 80 or 100 Marines bunched up and laying along the sides of the gully, I preferred being elsewhere.

I hadn't gone far when I met Major [Benjamin F.] Lee, the 2/5 Operations Officer (S-3). He was carrying a walking stick, passing Marines in the supply line, like a British Officer on his way to a picnic! Calm as you please.

I stopped the major and explained the situation I'd just left. I took him around the way I'd suggested. As he emerged past the far end of the open path and seeing so many bodies, body parts and equipment scattered along it, he almost fainted. "My God, man," he exclaimed, "Take me to that Captain!" I did and he ordered the Captain to get those men out of the gully immediately and headed around the way I'd shown him.[24]

The Last Counterattack

Along with its sister companies Dog and Easy, Fox Company 2/7 had been moved forward from division reserve but not initially committed. Then, the 5th Marines counterassault became stalled.

At 1300, while Dog Company 2/5 and the provisional company were pinned down on the slope of Vegas, and Easy Company 2/5 began its advance, Fox Company 2/7 received marching orders. 2d Lt. Theodore Chenoweth, the 3d platoon leader, was to lead his platoon in the next assault. The company commander, Capt. Ralph Estey, called a meeting of his three platoon leaders, the gunnery sergeant, and the mortar platoon leader. There, on the back of an open truck behind the MLR, he issued his orders and then sent his officers to the line to view the place that they were going to attack.

Lieutenant Chenoweth and the other officers hiked to an observation post on the MLR. Inside, the telephones were silent. Two officers from the 5th Marines did not speak or offer to help. They appeared benumbed from fatigue and mental trauma. Chenoweth writes:

> In front of the observation post, we observed a small spur leading downward, away from the MLR. At about the point where the spur petered out in the paddies, the trail turned around the spur toward Vegas and became observable to us. We could see most of the communication trail going along the east side of a wide shallow valley that had narrow rice paddies up its middle. The trail led out to the base of Vegas. The low hillsides of the shallow valley were dotted by bare trees and small brown bushes set in yellow grass. The bushes were too

small to give any concealment even though they retained their brown leaves. There appeared to be no cover or defilade in the entire valley, except possibly in the forward assembly area the Skipper had chosen and now pointed out to us.

Scattered along the side of, and on the communication trail for a distance of 400–500 yards, maybe more, we could see the bunched and the single green forms of several hundred dead, or wounded Marines. All appeared motionless. The Skipper ignored them. No one commented.[25]

Elements of Dog Company 2/5 had reached the right finger of Vegas but were pinned down by artillery and mortar fire. Easy Company 2/5 and the provisional company were lower on the hillside and equally stuck. For the Marines to move anywhere on Vegas meant certain death. Archival records do not explain why anyone would possibly think that, with nearly a full battalion pinned down, Fox Company had any better chance than the others. There is no indication of a change in tactics, of additional supporting arms, or of lessening enemy resistance. The third counterattack on Vegas was more like the last wave of an amphibious landing, reminiscent perhaps of Gallipoli.

Waiting behind the MLR, the men could hear only the intensified sounds of battle as the enemy tried to dislodge the 5th Marines. The men of Fox Company knew that something big was going on and that they would soon be in it. They were tense and nervous; some were getting sick. They waited, like Marines before them who had circled in landing craft as they waited for orders to hit a beach. Sergeants, wise beyond their years, began to exercise their men—calisthenics, movement, checking their gear, anything to stay busy and get their minds off of Vegas.

"Away the boats!" At 1530 on 27 March after three postponements, Fox Company 2/7 was committed to the battle. Three platoons left the MLR in a column with orders to pass through the pinned-down 5th Marines and take the outpost. Lieutenant Chenoweth continues his narrative when the company left the MLR gate at a slow double time in platoon order. Chenoweth's 3d Platoon picked up the rear:

The march file went over the hill past the observation post, turned left and went down. I could see several Marines sitting and standing in the MLR watching us. They were silent and looked at us without expression. They looked stupefied. The occasional mortar burst—Krump!—ahead of us didn't disturb their gaze. They never changed that look.

. . . The file of Marines ahead of us were jogging on the wide trail. They turned right around the little spur and went from our sight. I looked behind and saw Sergeant [Ralph] Wynne and the second squad on the hillside descending toward the gate. He gave me a recognition hand sign. The march was moving well. We jogged toward the end of the spur and moved out of the shade into the sunshine of that wide valley I had seen from the observation post.

Captain Estey was holding to his order. We were an attack force, not a relief party. We had been ordered to keep moving.

. . . With Sergeant [Wallace] Towne's squad in the lead, the 3rd Platoon moved in double time down the trail and into the wide valley. We jogged along with our weapons carried in hand.

Mortar shells fell erratically out in the dry rice paddies near the head and middle of the 1st Platoon. From the harsh Krump! that echoed off the hillsides, the shells sounded like Chinese 120-mm but that may have been only our fears. The Chinese could never get those heavy 120-mm tubes and base plates out here, could they? The ammo alone needed a truck to carry it! We didn't like the 120-mm mortars. These mortars were most likely Chinese 82-mm's.

The file kept moving but the mortars were having their usual effect. The forward file was getting dispersed. It was slowing down rather than speeding up. Combat wisdom insisted that we should speed up, run faster to get away from the beaten zone of the mortars.

The head of the column dispersed momentarily up the hillside when a mortar burst in the paddies and closer to them, like a school of fish attacked by a big mouth bass! Then I saw the file resume moving but slower now. They may have had some injured.

There seemed to be no method to the mortar bursts. Only one burst or two at a time, sporadically. They were not well aimed and fell out in the rice paddies. We noticed this fact and were grateful. The Chinese observer did not seem to be adjusting his rounds. . . .

My attention was outward, watching the mortars and the progress of the file ahead of us, but I was ignoring the valley of horror we had entered. Nearby and strewn out ahead of us were the bodies of many Marines, fallen like jack straws over the valley floor. Beside the trail, the lacerated, decapitated body of a Marine lay on his back. His flesh showed through the shredded dungarees. The sadness I felt, to see him so, was intense and twisted my stomach. . . .

He had taken a fatal wound through the line of his mouth. His lower jaw and chin were still attached to the stump of his neck on his body. His helmet, the strap still fastened, with the entire head, face and upper teeth in it, lay ten feet away, upside down, the eyes staring at us and the teeth gnawing the sky.

I couldn't take my eyes away from the poor fellow. My radioman, Pfc. Jim Crouch, cried out in shock. He stopped and stared and bent over mouth open, in fascination by the bloody awful sight. The men in front and behind me were stopped, stunned by the redness of death. Except for me and the NCO's, all of the men in the 3rd Platoon were only 18 or 19 years old. . . .

I have heard that it is rude to talk about the mutilation of our comrades, or even about the mutilated bodies of enemy soldiers for that matter. The bodies bloodied and shattered by lethal force are a secret. I agree that it is rude and better left unsaid. But, I have also heard that the horror of combat is something felt mostly by "weak sisters," who are impressionable or who become the neurotic rubble left behind by every war. These denigrations are not true of the greater number of us. Most of us are different from that.

What makes most Marines, or most warriors, different is that they can still function and carry out a mission when confronted by the horror caused by lethal force. Most of us can function without becoming neurotic. To make my point, even while feeling fear, a Marine is expected to function and does function. How is that achieved?

There is one aspect that I want to say here. If we are silent about the lethal force of war that caused the death and the manner of death of our unknown (to us) fallen comrades, then their death was quietly overlooked. It is made an in-group secret never to be discussed, and then quietly forgotten. The dead will be remembered only by their family. The death, caused by the lethal force of war, needs to be remembered. So, that is why I tell about it. I tell about it so those who have never seen the slaughter, the shredding, the bloody rags of war, will see what I can tell of it, and never forget.

I feel so sad when writing this because I know that in the long run, all of us will forget. We all do.[26]

Fox Company Marines continued their jog across the valley but now noticeably slower as mortars continued to fall. Around them and ahead lay bodies of more Marines, some dead, others wounded. They lay on the trail and beside it, some in paddies 40 or 50 yards away. Groups of eight to ten lay where they had fallen, quite dead, and recognizable only by their 782 gear (e.g., weapons, helmets) and shredded dungarees. In the dirt all around were the gray star marks of exploded mortar rounds amid chunks and splinters of burnt black and silver shards of metal. Utter devastation. These were men of the 5th Marines, remnants of Dog, Easy, and provisional companies that had counterattacked Vegas that morning.

Korean War chroniclers Lt. Col. Pat Meid and Maj. James Yingling write, "Within the first hour after leaving the battalion line, the Company F Marines nearly reached the advanced positions of 2/5, and Company D, which had been in the vanguard since 1100, returned to the regimental CP. During the next hour, however, heavy shelling slowed the Marine advance."[27] More mortars fell in the valley. Fox Company's 1st Platoon was dispersed from the trail by incoming fire. The men were in the paddies and on the hillside, but they continued to move forward. Captain Estey was leading the column with Sgt. Richard F. Rainbolt, 1st platoon leader. The men moved in fire team order. Like maneuver units on the attack, they advanced another 500 yards to begin the ascent to Vegas.

The 2d and 3d Platoons, still in the valley, were coping with mortar fire. In its haste to get away from the mortars, the 3d Platoon passed the 2d Platoon, only to encounter long-range machine-gun fire. On a low hillside, 75 yards ahead, the men could see an oval-shaped beaten zone of falling bullets. According to Chenoweth, "The sound was like a downpour of rain on dry leaves."[28] The men double-timed as best they could to the small hill at the base of Vegas; they had to get out of that deadly valley. Around them lay more fallen Marines, lying where they had been struck.

Near a creek bank, HM3 William Charette was treating the wounded. He was Fox Company's 3d Platoon corpsman. Surrounded by wounded men, he removed his flak vest and placed it over one of them. Earlier, he had left his steel helmet with another man.

While Charette was attending yet another Marine, an enemy grenade or mortar landed nearby. With no hesitation, he threw himself over the body of the wounded man. The force of the blast ripped into the corpsman without injuring the Marine. Miraculously, Charette survived and continued to work. He tore up his own clothing to fashion battle dressings because his medical kit had been destroyed in the explosion. William Charette was later awarded a Medal of Honor for the courage that he showed on Vegas. Charette is the only Navy corpsman to be awarded a Medal of Honor during the Korean War and live to receive it.[29]

The 3d Platoon, somewhat separated from the other two, worked its way toward the company assembly area at the base of Vegas. Leaving the men to search for an enemy mortar position, Lieutenant Chenoweth and Sergeant Wynne traveled along the topographical crest above the platoon. Chenoweth continues:

> I signaled Sgt. Wynne to move the platoon along with us while we maneuvered toward Vegas. We became, in effect, a left flank scouting unit for our platoon.

Soon we found two Marines standing in the lee of a five to six foot outcrop of rock. One was a captain, the other a Technical Sergeant. The captain had that same stupefied stare that I had seen before. He was talking into the handset of his radio, but the wire was not connected to anything. The radio was not to be seen. He never stopped talking. The sergeant had his arm around the captain's shoulder and gave us a long, sad look before turning back to his companion. They were the last Marines not of our company that we saw.[30]

Four hours into the battle, at 1730, Fox Company 2/7 was committed with orders to advance through the companies already engaged and to continue the attack. At the forward assembly point, the 1st and 2d Platoons formed into battle order for the attack on Vegas. The 3d Platoon remained in reserve. Captain Estey gave the assault order over the radio, "My frag order is unchanged. Fox 3 move out only on my order. Radio silence is lifted. Execute! Execute! Out."[31]

Lieutenant Chenoweth describes that assault:

The loudest, sharpest sound I have ever heard is the shock wave of a 90-mm shell from a tank cannon passing 150–200 feet over head. The shell moves at more than four times the speed of sound. The shock wave was a loud, splintering "Crack!" like the sound of an entire tree trunk cracking in two. The shock wave flapped our clothes and disturbed our insides. The sound is deafening.

When the skipper gave his execute order, the tankers back on the MLR began firing overhead supporting fire directly at Vegas. When the rounds hit Vegas they caused waves to roll outward in the rocks. (Later, when I could observe the strike of the rounds, I was amazed that rock would behave that way.) The punch of the tank rounds were tremendous. The rocks actually splashed upward. The armor piercing rounds hardly made a sound when they struck the trench. There was a "Thud!" and then the silent, upward splash of rock.

We were highly gratified. The tanks were firing at the trenchline and at any bunker entrance. The sound hurt our insides but it made us feel good to know that the Chinese on Vegas were now dealing with direct fire from our tanks.

The 2nd and 1st Platoons, left and right attack units, formed with their fire teams abreast, began running and maneuvering up the low hillside of Vegas. We moved into the assembly area and sat down.[32]

The assembly area where the 3d Platoon waited was hidden in a small valley at the edge of rice paddies on the slope of Vegas. Although the men could not see the rocky ridgeline of the outpost, they watched as the 1st and 2d Platoons began their ascent. Situated as they were in that small gully, they were in defilade and out of sight of the enemy. Consequently, the men received no mortar fire and were able to observe the beginning of the assault in relative safety.

The two assault platoons advanced in a wide skirmish line and maneuvered up the shrubby hillside of lower Vegas until they disappeared from sight. Chenoweth's 3d Platoon awaited orders to move out. While the men waited, they listened. They heard the popping explosions from hand grenades and police whistles; the sharp, shattering rounds of tank fire; the ripping sounds of burp guns; and the ponderous rhythm of BARs accompanied by the intermittent firing of individual M-1 rifles. Interspersed with the sounds of small arms were those of incoming mortar rounds, both Chinese and American. Machine guns both far away and close at hand sounded their continuous authoritative staccato. Around the waiting men, the sounds of war continued—a symphony of death.

Fortunately for their nerves, if not for their health, orders were not long in coming. The company executive officer trotted up beside Chenoweth, and they conferred. Chenoweth was to move his platoon into position at the edge of the paddy; it was being committed to the battle. His orders were to join the 1st and 2d Platoons on the hillside. Chenoweth continues his narrative from the time that his platoon enters the battle. He is more comfortable speaking in the present tense as he relives those events:

> Radioman Crouch and I, and Sergeant Towne are behind the center fire team of the first squad. The three fire teams of Corporal Warg's third squad are behind us and Sergeant Wynne and Sergeant Power are with Sergeant Thompson's second squad. . . .
>
> Our formation was intended to be fire teams abreast. Easier said than done, of course, as we run up the hillsides. We found the dirt bottoms of the gullies too narrow; they trap our boots. Also, the gullies don't go straight up; they twist back and forth and some are full of brush. They are not worth the trouble. We don't have mortars falling on us. Soon, we all are running up the slopes, looking right and left. The popping explosions and gunfire continue ahead of us. We clamber and run up the slopes through the brush. . . .
>
> Passing up and over the shoulder of the ridge, the ridgeline flattens out and the shrubs get thinner. The high mass of Vegas is in full view. . . . What a sorry sight Vegas is. Smashed white rock.
>
> Now for the first time I am able to observe first-hand the effect of these high velocity 90-mm armor-piercing shells. I can see the circular waves move outward in the rocks from the strike of the shell. They

Flame tank F-22 after being abandoned by SSgt. Kenneth Miller on the south slope of Outpost Hedy in January 1953. This photo was taken a year after the truce was declared. Sgt. Robert Caulkins of the 1st Demilitarized Zone Military Police Company looks over the wreck. LEATHERNECK

First Lt. Richard T. Guidera fought with George Company 3/1 on Outpost Hilda in January 1953. RICHARD T. GUIDERA

Sgt. Jess E. Meado, a machine gunner with George Company 3/1, in reserve. Meado also saw combat on Outpost Hilda in January 1953. JESS E. MEADO

Sgt. Tom McGuire (left), Item Company 3/7, and Lieutenant O'Connell, Company A, 1st Battery, Black Watch Regiment, British Commonwealth Division. In the background is a British Centurion tank. Sergeant McGuire received a Navy Cross for action in January 1953. TOM MCGUIRE

This photo of 1st Reconnaissance Company troops shows (left to right) Cpl. Arnold E. Allen, Pfc. Jack Biehl, Sgt. Allen E. Brown, Cpl. Edward E. Easton, and Pfc. Frank J. Benenati. Benenati was killed on 27 February 1953 during the fighting at Gray Rock Ridge. THE BENENATI FAMILY

Cpl. Richard L. Champagne, George Company 3/1, while in reserve behind the Jamestown Line, February 1953. Champagne was a squad leader during the fighting for Boulder City in July 1953.

RICHARD L. CHAMPAGNE

Second Lt. Joe H. Fox (left) and 2d Lt. Vince Walsh, Item Company 3/7, late February 1953. Lieutenant Walsh led the rescue effort from Outpost Dagmar that month to save a patrol that was pinned down in no-man's-land.

VINCE WALSH

The officers of Able Company, 1st Tank Battalion, in April 1953: (left to right) 1st Lt. Robert March, Capt. Ed Critchett (new commanding officer), Lt. Dick Smith, Capt. Clyde Hunter (old commanding officer), and Lt. "Herk" Harris. Hunter commanded the tank feint on Kumgok during Operation Clambake in February 1953. HANS HENZEL

Pfc. Bev Bruce, 1st Reconnaissance Company. Bruce was with the 2d Platoon, which participated in the search-and-rescue effort on Gray Rock Ridge, 27-28 February 1953. BEV BRUCE

Second Lt. James L. Day, 1st Reconnaissance Company. Day led the
search-and-rescue mission on Gray Rock Ridge. WILLIAM CLARK

Opposite: Mail call. Pfc. Chuck
Burrill, 1st Reconnaissance
Company. Burrill earned a Bronze
Star for valor and was wounded
twice during the fighting at Gray
Rock Ridge. CHUCK BURRILL

Sgt. John J. O'Hagan, Able Company 1/7, carrying a packboard and his
M-1 rifle. O'Hagan helped bring back wounded Marines from Gray
Rock Ridge. JOHN J. O'HAGAN

Sgt. Arthur Lipper III, 1st Reconnaissance Company, receiving the Purple Heart from Maj. D. H. MacDonald, company commander, in March 1953. U.S. MARINE CORPS

Opposite: Pfc. Luther R. Hudson, Fox Company 2/5, fought in the battle for Outpost Vegas, March 1953. LUTHER R. HUDSON

Above: "The Sons of
Italy." (Left to right) Pfc.
Patrick Luminello, Pfc.
Davey Armatrudo, and
Pfc. Carmine Schiapano,
all BAR men from Dog
Company 2/5, are
pictured here in March
1953. Schiapano holds a
BAR. PATRICK LUMINELLO

Above: Cpl. Tom Kennedy,
Fox Company 2/5.
Kennedy fought on
Outpost Reno and Reno
Block in March.

TOM KENNEDY

HM3 Paul N. Polley, a Navy corpsman with Charlie Company 1/5, on the Main Line of Resistance (MLR), 26 March 1953. The following day, Polley was wounded and evacuated. WILLIAM JANZEN

Opposite: TSgt. Jack Little, Charlie Company 1/5, recently off line and in reserve. Little's machine gun defense on Outpost Carson was critical in repulsing a fierce assault in March. JACK LITTLE

Above: Second Lt. Theodore Chenoweth, Fox Company 2/7, at the company command post behind the MLR. On 27 March, Chenoweth led the last assault on Outpost Vegas, successfully wresting the crest from the enemy. THEODORE CHENOWETH

First Lt. Robert March, executive officer of Able Company, 1st Tank
Battalion, pictured here in April 1953. The company command post is in
the background. March wrote the verse, "What America Means to Me"
(see p. 50). ROBERT MARCH

Opposite: Sgt. William Janzen, Charlie Company
1/5, after the Nevada Cities fighting on 29
March 1953. Sergeant Janzen saw combat on
Reno Block earlier that month. WILLIAM JANZEN

Sgt. John Camara (left), Recon Section, Headquarters Company, 1st Tank Battalion. This photo was taken in May 1953. Camara is visiting two Turkish soldiers at their command post on Outpost Vegas. The next day the Chinese overran the outpost. JOHN CAMARA

Pfc. Madison Crosby, Baker Company 1/5, on the Danish hospital ship *Jutlandia,* May 1953. Private Crosby was wounded on Ungok in March. MADISON CROSBY

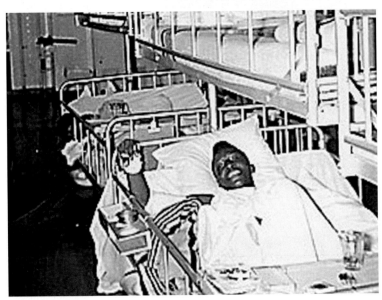

Machine gun section leaders, Dog Company 2/7, in reserve, June 1953. (Left to right) Sgt. Dennis Pryzgoda, Sgt. Robert Kreid, and Sgt. Jerry Roose. A month later, Pryzgoda and Roose were killed at Boulder City. ROBERT KREID

Cpl. Robert Hall, Weapons Company 2/5, in reserve at Camp Casey, June 1953. Hall is digging a machine gun position on the Kansas Line well behind the MLR. ROBERT HALL

Members of How Company 3/1 in July 1953 on Hill 111. From left to right, "Ski" (real name unknown), a machine gunner; George Broadhead, a wireman; and Don "Doc" Davies, a Navy corpsman. Ski is holding a Chinese "burp gun," and Davies has an M-3 "grease gun" with two magazines taped together. GEORGE BROADHEAD

Sgt. Robert R. Guertin (standing in the foreground facing the camera), Charlie Company 1/1, with the advance party to relieve the 7th Marines near Boulder City, July 1953. The other men are unknown.

ROBERT R. GUERTIN

Pfc. Alvin R. Smith, 3d Platoon, Dog Company 2/7, in Boulder City trench, July 1953. Smith is holding a captured enemy burp gun. ROBERT KREID

Reloading Able Company M-46 Patton tanks with 90-mm rounds from the company ammo dump. From left to right, SSgt. Ken Miller, Cpl. Lee Ballenger, Cpl. John Moody, and Pfc. William Abel. U.S. MARINE CORPS

While in reserve, Marines from 3d Platoon, Able Company, 1st Tank Battalion, take a dip and wash their tank in the Imjin River. JOE FERRARA

Sgt. James J. Everson, Jr., 3d Machine Gun Section, George Company 3/1, holding "Headspace," the platoon mascot. JAMES J. EVERSON

Opposite: Sgt. James R. Champlin, Charlie Company, 1st Tank Battalion. Champlin was a tank commander on Boulder City during the July fighting. JAMES R. CHAMPLIN

Sgt. Robert A. Gannon was the Irish poet laureate of the 1st Marine Division. He wrote "Sea Bags in the Rain" (see p. 16).

ROBERT A. GANNON

SSgt. Kenneth Miller (right), Able Company, 1st Tank Battalion. Miller is passing 90-mm rounds to Corporal Ballenger for loading into a tank.

AUTHOR'S COLLECTION

First Lt. Robert Montgomery, Charlie Company, 1st Tank Battalion. Montgomery was the executive officer of Baker Company while his company was attached to the Turkish Brigade in June-July 1953. ROBERT MONTGOMERY

Second Lt. Stanley Rauh, Able Company 1/7, while in reserve. Note the Able Company emblem on the hillside in the background. STANLEY RAUH

SSgt. Timothy Tobin, George Company 3/1, at the command post bunker on line. He is holding a piece of shrapnel from a round that exploded outside the bunker. Tobin fought on Boulder City, July 1953. TIMOTHY TOBIN

(Left to right) SSgt. Timothy Tobin, Pfc. Claude Wirt, Butler (first name and rank unknown), and Pfc. Edward Howze seen here in reserve. They were the machine gun section for George Company 3/1. GEORGE 3/1 ASSOCIATION

Second Lt. Robert Werckle, George Company 3/1, receiving a Bronze Star. The officer giving the award is unknown. U.S. MARINE CORPS

Pfc. Howard C. Davenport, at 1st Reconnaissance Company command post in the vicinity of Munsan-ni. Davenport was evacuated from Korea in December 1952 with severe wounds. The account of his return visit to Korea years after the war appears in Chapter 13.

are not hurled out in tiny pieces at high velocity, but in big chunks that splash upward and fall back in unison as if the rocks were water. . . .

The tank rounds are close to us. They are only 30−40 feet over our heads. The shock wave confuses us, upsets our sense of direction. We worry about them passing so closely overhead. They deafen us and push us aside or cause us to stumble. The explosions on Vegas are only a couple of hundred feet away. But, we still like them! . . .

Three Chinese soldiers, in green uniforms, are running in the main trench of Vegas from our left toward the middle of the outpost. . . . They are running for the entrance of a bunker. The tanker sees them. . . . One round hits behind the three soldiers, . . . and then two rounds hit the trench berm directly in their midst. The rocks and bodies arch up above the trench. The bodies rotate slowly through the air and fall on the slope of the trench.

When we reach the flat top of the ridge, we begin running through the men of the second platoon, lying on the hillside leading up to the communication trench.

Many are wounded. . . . I ask a Marine, where is the lieutenant? He points along the front to the west. In the shallow head of a gully nearby, the lieutenant and his staff sergeant and a Marine with a radio are kneeling and talking. Two other Marines are kneeling nearby.

The lieutenant looks up at me. I ask where are the positions on Vegas for us to relieve. I am told all around us.

. . . I report to the Skipper that we have reached the communication trench and that the second platoon has taken casualties. He orders us to move through the second platoon to the trench and on to Vegas. He advises that the Tank Commander on the MLR wants to have Fox Company direct his fire and that the Tank Commander is on the Company net. His call sign is "Alligator Six."[33]

The time was 1800. All Fox Company platoons had advanced to the lower communication trench of Vegas. Pausing to catch their breath, the men organized their drive to the main trench line, which, by then, had become a shallow ditch. The original fortifications circling the summit of the hill connecting the bunkers and fighting positions were all but destroyed. For the past few days, bombs, artillery, tank shells, and mortars had been pummeling them beyond recognition and turning defenses into white granite dust. Lieutenant Chenoweth continues his narrative describing that final push into the trench line:

Sergeant Towne's squad crosses the communication trench unopposed so, with one fire team jumping down in the trench, BAR blasting ahead, we wheel left and run along the ridge through the bushes toward a small flat area to the left front of Vegas. I called it "Little Vegas." Crouch and I press on to keep up with Towne's squad.

I will forever remember the image of the Vegas outpost, in the long light of the sunset, white, rising above us on our right, while we run on the ridge beside it. The tanks are firing at the trenchline over our heads. No enfilade fire on our right flank from any Chinese above us! The third squad follows closely behind us. Sergeant Wynne will wheel right and clear out the trench toward Rainbolt, make contact with Rainbolt's fire teams and then join us.

Grenades are thrown out of the trench at Towne's fire teams— some are duds—but we keep running right through the black clouds. I'm amazed that except for the blast, they don't do us more damage. The duds look like black and yellow toys lying on the ground. They are "potato mashers," much larger than American grenades. Burp guns fire briefly toward us. The Chinese are fast retreating to Little Vegas. Towne's riflemen are firing into the trench, and we move on but more slowly.

Sergeant Towne's squad has overrun the trench on Little Vegas. He looks back at me and gestures that there is another trench that encircles Little Vegas. I wave his squad to go to the right and to keep going up the main communication trench onto the slope of Vegas and clear out any opposition.

"Alligator 6" says that in his gun scope, he can see us on the left slope of Vegas and near the main trench. He warns that twilight will soon be gone. His tanks are still firing over Rainbolt's head.

The trench around Little Vegas is perhaps 100–150 feet in a rough diameter of a circle. This trench is less deep and narrower than the communication trench but serviceable as a combat trench. It makes a loop on the side of the communication trench that goes on to join the main trench of Vegas.

We have to get any Chinese out of that circular trench. The third squad is right behind me and I wave Corporal Warg and his squad to move past me and into the circular trench.

Then, for reasons still not clear to me now, I jumped down into the communication trench. Crouch stayed aloft because he had the radio to deal with. The trench is about 4 feet wide and maybe shoulder deep. It is dug into a granite-like rock but there is no time to examine it. . . .

The communication trench was wide. It had been dug straight but not for long runs. There were right angle turns—offsets of the straight run—every 50–60 feet. That is good. I ran toward Little Vegas and in the direction of the main trench of Vegas. I turned a corner and stepped on a dead Chinese soldier.

He wore green quilted clothing without any rank marking and had a quilted cap without a bill or visor on his head. Perhaps he was an ammo carrier. He was middle aged, partly bearded and in rigor. He had been dead 10–12 hours.

Almost blocking the trench, there was a chest-high stack of flat wooden boxes. The black letters "SKODA" and other indecipherable words were stenciled on all four sides of each box. A box lay beside the stack, its wooden lid had been thrown aside. The open box had two layers of grenades, some were missing. The grenades looked like the "potato mashers" used by the Germans in movies about WW I.

. . . Almost to Little Vegas, I ran past one spider hole. There seemed to be a dead body in it so I continued running, but as I ran down the trench and turned a corner, I saw a Chinese soldier, in green quilted clothing, climbing out.

I can't explain this. Instead of climbing out in the direction I had run past him, his head and his weapon and his entire attention was turned in the opposite direction, the direction from which I had come. He must have been confused or he was dyslexic! As he stood up in the trench and saw nothing, he turned toward me and saw me but his burp gun was still pointed the other way. He died from a .45 caliber bullet in the chest. His burp gun was lying on top of him. I wanted to get his burp gun but was anxious to join Corporal Warg and the third squad.

. . . Crouch and I run up the slope to join Towne. His troops are on the berm of the communication trench and are running up the slope toward the main trench of Vegas. Ascending the slope of Vegas, I look back to locate Wynne.

Looking eastward along the slope of Vegas, Rainbolt's fire teams are charging the main trench. In the twilight, I can see some of his troops silhouetted against the sky to the east. They have already crossed the little valley and no minefields.

Along the Vegas trenchline, a few Chinese are throwing grenades with both hands over the parapet of the trench. A Marine is standing on the berm of the main trench. His rifle is aimed downward toward the Chinese and I can see him recoil as he stands and fires again and again into the trench. Most of Rainbolt's troops are held up by the grenades and burp guns.

While all this action is going on, Wynne and the second squad have been clearing the communication trench. Some of the squad is a couple of hundred yards away. Wynne is calmly directing them while sitting on the berm, his legs dangling in the trench. The second squad seems to have finished checking out the trench toward Rainbolt's left flank. . . .

The line of Towne's squad is up to the main trench. A shower of grenades hurl out of the trench, live grenades and duds, all bouncing down the slopes, some to lie inert and others bursting in big puffs of black smoke amongst us. These grenades slow us down. This is when I got some European cast iron dust in my face and eyelids that I still carry to this day. These grenades are hard to ignore. We need to get up to that trench.

We cannot see the Chinese. Some appear for a second on their firing steps holding their burp guns high over their heads to fire a quick burst and disappear. We are running uphill. We are meeting stronger and stronger resistance. The Chinese are throwing grenade barrages down on Towne's squad and on all of us nearby. We have no grenades to throw at them. Now, we need "Alligator 6" but with the failing light he had signed off the net. It is fast getting dark.

Some men are falling or have to be helped back downhill. Using good judgment, Towne pulls his squad downhill and out of range. Towne and I, with the wounded men, fall back to the circular trench. . . .

Sergeant Wynne has arrived with the second squad. Rainbolt has pulled back from the Vegas main trench. . . .

Later, Sergeant Wynne told me that the second squad had passed the two dead Chinese soldiers. One of his Marines took the burp gun and the bandoleers of magazines to use "just in case." Both Chinese had been lifted out of the communication trench and laid nearby. After he had gotten the two squads set up around the circular trench, he had all the grenade boxes moved and some of the grenades distributed to the men. Each could only carry four or five of the unwieldy things. (He gave me and Crouch four apiece.) He used the empty boxes to make a temporary barricade in the communication trench back toward Rainbolt's Platoon. The men were alert but resting. We had minor casualties from the grenades, Corpsman [HM3 David] Porter was attending to the wounded in the 1st and 3rd squads. We are OK for .30 cal. ammo but we could always use more. The rations are OK because we haven't had time to eat. We need hand grenades.

Later, we became familiar with using the SKODA hand grenades. They were thrown at us, in abundance. The Chinese method, undoubtedly based on sorry experience, was to pull the string and throw, duds and all, not waiting to see before tossing them. On the receiving end, we didn't know which ones were the duds so we became anxious when handfuls of grenades would come tumbling at us.

. . . These infernal devices were simple to operate and, if they had been well made, they would have been a formidable weapon. A string with a metal ring on the end dangled from the hollow, yellow wooden handle. A black cast-iron cylinder about 3–4 inches long and about 4 inches in diameter was attached to the handle. The device was started by pulling on the ring which drew a match head through a black powder fuse train in the handle. The cast-iron body held more black powder.... [These were likely Soviet RPG-43 HEAT grenades, weighing about 2 ½ pounds. Effective fragmentation radius was 22 yards.]

There were about 6–8 seconds before a properly functioning grenade exploded with a loud splintering blast and a black cloud like a huge firecracker. They were dangerous but not always lethal even when they fell near you....[34]

It was then 1915, nearly dark. Fox Company organized for its final push to the summit of Vegas. Thus far, the counterattack had gone well. Captain Estey gave the platoon leaders their orders. There would be preparatory artillery fire on Vegas. When the fire lifted, the men were to attack and occupy the main trench, pursue the enemy by fire, dig in, and hold defensive positions.

Commencing at 2000, artillery preparation would last twenty minutes. When it ceased, Fox Company would attack. Chenoweth's 3d Platoon was to gain the main trench and split up, the first squad turning left and the third squad to the right. The second squad would provide overhead supporting fire. The men were tired but less apprehensive than before. They had seen the Chinese soldier and taken his measure; he was not to be feared. Hand grenades and whistles were no longer a mystery. The artillery barrage began and stopped twenty minutes later. Chenoweth continues:

Pop! Pop! Pop! Three flares began rocking back and forth above Vegas.

I stood up and Sergeant Wynne shouted, "Third platoon! Up!"

We ran the slope.... Crouch and I got almost up to the berm of the main trench before the hand grenades and burp guns began. We had surprised some of the Chinese. Towne had one fire team in the communication trench whose BAR was firing. Some hand grenades went over our heads to fall behind us and bounce downhill. We threw our supply of SKODA hand grenades at the trench ahead of us. No major effect....

The burp guns to the front of us were heavy and those fire-squirting, bottle-rocket grenades kept tumbling past our heads. Except for one.

A grenade thudded square on my chest and fell between my feet (or on my foot). The fuse was fizzing. If I kicked it away, then what? The explosion might get my head. I didn't want to bend over to grab it and throw it away for the same reason. There was no time to decide what to do. It exploded and my right foot and lower leg began to burn. I tested it. The foot and leg still worked so I had been lucky.

Mortars! Krump! Krump! To our right, along the main trench, mortar shells began exploding. If we didn't get into the main trench, we had no chance with mortars. Only part of Towne's squad had made it to the trench. The third squad was crawling up hill. That was not enough.

Krump! Krump! Krump! More mortars, now in the center of Vegas. The flares were gone. The outpost was dark. With mortars on our head, I decided that this was not going to work. I shouted to Towne to pull his squad back and get into the communication trench. I shouted for Warg to get the 3rd Squad to get back to the trench around Little Vegas. We pulled back to Little Vegas. Mortars were falling in our sector and the center of Vegas.

The mortars were regular now, 5–6 per minute but still up on the slopes of Vegas.

We had several casualties but no crisis cases, from each squad. Corpsman Porter was taxed but he tended all. . . .

Corpsman Porter looked at my right foot and lower leg. The leather boot was torn away from the sole from the arch to the big toe but the heel and the lacing were intact. The bones of the arch and the other foot bones seemed fractured or broken. There was some bleeding. No pain, only burning. Porter put compresses across the arch and reattached the boot to the sole with many bands of adhesive tape. The repair was good. It served until next mid-day.

The shin, near the knee was badly punctured. From the wound, he could see that both leg bones were splintered but otherwise seemed OK. The wound was not bleeding. A compress and more tape made all serviceable. He observed that the leg shrapnel came from a different direction than the boot shrapnel; there was a second grenade. The leg worked when I walked on it, I asked how are the other men? Mostly puncture wounds, like me, in the legs and body, some were disabled, We needed to get them off the hill. . . .[35]

The Marines had fought their way through small arms, grenades, automatic weapons, and, in many cases, hand-to-hand combat and finally through an intense mortar barrage. According to the Special Action Report, "By 1915 'F' Company 2/7 had elements of all three platoons in the lower trenches and by heavy fighting was able to remain in this position throughout the night."[36] The Marines held the reverse slope of Vegas, while the enemy held the forward slope. No one controlled the summit. By 2030, all elements of Dog 2/5, Easy 2/5, and the provisional companies not already evacuated had returned to the MLR. Fox Company 2/7 stayed behind to hold the hill.

Probes

By this time, it was plain that Outpost Vegas was central to the enemy's offensive, but the Chinese were wise enough to maintain pressure elsewhere on line, which kept the Marines on the alert and distributed over a large area. West of Vegas, the 1st Marines brought reserve units forward and prepared for the worst. About 2310, a minor probe to Outpost Kate was repulsed after a fifteen-minute firefight. Minutes later, two platoons of Chinese troops struck Outpost Dagmar defended at the time by eighteen Marines of Item Company 3/1. The attack was supported by mortar and artillery preparatory fire and a heavy volume of machine-gun fire from nearby hills.

At 0100, a nine-man Marine patrol reinforced Dagmar by entering the outpost as one side of the supporting box was lifted. This proved to be too much for the attackers, and they withdrew at 0122. Item Company reported fifteen counted enemy dead and fifty estimated dead or wounded.

Three days earlier and twenty-five miles northeast of the Nevada Cities, the U.S. Army also had been subjected to the wrath of the CCF spring offensive. On 23 March, battalion-sized Chinese forces attacked Outposts Pork Chop and Old Baldy. By the 25th, both OPs were in enemy hands, and the Army was fighting to get them back. Army 7th Division casualties numbered more than three hundred during two days of fighting on its outposts. One might speculate that the Chinese successes in those battles inspired them to try similar tactics with the Marines. Certainly, the battalion assaults on the Nevada City outposts were identical in scope, tactics, and objective to those on Pork Chop and Old Baldy.

With such widely disbursed attacks, planners at the Eighth Army level were having a difficult time in keeping up with enemy strategy and anticipating the next move. The initiative was definitely with the Chinese. UN troops could only play catch-up.

SATURDAY, 28 MARCH

Throughout the night on Vegas, enemy troops counterattacked but could not drive Fox Company 2/7 from the hillside. At 0405, Marines assaulted the summit and advanced within hand-grenade range before being pushed back. Assembling in the lower trenches, Fox Company reorganized for another assault, this time preceded by preparatory fire. Artillery, mortar, and tank fire was directed at enemy support positions and at the summit of Vegas. The men of Fox Company attacked but were again repulsed. This time, however, they returned to the MLR with a Chinese prisoner. He was a grenadier with the 9th Company, 3d Battalion, 35th Regiment. Subsequent interrogation confirmed that the original attacks on Reno and Vegas were each made in battalion strength.

Unable to regain the hill during darkness, Fox Company's 1st and 2d Platoons pulled back to a defilade position nearly 400 yards from the crest. The 3d Platoon remained at Little Vegas. The 1st and 2d Platoons counterattacked again at 0930 after another concentrated preparation by artillery, tanks, and mortars. Again, they were driven back. Advancing to within 15 yards of the upper trenches, they could go no farther against the strong enemy resistance. An item in the 29 March 1953 issue of *Pacific Stars and Stripes* notes:

> SEOUL, Mar 28 (INS)—The Marines charged up the slopes of Vegas last night and initially reported they secured the position. But a Chinese pocket held firmly to the north slope of the hill and laid down a curtain of fire that made the crest too hot for the leathernecks to hold.
>
> At last reports, Marines were crouching in their foxholes at the base of Vegas as artillery pounded the Communists on the north slope. The last attack against the Chinese positions on the north slope was made at 9:30 this morning.
>
> The Marines were subjected to the heaviest Communist artillery bombardment since last October. The Eighth Army reported Communist gunners fired almost 41,000 shells into allied positions . . . concentrating 36,000 in Marine defenses.

Until this time, air bombardment had not been employed against Vegas itself in the futile hope that the outpost could be retaken with its defenses intact. It was now apparent that this would not be the case. Defenses on Vegas would have to be reduced in order to take it, which was rather like killing the patient to save him, but defenses could be rebuilt. Consequently, Vegas was targeted for a heavy air bombardment. Within a period of twenty-three minutes, 28 tons of bombs were dropped.

At 1030, Fox Company 2/7 was relieved. Under fire, Easy Company 2/5 passed through Fox Company and slowly worked its way forward. By 1245, when the Marines were within 150 yards of the summit, supporting fire shifted to enemy assembly areas and avenues of approach from Hills 150 and 153 to clear the way for the Marines to push forward.

As Fox Company 2/7 withdrew, Cpl. Robert A. Hall, Weapons Company 2/5, was ascending the hill with a stretcher. He was part of a detail assigned to evacuate the wounded and the dead. Corporal Hall describes the toll taken on Fox Company Marines as they worked their way off the hill:

> Word was passed that F/2/7 was withdrawing from the trench area. Our platoon was told to move over to the eastern finger of the draw [Chenoweth's "Little Vegas"] and assist with casualties. We left the path and walked across the wide draw toward its other ridge. We were spread out like skirmishers. As we went up the slope on the other side, I began to see figures in the fog and early dawn light. It turned out to be 15 to 20 Marines and, as we got closer, we could see that they were all dead, victims of the first relief attempts. They were spread across the ridge and covered by a thin layer of grime.
>
> During the previous six weeks on the MLR, in a relatively stable situation, Marine policy was to remove our dead as quickly and quietly as possible. After patrols, raids, or a KIA from arty [artillery], the dead Marines were soon taken away. It might have happened only a few yards from your position, but unless you were there, the death was something that men talked about. Few actually saw the bodies. At Vegas I realized how efficient the system had been. During the Nevada's, it became evident to all involved that we were taking serious casualties. Logically, the first priorities were the wounded. The dead had to wait and so, for the first time during my experience in Korea, I saw large numbers of dead Americans. I saw a Corpsman with his medical bag open, on his knees over a man he'd been helping. It appeared they had been caught in the open. Some were crouched over as though to avoid incoming. Some had been wounded before being killed. . . .
>
> Up the ridge to the left we became aware of other groups of men moving down through the fog. They were survivors of a platoon from F/2/7. Some walked, some trotted, but they all were moving down away from the summit, off the hill. I took a stretcher up. Many of the men had "had it," but the withdrawal was orderly. I approached a group with a casualty. A corpsman was talking to a Marine with a badly mangled foot. As we put him on the stretcher, the Corpsman kept the boot propped up so that the boy wouldn't panic at the seriousness of the damage.
>
> I vividly recall a Fox Company lieutenant, one of the very last to come off in the mist. He wore a parka and was armed with only a pistol and a stick. He'd been wounded in the foot or leg and was hobbling

along on this cane in obvious pain. Over the years, my most impressive memory is that in all the confusion and his own hurt was the total lack of concern for himself and the concern for those shook-up troops. He talked to the Corpsman and reassured the wounded Marine we were carrying, who was crying by this time. The lieutenant kept turning and waiting, looking into the mist for any more people coming off the higher ground. He was in no hurry and seemed to be in command. It was his platoon and he was the last man down. I've often hoped that he made it, and that he was one who received a decoration out of the many who did. He certainly deserved it.[37]

The lieutenant was Theodore Chenoweth, the last of his platoon to leave Vegas. He had eight effectives left. Hit twice during the night, Chenoweth had grenade wounds in his foot, legs, back, and face. Walking with a stick he had picked up along the way, Lieutenant Chenoweth assured himself that his men were safe and then walked the entire distance to the MLR. He was later evacuated to Yokosuka Naval Hospital in Japan and did not walk again until May. He was subsequently awarded a Navy Cross for his actions.

Corporal Hall continues his recollections of the conditions on Vegas:

> During the 28th and 29th evac [evacuation] parties went back and forth sometimes with wounded, later with dead. What I saw was a number of men near the end of their string in the draw at the base of Vegas where the groups got back together. Troops slept, ate and "shot the shit" through the day. One CCF mortar round hit among a group heating C's [C ration] in one of the narrow gullies, killing most of them. But, for the most part, the steepness of the reverse slope of Vegas, and the height of the hill made it a relatively safe place. Only mortars could get in there. Most daylight casualties were taken in the open paddy areas between Vegas and the MLR.
>
> At the MLR end of the route our groups were using, the path led to an aid station where the wounded were deposited. The aid station was a good-sized, sandbagged bunker. We'd just place the wounded Marine that we'd been responsible for with the others on the dirt in front of the bunker alongside several others. Navy doctors or Corpsmen moved in and out administering to the casualties.
>
> ... As I sat, waiting to go back for another trip, I watched a Marine slowly, quietly die. He'd been badly hit in the upper body and was laboring with each breath. Doctors constantly checked the condition of the man and new arrivals, but he wasn't taken inside. I knew at the time what was going on, but it was years later before I formally learned the term "triage."[38]

At 1313, Easy Company reported that it was in control of Vegas but "still engaged in hard fighting." Six minutes later, the Chinese counter-attacked but failed to push the Marines off the hill. At 1455, Outpost Vegas, or what was left of it, was secure, once again in Marine hands.

Dog Company 2/7 was committed to follow Easy Company 2/5 up the hill toward the outpost. Sergeant Kreid recalls the events as he entered the battle:

> At 1230 we were told to saddle up. We were being committed to retake Vegas. When the company reached the MLR I could see the [Easy 2/5] column ahead of us, going through the barb wire gate out to what looked like a valley between our lines and Vegas.
>
> We kept meeting other Marines on the trail who were coming back from Vegas carrying their wounded and dead. Each man had a strained look on his face, like he had just seen over the mountain, and whatever was there was very bad.
>
> As we walked down the trail from the MLR, it only took a glance to see that ahead of us was a rice paddy, one large Chinese field of fire. As shells slammed in to the paddy we began to run and the more shells that fell, the faster we ran. New men like myself soon learned.
>
> Incoming shells make a quick hissing sound as they fall from the sky. If you are on your feet and hear the hiss, you have milliseconds to dive for mother earth. The bursting radius of artillery is up and out. If you are standing and a shell explodes near by, you are more likely to be hit. Hearing the distinctive hiss, we would dive to the ground—one, two, maybe three shells would explode and shrapnel whined over us. Chunks of dirt fell and we were up and running again.
>
> While crossing the paddy, I saw a bloody boot with its laces still tied, a foot was in it but there was no body. There were torn and twisted weapons, some with the stock or part of a barrel blown away. Bloody bandages were strewn along the trail. I saw a wounded NCO swearing while holding his crippled arm. He refused to be evacuated. He was yelling at an officer, "No Sir! I will not leave my people!"
>
> Finally we made it across the paddy to the base of Vegas. We moved in against the hill and were ordered to dig in. I heard our company commander on the radio a few yards from me yelling between explosions, "I don't give a damn about your other fire missions, give me counter battery fire now! This company is being cut up." In a short time Chinese fire began to slacken and we could hear our own artillery passing overhead to slam into enemy positions.
>
> Though enemy artillery fire may have been suppressed, we still had the mortars to contend with. Lying on my side, digging as fast and as deep as I could, I looked up as a shell hissed in. When it exploded, I

saw a Marine cartwheeling through the air and hit in a pile, like a rag doll. A Corpsman immediately ran to check him, but it was futile. The man was dead when he hit the ground.

Every one was hugging the ground and digging except our Corpsmen; they were upright in the fire running from one wounded man to the next. I don't know how the Navy picks its men to be FMF Corpsmen, but they are a special bunch of brave men. More shells came in, getting closer. The earth heaved beneath us and dirt was thrown high in the air. The smell of cordite and smoke was nearly causing us to choke.

One of my men yelled out, "Corpsman, over here!" A Corpsman was there immediately but the man was trashing about so violently that the Doc couldn't hold him. It took three of us to hold him down while the Corpsman put a patch over a sucking chest wound. The man was drowning in his own blood. The Doc said that he "might make it but we have got to get him out of here now." They loaded him on a stretcher and began the return trip to the MLR. I don't know if he made it or not.

Suddenly my platoon sergeant ran up to me and said, "Your section leader has been hit. You now have the section. We are pulling back the way we came. Be sure you have the entire section accounted for, bring all your casualties and weapons with you. Start now! Move!" I was shocked by the order.

Pull back? Hell we just got here, I hadn't even seen a gook. We came out here through all that fire, got shot up and now we were pulling back. It made no sense.[39]

Kreid was unaware that, shortly after 1300, Easy Company 2/5 had driven the Chinese from the summit. Now the outpost and the Marines on it were going to be subjected to even greater incoming as enemy artillery barrages would not have to avoid their own troops. Dog Company was pulled from the danger zone.

Consolidation and Defense

After Vegas was taken, Maj. Benjamin F. Lee, S-3 officer of 2/5, was sent out to organize the position for defense. Major Lee, with his walking stick, was a Marine icon of the period. Authors Meid and Yingling describe him: "At 42, he was a Marine veteran of 19 years, a former sergeant major from World War II and holder of the Silver Star and Purple Heart for service at Guadalcanal. Now he had volunteered for this hazardous duty of holding together segments of the Vegas enclave until the Marines could once again possess the entire hilltop outpost."[40] The following day, Major Lee would be carried down the hill.

Under Lee's direction, the men of Easy Company began to prepare for the counterattack that was sure to come. During the remainder of the afternoon, they dug and sandbagged trenches and fighting holes while they dodged sporadic incoming fire. Later that evening at 2015, the men of Fox Company 2/5 climbed the hill and reinforced Easy Company, which brought the garrison up to two companies. Fox Company had arrived in the nick of time. Small groups of Chinese began probing the Vegas defenses—such as they were. It did not appear to be a serious attack, and the Marines drove back the enemy after a brief firefight. At 2135 and again at 2250, the Chinese attempted more serious probes but were again driven off with effective defensive fire. A Marine flare plane remained on station throughout the night to maintain constant illumination over the area. Tank lights were used to spot targets.

The counterattack came at 2310. Approaching from Reno and supported by the usual mortars and artillery, two battalions of Chinese assaulted Vegas. The Marines fought hard to slow the advance, but Vegas was surrounded at 2348. Despite their numeric superiority, the Chinese assault failed to breach the wire. Boxing and direct fire from the MLR, coupled with fire from Vegas, created a deadly cross fire that was impenetrable. More than 10,778 rounds of artillery were fired at Chinese troops.[41] By 0100 on 29 March, the Chinese had had enough and had withdrawn with heavy losses.

SUNDAY, 29 MARCH

After falling back, the enemy reorganized and tried again to drive the Marines from Vegas. At 0033, two Chinese companies attacked, but the Marines drove them off with heavy casualties. Afterward, Chinese troops were taken under fire by artillery and mortars as they policed the battlefield of dead and wounded.

During the remainder of the night, the Marines consolidated and improved their defenses. KSC supply trains were kept busy in moving concertina wire, lumber, sandbags, engineering tools, water, rations, ammunition, and numerous other items required by the defenders. By 1050 that morning, 40 percent of the trenches were shoulder high and the remainder were waist deep. Somewhat earlier, Easy Company 2/7 had relieved Easy Company 2/5 on the position and reported that the "situation was well in hand."

Meid and Yingling report that battalion spirits were ". . . dampened, however, by loss of several Marine leaders in the early morning foray. Shortly before 0500, Major Lee and Captain Walz were killed instantly by a 120-mm mortar round during an intensive enemy shelling. Another Marine casualty early on the 29th was 1st Lt. John S. Gray. A forward observer from C/1/11, he was mortally wounded by an enemy mortar blast when he left his foxhole to crawl closer to the Vegas peak and thus better direct artillery fires on the enemy. At the time of his death, Lieutenant Gray was reported to have been at Vegas longer than any other officer."[42]

March 29 was Palm Sunday. Corporal Hall, still working with the evacuation platoon, continues his narrative:

> Coming back from one of the early evacs, it was still dark and cloudy, a couple of us met a group carrying Major Lee and Captain Walz. They were resting at the base of Vegas in the generally safe area before going across the exposed paddies to the MLR. Stretcher parties usually offered help to each other, but these men of F/2/5 wanted to make the whole journey. Under the ponchos, both officers had been decapitated by the round that had hit the CP. Major Lee was well known by most in the battalion. Their radiomen had also been killed at the same time when their CP hole had been hit.

> I have a couple of other vivid memories of Palm Sunday. One evac trip brought us back to the same supply area where the trucks had taken us on the 26th and 27th. Now there was much more evidence of the effort the battle was costing us. There were at least 20 dead Marine bodies on stretchers from the previous night's toll. We had just added ours to the poncho or blanket-covered rows and were waiting to go back to the hill. They were waiting for trucks to be taken to the rear. A jeep drove up with several officers. They were obviously staff. Their utilities and field jackets were clean and looked pressed and neat. They asked one of the corpsmen which corpses were officers; they'd probably heard of the death of Major Lee. The corpsman led them to some of the stretchers and pulled back the covering. One of these bodies had been severed near the mid-section and the stretcher-bearers, no doubt eager to evac, had placed the remains on backwards so that the upper torso was lying next to feet. The staff officers looked with quiet comments and drove away. One of them gagged and nearly threw up.

> During this same time, probably mid-morning, a Chinese prisoner was brought through the area, followed by a Marine from the OP. When the POW came upon the dead Marines lying there, he faltered. He was obviously even more nervous, looking from side to side at the

impassive enemy watching him. Then he smiled and began an ingrati-
ating shuffle, whining sound. The chaser thought he was laughing. He
cursed and pushed the Chinese; I thought he was near to shooting him,
but an officer moved in quickly, calming him and they moved on.[43]

To replace Major Lee, Maj. Joe [Joseph] Buntin, executive officer of
3/5, was sent to Vegas and assumed command of its defense. As dawn
broke and visibility began to improve, a smoke haze was placed around
Vegas to obscure the work of Marines working on evacuation of casualties. Under cover of the smoke Fox Company 2/5 retired to the MLR
to be relieved by Dog Company 2/5. In the meantime, Marine artillery
pounded suspected enemy resupply points. The artillery effort was augmented by aerial observers overhead until dusk when rain and a light
snowfall grounded the aircraft.

Typically, individual Marine morale remained high throughout the
fighting on Vegas. The Marines' training and spirit showed through time
and again during the hand-to-hand fighting in the trenches, during their
repeated frontal assaults up the slope of the outpost, and in their disci-
plined ability to follow orders and to be led by officers whom they
knew were willing to die alongside them.

In a *Leatherneck* article, M/Sgt. Robert Fugate quotes a Marine who
was on Vegas. Cpl. George Demars of Fox Company observed, "The guys
were like rabbits digging in. The fill-ins [reinforcements] gotten by the
company during the reorganization, jumped right in. We didn't know
half the people on the fire teams, but everybody worked together."[44]

Another Marine, 2d Lt. Irvin Maizlish, also of Fox Company, had the
distinction of being one of the few officers originally attached to the
company who had not been wounded or killed. He recalled, "I checked
the men digging in at Vegas. . . . I've never seen men work so hard. . . . I
even heard some of them singing the Marine Corps Hymn as they were
digging. . . ."[45]

Fugate also relates how M/Sgt. Gerald Neal of Dog Company 2/5
recalled a man reporting to his bunker in nothing but long johns:

> The remainder of his clothing had been cut away at the aid station
> to locate the many small shrapnel wounds he had suffered. Neal
> remembers him saying, "I may not be in the proper uniform but I'm
> reporting for duty and want to go back out."
>
> Another man from Dog Company wandered up to the bunker
> offering to help. He was apparently dazed from a concussion grenade.
> Neal asked, "Where have you been, son?"

"I don't know," was the answer.
"Well can you tell me your name?"
"Yeah, it's Vegas."[46]

That men could fight, face death, retain high morale, and seek out more danger is a phenomenon that defies description. Simplistically, one might attribute it to youth, but it is more complex than that. Whatever the reason, it is magnificent behavior, unmatched in any other human endeavor.

As the seesaw battle for Vegas continued, the tenacity of the Chinese army could not be underestimated. The Marine hold on Vegas was tenuous at best, and the enemy knew it. Once again, the Chinese prepared to retake the hill. At 1840, spotters observed large troop contingents heading toward Vegas from Reno and Hill 153. The show was on again.

The outpost called for boxing fire around it. Shortly afterward, two battalions of Chinese began their attack. Incoming fire on Vegas was a withering rain of steel as the enemy again surrounded the hill on three sides, left, right, and forward. Into this concentration of Chinese troops, five artillery battalions, massed behind Marine lines, poured more than six thousand rounds of high-explosive and steel shrapnel. The Marines observed another large enemy group approaching Vegas from Hill 67 to the northwest; two rocket ripples were fired into this group, and the Chinese troops all but disappeared. Even the Chinese, with their vast numbers, could not sustain casualties of this magnitude and continue the attack. The final assault on Vegas withered in place. The Battle of the Cities was over—or was it? Meid and Yingling note:

> The last direct confrontation with the enemy at Vegas occurred that morning [30 March], about 1100, when five Chinese unconcernedly walked up to the outpost, apparently to surrender. Then suddenly, they began throwing grenades and firing their automatic weapons. The little delegation was promptly dispatched by two Marine fire teams. Three CCF soldiers were killed and two taken prisoner, one of whom later died.[47]

SUPPORT OF THE INFANTRY

The Battle of the Cities was a contest of Chinese manpower versus UN firepower. The infantry strength of two battalions, heavily supported by artillery, was required to regain Outpost Vegas. The quantity and variety of firepower used to support those Marines over the four-day battle are difficult to imagine. There were three light and two medium artillery battalions, two 8-inch batteries (U.S. Army), one 4.5-inch rocket battery, two companies of 4.2-inch mortars, and a battalion of British 25-pounders. Together, they fired a total of 104,864 rounds. In addition, eighty-one flights of four aircraft each dropped approximately 426 tons of explosives in close air support missions. The Marines also fired 54,000 rounds of 60-mm and 81-mm mortar.

An example of the artillery effort was indicated by 2d Lt. Donald Spangler, ammunition platoon commander with the Marine 1st Ordnance Battalion, who had but thirteen hours of sleep during the entire five days of fighting. He proudly noted that his unit had "more than doubled the tonnage that the US Army says a man can handle in fourteen hours."[48]

As noted, Marine tanks also played a major role during the fighting. The 1st Tank Battalion's Command Diary reports:

> On the night of 26 March eleven (11) tanks were in position on the MLR ready to fire in support of an infantry raid to take place at dawn on 27 March. That night the enemy overran Reno and Vegas. The tanks, already in position and zeroed in on likely targets were thus in position to render very effective fire support. Throughout the period of attacks and counterattacks "A" Company maintained at least ten (10) in supporting fire positions at all times.[49]

The Diary also records that the tanks expended 18,425 rounds of 90-mm ammunition and 22,635 rounds of .50-caliber and 188,870 rounds of .30-caliber machine-gun ammunition.

A tanker who was on the MLR when the battle began on the evening of 26 March, and could well have been "Alligator Six," wrote:

> On the 26th our platoon had been brought up to the hill very early to lend fire support for a patrol the 5th Marines had planned that night [probably the patrol that went to Carson]. Well before dark we were held on the reverse side of the MLR waiting to be called.
>
> As it was getting dark the shit hit the fan. Surrounded with heavy incoming we buttoned up and rolled into our designated firing slot. Our position was atop the hill above the MLR, directly south of Vegas.
>
> For the next five days we slept, ate and lived in that tank. We crapped in ammunition boxes and pissed in empty 90-mm brass. We ate emergency C Rations stored inside the turret. This was one of those occasions when the infantry were quite happy to have us near by. They were getting so much incoming already that a few tanks made no difference.

Sometimes the incoming would get so severe that we would back out of the slot, or change positions to give it a rest. As we ran out of ammunition, we returned to our platoon CP for resupply and gas. On one occasion when we returned, I parked the tank, and while others in the crew ate and refueled, I grabbed a tray of hot food and dashed to the head where I sat and ate, accomplishing two functions simultaneously. Later during the operation, gas, food and ammo were shuttled to us in position so that the tanks did not have to leave their positions. By then we were rarely able to get out of the tank except to back off, take on more supplies and return to the slot to resume firing.[50]

To care for casualties, forward aid stations were established at the MLR and in makeshift facilities immediately behind the lines. Dr. William E. Beaven (USN) remembers his experience when he was a young medical officer assigned to the 5th Marines. On the last day of the Vegas fighting, Beaven found himself in a mess tent just behind the MLR that had been pressed into service as a forward aid station. The doctor and one corpsman were doing their best to keep up with the wounded men being brought in. At one point, there were more than two hundred wounded with more on the way. Doctor Beaven wrote:

By 2:00 A.M., Capt. [John] Melvin appeared through the far end of the tent flap, his arms thrown up in a gesture of utter futility. Unable to speak because of the incessant roar, he scratched out the following message, using a large black crayon: "Gooks by-passing Vegas; coming around your side. . . close to battalion strength . . . laying down smoke screen first. Can't bug out! Load walking wounded with grenades . . . send them down far path . . . pitch them into smoke screen! "

With that he abruptly turned, ran through the tent flap and scrambled back up the hill to his observation post.

It would be impossible for me to relate the emotions that went through my mind in the next few seconds: abject terror, to anger, to indignation, to a feeling of complete idiocy for having allowed myself to be caught in such an incredible position in the first place. [Medical officers were not supposed to be that close to the fighting. Earlier, Dr. Beaven had come forward to check out a proposed evacuation route and was caught up in the overwhelming need for medical care.]

Then, blessedly, a wave of compassion flooded my mind for this maimed and desecrated group of men before me. Blessedly, again, I began to reflect on the incredibly rich experiences I had accumulated, as a doctor, working with the body and spirit of men under maximum stress and hardship. I felt privileged to have witnessed the marvelous retaliatory faculties, both spiritual and physical, nature holds in reserve for the mortally wounded. It is axiomatic that he who cries most is by far the least hurt; but extending this to the extreme I had not expected to find an almost majestic dignity in the young who, though wholly conscious, are fully aware that death is but moments away.

The large cardboard on which Captain Melvin had scribbled his note to me had now been passed from hand to hand to each of the walking wounded around the tent. Their numbers were about 100. There was a moment's pause, then, spontaneously, the entire complement arose and without a word loosened the remaining hand grenades carried on their ammo belts. Deliberately, they filed out, traversed the 50 yard path to the end of the hill, entered a few yards into the thick smoke screen and pitched the grenades at the unmistakable garlic smell made by the advancing Chinese.

For more than an hour, there was a continuous procession of men jettisoning explosives down the far end of the path. The dead were stripped of all remaining grenades and loaded onto returning Marines who then returned to the edge of the smoke screen, and in a last act of defiance, hurled some 500 more grenades into the area. That was it. There was no more; and we waited for the end to come.

But the end never came. Miraculously, the screaming pitch of the artillery barrage dropped just perceptively, then dropped again, and again. The smoke screen began to drift apart, then disappeared completely. The garlic odor of the Chinese infantryman was no longer present. As if by a sign from the angels a beautiful, melodious trill from a Korean meadowlark pierced the air, and abruptly a hush enveloped the entire land.

Simultaneously, every man dropped to his knees and wept unashamedly. The Chinese had been stopped.

It was 2:30 A.M., and it was all over.[51]

Officially, the Battle of the Cities ended on the morning of 30 March. Although the Chinese had made no more attempts to retake Vegas by assault, the Marines continued to pound enemy positions with artillery and air strikes throughout the hours of darkness. Following the loss of Reno, a new platoon-strength outpost called Elko was established. The garrison on Vegas was beefed up from its former platoon strength to nearly a company, two officers and 133 men.

Also, on 30 March, the grisly business of policing the dead began. For morale and health reasons, not to mention just plain respect for fallen comrades, bodies and parts of bodies had to be removed from Vegas. Sgt. Roy ("Seabags") Seabury was part of the detail tasked with the gruesome job that night. He wrote:

> That night my fire team was assigned with about 40 KSC's (Korean Service Corps) to the body detail on Vegas. We went up to Vegas and what we were able to see was like something out of Dante's inferno. The hill was so pulverized from shell fire that you were up to your ankles in fine powder. There was the smell of dead bodies and rotting flesh and rats all over the hill. You could see shadows of Marines digging and repairing what was left of the trenchline from flares overhead. They were also digging for Marine and Chinese dead. There wasn't much left of these bodies. We put them on stretchers and the KSC's carried them to the MLR.[52]

The gamble to hold the Nevada Cities had succeeded. Against the odds, Vegas and Carson remained in Marine hands, but it had been a long shot. Reno was lost, but Elko remained. The price, however, had been high.

The Division Command Diary for March reports 169 Marines killed, 1,211 wounded, and 104 missing in action. Enemy casualties were 1,351 counted killed, an additional estimated 1,553 killed, an estimated 3,631 wounded, and 4 prisoners.[53] Beginning like a lamb, the month of March ended with the roar of lions.

CHAPTER 9
NEVADA CITY
AFTERMATH

*Infantry is the arm which in the end
wins battles. The rifle and the bayonet are
the infantryman's chief weapons.*
—British Army Field Service
Regulations, 1924

When March ended, the 5th Marines began moving off line to be replaced by the 7th Regiment. The Marines of the 5th Regiment had earned the change; their defense of the Nevada Cities outposts would be a landmark action of the Korean War.

The men remained on line for five more days until the replacement was fully effected. They used the time for work. In the first battalion sector, a new outpost had to be created to replace Reno. Consequently, on 1 April, gangs of KSC laborers trudged out and began the requisite digging for a fortified position. They created Outpost Elko, another Nevada city.

At 2021 that night, the Chinese made a token probe on Vegas. Easy Company 2/5, under operational control of 3/5, reported enemy soldiers on the forward slope of the hill. Within six minutes, a preparatory mortar barrage commenced and a Chinese platoon charged the outpost. After a fifty-minute firefight, the Chinese were repulsed. Later, the Marines drove off two more attacks as the enemy probed for weak spots and infiltration points.

For many of the men on Vegas, it was their last night; they were being relieved. The replacement was made in three consecutive nights, with a third of the men exchanged each night. By daylight of 4 April, the 7th

Marines were fully ensconced on the outpost, and the 5th Marines were on their way to reserve. There, they would enjoy a well-deserved rest while recovering from the Nevada Cities fighting. Corporal Hall remembers their arrival in reserve:

> . . . Back in the tents the cost of the last few days to our companies was another shock. We knew it had been bad, but the empty cots, the shortened chow lines told the story. Our section of the HMG Platoon had three killed and five or six wounded. The seriously wounded were evac'ed to aid stations, then sent to the Medical Battalions in the rear. Occasionally, a letter would be sent back from the hospital or the States weeks later, but frequently rumors were the only source of news about what had happened. The less seriously wounded men rejoined their units in reserve.[1]

MISSING IN ACTION

Meanwhile, the 1st Marines remained on line to defend the division center sector between Panmunjom and the Ungok hills. The 2d Battalion occupied the left, with the 1st Battalion on its right. With few exceptions, enemy contact in the area remained minimal, generally confined to minor engagements as patrols clashed in no-man's-land.

At 2100 on 5 April, Dog Company 2/1 dispatched a reinforced platoon of sixty men to set up an ambush in the vicinity of Hill 90. Five minutes before midnight, en route to set up, the platoon was ambushed by an enemy company. The lead fire team was overwhelmed by an enemy unit that opened fire from a distance of 6 feet and rushed through the team to attack the main body. Both sides used the full extent of supporting arms as artillery, mortar, and long-range machine-gun fire struck all around the combatants. A reinforcing platoon of Marines dispatched from the MLR reached the battlefield an hour later after first sweeping enemy troops from the Star, another nearby hill. Shortly, reinforcements reached the pinned-down platoon. The Chinese broke contact and withdrew, and the Marines returned to their position by 0218 on 6 April. Marine casualties were one killed, twenty-three wounded, and five missing. The reinforcing platoon returned and swept the area till daylight but discovered no sign of the MIAs.

On 7 April, in a bizarre twist, one of the missing men was recovered from the Chinese. At 0500, Easy Company on COP-2A (the Molar) reported hearing an enemy loudspeaker broadcasting in English. The message indicated that the Chinese had placed a wounded Marine in an open area and invited his buddies to come and get him. An account of what happened next is found in a *Pacific Stars and Stripes* article datelined 10 April 1953:

> . . . The 21-year old Marine, Pfc. Francisco Gonzalez Matiaz was wounded by burp gun blasts in his back and neck. . . . The dark haired rifleman said from his hospital bed that after he had been wounded Sunday in a fight near the Panmunjom Village, he didn't remember a thing "until I felt the Chinese kicking me. I figure I lay there on the ground for about three hours. I knew I was hit on the neck and the side."
>
> The Red Chinese infantrymen who found him, he said, "took me to a cave. And they beat me with the butt of their burp guns. They put the muzzles to my ribs and kept asking, 'What is the name of your company commander and the name of your squad leader?'" The Puerto Rican said the Chinese accompanied the beatings, insisting that 'you must answer all the questions we ask you.'" His captors spoke good English the thin Marine recalled. While the Reds hammered questions at him, they ripped his identifying dog tags from his neck. . . .
>
> Matiaz dimly recollected that he was dragged to another cave, near the first one and given first aid in the form of small bandages applied to his wounds. He related, "They gave me a drink of warm water, a few cookies and some cigarettes."
>
> The weary little warrior said he was held in this cave for about 12 hours. At about 6 P.M. Monday he was blindfolded. He said slowly, "They began marching me through the enemy trenches. They walked me all night until early morning. Then they put me in another cave and I collapsed again from loss of blood." The tired-toned voice continued, "The next thing I remember was that they were kicking me again. . . . They kicked me until I got up under my own power."
>
> The Reds stuffed his pockets with propaganda leaflets urging "peace" and told their victim, "Give these to your commanding officer."[2]

The *Stars and Stripes* reporter turned next to the Easy Company Marines on COP-2 for the remaining details on how Matiaz came to be rescued from his captors:

> . . . The Chinese apparently returned and placed the unconscious Matiaz on a stretcher in a Korean graveyard about 700 yards from Panmunjom. The Reds turned on their front-line loudspeakers and blared, "All attention. All officers and men, we have information for you. We have one of your wounded. Send two men as soon as possible forward of your left flank position. Everything was done for him that

was possible. We will allow you to come as far as the defiladed area without firing on you."

Marine outposts, peering through an eerie Tuesday morning fog, finally spotted a figure dressed only in a sweater and long winter underwear lying on a stretcher.[3]

A reconnaissance of the area surrounding Matiaz revealed the strong possibility of an ambush. Still, a recovery effort had to be tried. At 0925, a platoon from Fox Company was dispatched to get closer. Arriving within shouting distance, a Puerto Rican member of the patrol called out to Matiaz in Spanish and asked if he could walk. Matiaz waved an acknowledgment and staggered up. Struggling toward the outpost, he collapsed twice. Seeing him fall the second time, the patrol leader, Lt. Ken Clifford, shouted, "Oh hell! Let's go get him." Accompanied by four Marines, the officer ran out to Matiaz and brought him in while the Chinese held their fire. In addition to his original wounds, Matiaz had bruises to his legs and body. On reaching COP-2, he was evacuated.

The *Stars and Stripes* account concluded by reporting that, soon after midnight, the loudspeakers shouted again, "'Did you get your wounded buddy treated by us? What do you think of it? Write a letter and drop it at the base of the hill.' At last report the Marines had not replied."

After returning Matiaz to COP-2, the Fox Company patrol found a Marine's body and returned it to the MLR. Investigation revealed that the body was from a previous engagement in the area on 21 March. Later that night, four more bodies were located by a Dog Company patrol searching for the remaining MIAs of 5–6 April. In all, seven missing Marines were recovered on 7 April, and the 2d Battalion was able to account for all of its people.

LOUDSPEAKER WAR

Because the Outpost War remained static along relatively fixed lines, techniques of psychological warfare between the Chinese and the Americans became common across the area. Likely, the most highly developed "psy war" tactics were the loudspeaker broadcasts engaged in by both sides. Each was trying to convince troops on the other side of the futility of their own cause and the righteousness of the enemy's. The release of Private Matiaz was such an effort that was facilitated by the loudspeaker blaring out across the valley from one outpost to another.

The Chinese often broadcast hackneyed, comic opera speeches to the Marines in an attempt to convince individual Marines to surrender.

There is no record of any Marine ever succumbing to such enticements. As a matter of fact, most of the men found them to be entertainment, comic relief from the day-to-day monotony of living in dirt and mud.

A message, typical of the sort broadcast by the Chinese is repeated in Martin Russ's book, *The Last Parallel:*

> . . . "Ike is one of the leaders who could bring peace in Korea, but like the rest of the big-money boys, he is not interested in peace."
>
> A woman sang a song, a very sentimental piece but quite moving, "The Last Rose of Summer." I looked back at the other three men and could see the outline of their brush-covered helmets. They were listening too, not aware of each other and maybe for a moment unaware of the surroundings. When the song ended, a woman said, "Did you enjoy my song Marine? If so fire your rifle twice and I will sing another." A wag on the MLR fired an extremely long burst from a machine gun. It echoed for several seconds. A few miles to the east, in the Army sector, five or six parachute flares hovered above the mountains. Artillery rumbled in the distance, a kind of muffled thunder. The woman sang another song. It was unfamiliar, a semi-art song. This was followed by a haunting, 1920-type number played by an American dance band of that period. I listened hard for the sound of Bix Beiderbecke or at least Henry Busse. It may have been Whitman.
>
> I had an imaginary picture of the Chinese nearby, listening to the record, thinking how well it must typify the atmosphere of money-mad capitalist, warmonger infested modern America. Poor bastards really do need a new propaganda system. . . .[4]

With Chinese propaganda this poor and being ridiculed by the very people they were trying to convince, one wonders what the Chinese mind may have thought of American propaganda efforts. Were they any better?

Eighth Army psychological warfare units had cooperative South Korean and Chinese prisoners of war speaking over the loudspeakers to avoid American accents and syntax. "Psy war" people believed that this would make the messages seem more personal. Both sides tried to direct their messages to specific units and hoped to demoralize the troops by seeming to know names and units. A typical American message might greet a newly assigned enemy unit with: "Hello soldiers of the 340th Regiment, welcome back to the war! Sergeant Choi and Corporal Peng, what are your loved ones doing at home tonight? They will surely grieve when you fail to return." Nostalgic music, intended to make the soldier homesick, blasted out across the terrain from various UN positions. At night, eerie sounds were projected in the hope of playing on simple superstitions. Author William B. Breur reported:

> Two C-47 aircraft of the U.S. 21st Troop Carrier Squadron were equipped with loudspeakers mounted on their bellies. Designated "the Speaker" and "the Voice," the C-47's flew five thousand feet above Communist lines and blared propaganda messages about surrendering and empty stomachs and certain death. Flying loudspeakers often used South Korean WACs to gain propaganda mileage from an Oriental prejudice. It was humiliating to the Chinese and North Korean soldiers to have a woman fly back and forth over their front line without being shot down.
>
> On one occasion, "the Voice" called on a large Chinese group to surrender. Then the speaker said a smoke screen would be laid in front of its position by UN artillery and urged them to run through it to safety. The smoke screen was needed to protect surrendering soldiers from being shot by their own officers. Several Communist soldiers did bolt through the smoke to UN lines.[5]

If numbers of surrendered soldiers were a measure, it appears that American efforts at propaganda were far more effective than the Communist counterparts. The UN's POW camps in southern Korea were overflowing with Communist prisoners.

It became axiomatic with the outpost war that the Chinese army was unable to sustain an offensive for much longer than five days. This was not American bravado; it was a practical conclusion based on the fact that the Allies retained absolute control of the air. Chinese supply lines were lengthy and primitive. War materiel, moved by truck, train, and coolie labor, could travel only at night and in bad weather. On clear days, transportation in North Korea would lie doggo, hidden from the prying eyes of UN bombers and reconnaissance pilots. Hence, supplies to support an offensive—ammunition, food, medicine, and replacement personnel—arrived in a trickle. Then, they had to be hidden and stockpiled until the necessary accumulation was reached to support an offensive. Typically, such a process might take several months and, if used generously, would be depleted in three to five days of fighting.

The axiom was confirmed once again with the Nevada Cities fighting in March. Prior to that time, the last major action initiated by the Chinese was at the Hook in October 1952. Then came the attack on 26 March that lasted five days. If the Chinese were true to form, April should be a cakewalk. They had just lost more than 6,500 men and used tons of ammunition. How much more could they have stockpiled? Enough, it seemed, for another try at Outpost Carson on 9 April.

THAT EVIL LITTLE ISLAND

During the last six months of the war in Korea, Sergeant Bob Kreid fought on three outposts, Vegas, Carson, and Boulder City. Of these, he believed Carson to be the toughest experience of his life. It was there that he learned to conquer fear. Sergeant Kreid writes:

> To explain what Carson was like to me, I need to tell a short story about an unforgettable person I ran into one night in the States. I had been out of boot camp about eight months and assigned to the newly formed 3rd Marine Brigade at Camp Pendleton. I had been to a movie one night in San Clemente and stopped at the Sea Shore Cafe to get a cup of coffee before going back to Tent Camp Three. I sat down by what I thought was just another Marine enlisted man and said, "Hi." He turned and I thought, "Oh my God." I had sat down by a Marine Warrant Officer.
>
> Pfc.'s did not just go around saying "Hi" to Warrant Officers. Only God and field grade officers said "Hi" to them. To make it worse, he had been drinking and was carrying a pretty good load. When he turned to me, I saw five rows of ribbons covered with battle stars. I recognized the Navy Cross and Purple Heart with a star. I do not think he ever looked past my Pfc. stripe and said, "What do you know about it you God damn Boot." I replied, "Nothing sir." He spoke into his coffee cup. "I lost eighteen just like you on Iwo. Evil Little Fucking Island." With that I replied, "Yes sir! I am sorry sir." I left my coffee and got the hell out of there.
>
> It had been six years since Iwo Jima, but his Evil Little Island was there, tormenting his mind, remembering the eighteen young Marines he had lost on that island. Outpost Carson would become for me what Iwo Jima was to that Warrant Officer. In no way am I trying to compare a small platoon size hill in Korea to the epic battle of Iwo Jima where almost 6,000 Americans lost their lives taking it and over 20,000 Japanese died defending it. Yet, like the Warrant Officer, Carson was my "Evil Little Island." It stayed with me the rest of my life. [6]

In Korea, Kreid first laid eyes on his "Evil Little Island" through field glasses from the MLR in April 1953. He describes what he saw:

> Carson was approximately 900 yards to our left front. Through field glasses it looked like a city dump from all the refuse scattered

around. There was certainly no reason to hide the fact it was an out-post. It was so far out into Chinese territory every gun they had within range had long since been zeroed in on it. I could see geysers of dirt being blown into the air by exploding shells. Our platoon leader told us that if the garrison on Carson needed help, we were the platoon that would go. Also our platoon was to furnish a patrol twice a week escorting a supply train of KSC's out to the hill and back.

Our platoon Sergeant, a WW II veteran, told me, "Kreid, You go out to Carson every time you can with the gook train, and while you are there learn as much as you can about the bunkers, automatic weapon positions and fields of fire. Learn everything you can that might help us if we are ever sent out to retake it. I have a bad feeling about that hill." Hearing this from my platoon sergeant only added to my growing anxiety about Carson.

I learned a lot on my first trip out to the hill, none of it good. The winding trail made it well over 1,000 yards. It was a hill too far to reinforce in time to keep the platoon size garrison from being over-run. Reinforcements could too easily be ambushed on that winding trail on their way out.

With the loss of Outpost Reno in late March, the Chinese now controlled the high ground. This alone, it seemed to me, was reason enough for the Gods at I Corps Headquarters to declare Carson unten-able or retake Outpost Reno—they did neither. I told my platoon sergeant that Carson did not have enough barbed wire around it and there were not enough automatic weapons, especially on the west side where the attack would probably come. He told me he would talk it over with our platoon leader.[7]

On the afternoon of 8 April, the enemy began a slow, consistent preparatory fire on Carson and the MLR. Incoming fire continued throughout the afternoon until late evening when it shifted entirely to the outpost. In a Special Action Report, the 1/7 Command Diary recorded: "The mortar and artillery fire was very accurate and resulted in reducing much of the trench line on the north portion of the outpost in addition to knocking out the CP and two machine gun positions. The incoming continued throughout the night at a consistent rate of about one round/minute."[8]

The first sign of an assault on Carson was noted at 0315 when a lis-tening post on the forward slope reported movement across its front, west to east. Fifteen minutes later Outpost Elko reported movement between its position and Carson. Simultaneous with the Elko report, incoming fire on Carson increased sharply to a very intense barrage. The assault had begun.

Chinese soldiers stormed the north side of the hill in two groups, 100 yards apart. Easily breaching the wire, which had been severed in numerous places by the preparatory fire, the Chinese entered the trenches with the Marines, and hand-to-hand fighting erupted. The fight raged at point-blank range as enemy soldiers tried again and again to dislodge the defenders.

The platoon defending Carson was led by 1st Lt. George Yates. Though wounded early in the assault, Yates continued moving about his perimeter to check positions and provide encouragement to his men. As the enemy attained the trenches, he participated in the hand-to-hand struggle and personally killed several of the enemy. Taking advantage of a slight lull in the fight, Lieutenant Yates reorganized his few remaining men into a perimeter defense and called for protective mortar and artillery fire. When the enemy penetrated the other flank of the hill, he ran through the incoming fire to engage in more hand-to-hand fighting.

Meanwhile, at the Baker Company CP behind the MLR, communication with the outpost was lost except from a mortar forward observer. Boxing patterns were fired, and illumination flares lit up the area. By 0443, a flare plane was on station and dropping long-burning parachute flares.

More important, at 0500 a platoon from Dog Company 2/7 was dispatched to reinforce Carson. Sergeant Kreid was on phone watch in the platoon CP. He recalls:

> . . . [T]here was a call from battalion for our lieutenant. I gave him the phone and heard him say, "Yes sir, I'll be right there." In about 20 minutes, the phone rang again, the platoon sergeant answered and said, "Yes sir," and "Aye Aye sir." Then he looked at me. "Get your people ready to move and take extra ammo." I knew without question where we were going. The sergeant said, "Battalion has lost radio and phone contact with Carson."
>
> Ten minutes later the platoon was assembled at the Carson gate, the trail that led out to the hill. We were told that we would be moving fast, for it would be daylight soon. The night air was cold in April with frost on the ground. About halfway out it started to get gray in the east. We passed through a cut or what we call in Texas, a draw. With high ground on each side I rubbed my finger across the safety

of my rifle and thought of something I had heard my mother say, "Fools walk where angels fear to tread."

By this time it was light enough, I could see the outline of Carson about 200 yards away. The Chinese saw us too, and fired. When the incoming arrived, the earth seemed to buckle under me, and I was knocked down by the concussion. Rounds hit so fast the explosions melded into a roar. It was as if the earth was being blown apart. Shrapnel whined inches over our prone bodies. Chunks of rock and dirt fell from the sky. The earth heaved beneath me as I was trying to press myself into the rocky ground, anything to escape that maddening fire storm. I could hear the cry, "Corpsman, Corpsman Get Up Here!" I tried to fight back the terror that I could feel building inside of me. I began to cough because the smell of cordite was choking. We had been shelled at Vegas and I had been able to handle my fear, but this was so much worse. I could taste the fear in my mouth. It tasted metallic, like brass. I just knew the next shell would hit me between the shoulders and there would not be enough left to send home. My courage failed me that morning with my face in the dirt.

Then the command was passed back to move out. I wanted to scream, "No! We will all be killed!" I looked from beneath my helmet in time to see a Marine ahead of me jump up and start to run forward. The spell was broken, and I was up and running, yelling to my men, "Move Out!" I looked and my section was following. It was one of the proudest moments in my life. Marine discipline had taken over when my own discipline had failed. God bless every one of those mean ass Drill Instructors back in boot camp. Bless them for screaming, hitting, intimidating us into action. Teaching us to obey.

The shells still fell, but not as fast. After I was up and running, my fear was replaced by a strange high. It felt good to be alive and living on the edge. All at once, I saw Marines coming back from Carson yelling, "Pull back, pull back. Gooks are on Carson. Pull back to Elko and set up a base of fire." That made sense because we sure as hell could not attack Carson in single file.

It took awhile because the wounded and dead had to be taken with us. I stopped to help two Marines get a wounded man onto a stretcher. He had been hit in the crotch and was bleeding badly. I remember thinking, "Whata hell of a place to get hit." We left him behind on Elko with a corpsman.[9]

Records show that, as dawn came, the men on Elko watched Baker Company Marines on Carson throw grenades at the enemy while engaging in hand-to-hand fighting. Miraculously, the platoon on Carson was holding, but it badly needed reinforcement. Lieutenant Yates was still alive and attending to his men despite the enemy's incoming fire. Then his luck ran out. An exploding shell mortally wounded him while he was trying to reach yet another casualty. Yates was posthumously awarded a Navy Cross.[10]

The Dog Company platoon, now on Elko, had been too badly mauled to reinforce Carson effectively, so a platoon from Easy Company 2/7 was the next group to try. By 0800, the platoon reached the base of the hill and, ten minutes later, attained the crest. On reaching the defenses, the platoon found that Baker Company retained control of the hill and had defeated the attackers. Accompanying the Easy Company platoon as it arrived were the Dog Company machine gunners. Among them was Sergeant Kreid:

> The moment we left Elko the Chinese could see us. They still shelled us but nothing like that opening barrage. We crossed over to Carson, one and two at a time. I was about halfway across when two shells hissed in on Carson. One hit a winter sleeping bag and feathers flew high in the air as if it were snowing. As I passed through the wire into the trenches, I saw a dead Chinese soldier hanging across the barb wire.
>
> Carson had been so heavily shelled that most of its five and six foot trenches were caved in to about three and four feet. Just then a shell hissed in and I dove for the ground.
>
> . . . I came across a bunker that had caved in. I could see two legs sticking out with a pair of boots. I started to dig, removing the sandbags one at a time until I could see the bottom of his flak jacket. I knew he was dead, because his legs were stiff. I dug a little further and could see part of his right shoulder and arm. I thought I was getting used to blood and death, but I certainly was not prepared for what I found. I ran my hand through the arm hole of his flack jacket and pulled hard. The body came free and I sat there frozen.
>
> Mother of God! The man's head and neck were gone even with his shoulders. Something inside of me died. Sitting there on my knees, holding a headless corpse.
>
> I yelled at one of my squad leaders for help. His first name was Dennis [Pryzgoda] and we had become good friends. The pair of us lifted the body out of the sand bags and placed it on a stretcher.
>
> What happened next can only be explained as blind luck, or Divine Providence. Dennis and I bent over at the same time to pick up the stretcher. The instant our heads passed below the top of the trench a mortar round hit five feet from the edge of the trench where we had been standing. They say you never hear the shell that gets you;

we sure never heard that one. The concussion knocked both of us down onto the body. I buried my face in the stretcher and held onto the body's legs expecting another shell to follow. Dennis, disregarding his own safety, was up and by my side shaking me. I looked up and could see his mouth moving, but all I could hear was ringing in my ears. I nodded that I was okay. This fine young sergeant would be killed four months later on a hill called Boulder City.

A stretcher team of four KSC's was carrying a Marine KIA from Carson to Elko. A Marine was ahead leading the way when a far off machine gun fired. One Korean was hit in the back of his helmet and went down. The other three Koreans dropped the stretcher and ran. The Marine turned and hit a fleeing Korean with his rifle butt. Then the gun fired again and the Marine went down like he had been pole axed.

Dennis and I watched from Carson and ran to help the fallen Marine. We were halfway there when he got to his feet and staggered around like he was drunk. The bullet had ricocheted off the top of his helmet knocking him momentarily senseless. Dennis and I placed the KIA back on the stretcher. The machine gun would fire small bursts now and then, but the bullets were snapping high above our heads. Dennis asked, "What about the Gook?" I said, "To hell with him. His buddies bugged out and left him knowing he was hit. We will send them back to get him." We carried the Marine KIA to Elko. Our lieutenant asked, "Is that all the Marines off Carson?" I said, "Yes sir, all we could find except for a wounded KSC on the trail that is about half scalped." The lieutenant said, "He will have to be brought in." I said, "Sir, those three Gooks over there dropped this dead Marine and ran when their buddy was hit. Can't they go get him?" The lieutenant gave me that look that said, "Sgt., you have said enough." I said, "Yes sir" and made ready to go. A corpsman spoke up and said, "I'll go too." We went back and got the Korean. Checking him over, the corpsman said he would live.

The day had cost our platoon two killed and ten or more wounded, some seriously. I do not know how many KIAs and wounded the platoon had that was overrun, but it was a lot. Its casualties had been taken back to the MLR from Elko all during the day. The Marines on Carson had put up a hell of a fight. There were dead Chinese from one end to the other. It looked as if they had attacked the hill from three sides.

We picked up our dead and started back to the MLR. We were tired, dirty, bloody and sad. We took turns carrying stretchers with the handles on our shoulders. During my turn I felt something running down my arm. Dark blood had soaked through the stretcher and was running down on my arm. I whispered, "Lord God my Father, please help us through this day." He must have heard, because there were trucks waiting behind the MLR to take us to hot showers, clean clothes and a hot meal.

Like the Warrant Officer at the Sea Shore Cafe, I have never forgotten. Carson became my "Evil Little Island."[11]

The 1/7 Special Action Report indicates that successful defense of Carson was attributed to Marine artillery and mortar support, which totally prohibited enemy reinforcements from reaching the hill.[12] Because enemy artillery prohibited Marine reinforcements from reaching the hill as well, however, it would appear that the successful defense of Carson on 9 April more rightly should be attributed to the tenacity and valor of the men from Baker Company, 7th Marines.

The Marines sustained casualties of eleven men killed, sixty-four wounded, and three missing. Enemy casualties were sixty-five men counted killed and ninety estimated killed, with wounded estimated at seventy-four.

For three more days, Chinese troops attempted to take Carson. Like the 5th Marines before them, the men of Baker Company 1/7 were determined not to lose the outpost and fought back with massive doses of firepower. Unlike Vegas, the infantry did not have to assault and reassault the hill. Reinforcements were sent out, but much of the defense was accomplished with supporting arms.

Platoons of Able Company tanks, which were still on line from the Vegas fighting, returned to their firing slots on the MLR and again provided support. Elements of Baker Company tanks were brought up from forward reserve and, aided by tanks from the 7th Marines' Anti-Tank Platoon, expended nearly fifteen hundred rounds of 90-mm firepower. Throughout the month of April, Carson and Vegas remained in Marine hands.

AMBUSH

To the west, the 1st Marine outposts were also probed each night, and numerous small firefights and corresponding casualties resulted. On 15 April, the 3d Battalion replaced the 2d Battalion on line in the left sector. The following morning, Marines on Outpost Marilyn captured a Chinese soldier who was subsequently delivered to the Regimental S-2 (intelligence section) for interrogation and processing. Later that night, a George Company reconnaissance patrol was fired on by an enemy machine gun while the Marines were crossing the old tank road in front of Outpost Kate. The patrol countered by calling in mortars on the gun position.

During the early morning of 17 April, George Company 3/1 set out again, this time on an ambush patrol led by 1st Lt. Jack McCoy. The thirty-three man patrol, leaving the MLR on a moonless night, followed a well worn trail north into no-man's-land. At 0045, about halfway between the MLR and Outpost Kate, the Marines were ambushed. An enemy skirmish line, well deployed along a paddy on their left flank, opened up with machine guns, burp guns, and hand grenades. The range was close, and the Chinese took the Marines totally by surprise and decimated the patrol. One of the first Marines to be killed was Lieutenant McCoy. He died while speaking on the radio with Lt. Richard Guidera at the George Company CP. Guidera wrote:

> While I talked to Jack McCoy by radio, I could hear much confusion at the ambush site. He was asking for 81 mm mortar support and telling me the location of the patrol when communication stopped. His PRC 6 [a walkie-talkie radio affectionately called a "prick six"] went dead; he had been hit and evidently was killed instantly. . . .
>
> Jack had been a good and courageous man. It was a shock to hear him alive and vital, talking to me at one moment, and then not at all a moment later.[13]

With the death of Lieutenant McCoy, leadership fell to Sgt. Jess E. Meado. In the chaos, Meado organized the group and returned fire. Being ambushed in combat is not something that one readily forgets—the noise of burp guns, flying bullets, hideous explosions from grenades bursting among men, and a machine gun relentlessly sweeping back and forth. Men dived for the ground while others lay there dead or wounded. Sergeant Meado's recollection of that morning remains clear:

> . . . Next, they threw mortars right on top of us, wounding many more men. I too, was hit again but managed to take over the patrol when I learned Lt. McCoy and our platoon guide had been killed. We forced the enemy to withdraw and began looking after our wounded.
>
> Reinforcements finally arrived. Some of our men made it back to our lines on their own, but others had to have help. We had begun with a thirty-three man patrol, of which twenty-six were wounded and three killed. Those killed were Lt. John McCoy, Sgt. Homer Anderson and Pfc. Frouiler Cabera-Gonzalez from Puerto Rico. The front four men of the patrol were the only ones not wounded.[14]

At 0112, a green signal flare was fired from the vicinity of enemy-held Hill 64, and the ambush broke contact and charged through the Marine platoon toward its own lines. The Chinese left five men killed and carried away seven more. Their wounded were estimated at about fourteen.

For his part, Sergeant Jess Meado was awarded a Silver Star.

RECONNAISSANCE COMPANY RETURNS

Following the disaster on Gray Rock Ridge, the Division Reconnaissance Company had been organizationally ineffective. The first two weeks of March were spent recovering, reorganizing, returning the minor wounded, and obtaining replacements. New men, volunteers from the regiments, joined the company. All of the new arrivals had patrol experience and knew how to handle themselves in combat, but they had to train together and get to know one other. The last two weeks of March were spent in rear area patrols, honing skills, searching for infiltraters, and accustoming the newer men to the ways of Reconnaissance Company.

Beginning in April, patrols in front of the MLR began again; many were one- or two-platoon size. Although they invariably found evidence of enemy activity, the patrols seldom became engaged in combat. An exception occurred on 7 April when Patrol 99, consisting of thirty-nine men, departed COP-1 (Nan) in the KMC sector near Panmunjom. An hour and forty-five minutes later, they were fired on by what they believed to be irregular troops using American weapons. The patrol leader reported the familiar sounds of M-1 rifles and M-2 carbines, rather than the distinctive action of the Chinese PPSH "burp gun." He also noted that the enemy attempted to maneuver in such a fashion as to get between his patrol and the neutral corridor, thereby forcing the Marines to fire into the forbidden zone. Because of this tactic, the patrol broke contact. In his report, the leader, concerned about the resumption of peace talks at Panmunjom and in order to avoid an incident, "strongly recommended that no further patrol activity be carried out in this area."[15]

The recommendation was rejected. On 12 April, another patrol in the KMC sector was not as fortunate. Leaving Outpost Nan at 2005, thirty-nine Marines made contact with the enemy two hours later. Eighteen to twenty Chinese soldiers were lying in wait. The ambush was brief, fifteen minutes, but it was long enough to wound five Marines. After evacuating the casualties, the platoon returned to the scene of the fight to search for three men who were unaccounted for. Searching through the night, no trace was found until first light when, at 0530, two of the missing men were found in a shallow trench. Pfc. Horace Alford was dead, and the other man was wounded. Continued searching failed to locate the third missing man. On orders of the company commander, the platoon discontinued the search. Cpl. Zachary Piercy was never found.

Although Reconnaissance Company was back in the war, it was not yet as effective as it once had been. The men were still learning to work as a team. Patrol 120 was a disappointment. On the night of 18 April, thirty-seven men left the MLR from 1/7's area for the purpose of setting an ambush. En route, they engaged an enemy squad, killed two Chinese, and wounded three, but three Marines were evacuated for wounds. The patrol reorganized and continued forward. It deployed a squad on "Kirby," a small piece of high ground near the Ungok hills. On hearing noise, another squad went out to investigate, and soon another firefight took place. The Marines overran the Chinese position, killed five men, and wounded four, but four more Marines suffered minor wounds.

Continuing on, the patrol took up its ambush position at 0031 (now 19 April). The patrol leader sent two squads to organize a blocking position. About 25 yards away from the ambush position, the point squad leader fell and twisted his ankle. Returning to the ambush position to seek a corpsman, he was mistaken for the enemy and shot by one of the Marines. He survived but required evacuation to the rear. With help from men of 1/7, the patrol and all of its wounded retired to the MLR at 0315.

It was evident that the meticulous, one-step-at-a-time patrol techniques practiced by the recon Marines before Gray Rock were no longer in effect. The new men, though experienced, had a lot to learn about stealth and observation. They would learn, but the knowledge would come at a price.

OPERATION LITTLE SWITCH

Probably the most significant event of April, Operation Little Switch had little to do with outpost fighting. Humanitarian in nature, it was very good news for 18 Marines and Navy corpsmen, 471 South Koreans, 195 other American and UN troops,[16] and well over 6,000 Chinese and North Korean troops. Operation Little Switch was the mutual exchange of sick and injured prisoners between Communist and UN forces. Qualified prisoners of war were released to their own countries.

On 22 February, the U.N. commander, Gen. Mark W. Clark, had a letter delivered to North Korean and Chinese leaders through the Indian ambassador. Clark called for the immediate exchange of ailing prisoners. As expected, the reply was a loud silence. Peace talks had been stalemated since October 1952 when neither side could agree on anything. Then, on 5 March, the Communist hierarchy worldwide was stunned by the sudden death of Soviet Premier Joseph Stalin, which was followed by the creation of a new government in Moscow. On 28 March, an unexpected response to General Clark's query was received at UN Command in Tokyo. Korean and Chinese leaders agreed to the unconditional exchange of "sick and injured prisoners." After details were worked out, a week-long transfer of selected POWs was scheduled to begin on 20 April at Panmunjom.

Communist forces announced that they would release 600 prisoners, and the United Nations Command was prepared to release more than 6,000. Following negotiations, the numbers grew to 684 and 6,670, respectively. (Although the numbers appear enormously lopsided, they actually reflected about 5 percent of all POWs held by either side. In all, the UNC held 132,000 prisoners and the Communists held 12,000.)[17] As further evidence of a change in attitude, Communist and Allied representatives also agreed that truce talks would be resumed at Panmunjom after the prisoner exchange was completed.

UNC staging for the prisoner exchange would occur at Munsan-ni, with the actual transfer 10 miles to the northwest in Panmunjom. Because the area was entirely within the 1st Marine Division sector, the bulk of preparations and security fell to the leathernecks. In little more than one day, elements of Able Company, Shore Party Battalion, with help from H&S and Dog Companies of the Engineer Battalion erected the entire Freedom Village compound, a three-part complex:

> The command area comprised receiving lines, processing and press tents, and related facilities for United Nations troops. . . . Across the road from the UN site proper was the area reserved for South Korean prisoners, who would form the bulk of repatriates.
>
> Altogether the three camp areas represented some 35,100 square feet of hospital tentage, 84 squad tents, and five wall tents. Gravel to surface three miles of standard combat road, plus two miles of electrical wiring, was hauled and installed. More than 100 signs, painted in Korean and English, were erected. . . .
>
> Special area for ambulance parking; helicopter landing strips; five 50-foot flagpoles; graded access roads and foot paths; sanitation facilities; and storage areas for food, blankets and medical supplies were also constructed. . . .[18]

In addition to physical preparations for receiving prisoners, security arrangements were also augmented. The rescue task force on COP-2 was reactivated so that a tank and elements of a reinforced Marine rifle company could race into Panmunjom if needed. A platoon of tanks was moved to Hill 229 immediately behind the MLR and adjacent to the Neutral Corridor. Provisional platoons of 5th Marines were formed and placed on five-minute alert to respond as might be needed. Numbers of Military Police were increased at Panmunjom itself, and the road network in North Korea was placed under constant air surveillance by UN aircraft. As the humanitarian convoy of vehicles proceeded south from the various prison camps, UN pilots monitored progress. (It was highly suspected, but never confirmed, that interspersed among the trucks carrying prisoners were truckloads of ammunition and war supplies destined for stockpiles behind Chinese lines.)

The prisoner exchange began promptly on Monday, 20 April, in Panmunjom with the initial fifty Allied prisoners unloaded from the long line of CCF ambulances at 0825. The first Marine to be freed was Pvt. Alberto Pizarro-Baez of How Company 3/7, one of the men captured on Outpost Frisco in October 1952. Later that day, Pvt. Louis A. Pumphrey, also taken on Frisco, was released. By noon, the routine was moving along evenly as it would during the entire week. The Communist quota was one hundred prisoners freed daily, in two groups of fifty each. The Allies returned five hundred prisoners a day.

From Panmunjom, all Allied prisoners were taken to Freedom Village at Munsan-ni to begin their processing home:

> Each Marine prisoner was met by a 1st Division escort who gave him physical assistance, if necessary, as well as a much-prized possession—a new utility cap with its Marine Corps emblem. Recovered personnel received a medical examination. Waiting helicopters stood by to transport seriously sick or wounded Marines to the hospital ships *Haven* and *Consolation* riding at anchor in the Inchon Harbor. Chaplains chatted as informally or seriously as a returnee desired. Newspapers and magazines gave the ex-prisoners their first opportunity in months to read unslanted news. And a full set of utility uniforms, tailored on the spot for proper fit, were quickly donned by Marines happy to discard their prison blues.
>
> Although returnees received their initial medical processing at Freedom Village, no intelligence processing was attempted in Korea. Within 24 hours after their exchange, returned personnel were flown to K-16 (Seoul) and from there to Haneda Air Force Base at Tokyo.

Upon arrival at the Tokyo Army Hospital Annex, a more detailed medical exam was conducted, including a psychiatric interview....[19]

For UN forces behind the Imjin River, Little Switch had been a major project, a diversion from supporting a war that had become static and repetitious. For the press, it was big news, a welcome change from trying to report what to journalists had become a most uninteresting war. Noting this phenomenon, S. L. A. Marshall wrote in reference to a concurrent U.S. Army battle:

> ... Because Operation Little Switch was going on coincidentally at Freedom Village, and every correspondent rushed to that spot as if all life depended upon it, all that happened, all of the heroism and all of the sacrifice, went unreported. So the fine victory of Pork Chop Hill deserves the description of the Won-Lost-Battle. It was won by the troops and lost sight by the people who had sent them forth.[20]

Marshall was, of course, referring to the U.S. Army 7th Infantry Division's defense of Pork Chop Hill in April. But, his words apply equally to most months of the Outpost War. The press and, by extension, the people had indeed lost sight of the young men who were continuing the fight in Korea.

To men on the MLR and the outposts, Little Switch might never have happened. For the troops, it was business as usual—defend a position and seek out the enemy. The month of May would be considerably different for the Marines. Most of them would not be fighting at all.

CHAPTER 10

THE ARMY WAY

*Our Country will, I believe, sooner forgive an officer
for attacking his enemy than for letting it alone.*
—Lord Nelson: Letter during the attack
on Bastia, 3 May 1794

May 1953 would be a landmark month for the 1st Marine Division. It would leave the battle zone. Associated Press correspondent Robert Tuckman, announcing relief of the Marines from the Jamestown Line in a press release, reported:

> SEOUL, May 12—(AP)—The mighty U.S. First Marine Division has been pulled out of the Korean battleline to rest after 33 months of war.
>
> The famed Marine Division was relieved by the rested U.S. [25th] Infantry Division on May 5. The Marines came out under protest from commanders who wanted the Division to remain on the line.
>
> Starting with a Brigade on Aug. 2, 1950, the Marines have been in Korea's furious war ever since, with only 143 days out of line in all that period. . . .[1]

Strategic reasons for the move remain obscure, and, as implied in the news article, a number of Marine officers entirely disagreed with the move. Although the 1st Division had been on line for thirty-three continuous months, the statement was accurate only in the name of the division. Individual members—the officers and men—had not been on line anywhere near that time. With rotation policies, few Marines stayed in Korea longer than fourteen months. Further, those combat units on the MLR and outposts were regularly rotated from the line to reserve camps at regimental and division levels. As a consequence, the men remained fresh, aggressive, and ready to fight.

With few exceptions, the Marine MLR was manned by four battalions at any given time. The remaining five battalions were in reserve. A single infantry company's time on line approximated two months. Taken as a whole, the division's battalions and selected companies were in a constant state of monthly rotation. When all this is taken into consideration, one discovers that the individual Marine typically spent two months fighting the enemy and five months in reserve. Thus, during a full tour of duty, an infantry Marine might spend three to five months in combat. Recognizing this fact, many Marine officers saw little need for relief and cynically postulated that, during their absence, Army troops were likely to lose real estate that the Marines had fought so hard to retain. (Within a month, their fears proved correct.) The point, however, is irrelevant; the decision had been made. During the first five days of May, the Marine division came off line to be replaced by the U.S. Army's 25th Infantry Division.

The Kimpo Provisional Regiment, that composite mixture of U.S. Marines, U.S. soldiers, and South Koreans, remained in place and was transferred to control of the 25th Division. A few other Marine units, also remaining forward, did not join their companions in Corps Reserve. Most conspicuous was the artillery of the 11th Marine Regiment and the Marine 1st Tank Battalion, both of which remained.

Many Marines were dismayed at the Army's deployment and different "style" of defending ground that they had occupied for the past thirteen months. An example was the quantity of supporting arms. The 25th Division brought its own four battalions of artillery and then assumed control of the 11th Marines' four artillery battalions as well. It also doubled its tank support. Augmenting the Marine 1st Tank Battalion was the Army's 89th Tank Battalion deployed with the 27th Regiment west of Panmunjom. The Turkish Brigade, with four battalions of 5,455 men, relieved the 3,500-man 7th Marine Regiment and soon placed three battalions on line. Numerous differences, some good and others questionable, had veteran Marines watching in disbelief and awe as they wondered why they could not have had all that firepower on Vegas or the Hook.

Relief of the Marine Division began on 1 May when the 5th Marines closed its command post in Division reserve and moved to Camp Casey, the I Corps reserve area. Its replacement in Division reserve was the Army's 14th Infantry Regiment. On the same date, the KMC Artillery

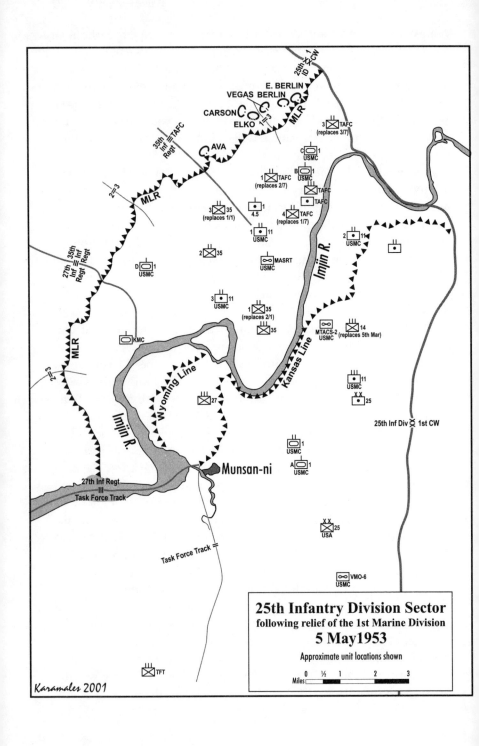

25th-XX-1
ID · CW

E. BERLIN
VEGAS BERLIN
CARSON
ELKO 1—3

MLR

3 ⊠ TAFC
(replaces 3/7)

35th Inf ≡ TAFC
Regt

AVA

C ▭ 1
USMC

B ▭ 1
USMC

2—3

MLR

⊠ TAFC
(replaces 2/7)

⊠ TAFC
• TAFC

3 ⊠ 35
(replaces 1/1)

4 ⊠ TAFC
(replaces 1/7)

• 1
4.5

1 ⊠ 35
(replaces 1/1)

Imjin R.

2 ⊠ 11
USMC

27th Inf 35th Inf
Regt Regt

1 ▭
USMC

2 ⊠ 35

D ▭ 1
USMC

MASRT
USMC

Kansas Line

3 ⊠ 11
USMC

1 ⊠ 35
(replaces 2/1)

MTACS-2
USMC

⊠ 14
(replaces 5th Mar)

⊠ 35

2—2

MLR

KMC

• 11
USMC

X X
• 25

Imjin R.

Wyoming Line

⊠ 27

25th Inf Div ⊠ 1st CW

• 1
USMC

A ▭ 1
USMC

Munsan-ni

27th Inf Regt
III
Task Force Track

X X
⊠ 25
USA

Task Force Track ≡

VMO-6
USMC

25th Infantry Division Sector
following relief of the 1st Marine Division
5 May 1953

Approximate unit locations shown

0   ½   1   2   3
Miles

Karamales 2001

⊠ TFT

Battalion came under Army control but remained in position. On 3 May, the Army's 89th Tank Battalion moved into the area. The following day, the 1st Battalion of the Turkish Armed Forces Command (TAFC) relieved 2/7 on line. Also, on 4 May, the 1st Marine Amphibian Tractor Battalion on the Han River was relieved by a provisional Army unit named Task Force Track. The Marine amtracs relocated in Ascom City near Inchon. On 5 May, the final relief of MLR units began, and, by 1045, relief of the 1st KMC Regimental Combat Team by the 27th Infantry Regiment was complete. At 1100, the 35th Infantry Regiment had relieved the 1st Marines, and the TAFC completed relief of the 7th Marines.

The U.S. 25th Infantry Division assumed full control of the James-town Line at 1120. The Marine 1st Tank Battalion and the 11th Marine Regiment remained forward and passed to control of the Army. With those exceptions, the Marine Division was officially, and actually, off line. Relocating the division required nearly twenty-four hundred truckloads of men and equipment. In the rear, Camp Britannia became the new home of the 1st Marines, with the 5th Marines at Camp Casey and the 7th Marines at Camp Indianhead.

On the MLR and the outposts, relief of men and positions took place in increments of about one third per day. During that period, men of both services worked together and were exposed to differences in doctrine and practices of the two often competitive services. The comparisons astonished young Marines who had learned, trained, and practiced behaviors that they had always accepted as gospel. 2d Lt. Robert E. Werckle of George Company 3/1 recalls an early encounter with an Army lieutenant who had come to his position to prepare for the movement. Werckle was concerned when he noticed that the visitor displayed his rank insignia prominently on his uniform contrary to Marine practice. Rightly or wrongly, Marines believed that officers displaying rank insignia within sight of the enemy created attractive targets for snipers. For that reason, Marine officers rarely wore indications of rank while on the MLR or an outpost.[2] Lieutenant Werckle recalls:

> I'll never forget the big shot Army lieutenant (West Point) when he came to our outpost to look things over. He had two gold bars (much larger than the bars we wore), one on each collar, and a large bar on his helmet. It was a sunny afternoon and he wanted to tour our outpost.
>
> I never wore bars on line. The Chinese would take pot shots during the day if we exposed ourselves. The sun shining on those bars

would have made the Chinese think some general was there and all hell would have broken loose. We about came to blows before I got the big shot to take off his damn bars.

When his platoon came to relieve us a day or so later, I was ordered to stay an extra day, which became the longest 24 hours I've ever spent. I went out on patrol with them—the noisiest group imaginable. Luckily, we didn't run in to anything.[3]

Enlisted men, too, were struck by differences in the way that things were done. For example, Cpl. Harvey Dethloff, a machine gunner, with George Company 3/1, wrote:

> After dark, when they [Army replacements] finally arrived, I was called into the CP bunker to meet my counterpart. Upon arrival at the bunker, where there was a candle burning for light, I was introduced to a black S/Sergeant who was the MG squad leader.
>
> The first thing I noticed was that he had his rank on his helmet and both collar points. As I started to show him our guns and their fields of fire, he asked me my rank. I told him Pfc. Then he wanted to know how long I'd been in the Corps and I told him 2 ½ years. I asked him how long he'd been in, knowing he wasn't very old and he said 13 months.
>
> Then I asked him about his rank, and he said he was the oldest man in time in Korea and was promoted from Pfc. to Staff Sergeant in one jump because that is what the T/O [Table of Organization] called for. (I finally made corporal one day before Boulder City!)
>
> Our standard procedure was to leave the MG tripods in place because they were sandbagged in. We always took the relieving outfit's tripods and our guns off with us. Well, this guy didn't want our tripods because they were dirty and probably had the paint chipped off and his were brand new.
>
> I tried for quite a while to get him to trade tripods, but he couldn't hear too good, I guess. Well after pulling out one tripod and letting him try to get his in, he was willing to trade the other two.
>
> After getting everything straightened out, we went into the cave to get to the back trench. We could barely get through because the cave was full of extra men and a rocket launcher team. Outpost Kate had been defended by a rifle and machine gun squad of Marines, the army must have manned it with a reinforced platoon.[4]

The Marines never did understand why combat methods that they had acquired through trial and error and had come to embrace as doctrine were not accepted carte blanche by the Army. Likely, their Army counterparts just as strongly reacted in ways that were quite the opposite and wondered why those crazy Marines did things the way they did.

To be fair, the Marines were no angels by any stretch of the imagination. Like military prima donnas, they are usually arrogant, frequently uncooperative, and sometimes just plain ornery. For example, a group of soldiers was gathered in a trench while waiting for some Marines to leave when a leatherneck suddenly threw a hand grenade into a living bunker that he was vacating. After the dust settled and as the astonished soldiers watched, the Marine dashed back into the smoking bunker. He soon emerged, triumphantly holding a dead rat by the tail. The bunker, of course, was now nearly uninhabitable.

Sgt. Bob Kreid recalls leaving the line with his machine gunners on 3 May:

> U.S. Army trucks rolled up to the MLR about 0430 that morning. The 2nd Battalion loaded quickly and we were ready to go. It was great to be leaving the line, but I came very close to getting in trouble that morning.
>
> Most of the truck beds were covered with canvas except the one carrying my gun section. I climbed into the cab with the driver and we were soon on our way. The sun wasn't yet up and it was still very cold. I was cold in the cab but the poor guys in back were freezing. The driver turned to me and asked, "Sarge, would you like to buy a fifth of whiskey?" "How much?" I asked, and he replied, "ten dollars." I gave him the money and he handed over an unopened bottle of Canadian Club. I took a long pull from the bottle and handed it back to sixteen cold and tired Marines who hadn't eaten in several hours.
>
> A little while later one of the men knocked on the cab and motioned for me to roll down the window. "Damn that was good, got any more?" he asked. The driver handed me another bottle and someone came up with another ten bucks.
>
> Before long the men in the back of the truck began to sing "Ninety-nine bottles of beer on the wall." The verse I remember best was:
>
> > "A fighting over yonder,
> > A fighting for my life,
> > Before I go to war again
> > I'll send my darling wife."
>
> Oh Great! My men were drunk!

It was starting to get daylight and the convoy was pulling up to an MP check point. I heard someone in the back yell out, "I can whip any rebel mother fucker in this truck." In response, a gunner from Alabama stood up and the fight was on. The truck began to shake and I sat still, thinking the squad leaders would soon get things under control, but it was too late.

Our lieutenant was in the truck behind us, and when I heard his door slam I too jumped out. Between the two of us we broke up the fight. He gave me a hard look, said nothing and climbed back in his truck. I knew then that I was in trouble. A drunk section of machine gunners could cost all of us our stripes and maybe brig time. I got to thinking that if I could get the men quiet now, and into their tents at the new camp, there might be a chance to keep this within the platoon. Things might not be too bad.

Then I decided, To Hell With It!! These raggedy ass Marines had been shot at, shelled, seen their buddies die, got wounded themselves, gone without sleep for nine days, only took their boots off long enough to change into another pair of dirty socks and eaten cold C rations while fighting flies coming from Chinese corpses rotting outside the perimeter fence of Carson. If I lose my stripes because I gave them a little whiskey while riding in the back of an open and cold 6×6 truck, so be it. They damn well earned the right to raise a little hell.

That settled, I felt better.

The convoy crossed the Imjin River and we arrived at our new home. For some strange reason it was called Camp Indianhead. The company gunnery sergeant came by, gave us our tent assignments and told me to unload. After the men were out of the truck, I read them the riot act and told them to get their drunken asses into their tents and stay there! One of the ammo carriers looked at me and said, "Aw fuck Sarge, ah ain't drunk." Whereupon he turned and tripped over a machine gun tripod, falling flat on his face. I pulled him to his feet, cussed him out and sent him on his way. That's when I saw a Marine major watching us. He was standing there with his hands on his hips looking mighty pissed off. I thought, "That rips it! We are all going to be run up with morning colors. I'll be lucky if I don't land in the brig."

For three days I waited, expecting any minute to be called to report to the company office. The call never came. Then I figured it out. Our officers were damn proud of their raggedy assed Marines and had turned a blind eye to our antics—this time. We had some fine officers in the second battalion. The kind men would die for—many in fact had.[5]

MARINE TANKS SUPPORT THE ARMY

When control of the Marine Tank Battalion passed to the U.S. Army's 25th Infantry Division, there were more changes. The Army's use of tanks differed from Marine methods. Baker and Charlie Company tanks were placed on the division's right to support the Turkish Brigade behind the Nevada Cities outposts. Dog Company tanks supported the 35th Regiment in the division's center sector, while Able Company was designated as the single reserve unit. On the left, formerly the KMC sector, tank support was provided by the KMC tank company, as well as a tank company from the U.S. Army's 89th Tank Battalion.

This deployment differed from the Marine system of maintaining two tank companies on line, each supporting an infantry regiment, and a third in forward reserve a short distance behind the MLR that was ready to move where it was needed. The fourth Marine tank company was located at the battalion CP near Munsan-ni, where Marine vehicles underwent maintenance. The Army deployment placed five Army and Marine tank companies on line compared with the Marines' two companies.

A change in tactics also took place. It had been Marine practice to retain its forward tanks at platoon and company CPs close behind the MLR. From there, the tanks could be moved to various positions at the request of infantry units. One tank might use any of several firing slots, and, in case of a major attack, tanks from forward reserve could rapidly move forward to reinforce. Further, using a variety of firing positions made it more difficult for the enemy to shift its artillery rapidly from one slot to another.

Under the Army concept, tanks were deployed to fixed positions on the MLR. Dug in and sandbagged, they never moved. In effect, they became pillboxes. The tank crews lived in bunkers next to their tanks and entered the vehicles only to fire a mission. Most Marines opposed these changes, but there was little that could be done—except complain. The grumblings of 1st Lt. Robert March in letters to his wife were typical of the dissatisfaction felt by other Marines:

[16 May 1953]. . . Tonight I had to go to back to the Army regimental briefing and boy was that a pain in the neck. They call it a briefing but there is nothing brief about it, it lasted 1½ hours. Everybody from the Col. on down talked and it was just so much bull sh—. If they ever get an attack in this sector like we had on Vegas or Carson I wonder how long the briefing will last, probably sev-

eral days. They never have any action over here because they are afraid
to patrol and push the Chinese. The goonies are free to do as they
please and are probably building up for a big attack. The doggies don't
like to patrol to see what's going on over there. They are afraid some-
body will get hurt. But if they let the goonies build up without both-
ering them with some aggressive patrols they are going to get kicked
hard.

. . . You should have heard my report at the briefing tonight. I told
them what we had done during the day and what we have planned
for tonight and then sat down. They looked at me like I had shirked
my duty because I didn't stand there for 15 minutes discussing the war
in general.

[18 May 1953]. . . Nothing ever goes off smoothly like it did with
the Marines, and everybody seems to be working against one another.
I have had to go to the regimental briefing for the last three nights
and they get worse all the time. It lasted two hours tonight. Nothing
was accomplished.

. . . As big and well equipped as the Army is, why do they insist on
being supported by Marine tanks and artillery. It's a big mess.

[23 May 1953]. . . The Marine method of support is by fire from
the MLR and outposts. Since the Army never raids or probes, we are
in a purely defensive role. Consequently we aren't very busy.

[25 May 1953]. . . Tank positions are way back about 7,000 yards
from the goonies. The Army won't use the positions that we used. They
say they are too close. I don't know whether they are just yellow or
over cautious, but I can't see what good they can do that far back. No
wonder we are losing this war, there are too many doggies over here.[6]

Like it or not, the Marines and the soldiers worked hard to make the
arrangement successful. The most awkward situation was with the two
tank companies placed under operational control of the Turkish Brigade
in the right sector. A situation report prepared by Marine personnel
described solutions to three immediate problems.

First, personnel and ammunition bunkers had to be built immediately
at each of the fifteen tank-firing slots. These slots were selected from the
thirty-four previously used by the Marines, and construction began
straightaway.

Second, until such time that the bunkers were constructed, the fifteen
tanks (one company) had to be maintained in position on the MLR
twenty-four hours a day without completely exhausting the tank crews.
The proposed solution was to keep one tank company in position daily
from 0600 to 1800 and another company from 1800 to 0600.

The third problem was the language barrier combined with the necessity for developing a workable system of fire coordination. Close coordination of tank fires apparently had not been maintained in other sectors in which the Turkish Brigade had operated. Evidently, if the brigade had ever worked with tanks before, the effort had been uncoordinated and each unit had fought its own war without regard for the other's activity. It was necessary, therefore, for the Marines to develop a system from scratch. They recommended the basic system of tank fire coordination utilized by the 1st Tank Battalion in support of the Marine Division, and the TAFC brigade commander enthusiastically accepted it. He directed that every assistance be provided in getting a fire coordination system into immediate operation. The system had to be modified, however, to overcome the language barrier.

As the battalion was the lowest TAFC echelon where interpreters were located, all requests for supporting fire were channeled through the TAFC battalion CP, where they were cleared. At the CP, a tank liaison agent, usually the tank platoon commander or platoon sergeant, transmitted the fire mission to one or more of his tanks. Each tank was connected by a complex system of telephone lines and radio backup to the battalion CP. In this way, fire missions were conducted rapidly and accurately on request from infantry commanders. The system was cumbersome but usually effective. One of the tank platoon leaders, S/Sgt. James Champlin, described his experience with the Turkish soldiers:

> . . . They thought our 90-mm guns were the greatest and would jump in front of the tank while we were trying to fire. They shouted, jumped and really went nuts. With communication being marginal at best, we ended up using pidgin Korean, sign language and even drew pictures.
>
> The biggest problem was the muzzle blast from the 90. The blast shot flame and shock waves for yards around. We had been told that it was so severe it could kill anyone caught nearby. We had a helluva time keeping the Turks away from the gun when we fired. The bottom line was that for them it was a sport. Men were blown completely off their feet, rolled over and over, and then jumped up laughing to do it all over again. It was crazy![7]

WITH THE ARMY ON COP-2

On COP-2, a company of Marines from 3/1 was replaced by George Company, 3d Battalion, 35th Infantry, and soldiers took over the gun positions and bunkers vacated by the Marines.

Since 1952, the Marines had continuously deployed a flame tank on COP-2. When George Company took over the outpost, the tank and its four-man crew of Marines remained on the hill now under control of the Army company commander. They, too, had some adjusting to do. One of the first problems to overcome was the presence of South Korean Army troops. Called KATUSA (Korean Augmentation to the U.S. Army), these regular ROK troops were attached to and intermingled with U.S. Army units. Army commanders generally liked the arrangement and found that the ROK soldiers performed well side by side with American troops. By contrast, the U.S. Marine Corps had assembled and trained a regiment of Korean Marines and assigned them as a self-contained unit to defend a sector of the MLR. Consequently, unless they were working in the KMC sector, Marines seldom came into contact with South Korean troops. For the Marine tankers on COP-2 there was a bit of culture shock.

Sgt. Jerry Ellis was with the flame tank remaining on the hill. On the first night of the relief, Ellis walked down the hill to the mess tent located within the Neutral Corridor. The night was pitch black. At the wire gate marking the corridor boundary, Ellis encountered two KATUSA guards. They looked oriental, smelled like garlic, and spoke Korean. Ellis was not prepared for this. Thinking they were enemy soldiers, he drew his .45 pistol. Fortunately, the Koreans knew enough English to convince Ellis that they were friendly, but there were a tense few moments.

As the Army redeployed Marine tanks, a platoon from Able Company went from reserve to a CP on Hill 229,[8] just behind the MLR. Marine tank A-13, an M-46 Patton with a 90-mm main gun and a fighting light, was pulled from the Able Company CP and assigned to COP-2. Two other 1st Platoon tanks were deployed to Outpost Marilyn. The reserve tank company was reduced to approximately two platoons.

In addition to the gun tank, the Army elected to further reinforce COP-2 with an M-16 quad 50 half-track from the 21st Antiaircraft Battalion. The quad 50 was a mechanism from which four .50-caliber machine guns fired in concert from the rear of a lightly armored truck, a half-track. The rear suspension was on caterpillar tracks like a tank, whereas the front was equipped with two-drive wheels like a truck. The quad 50 was originally designed as an antiaircraft weapon; in Korea it was found to be highly effective against troops in the open.

A Marine corporal who drove the gun tank deployed on COP-2 later wrote of his experience with George Company, 35th Regiment, U.S. Army, during May and June 1953.

We were in battalion reserve when we received this detached assignment to the Army. Our recent tank commander had rotated home and we picked up a new tank commander, S/Sgt. Kenneth Miller, former platoon sergeant of the Flame Platoon. Ken was the same man who had left his flame tank on Outpost Hedy in January and then a month later abandoned one on the Clambake Raid. In less than two months Miller had two tanks shot out from under him. We hoped that we would not become number three.

On 13 May the first platoon left our battalion reserve area at Munsan-ni. Our five tanks traveled north up Route 1 toward the front and crossed the Imjin River at Freedom Gate Bridge. We drove to our new platoon CP behind Hill 229 and spent the night. We would start for COP-2 at first light the following morning.

It felt good to be on the road again. Reserve duty got old very fast, it was too boring and predictable. Now we were back in the war. Our platoon was in high spirits. We had also picked up a new platoon leader, 1st Lt. Vern Sylvester, a popular and congenial officer. He replaced 1st Lt. Robert March, who became company executive officer.

At our platoon CP we met the crew of the Army half track and prepared for our trip across no-man's-land to COP-2. That night as we slept, engineers scouted and cleared the road we would use. We knew that we would be driving out in front of the MLR the following morning without infantry protection. Would we run into an ambush? Had all the mines been cleared? What might happen? Such thoughts weren't conducive to a good night's sleep.

The following morning at first light, we left the MLR and drove into no-man's-land. Our tank led the way. I had never been out there in daylight and was unfamiliar with this particular stretch of road. Ahead of me, I could pick Gray Rock, the scene of my firefight when I was with Recon Company in February. This time I was looking at it from the Chinese side.

We traveled unbuttoned so we could see better, and everyone was alert. If the Chinese were going to hit us, this is where it would happen. Behind us on the MLR, the remainder of our platoon was in position, ready to fire if enemy troops were sighted.

Traveling northwest on the rutted road, our route took us over the top of Outpost Marilyn, where two more tanks stood watch, and down the forward slope. We were now in plain sight of enemy guns. We drove through the dry wash at the base of Hill 90 without incident, hit the road to COP-2 and finally drove up the hill to the outpost. A piece of cake. Why were we ever worried?

Life on COP-2 turned out to be pretty typical of trench living. A little primitive, but rather lay back much of the time. Our main job consisted of driving to a tank slot on the crest of the hill once a day and firing a few rounds at a variety of Chinese targets; trench line, gun emplacements, observation posts and the like. We used the target practice to zero in on points of likely offensive fire. Reciprocating, the Chinese would fire a few rounds of mortar at our trench line, gun emplacements, observation posts, and us. After they finished I suppose they did the same thing we did, retire to the bunker to clean guns, maintain equipment, and visit with friends. There wasn't much night work on COP-2 as the army seldom made night attacks or ambushes that required a tank to standby on the hill for support.

On moonless nights the Chinese would occasionally fly over the hill in "Maytag Charlie," a small single engine airplane so named because its little putt-putt engine sounded as though it came from a washing machine, or lawn mower. Near as anyone could tell, Maytag Charlie did no harm whatever; it dropped no bombs and was too dark for photography. We couldn't see to shoot so I presume it had the same handicap. Maybe it was just trying to make folks nervous. If so, it failed.

Our most important day time activity, when not on a fire mission or sleeping, was seeing to the maintenance of the tank. While it didn't require much upkeep, there were a few chores required to ensure constant serviceability. Without the tank we were just another five riflemen.

While the crew tended to maintenance chores, the tank commander spent much of his time in the FO Bunker on top of the hill. The artillery forward observer was a Marine officer from the 11th Marines. His job was to direct all artillery fire to the area around us. He also suggested targets for tank fire missions. He and Miller frequently compared notes on enemy activity, targets and what each had seen through their high powered spotting scopes. Together they watched and observed the hills to our front. As Chinese positions were rebuilt, they were selected for disassembly by our main gun.

Life with the Army on COP-2 was not at all difficult and occasionally proved interesting. For example there was the day the soldiers made a truce with the Chinese, which, as Marines we felt it our duty to break up. The day developed as follows:

Early in the morning we were treated to some music and propaganda from the "Dragon Lady," a woman who spoke to us on infrequent occasions over loudspeakers. She often inquired about the love lives of our wives and girl friends and provided other items of irrelevant information. On this particular occasion, she suggested that the fighting on COP-2 wasn't serving any useful purpose and proposed that we call a little truce between ourselves. The speaker went on to say that if we on the outpost would not shoot at them, they wouldn't shoot at us, and we all could enjoy a little truce. If we liked the idea, we were to send someone to the top of the hill and signify our agreement by flapping a blanket. Several people did it. Rumor had it that the George Company Commander authorized the arrangement, but that was never confirmed. In any case the damage was done, the blanket was flapped and the "truce" began. Authorized or not, the Army troops, including officers, seemed to think that the "truce" was a marvelous idea and appeared quite content with it.

One must be familiar with Communist tactics to understand a move such as this. A truce by the Communist forces is not a peace move, it's a strategic tactic. It allows him to resupply, retrench and get ready for the next offensive. When he is ready, he will not hesitate to break the truce and attack.

Sergeant Miller had a short fuse, and when he heard of the private little "truce" he was incensed. He immediately called our company commander, Capt. Edward Critchett, for instructions. He told Miller that our tank was expected to expend a daily allotment of 90-mm rounds against enemy targets. The Captain implied that the fate of the entire UN war effort depended on those rounds being fired—today. He was advised to continue with his normal fire mission, immediately.

We were delighted. I cranked up the tank and off we went to our firing slot on top of COP-2. There we selected targets and shot hell out of everything Chinese that we could possibly find. It was a satisfying feeling and caused a lot of damage. We fired our allocation and a few more for good measure.

Our shoot that day apparently upset the Chinese because for the next couple of hours, the outpost received an inordinately large number of incoming mortar rounds. All of us were so well dug in that no damage was done, but there was no truce on COP-2 that day.[9]

Apparently, these small, localized truces were not uncommon among Army units along the line, another practice that baffled the Marines. In late May, the Marine Reconnaissance Company found a similar situation when the company moved to the banks of the Imjin River to replace an Army infantry company. Sergeant Lipper wrote home that, after their arrival, the Marines had slain sixty-nine Chinese and wounded twenty-four with artillery and .50-caliber machine guns. He stated, "The Chinese had become extremely careless as they had a sort of 'you don't fire at us and we won't fire at you,' arrangement set up with the Army. The doggies on either side of us can't figure out why we began shooting."[10]

This blatant lack of aggressiveness on the part of our Army just mystified the Marines. Institutionally, as evidenced by the behavior of officers and enlisted alike, the Army seemed to want to lie back and let the war happen around it. The soldiers conducted fewer patrols and virtually no ambushes or raids. For them, the war appeared to be strictly defensive with as few offensive actions as possible.

COP-2 IS ATTACKED

In late May, the men on COP-2 had to start earning their keep. The 35th Regiment Command Report for May 1953, in a monument to understatement, reads: "On the night of 28 and 29 May, CCF units estimated to be of battalion size attacked COP #2 held by Company "G" (reinforced). A firefight ensued, Company "G," employed hand grenades, shot guns, napalm, mortar and artillery in areas where proximity of neutral zones prohibited use of high velocity direct fire weapons. The accuracy and volume of all fire during the several phases of the attack was such that the enemy suffered casualties estimated to be fifty (50) KIA and sixty (60) to seventy (70) WIA. Company "G" sustained only two (2) WIA. Several men were cited for bravery following the action."[11]

The Marines on COP-2 were involved. The driver of tank A-13 reported:

> The early evening of 28 May was clear and warm. It was almost a summer night, we were standing by in the tank, lying just below the crest of the hill. [S/Sgt. Kenneth] Miller was in the FO bunker with the company First Sergeant and our forward observer. Suddenly from north, the arc of a falling green signal flare appeared, falling through the twilight. The flare was accompanied immediately by enemy machine gun fire to the outpost, and then mortar and artillery rounds began to fall all around us. It was 1800 and COP-2 was under attack.
>
> Miller dashed back to the tank and shouted at me to start up and roll into position. As we pulled forward and turned on the tank light Chinese troops were storming the hill. In the turret the gunner began firing his .30 machine gun, sweeping the hill in front, as Chinese infantry climbed toward us. Aerial flares burst overhead and while they were falling the night was bright as day.

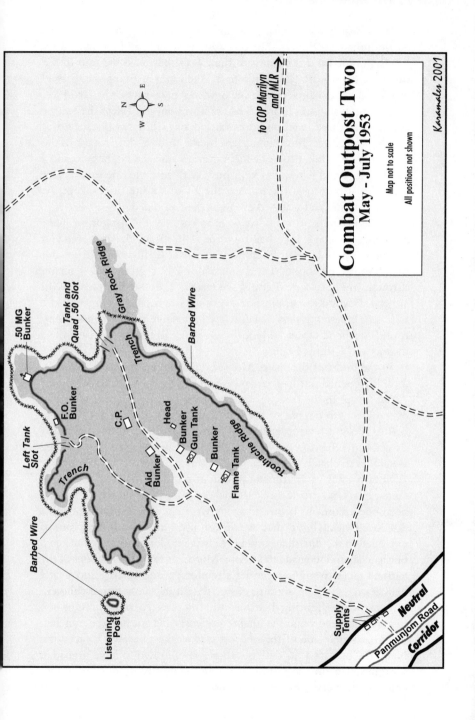

Combat Outpost Two
May – July 1953

Map not to scale
All positions not shown

Karamales 2001

to COP Marilyn and MLR →

50 MG Bunker

Tank and Quad .50 Slot

Gray Rock Ridge

Trench

Barbed Wire

F.O. Bunker

C.P.

Head Bunker

Gun Tank

Bunker

Flame Tank

Toothache Ridge

Left Tank Slot

Trench

Barbed Wire

Aid Bunker

Listening Post

Supply Tents

Neutral

Panmunjom Road

Corridor

We felt fairly secure inside the tank. We fired our guns and used the battle light until it was shot out. Our gunner, Sgt. [Thomas] Tom Jervis, pumped out tracers from the .30 caliber machine gun in the turret, while Moose [Pfc. William E. Abel], our assistant driver, used his .30 caliber machine gun in the bow to spray whatever he could see.

The din inside was nearly as bad as it was outside. I kept the engine running, as three machine guns rattled away. The rapid staccato of two light machine guns punctuated by the throaty, slower bark of the heavy fifty. We didn't fire our main gun because the Chinese infantry was so close and Jervis was kept busy with his machine gun. I kept the exhaust blower going to clear the air of cordite fumes, kept the engine running and watched events as they unfolded.

In the excitement we didn't seem to consider the danger, we were enjoying ourselves. Like hail on a tin roof, shrapnel, hand grenades and bullets bounced off the front of the tank. A rifleman told us later that, "Your tank looked like a Fourth of July celebration." Peering through my periscope, I could see tracers, flares and explosions all around. Beyond the explosions were enemy infantry climbing the hill. As Chinese gunners began to get our range mortar and artillery rounds dropped closer and closer. Over the din inside I heard their distinctive, "Crump, Crump."

In the midst of the chaos, Moose and I, caught up in the moment, foolishly opened our hatches and began to sing the Marines Hymn to Army troops in the trenches below. I have no idea why, we were just overcome with a sense of bravado that needed an outlet. I'll be the first to admit it a was pretty dumb thing to do. Fortunately, we didn't sit with open hatches for very long. Our brains began to function and we closed the hatches—in the nick of time.

Shortly after we buttoned up mortars got our range, and we began taking hits. One struck about six inches from Moose's hatch which had been open moments before. Damage was negligible, burnt paint and a destroyed head light that we never used anyway. Other rounds exploded in the dirt all around us. We were no longer tempted to open our hatches and serenade the troops. Moreover, for the remainder of the battle, I sat with my head under a reinforced steel casting and a steel helmet on my lap, an effort to ensure the future of my future children.

Meanwhile fighting became more severe. To our left Chinese infantry broke through the infantry defenses and got into the trenches. That particular side of the outpost was weakest because it faced the Neutral Corridor. Our defenses there were limited to hand grenades, shotguns, napalm and pistols, avoiding the possibility of stray rounds entering the nearby Neutral Corridor.[12]

After an hour and a half, the fighting lulled, The attack on COP-2 had merely been a feint. It was never intended to defeat the Americans or occupy the position. Having achieved their goal, the Chinese withdrew. The true objective that night was farther east, the Nevada Cities outposts.

THE NEVADA CITIES FALL

Other parts of the line were not so fortunate, specifically the outposts of Carson, Elko, Vegas, Berlin, and East Berlin. Occupied by Turkish forces, these outposts were hit at the same time as COP-2, only harder. The ferocious attack even spilled over to the Hook, now held by the British Commonwealth Division.

Always political, the Communists had reacted to a UN "final offer" made three days earlier at Panmunjom. Using artillery to punctuate their dissatisfaction with the ultimatum, Chinese forces commenced a buildup of fire to the outposts. When the first attack came on the evening of 28 May, Turkish units defending the outposts were well dug in. There were 140 men on Vegas, 44 on Carson, 33 on Elko, 27 on Berlin, and 16 on East Berlin.

On the heels of an intense artillery and mortar preparation, the Chinese 120th Division sent four battalions forward. Two attacked Vegas, one assaulted Carson and Elko, and the other went after Berlin and East Berlin. Like the attack on COP-2, the last attack was apparently a diversion because it halted and broke off early in the evening.

On Vegas, the Chinese succeeded in taking one small finger of the hill and clung to it tenaciously despite automatic-weapons, small-arms, artillery, and mortar fire. The Turks sent a reinforced platoon to bolster the defenders, and it arrived in time to help throw back a three-pronged enemy assault on the outpost. After reorganizing, the Chinese sent another force, again estimated at two battalions, to take the hill. Ammunition began to run low, and the Turkish 2d Battalion sent another platoon, accompanied by KSC personnel, to resupply the embattled troops. After a brief respite, the enemy tried again. This time, the Chinese pushed through, and hand-to-hand combat broke out in the trenches.

Meanwhile, the Chinese added a second battalion to the assaults on Carson and Elko. Bayonets and hand grenades were freely used as the Turks managed to throw back the attack. The battalion commander sent an engineer platoon and then committed the rest of the engineer company to reinforce Carson. Shortly after midnight, the pace slackened, but observers reported that a third enemy battalion was assembling to join the assault. Supporting arms were called, and the Chinese battalion was destroyed.

As the night wore on, the men on Elko held out against continuing Chinese attacks, but the Turkish soldiers on Carson were dying one by one. A few managed to slip over and join their comrades on Elko, but the majority died in the trenches and bunkers from enemy fire. By morning, Carson belonged to the Chinese.

Convinced of Chinese determination to take the Nevada outposts, Maj. Gen. Samuel T. Williams, 25th Division commander, moved a battalion from the division reserve, the 14th Infantry Regiment, to control of Brig. Gen. Serri Acar, commander of the Turkish Forces, which freed Acar to commit his reserves to the counterattack.

The fighting continued and the enemy gradually gained control of the northwest portion of Vegas. Turkish casualties were increasing. In a desperate effort to blunt the Chinese drive, the Turks began a counterattack to clear the hill. Savage fighting followed as the Turks slowly swept the enemy off Vegas with bayonets and knives.

The Chinese, however, regrouped, reinforced their offensive units, and returned. They edged their way up Vegas and met the indomitable Turks, who refused to be budged. Late in the morning of 29 May, the Turks launched a four-platoon attack that cleared Vegas with cold steel. The Chinese, in turn, would not accept defeat and sent wave after wave of men against the Turkish stone wall. Casualties on both sides sharply increased.

Meanwhile, the struggle for Elko continued throughout the night of 28–29 May as the enemy increased pressure against remnants of the Turkish force on that hill. On the morning of 29 May, General Acar ordered the 1st Battalion of the U.S. 14th Infantry to send a company to reinforce Elko and to retake Carson.

Using two platoons in the attack and two in support, Baker Company, 14th Infantry, advanced west on Carson. Midway between Elko and Carson, the company began receiving automatic-weapons, artillery, and mortar fire. The assault slowed and then halted. Withdrawing to Elko, the men of Baker Company tried twice to gather enough momentum to break through the Chinese wall of fire on Carson. Each time, they failed and were turned back. Artillery, mortars, and automatic weapons could not silence the Chinese weapons nor could they dislodge the enemy defenders of Carson.

After the third assault ground to a halt, the Chinese retaliated. Six times, they crossed from Carson to Elko and, on several occasions, managed to advance within hand-grenade range. Baker Company, supported by artillery, tank, mortar, and automatic-weapons fire, forced the enemy to break off the attack each time, and Elko remained in friendly hands.

The Turks conducted themselves well, in keeping with their reputation for courage and ferocity. When using bayonets and knives in close combat they had no equal, and, when possible, the Chinese tended to avoid close combat with them. Unfortunately, Turkish tactics were archaic. As raw infantry, with little thought given to the use of modern supporting arms, artillery, tanks, or mortars, they were superb assault troops. Deployed as a purely defensive force, however, the Turks were unaccustomed to the American "Army way" of defense and did not fit in well. They sustained enormous casualties.

ON THE MLR WITH THE TURKS

During the fighting of 28–29 May, both Baker and Charlie Companies of the Marine 1st Tank Battalion were deployed with the Turks. When the action began, fifteen tanks were in position on the MLR. As the battle developed and the objectives of the Chinese became apparent, additional tanks were committed until a total of thirty-three were on line. Throughout the night, fighting lights illuminated the battlefield while 90-mm tank guns pounded enemy concentrations. As tanks ran out of ammunition, they were replaced with others full of ammunition and fuel. The relieved tank returned to its supply point to rearm, refuel, return to the line, and replace another tank. Finally, targets became so plentiful that the tanks could not leave. To shuttle fuel and ammunition, the platoon of Marine APCs was pressed into service. The crew of each APC picked up a load of ammunition at the company CP, drove to the MLR, and maneuvered beside tanks in position to rearm them on the spot. Thus, uninterrupted tank fire continued with minimum lost time.

Marine 1st Lt. Robert Montgomery was executive officer of Baker Company during the fighting. He recalls that, on his assignment to the Army, the tank officer for the Army's 25th Division had some unusual ideas (at least to Montgomery) about the use of armor. He wanted to dig in the tanks and use them as stationary pillboxes on the MLR. Montgomery indicated, "The Army's tank battalion was still equipped with older M-4 tanks with less armor and firepower,[13] and this may have colored the officer's thinking on tank employment. It was only through intercession of an Army colonel, attached to the Turks as an advisor, that the problems were resolved. Still, our relations with the Division Tank Officer remained rocky at best."[14]

After pushing the Turks out of position, Montgomery adds, "continuous files of Chinese troops, reinforcing the outposts, were moving down the ridgelines to escape artillery fire. It was like shooting fish in a rain barrel. We used up our HE rounds faster than we could replenish them. Some crews ran out completely and switched to Willie Peter."[15]

According to the Command Diary of the 1st Tank Battalion, "In the course of the action Marine tankers actually killed seven hundred twenty-one (721) Chinese and wounded one hundred eleven (111) more. This was in addition to the estimated number of enemy casualties which totaled one hundred thirty-six (136) killed and twelve hundred (1,200) wounded."[16]

Lieutenant Montgomery describes portions of the battle:

> Moving tank 21 into position, the tank commander, Sgt. Page L. Keith, was forced, due to smoke and darkness, to raise his hatch to direct his tank's fire. The tank received a direct hit killing Sgt. Keith and wounding Pfc.'s Evans, Waldrip and Bruschi.
>
> Incoming on company tanks during the period was 4,000 rounds of mixed mortar and artillery. On the night of 29 May, the ammo dump for the Turkish artillery battery was hit by incoming and completely destroyed. Ten rounds found their way into our tank company CP, located directly in front of the dump.
>
> Later that day our 1st and 2nd platoons were relieved on line by the Army's 14th Regimental Tank Company. The remainder of Baker Company's tanks were relieved by Charlie Company.[17]

Both companies of Marine tanks were fully engaged during the battles for Carson, Elko, and Vegas. Later, when such things are attended to, the 1st Tank Battalion supply officer reported an expenditure of 4,294 rounds of 90-mm, 150,000 rounds of .30-caliber, and 25,000 rounds of .50-caliber ammunition used during the two-day period.[18] Some participants attributed this continuous and deadly accurate fire to be a major factor in preventing a successful penetration of the MLR. Consequently, on conclusion of this action, the Army awarded Baker and Charlie Companies each a Presidential Unit Citation.

None of the Army documents concerning the Nevada Cities battle mentions barbed-wire entanglements, box-me-in fires, VT, fighting holes, or other defensive measures found by the Marines to be so successful during the outpost war. It also appears from other reports that the

Turkish trenches were too deep and did not have fighting holes from which to return fire. Defenses on the Nevada Cities outposts left a lot to be desired.

By midafternoon on 29 May, Lt. Gen. Bruce C. Clarke, I Corps Commander, and Maj. Gen. Williams, concluded that the Chinese intended to remain on the offensive until the Nevada outposts were taken. By then, the strength on Vegas had been reduced to 40 men, many of whom were wounded; 20 men were left on Elko, and Carson was lost. Over the period, 150 men had been killed and 245 wounded while defending the outposts. Chinese casualties were estimated at 3,000 men.

The Army's basic perception at the time was that the war soon would be over. With that in mind, General Clarke believed that the Nevada Cities outposts had served their main purpose of uncovering and delaying the enemy attack. Subsequently, in the evening of 29 May, Clarke issued orders for the Turks to withdraw from Vegas and for U.S. troops to leave Elko. The outposts were to be abandoned to prevent further loss of life.

Two months earlier, the 1st Marine Division had sustained nearly 1,500 casualties in successfully holding those same outposts. (The loss included 104 Marines missing in action.) The Vegas high ground remained a viable protection for the MLR. General Clarke was now betting that the war would soon end and there would be no more attacks at that location. If he were wrong, the MLR would be left quite vulnerable. With no outposts to delay the enemy, the MLR could be directly attacked. Were it breached, a far greater loss of life could result from defending and retaking it. If loss of life was the deciding factor, why not abandon the entire country and go home?

The irony of the Nevada Cities loss did not pass unnoticed among Marines in Korea at the time, and the topic remains a matter of some debate. In a letter to the Director, Marine Corps Historical Branch, Headquarters Marine Corps, dated 20 May 1970, General Clarke reiterated his reasons for abandoning the outposts: "The outposts in front of the MLR had gradually lost their value in my opinion because, between the MLR and the outposts, minefields, tactical wire, etc., had made their reinforcement and counter attacks very costly . . . holding poor real estate for sentimental reasons is a poor excuse for undue casualties."

It has been shown time and again in battle that "minefields, tactical wire, etc." seldom survive the first bombardment; thus, they are rarely an impediment to reinforcements. Further, Carson, Reno, Vegas, and later Elko hardly could be described as "poor real estate." They were the only protection for the MLR, not to mention protection for the flanks of Outposts Berlin and East Berlin. General Clarke's reasoning is flawed.

Could the outposts have been held? The Army was not shorthanded. The Jamestown Line was better defended in May 1953 than it ever had been. Further, as the fighting became more intense on 29 May, the 1st Marine Regiment moved forward from Corps reserve and bivouacked behind the 25th Infantry to await orders to counterattack. Those orders never came.

The Marine Reconnaissance Company was also moved forward in order to replace the Army's Baker Company, 14th Regiment, which had been deployed to reinforce Elko. Though it was not directly affected, the loss of Vegas and Elko touched the morale of its men as well. Sergeant Lipper wrote home, "One thing that bothers us more than anything else are the Army's comments on the recent loss of Vegas. A lot of Marines got chewed up re-taking that hill. They had been told to take them 'at all cost.' Now they are no longer important. Losing outposts is no disgrace but not re-taking them is a damned shame. Those doggies are just worthless."[19] The Turks, too, strenuously objected to giving up the Nevada Cities outposts. They felt that the loss was a stain on their national honor and ability as fighting men. They argued that they should be allowed to retake the hills and believed that they were capable of doing so.

In addition to manpower, plenty of firepower was also available. The Army had four battalions of artillery from the 11th Marines. Together, they fired a total of 56,280 rounds during the period of 28–30 May, which accounted for almost half of the 117,000 total rounds expended by all of the Army's artillery assets. Marine air flew 119 sorties, and Marine tanks on the MLR accounted for nearly two thousand enemy casualties.[20]

The Nevada Cities outposts were not lost for a lack of manpower or because of inadequate firepower. They were lost because the American general blinked first.

In a note of irony, on 15 June, General Clarke, the man who abandoned the Nevada outposts, presented a Distinguished Service Medal to Maj. Gen. Edwin A. Pollock, Commander, 1st Marine Division, for his "outstanding success" in defending those same outposts in March. Lord Nelson was right—the officer who attacks his enemy is esteemed. (Note the epigraph at the beginning of this chapter.)

In 1920, Sir Ian Hamilton, the British general, wrote: "The most fatal heresy in war, and, with us, the most rank, is the heresy that battles can be won without heavy loss." The Korean heresy was that they were not trying to win the battle at all.

I CORPS RESERVE

For Marines, the May-June period of reserve was devoted largely to training. From general to private, emphasis was placed on using this time to maintain combat readiness. Whoever said that reserve was for rest and relaxation was dead wrong. It was for training, camp construction, and hard work. On 10 May, elements of the 5th Marines boarded ships at Inchon Harbor for a weeklong amphibious landing exercise, a MARLEX, on an offshore island.

The 1st Marines, approximately 3,500 men, remained bivouacked behind the MLR until 5 June in readiness to counterattack Vegas. On return of the 5th Regiment, officers and men of the 1st Marines began to prepare for their amphibious exercise.

From 2 through 11 June, elements of the 7th Marines participated in a MARLEX, while the remaining units continued training in other areas. Typical reserve activities included attendance at Machine Gun School, NCO School, and Mine Warfare School. Battalion-level instruction consisted of amphibious training, individual weapons training, military courtesy, and field problems, with at least 50 percent of all tactical training done at night. Sergeant Kreid relates the reserve experience of his unit, Dog Company 2/7:

> The first few days in Corps Reserve we were kept pretty busy squaring away our gear. Weapons were cleaned, oiled and cleaned again. Any combat equipment (782 gear) that needed replacing was exchanged.
>
> After we were combat ready, we were "turned to" improving our new camp. We lived in squad tents with room for twelve bunks. Staff NCO's had their own tents as did buck sergeants. I was bunked next to Dennis Pryzgoda, a tall blue eyed Polish lad from Yonkers, New York, who loved country music. He had a smile for everyone and was almost too good natured to be a sergeant, but he got the job done. Dennis was as brave as he was good natured.
>
> It was in reserve that most of us saw our first inflatable air mattress. We called it a "rubber bitch." They did make the folding cots more comfortable to sleep on.
>
> On days off from training and work, we would take our beer and our rubber bitch down to the Imjin river for a swim. One day as I lay in the sand, I thought, "It was hard to believe that only a few miles

north men were killing one another any way they could." As I lay there watching those naked Marines playing in the water like puppies, I began to count the ones who had been wounded. Those with ugly red scars on their bodies. Some scars were fresh enough to observe where the surgeons knot had been tied. It looked like every third or fourth man had been wounded.

Some of the best times I had in Korea were at night, sitting around in the tent, talking. The subject was nearly always the same—women. Tales of conquest, of failure, of moves we should have made and didn't, or stupid moves we did make and blew it, it was endless. Sometimes we would laugh until there were no more tears left in our eyes.

It was these bull sessions, coupled with the price we paid to become Marines, that pulled us together into a unit, that made us buddies. Each of us knew the other, had been in combat together, and knew that our buddy would risk his life if necessary for the other. This was how Dog Company became a brotherhood.

About mid-June we could tell it would not be too long before the Division would be going back to the MLR. The tempo of our training increased, and it seemed like everything was done with more urgency. We had the feeling that our rest in reserve would soon be over.[21]

At Panmunjom, negotiations appeared to be coming to a close, which would lead to a halt in the war. The Marine Division reactivated and updated its plans for Operation Little Switch in anticipation of the war's end and an exchange of large numbers of prisoners of war. A scheduled amphibious landing exercise by the 1st Marines was canceled when naval commitments were diverted to assist with the anticipated prisoner exchange. No one believed that the Marines would stay long in reserve, but no one could anticipate events that threw some Marines into action in the opposite direction to the south.

Long opposed to a truce that did not include reunification of the entire country, the ROK National Assembly passed a resolution on 6 June that demanded freedom for all anti-Communist North Koreans held in South Korean POW camps. In various cities, South Korean civilians emphasized their support with violent demonstrations against the proposed truce. Immediately, the 5th Marines began training for riot control, and response plans were formulated to quell the riots. Then, in the early morning hours of 18 June, approximately twenty-five thousand North Koreans were released from POW camps in the Pusan area. Unauthorized by the UN, the release was ordered unilaterally by President Syngman Rhee and carried out by his ROK troops.

That night, prisoners in Camp Ten near Ascom City, the enormous Marine supply depot at Inchon Harbor, rioted and launched a breakout attempt. Able Company, 1st Amphibian Tractor Battalion, was hastily thrown into the breach. In the ensuing melee, 41 prisoners were killed, most of whom were trampled and crushed against the wire. An additional 84 prisoners were wounded, but 469 escaped. One Marine was wounded by rifle fire.

The consequence of these actions, taken unilaterally by the South Koreans, caused diplomatic panic. The peace negotiations immediately ceased, and a truce suddenly appeared quite distant. It slipped even further as Chinese forces launched a particularly vicious offensive against ROK divisions in Central Korea. The war apparently had resumed with a fury and seemed destined to continue indefinitely. The 1st Marine Division prepared to return to the line, its reserve period coming to a close. Sergeant Kreid continues:

... We stepped up our preparations. Advance parties were picked to go ahead to our new positions on the MLR. The troops knew very little except that we were scheduled to relieve the Turkish Brigade and the relief would be at night. This meant that we were returning to our old area near the Nevada Cities outposts, except now they were no longer ours. This made old Luke the Gook closer to our MLR. It meant that patrols would be more dangerous, and with the Chinese creeping tactics of continuous digging, the enemy would be in our laps at no time. Damn the Army for giving up those outposts!

The rains came until it seemed that the earth could hold no more. It was still raining when we were told one afternoon that we would relieve the Turks that night. It was early in July.[22]

CHAPTER 11

RETURN TO WAR

Political power emanates from the barrel of a gun.
—Mao Tse-tung: *On Guerrilla Warfare,* 1937

During the 1st Marine Division's hiatus in May and June, activity around the truce table at Panmunjom intensified. The press, both Communist and UN, reported that the combatants were beginning to show signs of compromise. Rumors of a forthcoming armistice began to fly. Then Rhee freed the POWs, and no one knew what to expect.

July 1953 marked the anniversary of two years of negotiating, if one could call it that. The only substantive accomplishment in all that time had been an exchange of sick and wounded prisoners during Operation Little Switch. One could hardly blame the troops for being cynical; they were still facing a deadly enemy, patrolling no-man's-land, and taking shells from incoming artillery. Yet, if the shooting were to stop, few would complain.

As July opened, there were strong indications that an armistice would soon take place. Until it did, however, the war would continue. Preparations to relieve the Army's 25th Division on the Jamestown Line were under way. I Corps desired that the relief be effected during the night of 7–8 July, and the 1st Marine Division returned to the sector that it had vacated two months earlier.

The territory to which the Marines returned was altogether different from that which they had left in May. The Nevada Cities, Outposts Carson, Elko, and Vegas, were under enemy control. The only outposts remaining to protect the MLR's right sector were Berlin, East Berlin, and Ava. The effect was not to the Marines' liking. More than 4 miles of the MLR lacked an outpost screen. There was no way to alert the MLR to a sudden enemy assault or to slow it down. The line was terribly weakened, vulnerable. Commenting on the situation, Maj. Gen. Randolph McC. Pate, who had assumed command of the 1st Marine Division on 15 June, observed in his "Berlin Report," as quoted in Meid and Yingling:

> Vegas [had] dominated the enemy approaches to Berlin from the north and northwest and therefore made Berlin relatively secure. Berlin, in turn, dominated the enemy approaches from the north and northwest to East Berlin and made East Berlin relatively secure. The loss of outpost Vegas to the CCF placed Berlin and East Berlin in very precarious positions and negated their being supported by ground fire except from the MLR.[1]

The weakness was aggravated by terrain features. Both Berlin outposts were situated on separate fingers of a larger land mass known as Hill 190. The bulk of Hill 190 was a major enemy strong point. Its position enabled the Chinese to initiate sudden attacks on the Berlin outposts from behind ridgelines protected from MLR observation and direct fire. Outposts Vegas and Carson had formerly covered that approach. This was a perfect example of the "domino effect" caused by the loss of critical outposts forward of the MLR. Without outpost protection, the MLR and the Berlins were exposed to the full brunt of enemy attacks, which lessened the ability of superior UN firepower to reach out and pound the enemy before he came too close.

Of further concern were intelligence reports of a Chinese armored regiment deployed in the vicinity of Kaesong. Reliable sources reported the presence of at least thirty-six T-34 medium tanks, four JS-2 heavy tanks, and four JSU-122 self-propelled guns, all of Soviet manufacture. The vehicles stayed generally within the confines of the neutral zone where they were out of reach to UN air. On one occasion, however, a self-propelled gun was seen by a sharp-eyed Marine tank crew in a firing slot away from the Zone. The tank immediately fired, hitting the vehicle with a round of high explosive. The Marines could not determine the extent of damage as they watched the vehicle back out of its firing position and disappear.[2]

Strange as it might seem, many of the Marines were eager to return to war. Two months of garrison duty had made the men antsy, bored with the training, and tired of the hard work. They were tired, too, of attempts at spit and polish in the dirt, dust, and grime and the seemingly petty routine of military discipline that occurs in rear areas.

On 3 July, Cpl. Robert A. Hall, a machine gunner attached to Easy Company 2/5, was notified that he would be part of an advance party to relieve Army units. Corporal Hall wrote:

About a dozen men from each of the 2nd Battalion line companies, Dog, Easy and Fox, were to be taken to the portion of the MLR they were to occupy. There they were to make arrangements for the orderly relief of Army units then in position. The remaining one hundred-sixty or so Marines of each company, would follow in three days. Marine rifle company strength and size was somewhat different than the Army's. We had to plan bunker assignments, fields of fire, and patrol routes.

Personally, I was eager to get back to the line. The training and repetition of the same infantry skills had made us better infantrymen, but also brought out what was seen as "chicken shit." Reserve was wearing out for several reasons. Our depleted units had been built back up to near T/O strength by arrival of the 31st and 32nd Replacement Drafts. Because of the ongoing truce talks, there was some concern among the new men that the war might end before they could get in it.[3]

The full relief began on 6 July and was completed the next day. For those units that had stayed to support the Army, there was little change. The tank battalion resumed its former tactic of maintaining a forward and a rear reserve with two companies on line, each supporting an infantry regiment. Much to the satisfaction of Marine tankers, the Army's pillbox tactic was immediately abandoned.

The KMC regiment resumed its former positions left of the Neutral Corridor, and the 1st Marines moved into division reserve. The 5th Marines relieved the Army's 35th Infantry in the center sector, and the 7th Marines relieved the Turkish Brigade on the right. Sgt. Bob Kreid, the machine gunner from Dog Company 2/7, expresses his feelings when the 7th Marines left the reserve area for the MLR:

I felt good. I wasn't eager to go back, but neither did I have the anxiety I felt before Vegas and Carson. I now had the third machine gun section, Sgt. Dennis Pryzgoda the first section and Sgt. Jerry Roose the second section. All three of us were buck sergeants. Though the TO (Table of Organization) called for Staff Sergeants, line companies were never up to TO strength. . . .

It began to rain before we reached the trucks. A few four letter words were mumbled as rifles were re-slung with their muzzles down, and ponchos broken out. No one liked the rain when they had to live in it. After what seemed like hours, the wet torturous journey came to an end. The trucks stopped somewhere behind the MLR.

Members of our advance party met us to guide the platoons to their new positions, and as we moved out in a column of twos, it began to rain again. The scene reminded me of an old movie, "All's Quiet on the Western Front," the rain, the mud, soldiers bent over in the darkness carrying their loads. This was another western front, two world wars and thirty-five years later. It was eerie.[4]

BERLIN OUTPOSTS ATTACKED

The 7th Marines were not in an enviable position, and it did not take the Chinese long to exploit it. The men had hardly unrolled their sleeping bags when, at 2100 on 7 July, several companies of Chinese attacked East Berlin and Berlin, each a platoon-sized outpost.

To isolate the outposts from supporting fire, the enemy subjected the MLR to an intense bombardment. Sergeant Kreid describes the attack as he experienced it from the MLR that night:

There was a saying among Marines that the Chinese Army conducted a "Dr. Pepper War." They would attack at 10 O'clock, 2 O'clock and 4 O'clock at night. Sure enough, at 2200 we began receiving heavy incoming, mostly mortars. In the CP our lieutenant called for mortars to illuminate our platoon front. In seconds we could hear the 60-mm tubes behind us coughing out illumination rounds. In the CP bunker we waited.

Around 0200 our forward positions reported that they were getting white phosphorous smoke screens. Our listening post had almost zero visibility and asked us to place some machine gun fire over the top of their hole in case of any approaching enemy.

Nothing is worse than not knowing or seeing what was happening. In our cave-like CP we imagined we were going to be up to our ass in gooks very shortly. I sat at a makeshift table on the platoon phone watch. The lieutenant had the phone to the company net. I was facing the only door in the bunker which was covered with a wool blanket. The longer I sat there the more I could imagine old Joe Chink coming through that blanket with a blazing burp gun, or throwing in a grenade first.

I reached down, opened my holster and took out the Government Model .45 that my father and uncle had bought for me the last time I was home. I put the pistol on full cock, pushed the safety on and laid it on the table near my right hand. The pistol made me feel better just lying there. It also made me think of home and kin. I wondered if I'd ever see them again.

Finally, we got the word that the Berlins had been hit and East Berlin overrun. Company asked if we could lay machine gun fire into the rice paddy at the foot of Berlin. I got the .50 crew on the phone. The assistant gunner said that they could see part of the paddy through the smoke, and I gave the order to commence firing.

I was concerned about giving the position away by firing that big .50 at night. It had a thirty-six inch muzzle flash that could be seen for miles. But, orders were orders.

I could hear the methodical "chug, chug, chug" of the gun over the phone. Suddenly there was an explosion and the gun was quiet. I thought a grenade had been thrown into the bunker. I kept repeating the assistant gunner's name over the phone, finally he answered, "This son of a bitch blew up." "What blew up?" I replied. "This fucking gun, what else?" "Are ya'll OK?" I inquired. "I guess, but this gun has had the course."

I was able to replace the .50 with a light .30 from another position and continue the fire mission. The .50 was a goner. Apparently a cartridge had fired before the action was locked. The gun was ruined.[5]

On the MLR, no one could tell if either of the outposts held, but the situation did not look good. Elsewhere on line, Sgt. Roy Seabury operated a heavy machine gun for 3/7. He describes the action from his location overlooking the outposts:

The shells were coming in so heavy it was impossible to move. The Chinese infantry attacked OP East Berlin while their artillery pounded us. They were all over the OP like ants.

Our gun was knocked out early that night. Shrapnel had punctured the water jacket. The remnants of our machine gun section became riflemen. Most of us had only .45 caliber pistols, so we took weapons off dead or wounded Marines. I grabbed a BAR. . . .

All of our Corpsmen were dead. Pfc. Walter Eicholz laid down his rifle and started working on the wounded up and down the trench line while we laid fire down toward East Berlin. We had taken many casualties and were low on ammo and first aid supplies.

During the fighting, Eicholz jumped out of the trench and ran to East Berlin, right through the Chinese fire. He came running back to the MLR with a wounded Marine over his shoulder. On his next trip to the OP he brought back bandoliers of .30 caliber ammunition, a knapsack filled with grenades and another wounded Marine. He made seven trips to OP East Berlin before he was killed. There are many Marines alive today because of Walter's heroism. [Pfc. Walter Eicholz was posthumously awarded a Silver Star.][6]

Difficult as conditions were on the MLR, they were many times worse on the outposts. When Chinese infantry attacked Berlin on 7 July, the Marines discovered unexpected strength in the form of Turkish soldiers who had not yet departed. Consequently, there were twice as many defenders as might be normally expected. Further, a reinforced squad from Fox Company 2/7, returning from an ambush, was also on the hill. Even so, the reinforced Marines were heavily outnumbered, and, by 2345, the fighting was hand to hand in the trenches.

Lacking the reinforcements enjoyed by the men on Berlin, East Berlin quickly fell. Within ten minutes, Marines were desperately fighting in the trenches and slugging it out with everything they had, but to no avail. By midnight, the hill position was overrun and communication lost. Berlin held on slightly longer, but, by 0130, communication with it too was cut off. No one knew who owned the hill.

Throughout the night of 7–8 July, fighting continued. The Chinese continued to shell the MLR, and the Marines became concerned that they might be attempting a breakthrough. The Berlin outposts were only 325 yards from the MLR, well within range of a determined infantry attack. Consequently, 3/7, the reserve battalion, was moved forward to reinforce the MLR.

UN artillery fire was generously applied to known Chinese positions. Battalions of the 11th Marines, augmented by seven U.S. Army and Turkish artillery battalions that had not yet left the area, were employed. Reportedly, on Vegas, a Marine artillery fire mission landed direct hits on a full company of Chinese soldiers.

Two platoons of Baker Company tanks fired eight hundred rounds of 90-mm at enemy positions on Reno, Vegas, and Hill 190. In retaliation, the tanks received more than two thousand rounds of incoming mortar and artillery fire. The MLR was devastated, trenches crumbled, and bunkers fell. Fighting holes were destroyed faster than they could be dug.

The Marines on the Berlins, however, knew little of what was happening. Throughout the night, efforts to relieve the outposts were initiated to no avail. At 0438, a counterattacking squad clashed with the enemy on the slopes of East Berlin but could not gain an advantage. Another squad from Fox Company 2/7 attempted to reinforce the counterattack, but it was also repulsed. There were just too many Chinese.

Finally, at 0500, it was determined that East Berlin had fallen and was in full possession of Chinese forces. The counterattacking squads were ordered to withdraw to enable an artillery saturation of the outpost.

Of the original platoon on East Berlin, nothing was known. On this point, archival reports are vague. Officially, the platoon seems to have vanished from the face of the earth; however, at least one man survived. Sgt. Vernon Schmidt, a squad leader with Item Company 3/7, recalls in a letter how one of his men was wounded:

> ... The night East Berlin was overrun Pfc. "Moose" Moran had taken a gook train of supplies out to the outpost. Just after he arrived, they hit with overwhelming force. He told me about it the next morning while the Corpsman was working on him.
>
> I was sitting outside the aid bunker holding my injured head with both hands when they brought Moran to the Corpsman; he looked like hell. But he talked in a clear voice. He said that goonies came up to him and hit him with a rifle butt, then dropped a grenade between his legs. Thinking he was dead, they threw his body into the barbed wire. When he came to he couldn't get out of the wire without zipping out of his flak jacket. It took him all night to crawl about five hundred feet to the MLR gate.
>
> During this time the enemy threw mortars into the area keeping us from sending reinforcements to East Berlin. We likewise threw mortars to prevent the goonies from coming through the gate. Moran was caught in the crossfire.
>
> He had no water with him and said that he drank out of a puddle in a nearby paddy. At daylight someone saw him and went out to get him while under fire from the Chinese holding East Berlin. I'm not sure if he had been bayoneted or not, but he had shrapnel wounds all over and his upper legs looked like hamburger that was dropped in the mud. One eye was hanging on his cheek, the one hit with a rifle butt. When they came to carry him away he said, "I'm going back to New York if I have to crawl." He was some Irishman.[7]

Perhaps others on East Berlin were able to escape Moran's fate; unfortunately, no one knew. By dawn on 8 July, the Chinese were in full control of the hill.

To the west, meanwhile, Outpost Berlin had managed to repulse the attacks and remain in Marine hands—just barely. Eighteen Marines and a handful of Turks had held onto it. When it was determined that Berlin had not fallen, another eighteen Marines from Fox Company 2/7 were dispatched to reinforce the position. No more could be sent as the hill was simply too small to accommodate a greater number of people. Berlin remained in Marine hands.

Meanwhile, plans to retake East Berlin were formulated. On 8 July at 1000, the 1st Platoon of How Company 3/7 made the first attempt. While charging the hill, the platoon's strength was cut to twenty effectives. Twenty minutes later, the 1st Platoon of George Company 3/7 left the MLR to reinforce the attackers. Passing through the How platoon, it continued to press the attack and reached the first trenches at 1123.

Under a curtain of friendly mortar and artillery, augmented by tanks and automatic weapons from the MLR, the men of George Company forced their way to the top of East Berlin. As they climbed the slopes, tanks fired high-explosive 90-mm rounds from the MLR that impacted only yards in front of the Marines. The tank fire moved forward as the infantry advanced and provided a deadly screen of exploding steel leading the attack.

During the ebb and flow of fighting, Sgt. David Smith of Fox Company 2/7 realized that his squad had advanced too far and was surrounded. It became necessary to withdraw. He organized his remaining men, and they began to fight their way back through enemy soldiers in the trenches. Hearing a wounded Marine calling from the outpost, Smith ordered his men to continue on while he returned for the casualty. Trying to reach the wounded Marine, Smith again battled hand to hand with Chinese troops occupying the trench line until, finally, he was killed. The men from the George Company platoon witnessed the melee and, inspired by the courage shown by Sergeant Smith, counterattacked.

Charging up the hill, George and Fox Companies attained the trenches and fought for another hour with grenades, fists, and small arms before gaining the crest of the outpost. The Marines threw Chinese soldiers bodily out of the trenches and off the hill. Fighting like demons, they killed or routed every defender on the outpost. By 1233, with twenty men left in fighting condition, the exhausted Marines regained possession of East Berlin.

Sergeant Smith did not live to see the attack succeed, but his courage significantly contributed to the success of the counterattack. He was posthumously awarded a Navy Cross.

During the afternoon of 8 July, the Chinese were comparatively quiet. Marine artillery continued with fire missions on suspected enemy positions and assembly points. Observation planes, when they could get through the rain, reported no enemy movement, and the Marines were afforded an opportunity to regroup, resupply, and tend to their wounded.

Their most important task at this time was to continue with the Army's relief started two days earlier.

Although the infantry units on line had been relieved, many of the Army's supporting arms, tanks, and artillery were still in place. Their intervention in the fighting that followed had been quite valuable. The Chinese, by hitting during "shift change," found that they had to contend with twice as much artillery and tank fire. In all, Marine and Army artillery units fired more than twenty thousand rounds during the two-day battle for the Berlin outposts. This figure did not include tank support or air strikes.

Along with relieving the Army as scheduled, the Marines also had to relieve George and Fox Companies on East Berlin. At 1300, Item Company's 1st Platoon was dispatched. The platoon guide was Sgt. Tom Parlin, the platoon leader was Lt. Paul Giordani. Sergeant Parlin wrote of his experience during the relief on East Berlin on 8 July and the morning of 9 July:

> The George Company platoon leader told us that there were still enemy troops on the forward portion of the hill. He did not have enough effectives to handle them, and was moving back to the MLR. We consolidated the entire outpost with no casualties and prepared ourselves for immediate counter attack. We had been told we would be relieved shortly after we replaced the George Company platoon. In late afternoon. We learned by radio that we would be relieved after dark. A later radio message advised we would stay on the hill all night. Lt. Giordani, Sgt. Al Joyce and I put our heads together to decide on a course of action, We knew we would be hit hard sometime soon. Our packs with our entrenching tools were back at the MLR and our ammo supply was low. We started digging in with hands, helmets and two Chinese shovels. I asked Lt. Giordani if we couldn't get some supplies. "Go for it," he said. I radioed for water, a case of C ration, MG and rifle ammo, and case of grenades. These came in after dark, carried by four volunteers. The water and ammo were to prove lifesaving.
>
> We had been receiving sporadic artillery fire since our arrival, now shelling intensified. We had our first KIA, Pfc. George Yerger. Another radio to Lt. Giordani ordered him to hold the hill at all costs. We could expect no help except artillery and mortar support, also mortar illuminating rounds were in short supply. Lt. Giordani decided that he would direct and fight from the right side of the outpost and Sgt. Joyce the left. I was to stay on the backside of OP East Berlin with the PRC 6 radio. Our sound power phone line was out. The lieutenant sent two riflemen to find the break and repair it.

Reports began coming in that the enemy was coming in on our front and from both flanks. Lt. Giordani told me to radio our CP to stand by to shoot, on our order, a mortar box barrage with illumination shells around our positions. All hell broke loose as the Chinese launched their attack. Our MGs and riflemen opened fire. I called for mortars. The men were yelling for more illumination; the cry "Corpsman" could be heard. So far no enemy had gotten into our positions. I noticed two men at the backside of the hill. At first I thought they were our two men sent to repair the phone line. As they drew closer, I could see their burp guns. I opened up with my TSMG [Thompson submachine gun] and at that range I couldn't miss. More enemy troops hove into sight. I lobbed three grenades into them. No further enemy tried that route, but I would periodically spray the area anyway, as a safety precaution.

An assistant machine gunner from the very top of the hill came looking for more ammo. I gave him several cans. He started back up, had not gone far when he yelled "look out." I turned to see a single Chinese soldier throw something at me. There was a blast which knocked me down. My right leg went numb. Amazingly, the Chinese stood looking at me, I guess trying to decide whether I was dead or not. I had not dropped my Tommy Gun so it was no problem killing him with a short burst. My leg began to get a little feeling in it. I was able to stand up. Wobbly, but up. I went back to my position. Looking down the hill, I could see two men coming up. I almost opened fire, but in good time realized they were our two men from the wire patrol. They told me that in tracing the broken wire they saw the enemy coming. Since they were in the open paddy with dead bodies lying around, they played dead and let the Chinese run by them. When the firing abated, they came back up the hill. They had not been able to find the break in the sound power phone wire. The enemy started pulling back from their attack. Small arms fire slackened, then ceased. Mortar and artillery fire continued, although moderated from its previous peak. That fire continued throughout the night. A platoon head count showed we had thirteen dead, including one corpsman, and three WIA. A plane appeared, circling overhead, dropping flares the rest of the night.

The next day was a continuation of artillery and mortar fire plus long range harassing machine gun fire. Shortly before night fall the radio brought word that the second platoon of our company would relieve us after dark. That did not happen. In the move up, the second platoon came under intense small arms fire resulting in the loss of the platoon leader and four men.

The second night passed with several minor probing attacks. Just after dawn, covering smoke was fired to mask movement of the relief platoon while they climbed the back side of OP East Berlin. A mortar round landed in the midst of four men of our platoon, killing three, and wounding the fourth who would die shortly. His name was Pfc. Alton Ray. He was our last platoon casualty of that engagement. Three of the eight of us that came off that hill were wounded, three of that eight would die later in the month.[8]

Throughout the early morning hours of 9 July, Chinese troops continued to probe the outposts. Each assault was preceded by quantities of artillery and mortar fire. The enemy persisted but on every occasion was beaten back. Each attack cost a few more men on either side. The last attack on Berlin broke off at 0130. During the next two hours, East Berlin suffered five more attacks and secured finally at 0300. Then, it was over. The Berlin outposts remained in Marine hands but at a cost— 9 Marines died, 12 were missing, and 140 were wounded. On the Chinese side, estimated casualties totaled more than 600.[9]

Several days later, in an Associated Press release dated July 20, 1953, Capt. Verle E. Ludwig, a Marine combat reporter, interviewed Sgt. Robert E. Rich, who had escaped from Outpost Berlin during one of the early assaults. Sergeant Rich related that, as the outpost came under heavy shelling from both sides, he had taken refuge in a nearby bunker:

"The next thing I knew Goonies were walking all around me. They'd moved in right under their own artillery. They started yelling for me to lay down my weapon and surrender. I guess they were the only English words they knew. One Goonie stuck his head into the caved in bunker, and I shot him in the face with my .45. Then there was another one and I blasted him at point blank range. I guess they didn't know that shot finished off my ammo, because there were no more to stick their heads in. But at least they knew I wasn't about to surrender because they threw a grenade in with me. It had a long fuse on it, though, and I had time to pitch it back before it went off. Next came a charge of explosives packed in a long iron pipe and I was just shoving that back out the opening when the thing went off."

The blast knocked the sergeant back across the bunker and dazed him. He was cut on the face, arms and hands by fragments. When he regained consciousness he looked outside and the Chinese saw him. A Red soldier stuck his head and shoulders inside the bunker opening and began to fire at the Marine.

Rich escaped by sliding out a rear opening of the bunker and working his way down the slope of the outpost hill toward enemy territory.

The squad leader, who has been in Korea since February, hid the next day near an abandoned rice paddy where he could get some water. He had no food.

The following night Rich again took to the darkened trails.

He climbed a hill toward what he thought was the Marine front line and shouted his identity. But then he discovered he was deeper in enemy territory. He walked under the muzzles of two Chinese machine gun nests.

"They began to shoot at me and fire mortars around me. So I knew I was still a little off base. I circled around and started working my way up over the shoulder of East Berlin."

Rich found his escape route blocked on East Berlin, so he doubled back, deeper into enemy country. There he switched toward Allied lines in the saddle between the fallen outposts.

He spent the day hiding in a rocky niche only a few yards from a Chinese soldier working on a gun emplacement. And in daylight he was able to regain his sense of direction.

Under cover of darkness Tuesday night [July 9] Rich worked his way cautiously across the paddies toward the Marine front lines. He reached an abandoned bunker forward of the Marine line shortly before day break and there he found the first food he had eaten since Sunday night—a single can of C rations.[10]

Sixty hours and two nights later, Sergeant Rich found his way to safety behind Marine lines. Medical personnel treated his wounds and praised his constitution, which they said enabled his survival.

A REST BETWEEN BATTLES

After the 7–9 July flare-up on the Berlins, action lulled. The 7th Marines had an opportunity to reorganize and prepare for the next assault, which they knew was bound to come. The 2d Battalion was removed from the line and replaced by 3/7, which had been pulled up from regimental reserve. Although some 3/7 platoons had participated in the recent fighting, most of the troops were well rested and eager. The 2d Battalion, which had taken the brunt of the three-day battle for the Berlins, was beat up.

Also in need of rest were the Baker Company tanks. The crews and vehicles had been on line continuously for more than sixty days, since before the Army relief. Vehicles, particularly, required extensive repair and maintenance. It was ironic that the big, cumbersome, seemingly invulnerable armored machines were so delicate as to require more frequent attention than the men who crewed them. Perhaps it had something to do with their maker.

Charlie Company tanks replaced Baker's in supporting the 7th Marines, while Able Company tanks continued to support the 5th Marines in the center sector. For the next week and a half, activity on the Jamestown Line was sporadic and consisted of a few patrol clashes and ambushes. Incoming fire on Marine positions was minimal.

During the second week of July, torrential summer rains fell virtually nonstop throughout South Korea. Roads turned to mush, streams and rivers overflowed, and bridges washed out. The Imjin River at Libby Bridge crested at 26 feet. Spoonbill Bridge was under 11 feet of water and finally washed away. Roads were impassable for three or four days at a stretch. Transportation between the line and rear supply areas was completely bogged down.

To many of the men, it seemed as though the rain would never stop. Vehicles were unable to move. Tanks in position atop hills could not fire because gunners were unable to see targets through low clouds lying in the valleys below them, nor could they leave their positions on the slippery, eroded roads.

Rain, continual haze, and ground fog for most of the days through 18 July reduced the effectiveness of ground patrols and Marine air observers. Few enemy troops were seen, but Marine patrols reported finding numerous new minefields in and around commonly used trails. On 12 July, six Marines from one squad of Baker Company 1/7 were wounded when they detonated newly laid mines.

Later that night, a two-squad patrol from Baker Company was within 15 yards of the trenches on former Outpost Elko when it was attacked with machine-gun fire from Carson. The fire was followed by a barrage of grenades from Elko. After an hour-long firefight, the Marines withdrew under mortar fire with one casualty.

Near 0100 on 17 July, a two-squad patrol from Able Company 1/7 got into trouble when it encountered an enemy patrol twice its size. After a brief firefight, the Marines broke off and returned to Outpost Ava. A muster of the patrol revealed that four men were missing. A group was organized and left the outpost immediately to search the area. By dawn, the search party had recovered three bodies but was forced to return before daylight revealed its presence to the enemy.

On the division center, the 5th Marines did not escape enemy attention. At midnight on 16 July, a fifteen-man reconnaissance patrol from 2/5 was ambushed by a group of thirty to forty Chinese near Hill 90, two miles east of the Neutral Corridor. Surrounded, the Marines beat back the Chinese with rifles, BARs, hand grenades, and fists. A relief squad left the MLR to reinforce the badly outnumbered patrol but was intercepted by a mortar shelling that wounded every man in the detail. A second relief squad entered the area, but it also came under mortar bombardment. Taking cover, the Marines engaged the enemy in a vicious firefight that lasted two hours.

Before breaking off, Chinese troops made several attempts to capture prisoners. When the Marines withdrew, a quick head count revealed that seven men were missing. The following night, a search platoon scoured the area and returned with six Marine bodies.

Pfc. Roy Stewart was a member of the reconnaissance patrol. When the ambush occurred, half of the men were immediately wounded. Protecting the casualties while fighting for his own life, Stewart repeatedly exposed himself to fire as he repelled the attacking Chinese soldiers. When he saw a live hand grenade fall among the wounded, he scooped it up and hurled it back toward the enemy. Finally, as everyone in the patrol was wounded, Stewart was the last man able to fire. Standing upright amid the charging Chinese, he managed to kill five more of them before he was seriously wounded. Still, despite his weakening condition, he continued to fire his weapon and single-handedly held off the advancing enemy until reinforcements finally arrived. Miraculously, Stewart survived and was awarded a well-deserved Navy Cross.[11]

The following night, candidly expressing himself in a letter to his wife, a Marine tank lieutenant wrote:

> One of the infantry patrols was really clobbered last night and they are out trying to get some of the dead back now. There are still about six out there. Every day I realize how lucky I am not being in the infantry. They rate all the glory they get and then some.[12]

Glory was not exactly what the infantry received. It was more like death, hardship, and minimal appreciation. They did have their moments, however. A combat patrol from 1/7's Charlie Company, for example, ran into a little trouble in the Ungok hills. Not to be outdone by Chinese efforts at psychological warfare, the Marines, according to the 1/7 Command Diary, reportedly left a souvenir for the enemy to ponder: "During the action the patrol planted a Marine Corps recruiting sign at their FPOA [farthest point of advance] facing the enemy."[13]

One of two men wounded on that patrol was Sgt. Stephen Walter of Charlie Company 1/7. Sergeant Walter was credited with maneuvering his squad through a shower of bullets and enemy hand grenades to destroy a critical machine-gun position. He then turned his men to engage another group of Chinese moving to outflank them. During the ensuing firefight, he was critically wounded by fragments from a hand grenade but continued to lead and control his squad as the patrol began to withdraw.

Weak from loss of blood, Sergeant Walter offered to stay behind and hold off the pursuing enemy while the rest of the patrol escaped to the MLR, but the patrol leader refused his sacrifice. As it became dark, the returning patrol became disoriented. Walter suggested that a WP grenade be thrown from the MLR for them to guide on. This tactic enabled the patrol to reach Marine lines safely without further casualties. Upon reaching the MLR, Sergeant Walter was immediately evacuated by helicopter to a medical unit, but he died before arrival. He was posthumously awarded a Navy Cross.[14]

THE BERLINS FALL

It soon became obvious that the previous week's calm was merely a temporary respite, a valuable time for the Chinese to build up strength. On 18 July, they again struck the Berlin outposts in overpowering numbers. According to conservative estimates, the Chinese employed a reinforced battalion for the initial assault and used a second battalion to hold the ground that they captured.[15] Forty-four Marines holding Berlin and thirty-seven on East Berlin, all from Item Company 3/7, were hardly a match for two battalions.

The Berlin outposts were attacked at 2200. After a very heavy mortar and artillery preparation (at one time reported to be one round per second), 1,000 Chinese troops swarmed the slopes of Berlin and East Berlin in waves of screaming, yelling, shooting humanity. Within the hour, they were halfway up the slope of Berlin. Fighting continued as fire from Marine 60-mm, 81-mm, 4.2-inch mortars, and artillery rained on the approaches to the hills to box in the defenders.

Marines on the outpost were still holding at midnight, but their prospects looked dismal. Fighting spread to the MLR, which was providing much of their fire support. Hill 111, the right anchor of the MLR that abutted the Australians in the British Commonwealth Division, received a probing attack shortly after midnight. Aussies and leathernecks repulsed it with small-arms and machine-gun fire.

On the outposts, according to the 1/7 Command Diary, the Marines "fought with grenades, small arms and machine gun fire until they were overwhelmed by sheer force of numbers. The outposts were declared officially lost at 0146."[16] It is hard to believe that, for more than four and a half hours, seventy-seven Marines stood off over a thousand enemy soldiers intent on destroying them.

Although official records do not report what became of the original defenders, an Associated Press release of the period helps to describe the intensity of the Chinese assault on the Berlins and the last desperate defense fought by the Marines on those hills:

Seoul-(AP) Jul 20—Recklessly attacking Chinese engulfed two vital western front outposts defended by U.S. Marines last night and the first Leatherneck survivors staggered back to Allied lines today.

In their last act, before the radio went dead, the trapped Marines— back in the battle lines only three weeks—called in their own artillery on top of them in a desperate effort to halt the violent onslaught. . . .

Fourteen Leathernecks of the 1st Marine Division were the first known survivors of the bloody battles for outposts East Berlin and Berlin, part of a key hill area on the western front.

Fatigued and wan, they staggered back into Marine lines. Eight were from outpost Berlin and six from East Berlin.

A Marine Second Lieutenant told the tragic story.

"They swarmed all over us before we could get our guns set up and our men in protective cover," said the lieutenant, as he sat on the edge of his cot at a front-line medical aid station.

The lieutenant had just led his unit up the slopes of East Berlin to relieve another unit when the Chinese struck—"They came through their own artillery fire and into our trenches. We were mowing them down but they kept on coming. There were so many we couldn't stop them. They came from all around us and as they came the Red guns pounded us with 120s and 76s. The first round hit my command post. Two of my men must still be there. They were killed—that I know."

"As soon as I saw the attack was on us I called for box-me-in-fire. I got it almost immediately, but it wasn't soon enough. Already they were on us. In our trenches, throwing hand grenades at the men in the holes, clubbing and shooting men who were on the machine guns and BARs."

"Then we lost all of our communications and when we finally had to pull off we had to make it through our own artillery box fire."

The lieutenant's sergeant, wounded when a Chinese pitched a grenade into the hole where he and another Marine crouched, told how the lieutenant personally manned one of the machine guns against the advancing Chinese.

The Sergeant said that the first Chinese came up the trail with the Korean service troops that carry supplies and ammunition at the front.

"Those first Chinks just walked up the hill path. They didn't seem to be in any hurry. Then they started hitting us, and there were Chinks all around us, in all our trenches, behind us, in front of us, on each side."

"We would keep firing until they were right on us. Then we would slam out, swinging our rifle butts, catching two or three sometimes with a single swing."

"All this time they were still shelling us. A 76 [76-mm artillery round] landed near me and I caught some of the fragments. One of my men pulled me into a hole. Then he crawled into it to pull me in farther and tried to get me out of the range."

"Then a gook put a burp gun into the hole and pulled the trigger. I heard my buddy let out a small moan. That was all. But that gook can never live to brag about it. The lieutenant shot him down on the spot."

The Red victory—won with staggering casualties—gave the Communists full control of a vital hill area made up of outposts Reno, Carson, and Vegas, East Berlin and Berlin.[17]

During the assault on the Berlins, two platoons of tanks provided continuous supporting fire on enemy troops and positions, as did four battalions of artillery and all direct-fire weapons on the MLR. Also dug in on the MLR, some 70 yards across from East Berlin, Sgt. Roy Seabury, a heavy machine gunner with Weapons Company 3/7, watched the attack from the aperture of his bunker:

> . . . All of a sudden, around 2200 hours, it seemed like a thousand lightning bolts struck. A mortar round hit right in front of our gun, blowing me back into the bunker. When I came to a short time later, I returned to the gun. As far as the eye could see there were Chinese. They were on the saddle going up to Berlin and in the rice paddies in front of us. Because of the light from all the shells and flares, we had 100% visibility. As I looked to the left front, I was able to see the sky- line of OP Berlin. I saw three Marines try to surrender and watched helplessly as the Chinese beat them with rifle butts and then bayo- neted them.
>
> Firing "Sudden Death," [a heavy .30] John and I mowed down Chinese on the saddle and in the rice paddy just below us. I didn't want to fire on East Berlin for fear of hitting Marines there, even though I could see Chinese all over the hill. . . .
>
> I don't know how many rounds we fired from 2200 to 0600 hours, but we changed the barrel twice. We engaged a Chinese machine gun from East Berlin. I saw the red tracers hammering right at me, finally realizing that East Berlin had fallen and that the Chinese were firing

one of our own guns at us. I fired a burst just above where the tracers were coming from and that silenced him.

. . . We fired that machine gun for eight straight hours . . . we covered the slopes on Berlin—the saddle in front of us, East Berlin much later in the night, and the rice paddy in front. . . . The trench line around us was nearly waist deep with empty shell casings.[18]

On 20 July, two companies of 7th Marines, Easy and Dog, assembled to retake the outposts. The plan called for a two-company assault in columns of platoons. Easy Company would take Outpost Berlin, and Dog Company was to take East Berlin. Four other companies; George, How, Item, and Weapons, would support the attack by fire from the MLR. The time of attack was set for 0730.

The Marines assembled on a road about 500 yards behind Hill 119. Gathered temporarily on a piece of flat ground, the men of Dog Company were suddenly subjected to incoming fire when three rounds of 76-mm screamed over the MLR and detonated 100 yards behind them. Sergeant Kreid describes his difficulties:

. . . My section was already moving. I turned to run, took two steps and fell flat hard on the ground. The lace hooks on my field boot had become entangled in comm wire. Lying there, with mortars starting to walk down the road, I remember wishing that the genius responsible for putting hooks on our boots was there in my place. I was scared shitless, but something gave me the good sense to grab the wire and jerk all the slack out of it. Though not much, it was enough for me to roll the five or six yards to a ditch alongside the road. I was in defilade as the next mortar round sent dirt into the ditch with me. I finally calmed myself enough to get free of the wire and ran to join my section, which was busy digging in.

As I dug I noticed that a machine gunner a few yards away had his hole almost dug. All at once he came out of his hole spitting and swearing. He looked at me and said, "Kreid, that's an old shitter! I thought it was too easy digging. Look at this shit!" pointing to his trousers, which were damp and stained from the knees down.

Those of us that heard him all began to laugh. "It's not funny you bastards. I'm not getting back in that fucking hole and I'm not digging another one," he protested. About that time another 76 cut through the air above us, and he went back into the hole, like a prairie dog with a hawk after his ass. We laughed until tears came to our eyes.

The young man cussed us, the 76's, the gooks, the Marine Corps and the war that got him here. I am happy to say that this young

Italian kid from Chicago made it through the war OK. He turned out to be a damn good Marine.[19]

As Dog Company prepared for the counterattack, word was passed for all platoon leaders, platoon sergeants, and section leaders to assemble at the company CP for briefing. Kreid continues:

> I found the company CP as the officers and NCO's were arriving. We knelt in a circle around the Company Commander while he explained the plan and our deployment. The word was that Dog Company was to retake East Berlin. Retake it, hell we didn't know it had been lost. I glanced across the circle to my buddy, Sgt. Dennis Pryzgoda whose first section of machine guns was attached to the first platoon of riflemen. He gave me a half grin. Dennis had a stressed, puzzled look on his face that I had never seen before, like he was trying to figure something out.
>
> Dog Company moved up the back side of Hill 119 single file in a column of platoons. I don't recall what order we moved out in, but Pryzgoda's section, with the first platoon was ahead of me. As we started the incoming increased. Up ahead I saw Marines drop their packs and begin to run forward.
>
> The communication trench on the reverse side of Hill 119 was a good trench, five to six feet deep, dug into hard ground. As we ran into the trench and started up the hill, two rounds came in, one behind the other. I dived for the bottom of the trench. When they exploded, it felt like the whole hill moved. White hot shrapnel growled and whined over the trench.
>
> Military ordnance detonates between sixteen and seventeen thousand feet per second. This sudden energy turns splintered shell cases into white hot shards of metal, razor sharp and jagged.
>
> We hated mortar and artillery barrages. The shell could, and did, turn men into hamburger meat. We also hated them for what they did to our minds. As incoming shells hiss in, one gets the feeling of utter helplessness. There is a millisecond between the time you hear it and it explodes. This time lapse is like an eternity. Each round sounds as though it will hit on top of you.
>
> We crawled up the communication trench on our stomachs as the rounds shook the hill. They were the largest caliber rounds any of us had ever seen, or felt. I had my Saint Christopher medal in my mouth. Every time a shell exploded I would bite hard and say part of the Twenty-third Psalm.
>
> As the trench reached the military crest, it began to shallow out to about four feet and turn to the left. I reached the turn and encountered

a large puddle of blood in the bottom of the trench. It was frothy with lung foam. "Damn" I thought! Someone's not going to make it. As a boy in Texas my father had taught me to deer hunt. I had seen too many lung shot deer. None had ever required a second bullet.

Not wanting to get blood on my clothing, I raised from my stomach and crawled over the puddle on all fours, like a crab. There was a Marine helmet near the blood. The helmet cover had slits cut in, like some Marines did to hold leaves for camouflage.

We moved around and across the hill into the forward trench that faced Berlin and East Berlin. The machine gun crews stayed down, ready to move to the top of the trench when the time came for the attack. No use exposing the guns over the top of the trench until their fire was needed. I don't know how long we waited there, ready to move out on East Berlin. Then we were told that the attack had been called off. No explanation, military orders seldom are explained. Just that it was over and we'd be going back.

The company runner came down the trench toward me. "Kreid," he said. "Did you hear? Sgt. Pryzgoda was killed." "What? Did you see him?" I replied. "Naw," he continued, "the doc that worked on him told me he was hit in the chest with some of that big shit they were throwing at us on the way up here. He never had a chance."

I began to recall, "Oh God! That was Dennis' blood and helmet I crawled over back there. That blood was a chest wound and he had slits cut in his helmet cover." I knew the first platoon was ahead of us in that trench. I felt sick. I wanted someone to tell me it wasn't true. I wanted to look up and see Dennis coming down the trench with that shitty little grin of his.

I wanted to yell out every vulgar, profane oath I knew. Yell it at the gooks. This fucking no win war. I thought, "This whole fucking country is not worth one life like yours, Dennis." All I could do was sit there and watch a big green blow fly crawl around on the toe of my boot. I thought, "nobody wins in this shitty war except rats, maggots and these frigging blow flies."

I noticed my Saint Christopher medal hanging outside my flak jacket and remembered Dennis was a devout Catholic. Though I wasn't, I repeated something I had heard at Mass, "Oh Holy Mary, Mother of God. Pray for us sinners now and at the hour of our death. Amen!"

I felt old, and so very tired.[20]

That morning, the operation to retake the Berlins was placed on hold. At 1230, it was canceled. Against objections of Marine brass, Lt. Gen. Bruce C. Clarke, USA, directed that Outposts Berlin and East

Berlin not be retaken. This was the same general who had canceled the Turkish counterattack on Outpost Vegas in May. He was now having to live with the results of that decision. The former Outpost Vegas was used extensively by the Chinese to stage their attacks on the Berlins. Some Allied observers speculated that the Reds took the Berlin outposts in the belief that no effort would be made to retake them with an armistice apparently imminent. The observers were correct. The Chinese were better at reading their enemy's intentions than were the Americans.

After cancellation of the counterattack on the Berlins, heavy, destructive missions by air, armor, and artillery devastated the hills in an effort to make them untenable for the enemy, a tactic tried before on the Nevada Cities. These missions were equally unsuccessful on the Berlins and remained a monumental waste of ordnance.

In an awesome display of firepower, a series of air strikes dropped 9 ½ tons of ordnance on the two little hills. Artillery fired 3,600 rounds of 240-mm and 8-inch howitzers, plus four rocket ripples. Charlie Company tanks expended 200 rounds of 90-mm and more than 6,000 rounds of machine-gun fire. The following day, additional air strikes dropped 69 tons of bombs and 6,500 rounds of 20-mm ammunition on the Berlins and surrounding enemy positions.

Casualty figures for the two-day period, 19–20 July, attest to the severity of fighting. In *Marine Operations In Korea 1950–1953,* volume V, Meid and Yingling report an estimated 375 Chinese killed and wounded and 124 Marine casualties. An additional 56 Marines were listed as missing, many from the original garrison defending the outposts.[21]

On 24 July, the Chinese attacked Outpost Esther in the right battalion sector of the 5th Marines. At 2115, the enemy probed the outpost held by elements from How Company 3/5. The fighting was heavy and lengthy. By early morning, the enemy had overrun part of the front trench line, but the Marines still controlled the rear trenches. Attempting to prevent reinforcements, the enemy tried to isolate the hill with heavy shelling and patrols in the area between Esther and the MLR.

From the MLR, the Marines answered with heavy supporting fire, including machine guns, 81-mm, and 4.2-inch mortar boxes. Three tanks neutralized enemy targets with direct fire, and artillery units hurled nearly four thousand rounds. The outpost held.

In late July, the war would end, but the Chinese army was still trying to improve its position and was willing to fight for it. What preceded the end was arguably the worst battle of the outpost war, a clash all but ignored by the press and the historians. Overshadowed by the good news of an armistice on 27 July, there was no room for talk of tragedy. Few people today, or even then, were aware of the awful tragedy that occurred during the final four days of war at a place called Boulder City. During that battle, 1,892 Marines became casualties while fighting for a piece of land that was soon to be yielded and turned into a tenuous border zone. The battle was the kind from which movies are made, a heroic last stand by a company of outnumbered Marines standing their ground, like Rourkes Drift or Camerone. The story was all true, but who has ever heard of Boulder City in Korea?

CHAPTER 12

BOULDER CITY

At this stage of the war,
. . . when the talks were nearing their final stage,
what was to be gained by all this?
—Edwin P. Hoyt: *The Bloody Road*
to Panmunjom, 1985

The shooting would stop in July but not without the loss of a great many more men struggling in a victory that could be described only as hollow. The fighting on the MLR at Boulder City was equally marked by its ferocity and by its necessity. During this final battle of the war, like much of the agony endured before it, men died with nothing gained.

Without the twin sentries of Berlin and East Berlin standing guard, the MLR was naked, exposed to assault. Thanks to General Clarke's earlier decision to "spare lives" and not retake Outposts Elko, Carson, Vegas, Berlin, and East Berlin, the MLR was unprotected from the Ungok Hills to the Hook. This region constituted the entire right sector of the Marine MLR.

For the enemy, Hill 119 on the MLR was tactically and strategically the logical point of attack. An exposed salient of the MLR, it jutted north to meet the former Berlin outposts. With no protective outposts, Hill 119 became critical to UN defenses because of its height and access to the Imjin River valley. It commanded a major route to Seoul, straight down a valley known as "76 Alley" and thence to the great bend of the Imjin. From there, it was open ground to the UN rear, the capital city of Seoul—and disaster. Had the Chinese captured Hill 119, they would have surely broken off truce negotiations and continued to exploit their gains. A victory there would have been decisive.

Because of a conspicuously large outcropping of granite, Hill 119 came to be known as "Boulder City." Its loss was unthinkable. It would have to be held at any cost. The battle for Boulder City, beginning on 24 July, was arguably the single bloodiest battle of the outpost war—a fight to the finish. It was one of the few occasions when Chinese troops penetrated the MLR in strength and held their ground. The fighting to get it back rivaled the ferocity of the Nevada Cities battles and surpassed the fighting to retake the Hook. It was a ghastly four-day affair.

COUNTDOWN TO THE END

After the Chinese successes on the Berlin outposts earlier in the week, Marine planners believed that the enemy would continue its thrust south and attempt to seize Boulder City. Acutely aware of the danger, the Marines moved their reserves forward. On 20 July, the 2d Battalion, 1st Marines, was moved on line to reinforce the 7th Marines. The following day, a sister battalion, 3/1, was moved to a standby position. Because of the casualties sustained by George Company 3/7 during the Outpost Berlin fighting, it was decided that a company from reserve would relieve it at the Boulder City position. George Company 3/1 was selected. At 2000 on 22 July, an advance party of one platoon took up defensive positions on Boulder City under control of George Company 3/7. The remainder of the company made ready to effect a relief the next day.

In preparation for the move, 1st Lt. Oral R. Swigart Jr., CO of George Company 3/1, met with his company officers and key NCOs. S/Sgt. Timothy A. Tobin was there when Swigart laid it on the line. He remembers Swigart saying:

> I have some important news to convey to you. I received word that the representatives of North Korea, once again, have walked away from the peace talks at Panmunjom. The enemy has been reported to have massed in great numbers in the corridor leading to Seoul. Outpost Berlin and East Berlin have been overrun and are now in the hands of the enemy.
>
> The Chinese have shelled Boulder City and have probed it with its troops. The Marines on that hill have held on to it so far, but the enemy is determined to seize it. They feel we value the lives of our men and will not sacrifice them to hold this key position. It is only a matter of time before they throw everything they have at us to prove that they are right.
>
> Gentlemen, we have been ordered to reinforce Boulder City and hold it at all costs. If worse come to worse, and we can not kill the enemy fast enough and if it appears that he will overrun us, we have a prearranged signal that will call in all of the fire power we have in our

area to blow up the hill. With Boulder City in the hands of the enemy, they would be in a position to take Seoul without too much to stop them. Pass the word to your men to be ready to move out as soon as we get the word.[1]

The following morning, Thursday, 23 July, George Company 3/1 joined George Company 3/7 on Boulder City and dug in. Lieutenant Swigart, the senior officer present, took command of the two-company defense. There was no enemy ground activity, and the Marines received only sporadic mortar and artillery fire that evening. The men spent their time in improving fortifications, watching—and waiting.

Day 1 of Battle—Friday, 24 July 1953

Friday, 24 July, was three days before the signing of an armistice that ended the war. Although no one could have predicted such a thing then or even believed it had it been predicted, it makes the fighting that followed all the more tragic.

The relief of Boulder City continued. By 0400, all men of George Company 3/7 had withdrawn to their battalion CP and safety. George Company 3/1, under operational control of 3/7, had taken its place on the MLR. It was the sole company defending Boulder City.

At 0900, enemy mortars began falling and were soon joined by artillery. By 1030, incoming fire was falling at the rate of three to five rounds per minute, and by 1100, wire communication was out between Boulder City and the 3d Battalion CP. Radio communication was poor, and the only dependable means of communicating was through the artillery FO net. Cpl. Harvey Dethloff Jr., a George Company machine gunner, wrote:

> By mid day we knew something big was going to happen soon because the enemy was sniping at us with "76's" every time we moved. Pfc. Timothy Gilmore, my gunner, had arrived in Korea with me several months earlier. He decided he wanted some hot C-rations, so he made a dash to our other gun because he knew they had a stove.
>
> As he backed out of their bunker entrance, a "76" round landed about three or four feet behind him. We carried him out in a poncho. . . .[2]

It was apparent that the enemy was registering mortars and artillery on Boulder City and that an attack was imminent. 1st Lt. Robert Fleischner, 3d Platoon leader, reported mortar concentrations believed to be

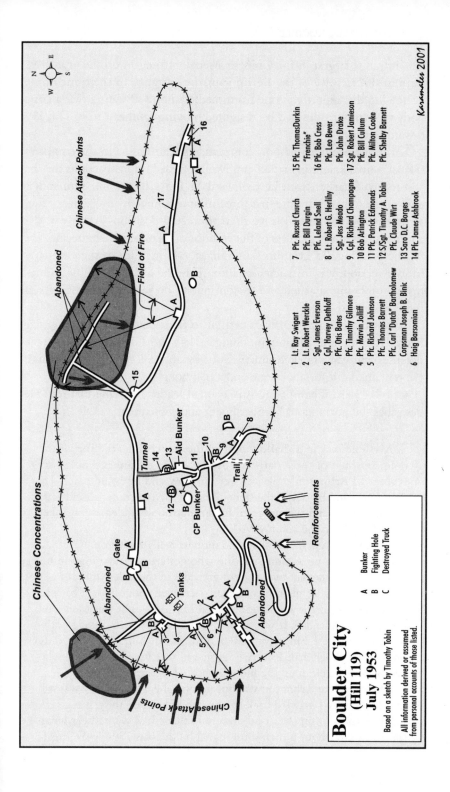

Boulder City
(Hill 119)
July 1953

Based on a sketch by Timothy Tobin

All information derived or assumed
from personal accounts of those listed.

A   Bunker
B   Fighting Hole
C   Destroyed Truck

1 Lt. Roy Swigart
2 Lt. Robert Werckle
   Sgt. James Everson
3 Cpl. Harvey Dethloff
   Pfc. Otis Bates
   Pfc. Timothy Gilmore
4 Pfc. Marvin Jolliff
5 Pfc. Richard Johnson
   Pfc. Thomas Barrett
   Pfc. Carl "Dutch" Bartholomew
   Corpsman Joseph B. Binic
6 Haig Barsomian

7 Pfc. Russel Church
   Pfc. Bill Durgin
   Pfc. Leland Snell
8 Lt. Robert G. Herlihy
   Sgt. Jess Meado
9 Cpl. Richard Champagne
10 Bob Arlington
11 Pfc. Patrick Edmonds
12 S/Sgt. Timothy A. Tobin
   Pfc. Claude Wirt
13 Soro D.C. Borges
14 Pfc. James Ashbrook

15 Pfc. ThomasDurkin
   "Frenchie"
16 Pfc. Bob Cress
   Pfc. Leo Bever
   Pfc. John Drake
17 Sgt. Robert Jamieson
   Pfc. Bill Cullum
   Pfc. Milton Cooke
   Pfc. Shelby Barnett

Karamales 2001

120-mm, the largest in the Chinese arsenal, zeroing in on the protective wire in the vicinity of the Berlin gate, the entrance to the trench line. Following this report was one from the battalion CP stating that a large body of enemy troops had been sighted moving southeast from Hill 139 toward Berlin.

Early that evening, platoon commanders were called to the company CP for a final briefing. Lieutenant Swigart passed on instructions that he had received earlier from Lt. Col. Paul M. Jones, battalion commander, emphasizing that "after the first three minutes of enemy preparatory fire, all troops would have to leave their protected positions and fire at the advancing enemy, regardless of the amount of incoming being received."[3] At the briefing, 2d Lt. John J. Leonhard, commander of the company mortar section, was instructed to illuminate the forward hillside immediately on being attacked and to continue to do so until the enemy was repulsed.

When the company officers retired to their platoons, incoming fire began to increase. Lieutenant Swigart left the CP bunker to check defenses and was knocked unconscious by an exploding mortar round. He remained out for about one and a half hours.

Cpl. Richard Champagne was a squad leader in a rifle platoon. He describes the horrendous bombardment and subsequent assault:

My hole was in a shallow part of the trench line; the top of the hole consisted of three barbed wire stakes and a blanket. Bob's [Pfc. Robert C. Arlington] hole was very narrow, and he could barely lay down in it and be out of the trench line. In my crab hole I could only sit straight up, and whenever an incoming round landed, the blanket shifted dirt onto me and my M-1.

About 8:00 P.M. the artillery and mortars really rained on us. I recall having to clean up a young Marine who got an artillery round in his hole; when hit, he had two cases of grenades in the hole with him.

As the heavy bombardment began, I crawled about 30 feet back to the open end of the horseshoe shaped hill. I thought this open end might be undefended. It was so dark that I could see absolutely nothing but blackness. Since we had arrived on this hill, I had seen only one person other than Bob Arlington and that was a lieutenant who had helped me clean up the kid who had taken the direct hit.

I knew where Arlington was but no one else. The artillery was still murder. Slowly I crawled back to my crab hole when there was a very bright explosion in the good crab hole that I had wanted earlier in the day. I saw about 8 men illuminated by the blast. Suddenly, I realized they were Gooks. One was particularly large, perhaps a Mongolian. As I got into a sitting position, one of the Gooks pointed me out to the big one. I nailed this big guy and squeezed the trigger for the next one, but my M-1 didn't fire. Apparently there was too much dirt dumped by the artillery from noon to 8:00 P.M.

It took a few seconds to realize my M-1 could only fire single shots, and I must work the bolt by hand. By then the Gooks were all down and out of sight at a turn in the trench line. They started throwing what appeared to be concussion grenades. Three went off within a foot or so of me, but I kept on firing, every time they appeared above the shoulder of the trench. I was firing right past Bob Arlington.

Arlington yelled, "Where the hell are they?" I yelled back, "They're standing on top of you." I saw Bob roll out into the trench line as a concussion grenade went off in his face. His BAR went end-over-end down the side of the trench, and I was certain Bob was dead just 15 or 20 feet from me. Suddenly, Bob got up and ran to his BAR; he grabbed it, but then threw it away.

Then a green flare went up and the gooks threw a frag grenade in on me. It was lying a few inches from my left boot. It was of Gook manufacture, no fuse as ours had, and it was serrated and rusty. . . . It finally went off, and I felt a sharp blow to my left chest and right leg.

In the meantime, Bob had apparently run to get some grenades that were in a hole just between us. He was throwing them, one after another, which succeeded in clearing the Gooks out.

Arlington came over to me and we decided to get better cover. I couldn't walk, so Bob dragged me toward the top of the hill. We finally got to the fork in the trench line just south of where we had been fighting.

At this point the trench line was blocked by the bodies of 2d Lt. John Leonard [Leonhard] and Pfc. Patrick "Dumdum" Edmonds. They had been killed only about 20 feet from me, and I never knew that they were even there. They had apparently been killed by Gook soldiers who had gotten into our trenches because neither of them had any weapons. It did occur to me at that time that if the Gooks were that close to me, why hadn't they killed me too?

We crawled over their bodies; they were both still warm. Eventually, we found an unoccupied bunker. We knocked out a sand bag to have a field of fire to the north, down the trench line.

Somehow, a corpsman made his way to our bunker and asked if we had been hit. We replied that we had been and needed some morphine. He apparently had none and told us to evacuate.

Bob and I looked at each other. I didn't want to take a chance of being shot in the back as I crawled down the trench line as may have happened to Lt. Leonard and Dumdum Edmonds. Arlington asked me what I wanted to do. I said I wanted to stay to see who owned this fucking hill come day break. Bob said "OK" to this and we stayed in the bunker until day light with only my M-1 between the two of us.[4]

At 2045, a reinforced enemy company charged Boulder City from two approaches. At the same time, there was a diversionary attack at Hill 111, 1,500 yards to the right. Hill 111 was the Marine Division's far right boundary. Chinese troops temporarily penetrated the MLR trenches of Hill 111 defended by men from How Company 3/7.

It was soon apparent that the main Chinese attack was being directed on Boulder City, specifically at the Berlin gate on George Company's left flank. There was a secondary attack on the right flank at the East Berlin gate. These assaults were repelled with heavy enemy casualties. According to Champagne,"Of particular assistance in repulsing it [the attacks] were 81-mm Mortar and Arty barrage[s], and the direct fire support from four M-46 Tanks positioned in direct support of Company G. Illumination fires from the 60-mm Mortars allowed the effective employment of small arms and hand grenades."[5]

Enemy preparatory fire, preceding the attack, had knocked out four machine guns and two 60-mm mortars. Five Marines had been killed and ten wounded. Among the dead was Lieutenant Leonhard of the mortar section, mortally wounded while getting one of his damaged tubes back into action. Corporal Dethloff and Pfc. Otis Bates crewed one of the machine guns that was hit. Dethloff, who was subsequently awarded a Silver Star, recalls:

> As it got dark, all hell broke loose, the big stuff came down like rain drops in a storm. Not far from Bates and me was Pfc. Marvin Jolloff on a 30 cal. MG [machine gun] which was out in the open, protecting our left flank.
>
> Just in a matter of minutes, a rocket round hit the right corner of the aperture and the concussion was so bad that it bent the cover of the "50" leaving it useless. At almost the same time, the "30" was hit and blown out of Jolloff 's hands, injuring him.
>
> As we got out of the bunker, I remembered that there was a flame thrower sitting there, probably left by a previous outfit. I had seen flame throwers demonstrated before, so I knew how to turn it on. For some reason I couldn't get the striker to work at first. When it finally did, a lot of gas had shot up the dead trench which extended out to the knoll and the whole area really lit up. At almost this exact moment,

a concussion grenade came in on me rendering my right arm useless and blowing the hose off the tank of the flame thrower. Fortunately, the two tanks behind us could now easily see the Chinese almost on top of us and they opened up, which allowed us to pull back to the block in the trench.

Bates was helping Jolloff, so I tried to get to the other "30" cal. gun, but the enemy was coming over the trench between them and me. Because of this and the fact that my right arm couldn't be used, I decided I had better help Bates and Jolloff get back.[6]

The machine gun to the left of Dethloff was manned by Pfc. Richard Johnson, Pfc. Thomas Barrett, and Pfc. Carl E. ("Dutch") Bartholomew. Adding his view of the experience, Private Johnson wrote:

> . . . There was no trench left, except from my gun down to the "50" cal. MG. I went up the trench looking for people, and all I found were shell holes and broken and twisted weapons. Also, there just was nothing that even resembled a trench.
>
> We heard horns, yelling and whistles and we knew they were coming. I remember telling "Dutch" to put the gun in the trench, pointed in the direction of the "50" MG. He said no because Dethloff was there. I kept hollering for those guys to get out. Dutch started firing from the area in front of the "50" to as far to our left as he could go.
>
> Out of nowhere a corpsman showed up. I guess he was the one that told us Dethloff got out with his people. He asked if we were all right. We told him yes and for him to get out, and we would start falling back. The only trouble was that it was too late for us. We couldn't go any place, so we made up our minds that we would either hold or die. I guess we all figured we would die.
>
> I know I wasn't scared any more. At some point, Dutch said for us to get in the bunker and be still. In a matter of minutes the Chinese were in the trench and were throwing grenades into our bunker. Dutch tried to cover up one, but only got a leg near or partly on it. The next time it was his arm. This one blew off both of Pfc. Thomas Barrett's feet. He died in my arms. We didn't even know his feet were gone. He was checked, but not his feet, and he didn't say anything. I got a tourniquet on Dutch, and then I got hit by a grenade.
>
> When I came to, I was looking up the barrel of a burp gun and was waiting for him to pull the trigger. Someone, perhaps an officer, dressed like a corpsman, stopped him.[7]

That night Private Johnson became a prisoner of war.

Pfc. Russell W. Church's machine gun section was set up on the left side of the horseshoe that was Boulder City. At roughly 1930 that night, he was helping set up a 30-caliber machine gun between some sandbags in an open part of the trench. Church, who was awarded a Bronze Star, recalls:

> ... Pfc. Bill [William L. J.] Durgin yelled a few seconds after the barrage lifted to get out of our holes as the Gooks were in the trenches. I quickly looked to the front of my lane of fire and saw a very large number of Gooks coming upon us. They were all bunched up, an easy target. I fired my MG and could see my red tracers hitting them. On my right I could see Pfc. Leland ["Lee"] Snell, my assistant gunner, using his M-1 to stop them from getting in back of us. I grabbed my M-1, and we stopped them about two or three feet behind us.
>
> One Gook a short time later tried to sneak up on us with a bangalore torpedo. I was standing there and surprised him. He stopped about 5 or 6 feet away from me, dropped the torpedo and ran like hell down the trench. It almost seemed comical to me as he was over weight and his ass kept bouncing off the side of the trench. I did manage to nail him, though.[8]

An hour or two after the Chinese assault began, Church turned his machine gun over to his assistant, Private Snell, in order to help Durgin to get to an aid bunker. The initial Chinese thrust had been stopped by Church's gun in the left sector, but there were still plenty of Chinese. Snell gives the following account of some anxious moments:

> I took over the gun while Church helped evacuate Bill Durgin. SSgt. Willard Covert of the 3rd platoon sent Pfc. Ronald Borges to help protect the gun. It was a God-send when Russ Church returned because things were getting real rough. We were using the machine gun, M-1 rifles and grenades to stop them, but they just kept coming, like a human sea.
>
> We were firing our weapons as fast as we could. I remember one who came right up to us before I let him have it. I was afraid of hitting a Marine, so I kept yelling to him asking him if he was a Marine. Suddenly a flare went off and I noticed that he had sneakers on; at that point, I let him have it.
>
> A few of them got together and started throwing grenades into our position. We were catching them and throwing them back. One landed between Russ Church and me, I yelled at Russ to watch out and scooped it up with my hand. Just as I threw it back, it went off sending some shrapnel into my face and eye.[9]

At approximately 2100, a second enemy attack was hurled against Boulder City in the strength of two companies supported by more mortar and artillery fire. This attack concentrated on the Berlin gate with secondary attacks on the forward-most positions (Dethloff's and Johnson's machine-gun emplacements) and the right flank of the hill mass. All of the attacks were repulsed except the one directed at the Berlin gate. The gate was defended by the 1st Squad, 3d Platoon, and Cpl. Paul J. Himmels, squad leader. The official account indicated: "This squad held its position in line until it was completely annihilated in savage hand to hand combat by a numerically far superior enemy force."[10]

Lieutenant Fleischner and Platoon Sergeant Covert organized and led squad-sized counterattacks to restore the critical section of the line. Each time, they were repulsed with heavy casualties. Covert was seriously wounded by an enemy hand grenade but insisted that he was all right and refused evacuation. He continued to assault the enemy strong point aggressively until he became too weak to continue. Sergeant Covert was awarded a Silver Star for this action.

The Chinese continued to reinforce their foothold at the Berlin gate with squads and smaller units. Hand-to-hand fighting was the order of the day, but there were too many Chinese and too few Marines. By 2120, the situation on the left flank was acute and casualties were increasing by the minute. The breakthrough enlarged and developed all along the forward trench line. Just as the situation became bad, it got worse.

At 2130, Battalion Headquarters received word that the enemy was reinforcing its attack on the right flank. Reports came in from the forward platoons that Marines in the trenches were down to half of their original numbers.

Sergeant Tobin, situated closer to the platoon CP, was somewhat back from the forward trenches. As the shelling slackened, he moved toward the top of the hill where he could better observe the situation. He wrote:

> . . . One of my machine gunners, Pfc. James Ashbrook, came running out of the tunnel and yelled that the Chinese were right behind him. He turned and fired back into the tunnel. When he did this, it looked like three Gooks came over the top. They were silhouetted by a flare behind them. I shot the one on the left, who was the farthest away from James, but he didn't fall. I realized I had shot at a shadow. I shot at the one in the middle and he bounced slightly. They were still coming toward me. I switched my carbine to full automatic and put the rest of the rounds in the one that had bounced. The Gook on the right started to hit the deck. Before he could, I put in a new magazine and caught him in the chest just as he was ducking down. The force of

my rounds lifted his body up into a standing position. I had emptied my 30 round magazine into him. When the last round hit, he sagged to the ground like a limp rag.

I turned to see how Ashbrook was making out. He had killed the Chinks in the tunnel, but he was dead. I don't know if one of the Gooks got him or if he was hit by shrapnel.

I asked Pfc. Claude Wirt to help me check out the situation. We found Chinks all over the hill, in front of us and behind us. Wirt told me there was no one alive in the front trench. He said he was running on top of dead Gooks and had just gotten off one when he moved. Wirt starting shaking and pointing his 45 pistol in my face. He was yelling, "he (the Gook) was dead, but he tried to shoot me. I put the 45 to his head and shot him and shot him and shot him." Wirt was cracking up; I took the pistol away from him and that's when I noticed his hand was all messed up. I headed him toward the aid bunker to get it patched up and report the situation.

I headed for the company CP where the skipper was getting the bad news from some of his key NCOs. It appeared we were about to be run over. There was a loud explosion. Two or three of the roof joists broke and fell into the bunker. The skipper said to pass the word that he was calling our artillery to come in on top of us.[11]

At 2145, Lieutenant Swigart requested VT on the forward slope of Boulder City to stop the enemy buildup slowly massing there in preparation for a final thrust to take the hill. The artillery immediately filled his request and decimated enemy troops caught in the open. As the VT lifted at 2155, the Marines counterattacked. Although they gained a partial restoration of the trenches, it was too little too late and they could not check the enemy advance. Lieutenant Swigart called for reinforcements. George Company alone, or what was left of it, could not hold the MLR.

At 2230, 2d Lt. Norman Farrington, commander of George Company's 2d Platoon, advised that the enemy was slowly pushing in his flank and that his casualties were extremely heavy. By this time, ammunition was getting critically low because of a lack of personnel to carry it forward to the troops. Worse yet, one of the company ammunition dumps had been hit by enemy fire and partially destroyed.

Evacuation of casualties had become nearly impossible. Wounded Marines lay about the position because no one could be spared to drag them to safety. Two of the eight corpsman were dead, and at least half of the remainder were wounded. The company CP bunker and all platoon CPs were filled with wounded. With the shortage of corpsmen, the walking wounded moved about and administered to the more severely injured. Sgt. James Everson Jr., and Pfc. Oscar Brown were in the former category. According to those present, they, "seemed to be in a thousand places at once," administering to the wounded and checking the enemy advance with small arms.[12] Pfc. Brown died of wounds and was awarded a Silver Star. Sergeant Everson survived the experience. He wrote:

> Sometime before midnight, I volunteered with a SSgt. whose name I can't remember, to help carry the wounded from the 2d platoon bunker. They had no room for the increasing casualties. I don't remember how many times I went up there, but I remember a tunnel and a very heavy guy who bled profusely. The SSgt. with me was hit in the back. Lee Snell found me the next day when he was being evacuated. I didn't have a helmet or flack jacket on—they must have thought I was goner. Lee had a corpsman check me out. I eventually woke up in Battalion Aid in a large tent with the CO of George Company and about ten others. My 3rd machine gun section had 3 KIA and 1 man taken prisoner.[13]

Meid and Yingling report that the George Company 3/1 machine gunner, Pfc. Richard Johnson, was possibly the last prisoner taken in the final battle of the Korean War.[14] Johnson described his capture and subsequent captivity:

> They took "Doc" [HM3 Joseph B. Bennet] first, then "Dutch" [Pfc. Carl Bartholomew] and last me. They carried me back to a field hospital in a cave. This was on the day of the night they signed the cease fire. Just before we got to the hospital, one of our jets came over. I guess the pilot thought we were all Communists because he made a strafing run. The Chinese carrying the stretcher dropped it and ran for cover. I waved like crazy, but the jet kept on firing. I don't know how I didn't get hit! He "stitched" right up both sides of me. If he had used his cannon, I wouldn't be here today.
> The next day, I was taken to an interrogation center in North Korea. They thought I was the son of Senator Lyndon Johnson. As a result of that, I was taken to another place, and they finally got the truth from their intelligence people, and sent me to POW camp #10. While there, I was threatened and abused both mentally and physically.
> It was in Camp #10 where the Chinese operated on my knee. That wasn't much fun because they didn't have anything for the pain before, during or after the operation.
> Twenty-eight days later we were sent back to our side. That was the last time I saw or heard anything from "Dutch."[15]

At 2300, Lieutenant Swigart's hour-old request for reinforcements was being fulfilled. The George Company CP received a message that Item Company 3/1 was on its way. Despite the fact that the good news was sent in code, enemy artillery fire immediately shifted to the rear approaches of Boulder City. The unexpected incoming fire, received while Item Company approached the MLR, delayed its arrival and caused thirty-five casualties, including Capt. Louis J. Sartor, the company commander.

The general situation at 2300 was that the 3d Platoon, on the left, had lost all but 20 yards of the forward trench line, and the enemy had succeeded in penetrating defenses on top of the hill in several places. The 2d Platoon on the right flank had lost all of the forward trench line and was conducting a defense from the high ground on the right. The 1st Platoon, in the rear of the position, had sent two groups of reinforcements forward to bolster critical areas. The remainder of the platoon, with the company antitank section attached, protected the company rear and flanks.

By midnight, the forward portion and both flanks had been pushed back to the reverse slope of the hill. Only the Marines' never-say-die resistance was keeping the Chinese from seizing the rest of Boulder City.

Day 2—Saturday, 25 July 1953

Sporadic fighting and heavy incoming fire also continued on Hill 111. During one ten-minute interval, sixty to seventy rounds per minute were counted falling on the position. Although the Chinese had once again penetrated Marine defenses, assault teams with flamethrowers and rocket launchers drove them back.

At 0015, Item Company began moving into position on Boulder City. Its arrival occurred in the proverbial nick of time as George Company had been reduced to approximately 25 percent effectives, less than a hundred Marines, many of whom were walking wounded. The arrival of reinforcements was heartily welcomed by the survivors and seemed to bolster their determination to fight despite the odds.

Chinese troops continued to charge the hill as they tenaciously tried to wrest away the trenches. Still the Marines prevailed. The Chinese troops were stopped in midassault by resourceful Marines, such as Pfc. Harry Cowle, a BAR man from Item Company, 3/1. While firing his weapon at enemy troops assaulting the hill, Cowle was wounded and his automatic rifle damaged. Refusing evacuation, he searched the trenches for another BAR. Locating three others, he found that they were also inoperable. As the hill continued to receive incoming fire, Cowle calmly hunched down in a nearby trench and worked to salvage a workable automatic rifle by using parts from the broken ones. He succeeded and returned to his position to continue the fight. Cowle was now the only man remaining in his fire team.[16]

As the senior officer present at Boulder City, Item Company's Captain Sartor, though wounded, assumed command. Within five minutes, the Marines counterattacked and began forcing the enemy back from the high ground. By 0130, the combined efforts of Item and George companies had driven the Chinese from all but a couple of isolated sectors of trench line.

The enemy, however, still controlled Berlin gate in strength. This was the most critical sector of defense because it was the best avenue of approach to the forward-most portion of Boulder City. At 0200, an enemy company launched a third attack at the gate. As before, the attack was supported by a barrage of mortar and artillery fire, much of which was directed at those Chinese units still occupying portions of the hill.

The attack was unsuccessful. With counterfire from Marine artillery batteries and mortar sections slamming into the forward slope, the men of Item and George Companies drove the enemy from the hill. By 0300, with the Chinese attack repulsed, the Marines were proceeding with mopping-up operations. During the mop-up and corresponding lull, more Marines were dispatched from behind the MLR. Easy Company 2/7 and Easy Company 2/1 each sent two platoons to reinforce the flanks of Boulder City.

Although their large attacks had been driven off, the Chinese were not giving up. While darkness lasted, they made ineffective attempts at infiltration. Piecemeal units of squad size or smaller, armed with burp guns and hand grenades, continued to harass the forward positions and kept the Marines on their toes. When daylight broke, however, the men on Boulder City watched as the Chinese began withdrawing the majority of their forces from the hill mass. The after action report states, "Friendly arty and mortars took a great toll of the enemy as he started this retrograde movement, and all approaches to Hill 119 were piled high with enemy dead."[17]

At 0800, after regrouping, the Chinese came again to hurl the first of two unsupported daylight attacks against the Marines. The attack was limited to two enemy platoons and, after a five-minute firefight, they were driven back with heavy losses. The Special Action Report states,

"The attack was characterized by a sluggish enemy advance to the Berlin trenchline, and little if any attempt by the enemy to return the fire of Marine defenders. The enemy seemed to be completely dazed."[18] About an hour later, the second attack commenced. It was even weaker than the previous one, but it had the same characteristics. Again, enemy losses were great.

During the early evening hours, elements of Easy Company 2/1 arrived on position to relieve the exhausted remnants of George and Item Companies 3/1 that had so resolutely absorbed the brunt of the Chinese assaults. By 1940, the relief had been effected. Easy Company 2/1 and Fox Company 2/7 occupied the hill under command of Maj. Robert D. Thurston, the 3d Battalion S-1, (Personnel officer,) 1st Marines.

Two hours later, the reinforcements were attacked by two enemy companies trying again to seize Berlin gate as well as Hill 111 on the right. Fire from the trenches, supported by artillery, mortar, and tanks, drove off the attackers. Boulder City held.

On Hill 111 to the east, How Company 3/1 attempted to relieve How Company 3/7 and assist in clearing enemy from the trenches. Slightly delayed, the relief was completed at 1815.

Supporting Boulder City throughout the attacks were four tanks from Charlie Company, five from the 1st Marines Anti-Tank Company, and one from the 7th Marine Anti-Tank Company. All were credited with dispersing major enemy concentrations. At the peak of the fighting, two of the tanks were surrounded by enemy forces, yet their crews continued to radio timely tactical information to the rear. S/Sgt. James Champlin was inside one of the tanks on Boulder City. In a letter to the author, he describes enemy antitank tactics:

> . . . The gooks started massing around the large boulder that gave the place its name. When we saw them we started firing Willie Peter at the boulder to make air bursts and every now and then a round of HE. That seemed to stop the activity for a while.
>
> Their anti-tank squads would start running for our tank (usually about three or four men) from about thirty feet apart, spacing across our front. They would come together about fifty feet in front of us. All the time they would be throwing AT grenades with white cloth streamers fixed to their handles. They would have at least a dozen attached all over their bodies. They came at us throwing with both hands. We had it happen quite a few times and it became quite unnerving to say the least.

By the end of the day all of our wire was gone and most of the trenchlines and bunkers were caved in. I swear every inch of ground on the hilltop had been turned over at least once.[19]

The Tank Battalion Command Diary reports, "On the occasion when the enemy temporarily occupied the top of Hill 119, the tanks were isolated but remained on position and continued fighting and reporting enemy activity even though they were surrounded by the enemy for a considerable period of time and were the only effective friendly forces in that area."[20]

Day 3—Sunday, 26 July 1953

During the early morning between 0130 and 0300, the Chinese launched another company-sized attack against the Berlin gate and Hill 111. Although they met a solid wall of defending fire, about half of the attackers managed to reach the gate and remain there. Again, they held a portion of the forward trench line. That fighting is summarized in Intelligence Reports, Appendix IV, of the 3/7 Command Diary:

> ... At 0030 [26 July] friendlies on Hill 119 requested a "box me in." At 0400 Australians reported a large mass of enemy troops approaching Hill 111 and five minutes later Hill 119 reported a small group of enemy on Berlin Gate and requested illumination. At 0110 Australians report large number of enemy coming from "Betty Grable" toward Hill 111 and enemy on Hill 125 heading toward their left. At 0125 Hill 119 reported enemy approaching the hill and requested a "box me in" an estimated enemy company headed towards them from East Berlin. At 0135 Hill 119 reported that the enemy is in the trenches on the left flank and hand to hand combat commenced. The enemy is in the trenches on Hill 111. At 0225 Hill 119 reported enemy attack repulsed and enemy casualties estimated at about 110 KIA. At 0330 3/7 with elements of 2/7 and 3/1 were engaged this date by about one battalion of enemy infantry. One company attacked H-3-1 on Hill 111 and 126. Two companies attacked Hill 119. All the attacks were repulsed. [21]

For 26 July alone, 3/7 reported enemy casualties estimated at 545 killed and 507 wounded. Incoming received in the battalion sector was estimated at 7,677 mixed rounds. Based on these numbers alone, the Chinese lost over a battalion of men trying to take Boulder City and Hill 111.

But there was more. As indicated in the 3/7 Command Diary, Australian troops were also involved. Abutting Hill 111 on the right was the

British Commonwealth Division sector of the Jamestown Line. In November 1952, this division had assumed responsibility for the Hook when the Marine sector was compressed to the left. (See *The Outpost War, Vol. 1,* chap. 10.)

Next to the 3/7 Marines on Hill 111 was C Company of the 2d Royal Australian Regiment (2 RAR). The following excerpt is from an Australian publication:

> The Contact Bunker, between the Marines on Hill 111 and C Company, was the scene of heavy fighting on the night of 25–26 July. It was manned by six Australians under the command of Lance Corporal K. H. Crockford. When the Chinese attacked Hill 111 they also penetrated the undefended space between it and the Contact Bunker and attacked Crockford's group from several sides at once. Bitter hand-to-hand fighting followed in the trenches around the bunker and the Australians threw the Chinese out of the position, preventing them from penetrating any substantial distance between Hills 111 and 121.
>
> The Chinese fired some 4200 mortar and artillery rounds onto the 2 RAR position that night, 25–26 July, killing three Australians and wounding nine. In the two nights of fighting, the artillery supporting 2 RAR and 3 RAR fired 23,000 rounds against the Chinese. As on the previous night, 3 RAR was not attacked.[22]

Cpl. George Broadhead, a Marine wireman with How Company 3/1 when it relieved How Company 3/7 on Hill 111, wrote:

> I was company wireman and was therefore not stationary. I always felt badly for the guys who were stationary in a fighting hole because they had no way to keep their minds off the incoming. They simply waited in a bunker or hole for one to land beside, or on top of them. That was when landline communications were being blasted to hell.
>
> Wiremen, on the other hand, were seldom under cover. During a heavy bombardment was when they were most needed, moving from platoon to platoon repairing breaks in the wire. Here and there on my rounds I saw an Australian voluntarily involved with our troops.
>
> The Aussies, so far as I know, were not actually on Hill 111. They were manning the Hook. and their position gave them an advantageous view of enemy flanking movement towards 111. Their presence was most beneficial. . . . The Aussies sent small units of infantry, 4 or 5 men, as they deemed could be away from their primary position, the Hook.
>
> On one occasion, I was racing along unreeling wire from the spool (Donut or Cheesecake) when I came to an embankment, and couldn't

believe my eyes. There was a huge stainless steel kettle with Aussies and KSC's around it. They were making a huge vat of tea for everybody. . . .

Parts of our trench were overrun, and there was no telling where a Chinaman might pop up, which is probably why some jarhead [Marine] shot an Aussie by accident. We heard later that the Aussie was poking around looking for a souvenir among the scores of dead. I have no idea how accurate that was, or badly he was wounded.

One thing I can remember very clearly, was running with a spool of wire between the company CP and a platoon. For long stretches I was actually running on top of dead bodies. Every once in awhile, I would hear a "whoosh" where my stepping on the body must have released the pent-up air or gasses.

I have never been a big church-goer, and I still am not, but I went to a Catholic grammar school, and one thing I could never reconcile, was that I know I finished a complete prayer as each foot hit whatever surface was beneath me. (Mostly "Hail Mary's" and "Our Fathers"). (Later, I tried repeating the same prayer when running, but I have never been able to achieve that again.)[23]

In a letter years later, Brig. Gen. Sir John Wilton of the British Commonwealth Division described the scene:

The floor of the valley between the Hook and the Chinese position was almost covered with dead Chinese who had been caught by our deadly defensive-fire artillery concentrations. On the immediate approaches to 2 RAR the bodies literally carpeted the ground sometimes two deep. These were obviously caused by mortar fire and machine-guns of 2 RAR in addition to the artillery concentrations. Most of the bodies had been there for two or three days and in the hot, humid weather had commenced to putrefy and there was a strong nauseous stench of death. It was a terrible sight which I will never forget.[24]

It was no different, and possibly worse, in front of Boulder City and Hill 111.

During the night of 26 July, Dog Company 2/7, under operational control of 3/1, relieved Fox Company 2/7. During the darkness, Chinese forces renewed efforts to gain the top of Boulder City. Three more times, at 2140, 2158, and 2220, they attacked the Berlin gate under barrages of artillery and mortar fire, followed by platoon-sized probes. On each occasion, the enemy was driven off.

Sergeant Kreid describes Dog Company 2/7's relief of Fox Company. For Kreid, it was a déjà vu experience, another ride to the backside of Boulder City but this time in an armored personnel carrier. Dismounting under the light of illumination flares in the sky with the noise, sights and sounds of artillery in front of them, the men entered the same communication trench that they had walked in during the prior week. Kreid recalls:

> As we came out of the trench, still on the reverse slope, there was a Marine major standing out in the open like a cop directing traffic while the hill shook from exploding shells. Shrapnel growled its welcome to Dog Company Marines. It was bright as day from our parachute flares. I was close enough to see gold oak leaves on the major's collar. "Third Platoon Dog Company?" He yelled above the noise. "Yes Sir," someone answered. He pointed to his right and called, "Berlin Gate, Go!" Without missing a step we turned in the direction indicated and kept running at the double. When I first saw the Major, I thought, "You are a brave bastard, but you'd better get your ass down." I heard later that he had been hit and would probably lose an arm. He was standing just a few yards from where Dennis had been killed. [On July 26, during the final attacks on Boulder City, Major Thurston was seriously wounded and evacuated.]
>
> Shells hissed in and we dove for the ground. After they exploded, I raised my head. There, close enough for me to reach out and touch, was a dead Chinese soldier. He was lying on his back, his sightless eyes staring at the heavens, off into infinity. In the glow of flare light, he looked green. He had pretty white teeth with lips that pulled back nearly into a grin—as if he knew something I didn't.
>
> Then we were up and running again. We didn't stop until we reached the Berlin Gate. It was a gate in name only, a place where the gate had been. The barb wire had long since been blown away by Chinese artillery rounds.
>
> Our platoon runner found me and relayed the lieutenant's instructions to position machine guns where they had interlocking fields of fire directed down the finger that led to Berlin. This was where the last attack had come from.
>
> We had far too many Marines crowded into the area of the Gate. The third platoon had arrived earlier and deployed in the trench. My two machine gun crews only congested the area worse. I kept the squad leaders and first gunners and told the remainder of the section to go the trench behind us and seek cover, as more mortars were beginning to come in.
>
> One of the second gunners, a gung ho young Marine named Talarico turned to me and objected to leaving his gun. I told him,

"Goddamit, don't argue, move!" He turned and went off with the rest to find cover about twenty yards behind us. For the rest of my life I have regretted that decision.

The tempo of Chinese shelling increased. Boulder City, Berlin and East Berlin remained under constant illumination from our artillery and mortars. Small arms fire broke out to our right. Both machine guns and more riflemen joined in. Was that what I thought it was? A figure dashed across the Berlin finger. Then there was another. Then more. We were being probed by enemy infantry moving in under their own mortars.

There were more. The artillery also reached out, pulverizing terrain where the enemy could gather. To prepare an attack the enemy had to first assemble and mass his troops someplace. Marine artillery sought out those places and saturated them with explosives. Thanks to the 11th Marines, Chinese attackers couldn't get close enough to the MLR to represent a grave danger. Those few soldiers that made it to the finger were cut down by our guns and that close in artillery support.

The incoming slowed as did our outgoing. The fighting was over, at least for a while.

One of my ammo carriers that I had sent back crawled up beside me. I asked if the guys were OK. With a pained look on his face he replied, "Talarico is dead." I was stunned. I couldn't believe it. I jumped up and ran back down the trench to the first rabbit hole I could see. There he was, curled up in the hole with his back to the trench. I knelt and could see shrapnel holes in the back of his flak jacket. When I put my hand on him, I knew he was dead. Looking around I saw that a mortar round had landed right in the trench with him.

We began receiving more shells. Now the reverse slope was under mortar fire. Two of Talarico's buddies asked me if they could carry his body back behind the lines. I said, "No, cover him with a poncho and do it after daylight." I knew the Chinese still had enough darkness to launch another attack. If they did we would need all hands right here. I did not want to risk four more lives in the open, carrying a stretcher to evacuate a KIA. I liked Talarico too, but I had to take care of the living first.

We sat in our holes and waited for daybreak. I felt like crying, but tears wouldn't come. Did I cause the death of this nineteen year old Marine when I sent him back for cover? Like Dennis, Talarico was Catholic, and once again I whispered the prayer to Virgin Mary.

To this day I hurt. Nothing, except the death of my mother, has pained me more than the deaths of Pryzgoda and Talarico, there in the trenches of Boulder City. They have haunted me over the years. I have searched, playing the "What if" game with myself. What if I had not been moved to the third section which formerly was Dennis'? Would I have been killed and Dennis live? What if I had let Talarico stay with his gun like he wanted to do? Would he have lived and someone else die in his place? What if this? What if that?

When daylight came, I almost wished it had remained dark. The death that surrounded us was hideous. Dead Chinese were lying all over. They were at the Berlin Gate, in the trench that led to Berlin, they were on the crest of the hill and even on the reverse slope, behind us. Off to our left about fifty yards there was a Marine tank with enemy dead piled all around it. I don't know which company held the hill before us but it was obvious that the fighting had been a vicious hand to hand battle. The Marines had not yielded an inch. It had been a fight to the death.

Also with the sun came the flies. They came buzzing in swarms around the dead, flying into the C-rations of those that had the stomach to eat. A few hours in the sun turned the bodies into something other than human. First they bloated, then they turned black. The flies laid eggs in every opening they could find, and in hours the bodies were crawling with maggots. The stench saturated our nostrils and no one could eat. Those in the open we left where they lay. We could not risk exposure to remove them. I looked away thinking, "even old Luke the Gook deserves a burial."[25]

Day 4—Monday, 27 July 1953

During that last night, the Chinese committed three thousand troops across the division front but gained no new ground for their efforts. Still, they were willing to try again. At 0035, a fourth platoon-sized probe was thrown against Boulder City. The firefight lasted over an hour, but the enemy could not attain a foothold. At 0151, the Chinese troops withdrew but continued to shell and machine-gun Boulder City. For the remainder of the morning and on into the afternoon, bullets, artillery, and mortar rounds continued to search out Marine defensive positions.

At 1000, 27 July, a truce agreement was signed at Panmunjom. It was to take effect twelve hours later at 2200 hours that night. Still, the fighting continued.

At 1430, a reinforced platoon from Charlie Company 1/1 was shifted to operational control of the 3d Battalion and moved forward to reinforce Dog Company 2/7. Sgt. Robert Guertin, a Charlie Company squad leader, describes Boulder City as he found it that afternoon:

> Out of the dust and chaos a Dog Company guide appeared to lead us to our positions. Climbing up the hill we passed litter bearers com-

ing down, evacuating wounded from that last barrage. Carried by "yo-bo's" [KSC laborers], the muddy, blood soaked stretchers held bleeding and broken Marines. Some were moaning, others were deathly still. We moved on up to Boulder City.

The smell of rotting bodies and the sight of ground littered with dead Chinese and shattered equipment gave evidence of the ferocious fighting that had occurred there over the past few days. Viewing that horrible devastation and death suddenly struck me with fear. My knees weakened till they could barely support my body and I remember thinking, "Don't fall. Don't give in to this fear of what is probably to follow." More waves of weakness washed through me and I hoped no one could sense my feelings of terror. Then, as suddenly as it came over me, the fear vanished, and I began to focus on the job at hand, and my squad.

Our guide led us to the Dog Company CP bunker and went inside apparently to receive instructions. I was startled to see more dead Chinese, some were on top of the bunker, others were crumpled beside it. Soon the guide emerged and led us to the left. I positioned my squad in a large depression about forty yards to the right rear of a Marine tank. We were receiving sporadic enemy fire, mortars and small arms but took no casualties. The tank seemed to be the primary target.

As it was elsewhere on the hill, Marine and Chinese corpses were lying everywhere. From my position I could reach out and touch one in just about every direction. One in particular, just over the rim of my hole, would move in a grotesque fashion from time to time, and I would hear the expulsion of gasses, engulfing me in the odor. The movement, I determined, was caused by a length of comm wire under the body which ran through our hole in such a way that we would occasionally catch on it. Each time the wire was pulled the corpse would move, like a macabre puppet on a string. The overall odor of death and decay saturated the hill and penetrated our clothing and nostrils.

It soon became evident to us that the Chinese artillery was after the tank and was not going to let up. Staff Sergeant Harold Wyndham, our Platoon Sergeant, ordered a man to run out to the tank and request that he withdraw to avoid casualties among the exposed infantry. The man tried but was down before he got there, another tried and he, too, was wounded.

Thinking that someone from my squad might be more successful I was directed to send a man. I turned to one of my men and told him to make the run to the tank. I was shocked at his response, the man simply crumpled before my eyes, and practically sobbing pleaded, "Christ, not me. I'd never make it." I was absolutely stunned.

Here was a Marine breaking down in front of me, refusing an order. I didn't know what to say, or do. Then I remembered a pledge I had made to myself when I first became squad leader, that "I would never ask my men to do anything I wouldn't do myself." It was settled. I would go out to the tank and deal with this man later. I grabbed his carbine in exchange for my heavier M-1 and jumped out of the hole.

Crouching and zig-zagging, I ran toward the tank. Later they told me that I drew a lot of fire, but I was unaware of it. I was so angry and disappointed with that Marine, and cussing the tank for being there, that I was oblivious to the incoming.

Stumbling over broken gear and dead Chinese soldiers I ran to the tank. The infantry phone on the back did not occur to me. I jumped on the back and ran over to the turret. I recall the ping and clang of metal hitting metal, but nothing hit me. At the turret I began beating on the tank commander's hatch with the butt of my carbine. He opened his hatch and I delivered the message. Then I leaped off the tank. I must have landed simultaneous with the detonation of an incoming round because I was engulfed in noise, dirt and shock wave, and felt pain in my side.

Scrambling around for my helmet and carbine I made a bee line for the safety of my squad in the hole.[26]

Sergeant Guertin was uninjured that day and remained unrecognized for his risky dash to the tank. No one knows the identity of the Marine who refused Guertin's order. Guertin did not report him, and who among the Marines on that battlefield, except Guertin, could say with certainty that he would have acted differently.

ARMISTICE

During those last days of fighting, UN forces had been ordered to ease off on their aggressive tactics and simply fight a defensive war, sometimes even to yield strategic high ground rather than lose more lives. (This situation occurred in eastern Korea, a sector controlled by ROK troops.)

Conversely, Communist forces were obviously trying to improve their position prior to establishment of a fixed demilitarized zone (DMZ). They succeeded in many areas by fighting right up to the last minute. On 27 July, the 5th Marines, for example, reported receiving "fifty-six rounds of enemy mixed mortar and artillery fire,"[27] the last of which arrived at 2200, the hour of truce.

Lest one fault the Chinese too harshly in this regard, it should be noted that the Marines, too, expended a little ammunition at the last minute. At 2138, in what might have been the final rounds fired by the Marines, How Battery 3/11 let go with a salvo of 105s directed north.

Exactly twenty-two minutes later, at 2200, each Marine company on the MLR fired a star cluster in the air to proclaim that it would observe the cease-fire order. From the Communist side, there was nothing.

During the battle for Boulder City, British artillery batteries from the Commonwealth Division were a great help in fulfilling a large number of fire missions. Unlike American artillery units, the British ammunition allocations were unrestricted; their gunners could fire as many rounds as they wished. Meid and Yingling quote an interesting letter found in the files during their research that epitomizes the cooperation and working relationships formed between the Marines and British in Korea.

> After the battle of 24–25 July, a young British artillery officer arrived at a Marine regimental CP. He identified himself as being from the unit that had provided artillery support to the Marines the previous night, for which he was profusely thanked. Before his astonished audience he then unrolled an impressive scroll. This proved to be a bill enumerating the various types and amounts of projectiles fired and specifying the cost in pound's sterling. When he felt the Marine staff was properly flabbergasted, he grinned and conceded waggishly: "But I am authorized to settle for two bottles of your best whiskey!"[28]

Boulder City was, in the author's opinion, one of the most crucial battles of the Korean War. Had it been lost, the entire outcome might have been different. Made vulnerable by its earlier loss of outposts, the MLR was easily penetrated by the enemy. Resistance, though heroic, was comparatively weak in terms of men—one Marine company against battalions of Chinese. But for the courage and determination of a few Marines, Boulder City would have been a catastrophic loss for the UN.

One can consider the effect, for example, if the Pusan perimeter had collapsed in 1950 and the Americans had been pushed into the sea or the consequences if the Inchon landing had failed? Strategically, either event would have been disastrous. If the Chinese had broken through at Boulder City and swept aside the defenders, as they had done many times earlier in the war, would they have stopped there? If they had exploited the break, advanced into UN rear areas, and consolidated, they most surely would have broken off peace talks and continued the fight.

One could argue that the Chinese did not have the logistical tail to sustain an advance into South Korea for long. That would have been true, but it begs the question. The damage would have been done, territory lost, more blood spilled, and truce talks terminated until another, more favorable time for the Communists.

Exposing Boulder City by conceding the screening outposts was a terrible and inappropriate risk. The battle stemmed from the conceding of outpost positions. The concession was intended to spare lives, but more were lost and a great many more were put at risk, along with the outcome of the war.

In numbers of casualties, July 1953 was a costly month for the 1st Marine Division: 181 killed and 1,611 wounded or missing, a close second to the month of October 1952, which recorded 186 killed and 1,798 casualties and reflected the fighting that reclaimed the Hook.[29] Of the July numbers, the 1st and 7th Marines alone sustained 118 killed and 1,398 wounded and missing.

Eighth Army statisticians estimate that, across the entire front for the month of July, Chinese Communist forces lost 25,000 killed and 72,000 wounded. Total Communist losses for the entire war are estimated at nearly 1,500,000 troops killed and wounded—a staggering loss of men.

The U.S. Marines first landed in Korea on 2 August 1950. By the end of July 1953, the fighting was concluded, ending thirty-six months of war for the leathernecks. During that time, 4,262 Marines were killed in action, an additional 26,038 were wounded, and 221 became prisoners of war.

It was over.

CHAPTER 13

The Warrior's Return

Each face will lose its name and time will not defer. But the bond will not be broken between who we are and what we were.

—Anonymous

No man who has survived combat ever forgets it. Be he coward or hero, it is a unique experience. For a brief period in his lifetime, he had a place in history as a participant in a cataclysmic event. Most men faced their fears and won; others might have lost, but none forgot.

In 1951, at Camp Pendleton, California, three young Marines were the best of friends. For months, Pfc. Howard Davenport, Pfc. Chuck Burrill, and Pfc. Frank Benenati lived and trained with each other. They went to schools and pulled liberty together. They grew close—close as only soldiering can do to men. Ultimately, the three Marines boarded a ship in San Diego. April of 1952 found them in the hills of western Korea and assigned to Reconnaissance Company, Headquarters Battalion, 1st Marine Division. There, among others in the company, they found and grew close to a fourth young man, Cpl. Robert Bush.

Together, the four Marines entered the war. They went out on night combat patrols, ambushes, and raids against the enemy. They were shot at, and they shot back; they learned to know fear and to overcome it. Off line, the four young men shared companionship with endless hours of talk, sports, horseplay, and togetherness.

The first tragedy struck on December 8, 1952. Private Davenport, with an eight-man patrol among the hills and paddies west of OP-1, was attacked by Chinese soldiers and seriously wounded. His squad leader,

Sgt. Lloyd Smally, despite being wounded himself, somehow managed to drag Davenport to safety and save his life. In the process, however, Smally was hit twice and died. Davenport's wounds were severe, and he was evacuated from Korea to hospitals in Japan and the States for intensive treatment and rehabilitation.[1] Three of the buddies remained. Burrill, Bush, and Benenati grieved their loss but took comfort in knowing that Davenport was alive and would recover.

On February 27, 1953, Corporal Bush and Private Benenati were killed in the fighting on Gray Rock Ridge near OP-2.[2] During the battle, Private Burrill was wounded a third time but remained in Korea.

Burrill was discharged when he returned to the States after the war. Davenport had received a medical retirement because of his wounds. The two friends reestablished contact and remained close. Over the passing years, they often met for Reconnaissance Company reunions and other occasions. Each was best man at the other's wedding. The two of them never forgot their buddies who had died in the hills of Korea. Davenport located Lloyd Smally's mother and continues to pay his respects with flowers and a card every Mother's Day. He also acknowledges the families of Robert Bush and Frank Benenati each year.

Thirty years later, in 1983, Davenport and Burrill, accompanied by their wives, returned to Korea but, this time, armed with passports rather than guns. They went to look, to visit, to remember, and to pay tribute to buddies who had died there. The trip, sponsored by the Korean Veterans Association of the Republic of South Korea, was specifically organized to honor United Nations troops who had fought so tenaciously for their country in the years 1950–53. During the trip, Davenport tape-recorded his observations and thoughts. Later, he transcribed the tapes and committed his feelings to paper. It is fitting that this narrative be concluded in Howard Davenport's words, a poignant tribute to his friends but applicable to all the troops who fought, died, survived, or were captured during the war:

> It is 3:30 A.M., Sunday, September 4, 1983. In just over two hours I will again be in Korea. Thirty years ago, on December 8, 1952, I left this country on a stretcher in a casualty helicopter. I have not been back since.
>
> I first arrived in Korea on May 5, 1952, at 8:48 P.M. . . . Frank Benenati and I touched Korean soil at the same time. He held on to me as I looked at my watch as we stepped from the landing craft together. We vowed to leave the same way—but we didn't. Frank left in a flag-draped casket three months after I was evacuated.

... I am beginning to feel the emotions of this revisit. ... I could never explain it. It's something one must experience. ... you see a war-torn country with all of its sad people, hungry and dirty, with hardly a place to live. You serve with buddies closer than brothers, and see blood, pain and death. I came to this country young, trained for war, and wearing a uniform, but it was here that I grew to manhood and became a Marine. I grew up in Korea—the most significant period of my life.

On Monday morning, September 5th, we left our hotel for Inchon Harbor, where, in 1950, men of the 1st Marine Division landed, changing the course of the war for the North Korean invaders. The first step in driving them from South Korea, Inchon was where I also first entered Korea.

En route to the harbor, we stopped at the Korean National Cemetery. Awaiting us was a military honor guard and, as we passed, they came to Present Arms, saluting us. The guard looked sharp and well drilled. We walked to the monument for the Korean War Dead and placed a wreath on it. Inside were the names of the missing and a shrine to some six thousand unknown Korean people buried there. The ceremony was very moving and helped me to realize the price these people paid resisting a Communist takeover of their country.

By 11:20 A.M., we arrived at Inchon. Overlooking the harbor is a monument. A statute of three Marines, built in 1980 to honor the men of the United States Marine Corps who landed there and fought in Korea. This is where we came ashore, Chuck, Frank, and I. It is difficult for me to capture the moment, standing there with pride—thinking of just what the monument means to me; I felt tears welling up inside. I had to walk away from the group so others wouldn't see the profound effect on my emotions. For me this was a sacred place, and I think of Frank Benenati, Lloyd Smally, Bob Bush, and John Allen. These men paid it all.

While standing there looking out to sea, a thought occurred to me, and lingers today—the Korean people really care. They appreciate what we did and the sacrifices those men made. They have honored us all in such a special way.

Right where I'm looking, in Inchon Harbor thirty years ago, the hospital ship USS *Repose* was docked to receive casualties. The helicopter landed us on the ship, Lloyd Smally on one side of the chopper, dead, and me, near death on the other side. I was blind, but I can picture what it was like. How close I came to dying—now God has given me thirty additional years—I utter a prayer of thanks.

Later that day, we dropped by the Korean Meeting Plaza. A place with signs on both sides of the street for blocks. Here the people post the names of loved ones and family members in hopes of locating the lost and unaccounted for. Hundreds of others were milling around, reading names and searching their memories, trying to help. We were told that many of the people whose names are posted remain in North Korea, unable to cross the border and be reunited. It was sad.

The next day was the highlight of our visit, a trip up Freedom Road past OP-2, to Panmunjom. First, we visited the Eighth Army Headquarters at the United Nations Command in Seoul. There an Air Force Major briefed us, explaining how strong the South Korean Military is now, and then he described the strength of the opposing North Korean forces. He adds that Seoul will never fall again.

Remember, the war has never been concluded. To this day, North and South Korea exist only under a temporary truce. Technically, they are still at war.

En route north on Freedom Road, our expectations rise. Chuck and I asked ourselves if we would see the Freedom Gate Bridge, OP-2, Outpost Nan [COP-1], and Hill 90. Would we see the place on Highway One where we came out from a stream bed one night to the safety of the no fire zone? We would look for the small bridge over the stream where we carried out the wounded and dead of October 4th and 5th, 1952.[3]

The bus stopped briefly at a Memorial Park within sight of the Freedom Gate Bridge. An honor guard of about thirty men was formed in front of a statue of Harry S Truman. As we passed, the men came to attention and presented arms, very sharp. We stood before the statue while a soldier played taps, accompanied by an echo on another bugle in the distance. It was a solemn moment and an impressive tribute. Again my thoughts turned to the men who died there. As at Inchon, I had to fight back the emotions.

Turning to Freedom Gate Bridge, now called simply Freedom Bridge, I note that it hasn't changed much at all. It's the same one-lane bridge over the Imjin River that we traveled across so many times before. The former bridge to the right is just as it was then . . . blown away with only the concrete pilasters standing . . . chips from the same bullet holes still there. Now there are wire and machine gun towers on both sides of the river. We were advised that for security reasons, no photographs could be taken from this point on.

Crossing the river, we were briefed again at a Korean Military Camp. They ran a movie showing a tunnel that the North Koreans had dug under the DMZ after the war. We were able to inspect the "third" tunnel, dug in 1978. It was some 70 yards below ground through solid rock. Inside, they had machine guns emplaced to cut off any invading North Koreans. A Korean Army Captain in combat dress, his eyes moist with emotion, thanked us for saving his country.

He said that if it hadn't been for us, "we would be under Communist control now."

At the U.S. Army base, Camp Kitty Hawk, we were briefed about the conduct expected from us while visiting Panmunjom. They also showed a movie concerning the ax murders of three U.S. soldiers by 35 North Korean soldiers at a tree in Panmunjom. We were told to refrain from any gestures or provocative activity while in the village and within sight of North Korean forces.

Boarding a U.S. Army bus with an American soldier as a guide, we left for Panmunjom, inside the DMZ. Talking with our guide, we learned that OP-1 is now called OP Collins and OP-2 has been renamed OP Ouellette. Passing through more checkpoints, I began looking for the bridge with a small stream that crossed under the bridge. It should show up just before OP-2. Hill 90 was south of the Outpost, rather close to the MLR. I recalled that day in 1952 when I got hit. There was a Chinese tank killer team of about 50 men on Hill 90 when 15 of us hit the reverse slope to capture a prisoner. It was an ambush and, after a one-hour firefight, we pulled back, carrying our wounded and dead. Joey Shockley was captured, I was wounded, and John Allen was killed. Moving west into the stream bed, we managed to reach the safety of the Panmunjom Road and its neutral corridor.[4]

We are there! I can see it! OP-2! Chuck sees it too! Tall and bald . . . an area that I knew better than any other in Korea. I made most of my patrols there. I see Hill 90. It is just as I remember it. There is the small bridge and the stream. There is more water in it now. I see the place where we laid John Allen, waiting for the ambulance and transportation to come for us.

I can't see OP-1 as well as OP-2, it has grown up so much that you can hardly see it from the road. Viewing OP-2 again, all the fears of patrols in front of that hill sweep over me. I don't know where we got the courage. I think of different patrols and those Marines I was with . . . little things that happened . . . the dead Chinese soldier that I got the burp gun round from that I would carry on patrol . . . and the money I got from him. The hill reminds me of Bob Bush and Frank Benenati killed on Gray Rock . . . seeing it all again and being so close was an awesome experience.

The bus took us on in to Panmunjom Village, site of the truce talks. I remember 1952 when the area was closed to combat troops. It had large balloons at each of four corners and a searchlight directed straight up in the air at night.

Looking to the West, I keep trying to locate Hill 37. I want to go there and find the exact spot where I was wounded. I know I could find it if I were allowed. I wondered if the weapon that was blown from my hands would still be there. The experience of looking at it from where I stand is difficult to describe. Just a short distance away, I spilled a lot of blood in the snow . . . and Lloyd Smally gave his life for me. My buddies brought me out of there, just as I would have done for them. We used to say "everyone comes back or no one comes back." I knew they would die rather than leave me, and it all happened just a few miles west of where I was standing that moment. It gave me a sense of pride, a sense of humbleness, and a lump in my throat.

We returned to Seoul on the bus and spent three more days in Korea, shopping and looking at the sights. One evening, we attended a very impressive cocktail party and reception given in our honor. They had an Army band, vocalists sang "God Bless America," and a four-star General was in the receiving line.

At 6:20 P.M. on Friday, September 9, 1983, we left Korea for the second time. The trip of a lifetime was over—a dream fulfilled. I shared it with my Marine buddy . . . no other one, no other Marine that I served with could have shared the significance of this trip. Chuck Burrill and I went through a lot of bad times together; it's fitting that we shared this good one.

I was so impressed with the progress and development of Korea. When we were there in 1952, there was only one bridge across the Han River into Seoul. Now there are 14. The city is like any large U.S. city. In downtown Seoul, there is a sixteen-lane highway. The Koreans are a hardworking people, very emotional and so appreciative. All the roads were paved, even near the front lines. In 1952, I only saw one paved road. They have accomplished so much. Other Marines that I tell about our visit won't be able to believe the development. They will only remember the straw and mud houses, and the fences.

The one thing that impressed me most was that the Korean people are happy now, and laugh. They are not hungry in a land ravaged by war. I was often moved at their saluting our bus, and telling us their thanks for defending their country. I was impressed at their sincerity, and how they truly appreciated us.

Was it worth it thirty years ago? The loss; the hardships; the fears; the longing to be home; the pain from wounds, the ten months of hospitalization and the fact that the pain from my wounds is still quite severe at times—yes, it was worth it all. God brought me back. I feel proud to have been a part. Proud to say that for eight months in Korea I played a small part toward what we saw achieved in 1983.

The Land of Morning Calm has found its calm. Blood no longer flows from its wounds. In America, the telegrams of "Deeply regret to inform you that . . . " are no more. I thank God for all of this.[5]

POSTLUDE

This work had its beginning as an effort to capture lost memories, details of a period not readily available. The work expanded and gained a greater purpose—a tribute to those men who were there.

Nothing more can be said about those who died in Korea; it has been said many times over by people far more articulate than I. But what of the living? Why were we spared? We were in the same battles, frightened by the same situations, and missed by the same bullets.

I would like to think that we were spared so that we would not forget. So that we can honor those who didn't survive, but most of all to keep the faith with ourselves, to continue to support one another, our Corps, and our country. We aren't always right, but we are always real. Those values exist and need to endure—only the living can make that happen.

> I have fought the good fight,
> I have finished the race,
> I have kept the faith.
> —2 Timothy 4:10 (NIV)

SEMPER FIDELIS

Lee Ballenger, Sergeant USMC (1951–57)

Marine Corps Casualties
Korean War 1950–1953

Date	Killed in Action [KIA]	Killed, Non-battle	Wounded in Action [WIA]	Total	Average Monthly Total
Grand Total	4,262	244	26,038	30,544	848
					100%
August–December 1950	1,526	30	6,229	7,785	1,557
January–December 1951	960	82	7,924	8,966	747
January–March 1952	87	19	600	706	235
Cumulative totals, August 1950–March 1952	2,573	131	14,753	17,457	873
			Percent Total Casualties:		**57%**
Outpost War					
April–December 1952	960	66	6,815	7,841	871
January–July 1953	729	47	4,470	5,246	874
Cumulative totals April 1952–July 1953	1,689	113	11,285	13,087	818
			Percent Total Casualties:		**43%**

Source: Lt. Col. Pat Meid and Maj. James M. Yingling, *Operations in West Korea,* vol. 5, *Marine Operations in Korea, 1950–1953,* Appendix E, 575.

APPENDIX II

Western Korea, 1952–53
Hill, Outpost, and Military Sites:
Grid Numbers and Place Name Cross-Reference

Place Name	Comments
Allen/Carson/Hill 27★	See Carson
Ambush Alley (CT068073)	Supply trail to Carson
Arrowhead/Hill 67 (CT063080)	CCF hill N of Carson
Ascom City (Bupyong)	USMC supply center
Ava/Stromboli/Hill 48A (CT044059)★★	USMC OP
Berlin/Donald/Hill 19 (CT082082)	USMC squad + OP
Betty Grable	CCF hill
Black (CT019039)	USMC OP, June 1952, later became MLR
Blue/Hill 88 (BT997026)	USMC OP (June 1952)
Boot/Hill 70A (BT996030)	CCF hill, vicinity OP-2
Boulder City/Hill 119 (CT085077)	USMC MLR
Bronco/Detroit	USMC OP, June 1952
Brooklyn (CT089109)	CCF hill
Bruce/Reno/Hill 25	See Reno
Bulb (CT050067)	E side of Kumgok
Bunker Hill/Hill 122 (CT017046)	USMC platoon OP
Camp Brittania (CS259916)	Regimental reserve area

Numbers are elevations in meters; for feet, multiply by 3.28.
Map references refer to 1:25,000 AMS Series L851.
(Coordinates correspond with gridlines on endpaper maps.)

Place Name	Comments
Camp Casey (BT307984)	Regimental reserve area
Camp Doughtry (CS103973	Battalion reserve area
Camp Indianhead (CT372093)	Regimental reserve area
Camp Lee (CT090034)	Battalion reserve area
Camp Matthews (CT079063)	Battalion reserve area
Camp Meyer (CT047013)	Battalion reserve area
Camp Pope (CT371108)	Battalion reserve area
Camp Rose (CS078994)	Battalion reserve area
Carson/Allen/Hill 27 (CT064076)	USMC OP, 1 off., 38 men
Chicago/Elmer (CT082094)	See Elmer
Clarence/Vegas/COP-5/Hill 21	See Vegas
Claw/Hill 70 (BT994034)	CCF hill, vicinity Marilyn
Command Post, 1st Marine Div./Yongji-ri	
COP-1/Nan (BT975012)	USMC 2 squad OP
COP-2/ Hill 84 (BT970028)	USMC OP reinf. company
COP-2A/Toothache/Molar (BT965025)	Covered rear of COP-2
COP-3 (BT987043)	USMC OP, abandoned
COP-4 (CT020050)	Same as Hill 120, abandoned Apr 1952
COP-4 (CT034057)	
COP-5/Hill 21/Vegas★	
COP-6/Hill 104	
COP-7/Hill 201 (CT021038)	May 1952, later became MLR
COP-19/Berlin	
COP-19A/E. Berlin	
COP-21/Vegas★	
Corinne/Dagmar (CT039050)★★	USMC 2 squad OP
Dagmar/Corrine (CT035050)★★	USMC 2 squad OP
Detroit/Felix/Bronco/Hill 15 (CT087089)★	USMC OP, July 1952, lost 7 Oct.
Digger (CT074078)	USMC OP (possible early name for Vegas)

Place Name	Comments
Dike (CT053071)	CCF position, vicinity Ungok
Dinosaur (BT981019)	Hill in no-man's-land
Donald/Berlin	USMC OP (July 1952)
East Berlin/Hill 19A (CT088082)	USMC squad OP
Elko/Hill 47 (CT067075)	USMC OP
Elmer/Chicago/Hill 190 (CT082093)	USMC OP, lost 7 August 1952
Esther/Samoa/Hill 56A (CT029048)★★	USMC squad OP
Fan (CT013037)	Saddle between OPs Bunker and Hedy
Felix/Detroit/Hill 110	See Detroit
Frisco/Gary	See Gary
Gary/Frisco/Hill 13 (CT090104)	USMC OP, lost Oct. 7, 1952
Gertie	USMC OP, abandoned June 1952
Ginger/Hill 100 (CT022044)★★	USMC squad OP
Green/Ingrid	See Ingrid
Harlow (CT051065)	CCF hill contected to Kumgok
Hedy/Yellow/Hill 124 (CT014036)	USMC OP, 2 squads
Hedy Gate (CT150032)	Trail to Hedy from MLR
Hilda/Queen (CT091099)	USMC OP, lost 11 Aug. 1952
Honker Bridge (CS067953)	Bridge over Imjin
Hook/Point Fox (CT103104)	Salient on MLR, right sector
Horseshoe (BT989031)	Approach to Hill 90
Ingrid/Green/Hill 64A (CT011030)	USMC 2 squad OP
Irene/Rome/Nan/Hill 41 (CT097103)	USMC OP, lost 17 Aug. 1952
Island (BT976028)	Terrain, vicinity OP-2
Jersey Ridge (CT084087	CCF trench line

Place Name	Comments
Jill/Pete/Seattle	See Seattle
Kate/Hill 128 (BT999021)	USMC 2 squad OP
Kirby (CT058067)	Hill vicinity Ungok
Kumgok/Hill 35A (CT050067)	CCF-held OP
Libby Bridge	Across Imjin, formerly X-Ray
Little Frisco (CT088093)	USMC OP
Little Rock (CT084086)	CCF-held hill
London	CCF hill
Marilyn/Hill 92 (BT992015)	USMC platoon OP
Molar (BT963028)	Hill vicinity OP-2
Nellie	USMC OP, abandoned June 1952
New Bunker/Hill 122A	Bunker Hill relocated
New York	CCF hill
No Name Ridge (BT977028)	Hill, vicinity OP-2, possibly Gray Rock
Paris	CCF hill
Pentagon (CT013036)	South slope of Hedy
Pete	Name changed to Jill (July 1952)
Pheasant (CT113113)	Hill mass, vicinity Hook
Point Fox	See Hook
Queen/Hilda	Name change (July 1952)
Red Hill, Hill 33B (CT056068)	
Reno/Yoke/Hill 25/Bruce (CT068079)★	USMC OP, approx. 40 men, lost Mar. 1953.
Reno Block (CT068077)	Reno support position
Rome (CT096104)	CCF hill
Ronson/Hill 41 (CT101102)	USMC squad OP
Rose Bowl/Stadium (BT958013)	Terrain feature in KMC sector
Royal	USMC OP, abandoned June 1952

Place Name	Comments
Samichon River	Boundary between USMC & British Div. till Nov. 1952
Samoa/Esther★★	
Seattle/Jill (CT100103)★	USMC OP, lost 6 Oct. 1952
76 Alley (093080)	Road east of East Berlin
Siberia/Hill 58A (CT023048)	USMC squad OP, lost Aug. 9, 1952
Spoonbill Bridge (CS088972)	Bridge across Imjin River
Stadium/Rose Bowl (BT958013)	Terrain feature, vicinity OP-1
Star/Hill 132 (BT 986017)	Hill, vicinity OP-2
Stromboli/Ava/Hill 48A (CT045059)★★	USMC squad outpost
Three Fingers/Hill 80 (BT985032)	CCF hill, vicinity COP-2
Toms Thumb (CT076082)	Vicinity, Vegas
Toothache/COP-2A	
Toryum	Burnt village in right sector,
Tumae-Ri Ridge/Hill 40D (CT45073)	CCF-held, vicinity Hill 104
Ungok/Hill 31 (CT059072)	Major CCF hill mass w/31A, 31B, 31C
Vegas/Clarence/Digger/Hill 21 (CT074078)	OP-5 in Mar. 1952, USMC OP, lost July, 1953.
Verdun (CT132095)	USMC OP, abutting British Div.
"W" (CT014037)	Opposite Fan on Hedy/ Bunker
Warsaw/Hill 137 (CT104108)	USMC 2 squad OP
White/Hill 90 (BT987024)	OP until lost
Widgeon Bridge (CT151034)	Bridge across Imjin
William/COP-3 (BT987043)	Abandoned, early 1952
X-Ray	USMC OP, abandoned June 1952

Place Name	Comments
X-Ray Bridge (CS096013)	Bridge across Imjin
Yellow	Early name for Hedy
Yoke (CT069079)	USMC OP, June 1952, early name for Reno
Yoke/Hill 159 (BT001037), 2d hill, same name	CCF hill near corridor
Yongji-Ri (103886)	1st Marine Div. CP

Cross-Reference by Hill Number

Number	Name	Comments
13	Gary/Frisco	See Gary
15	Felix/Detroit	USMC OP until Oct. 7, 1952
19	Berlin	
19A	East Berlin	
21	Vegas★	
21B	CT071082	CCF-held
23	CT072087	CCF-held
25	Reno/Bruce (CT068079)★	
25A	Hill 150 (CT069083)	CCF-held
27	Allen/Carson★	
29	CT063085	CCF-held
31	KMC OP	
31	Ungok (CT059072)	Major CCF strong point in 1953
31A	Part of Ungok (CT058072)	
31B	Part of Ungok (CT061070)	
31C	Part of Ungok (CT059070)	
33	KMC OP	
33B	Red Hill (CT056068)	
35	KUMGOK (CT052064)	CCF-held
36	KMC OP	
37	COP-67/COP-37	KMC OP
37	BS964983	CCF OP
39	KMC OP	
40		CCF-held
40A	Ava/Hill48A (CT044059)★★	
40D	Tumae-Ri (CT045073)	CCF-held
41	Ronson (CT100102)	Called Seattle in Sept. 1952
41	Irene (CT097103)	USMC OP
44	CT034057	OP-4 (in May 1952)
45	CT063085	CCF-held

Number	Name	Comments
47	Elko	
48A	Stromboli/Ava/Hill40A (CT044059)★★	USMC OP
50A	Corrine★★	USMC OP, 21 men
51	KMC OP	
52	Dagmar (CT035050)★★	USMC OP, 1 off., 27 men
56A	Samoa/Esther (CT029048)★★	USMC OP, 18 men
57		CCF-held
57A	CT080085	CCF-held
58A	Siberia (CT023048)	USMC squad OP, lost Aug. 9, 1952
64	CT007032	CCF-held, vicinity Ingrid
64A	INGRID (CT011030)	
66	Hill 123 (CT 006040)	CCF OP, opposed Bunker
67	Arrowhead (CT063080)	CCF-held, N of Carson
70	Claw (BT995035)	CCF OP
70A	Boot (997030)	CCF OP
80	Three Fingers (BT985032)	CCF-held (vicinity OP-2)
82	CCF MG position (BT975035)	Vicinity 134
84	COP-2	USMC OP, Reinf. Co
86	COP-1(BT975012)	KMC OP, 27 men
87	BS955930	CCF-held
88	OP Blue (BT996026)	CCF-held
90	White (BT986024)	CCF-held
92	Marilyn (BT992015)	USMC OP, 1 off., 29 men
95	BS964948	Chinese gun position
98	CT093097	CCF-held
100	Ginger★★	USMC OP, 16 men
104	(CT044065)	CCF-held 850 yd. N of Stromboli
110	Felix	
111	MLR (CT098094)	Used in Berlin fighting
114	CT029050	CCF-held

Number	Name	Comments
116	CT025052	CCF hill N of Siberia
118	CT17044	CCF hill, vicinity Hedy
119	Boulder City/MLR (CT084078)	Used in Berlin fighting
120	OP 4 (CT020050)	CCF-held
122	Bunker Hill (CT017046)	CCF till 11 Aug. 1952, USMC OP, 1 off., 31 men
122A	New Bunker (CT016040)	Relocated Bunker Hill, same ridge
123	Hill 66 (CT006040)	CCF-held, opposed Bunker
124	Hedy (CT013036)	Extension of Bunker, USMC OP, 1 off., 17 men
125	CT081087	CCF hill N of Berlin
126	CT089065	High point, rear of MLR, Co CP
128	Kate (BT998021)	USMC OP, 1 off., 30 men
132	Star (BT986017)	Between OP-2 & Marilyn
133	CT07091	Chinese hill, used July 1952
134	BT978032	CCF-held, between Three Fingers and Hill 67, vicinity OP-2
139	(CT080085)	CCF-held Used in Berlin fighting
144	CT029051	CCF hill, vicinity Dagmar
146	USMC MLR	Right sector near the Hook
148	Bruce	
150	Same as 25A (CT069085)	CCF-held
153	CT073082	CCF-held, N of Vegas
155	Prominent hill on KMC MLR	
155	CT071082	CCF-held
157	Warsaw (CT105107)	USMC OP, near the Hook
159	Yoke/Hill 159 (BT001037)	Major CCF OP, 5 mi. N of Imjin River; former USMC OP prior to July 1952.

Number	Name	Comments
161	Omaha (CT090108)	Chinese-held, about 1 May 1952
163	CT090107	Chinese-held
185	CT098131	CCF-held, near the Hook
190	Elmer (CT083093)	
190.5	Same as 191 (CT073088)	Chinese-held in Aug. 1952
191	Same as 190.5	
201	MLR (CT020039)	High point S of Bunker Hill
225	Pork Chop Hill	U.S. Army OP
229	Paehok (CT014017)	USMC high ground behind MLR, tank & artillery CP. Regimental observation post
236	Taedok-san	CCF high ground opposing 229
266	Old Baldy	U.S. Army OP
355	Little Gibraltar	U.S. Army OP (2d Div. in 1952)

*In September 1952, 7th Marines changed OP names to Reno, Carson, Vegas, Detroit, and Seattle.
**In November 1952, 2/5 changed OP names to Ava, Corinne, Dagmar, Esther, and Ginger.
Source: Lee Ballenger, © 1995.

NOTES

PREFACE
1. McKenney, "Recognition Delayed."
2. Riddle, "Depot Bids Farewell."

INTRODUCTION
1. Transcript of Proceedings, 122d Session, Military Armistice Conference, 8 Oct. 1952. Far East Command Main Delegates Meetings, vol. VI, 24 July 1952–15 May 1953. Quoted in Hermes, *Truce Tent*, 281.
2. Marshall, *Pork Chop Hill*, 15.
3. Meid and Yingling, *Operations in West Korea*, 532.

CHAPTER 1
1. Later in the war, the Marine Corps accepted draftees, but even they were volunteers of a sort. After being drafted, the men could volunteer for the Marines or go into the Army.
2. ITR was the forerunner of what is now the School of Infantry (SOI). It is still located at Camp San Onofre but in far more comfortable quarters.
3. Adapted from Gartz, "Staging Regiment," and from Coggins, "Replacements."
4. Adapted from Wood, "Pickel Meadows."
5. Quoted in Ballenger, *Of Men and Machines*, 19.
6. Ibid., 20.
7. Ibid.
8. Gannon, *Laughter and Tears*, 26.
9. Quoted in Berry, *Hey, Mac*, 284.
10. Hall, letter to Mr. Don Knox, author of *Korean War, Uncertain Victory*, 20 Jan. 1986. Used with permission.
11. Richard Champagne, quoted in Byrne and Pendas, *Bloody George*, 22.
12. Little, letter to author, 7 Nov. 1997.

CHAPTER 2

1. 1st Marine Division, Command Diary, Jan. 1953, 3.
2. The 7th AT was a platoon of five tanks from the Regimental Antitank Platoon. Although it belonged to the infantry regiment, the platoon was often attached to the tank battalion.
3. McGuire, letter to author, 14 July 2000.
4. Saluzzi, *Red Blood,* 144.
5. Lipper, letter home, 15 Jan. 1953. Used with permission.
6. A dozer tank is regular gun tank equipped with a movable bulldozer blade. Although not as versatile as a regular bulldozer, it could operate under fire.
7. Williamson, *Dearest Buckie,* 152.
8. Russ, *Last Parallel,* 265, 283.
9. Jess Meado, quoted in Byrne and Pendas, *Bloody George,* 21.
10. Guidera, letter to author, 6 Jan. 1997.

CHAPTER 3

1. Hall, letter to Knox, 20 Jan. 1986.
2. Quoted in Ballenger, *Of Men and Machines,* 114.
3. O'Hagan, letter to author, 9 Dec. 1996.
4. Luminello, letter to the author, n.d.
5. O'Hagan, letter to author, 9 Dec. 1996.
6. Matthias, *The Korean War,* p. 76.
7. Marshall, *World War I,* 210.
8. O'Hagan, letter to author, 9 Dec. 1996.
9. Hall, letter to Knox, 20 Jan. 1986.
10. Hicks, *U.S. Marine Operations,* 173.
11. 5th Marine Regiment, Command Diary, July 1952.
12. Rauh, letter to author, 4 July 1997.
13. Hall, letter to Knox, 20 Jan. 1986.
14. Hermes, *Truce Tent,* 354. Also note, the effects of ammunition shortages described in Ballenger, *The Outpost War,* chap. 10.
15. Ibid.
16. Hicks, *U.S. Marine Operations,* 175.
17. Keene, "A Thaw in the Freeze."
18. Janzen, letter home, 1953. Used with permission.
19. March, letter home, 1953. Used with permission. The lieutenant received his promotion and remained in the Marine Corps. He retired as a lieutenant colonel after commanding a tank battalion in Vietnam.

CHAPTER 4

1. Berry, quoted in *Hey, Mac,* 263.
2. Miller, interview by author, 15 Sept. 1992.
3. Russ, *Last Parallel,* 87.

4. Williamson, *Dearest Buckie,* 143.
5. Ibid, 144.
6. Ibid, 147.
7. Ibid, 148.
8. Ibid.
9. Adapted from the 1st Tank Battalion, Command Diary, Feb. 1953, App. IV, "Tank Action in Support of Operation Clambake," and from Miller and Hunter, interviews by author, September 15, 1992.
10. Quoted in Berry, *Hey Mac,* 263.
11. Coleman, "Ungok."
12. Saluzzi, *Red Blood,* 146.
13. Murphy, *Korean War Heroes,* 259.
14. 1st Tank Battalion, Command Diary, Feb. 1953, App. IV, 6.
15. Janzen, letter home, 13 Feb. 1953. Used with permission.

CHAPTER 5
1. Hermes, *Truce Tent,* 389.
2. Ibid., 513 (statistics for July 1953).
3. 3d Battalion, 7th Marines, Command Diary, Feb. 1953, 3.
4. Ibid., 32.
5. Scholten, letter to Richard Suarez, 19 Apr. 1991. Used with permission.
6. Sgt. Joe Ogden, statement from personal files of Vincent Walsh, n.d.
7. Ibid.
8. John Rogers, letter home, 23 Feb. 1953. Used with permission.
9. Vincent Walsh, letter to Robert Farrell, n.d. Used with permission.
10. 3d Battalion, 7th Marines, Command Diary, Feb. 1953, App. IV, 32.
11. Walsh, letter to Farrell, n.d.
12. 3d Battalion, 7th Marines, Command Diary, Feb. 1953, n.d.
13. 3d Battalion, 7th Marines, Command Diary, Mar. 1953, App. IV, 3.
14. Ibid., 7.
15. Scholten, letter to Suarez, 19 Apr. 1991.
16. Special Action Report, 23–24 Feb. 1953 in 1st Battalion, 7th Marines, Command Diary, Feb. 1953.
17. Ibid.
18. After Clambake, the Tank Battalion Reconnaissance Section, which should have checked Hill 90, did not exist. Ironically, a new and larger Reconnaissance Section had been formed, but the men were in training with the Division Reconnaissance Company. Some of them were with the Reconnaissance Platoon on COP-2 and watched events unfold.
19. 1st Tank Battalion, Command Diary, report of tank-infantry action on Hill 90, Feb. 1953, App. 4.
20. Special Action Report, 23–24 Feb. 1953, 2.
21. Ibid.

22. Williamson, *Dearest Buckie,* 164.

23. 2/5 Special Action Report, 25 Feb. 1953, 3. Also see 2d Battalion, 5th Marines, Command Diary, Feb. 1953.

24. Quoted in Knox, *Korean War,* 469.

25. 2/5 Special Action Report, 25 Feb. 1953.

26. Meid and Yingling, *Operations in West Korea,* 258.

27. Geer, *Reckless Pride,* 168.

28. Hall, letter to Knox, 20 Jan. 1986.

CHAPTER 6

1. Headquarters Battalion, Command Diary, Feb. 1953, App. IV, x.

2. Bev Bruce, letter to author, 20 Jan. 1994.

3. Ballenger, *Of Men and Machines,* 51.

4. Headquarters Battalion, Command Diary, Feb. 1953, App. IV, ab.

5. Lipper, letter home, 28 Feb. 1953. Used with permission.

6. John J. O'Hagan, letter to author, 9 Dec. 1996.

7. John L. Camara, personal diary, entry for 27 Feb. 1953. Used with permission.

8. Lipper, letter home, 28 Feb. 1953.

9. Burrill, letter to Howard Davenport, 9 Mar. 1953. Used with permission.

10. Finn, letter to author, 13 May 1992.

11. Burrill, letter to Davenport.

12. O'Hagan, letter to author.

13. Lipper, letter home, 3 Mar. 1953. Used with permission.

14. MacDonnell, letter to Joe Benenati, 21 Mar. 1953. Used with permission.

15. Williamson, *Dearest Buckie,* 168.

CHAPTER 7

1. Hermes, *Truce Tent,* 392.

2. 1st Marine Division, Command Diary, Mar. 1953, 2.

3. Jess Meado, quoted in Byrne and Pendas, *Bloody George,* 25.

4. Williamson, *Dearest Buckie,* 172.

5. Crosby, "Hill 31A—Ungok." Crosby retained his arm, somewhat the worse for wear and without full movement, but he does not carry an empty coat sleeve. He was medically retired from the Marine Corps for wounds received on Ungok.

6. 1st Battalion, 5th Marines, Special Action Report, 19 Mar. 1953. 6.

7. Ibid.

8. Ballenger, *Of Men and Machines,* 78.

9. At this time, the Marines were manning sixteen permanent outposts, ten in the center sector and six in front of the right sector. KMCs on the far left also maintained a small number of outposts in front of their positions.

10. Special Action Report, 18–28 Mar. 1953, 3. 1st Marine Regiment, Command Diary.

11. Gene Thomas, quoted in Byrne and Pendas, *Bloody George,* 26.

12. Special Action Report, 18–28 Mar. 1953, 3. 1st Marine Regiment, Command Diary.

13. Special Intelligence Report 2d Battalion, 1st Marine Regiment, Command Diary, Apr. 1953.

14. Ibid., 10.

15. Ibid.

16. Williamson, *Dearest Buckie,* 182.

CHAPTER 8

1. 1st Marine Division, Command Diary, Mar. 1953. 1.

2. Little, letter to author, 11 July 1997.

3. Geer, *Reckless Pride,* 171.

4. 5th Marine Regiment, Command Diary, Special Action Report, "Battle of the Cities," Mar. 1953, 2 (hereafter cited as 5th Marine Regiment, "Battle of the Cities"). Also, see outpost inspection reports included in the report.

5. Meid and Yingling, *Marine Operations in Korea,* 280

6. Ingalls, letter to William Janzen, Jan. 1998. Used with permission.

7. Ibid.

8. Ingalls, letter to author, Mar. 1998.

9. 5th Marine Regiment, "Battle of the Cities."

10. Janzen, "Reno Block," 6.

11. 5th Marine Regiment, "Battle of the Cities," 3.

12. Janzen, letter to Lee Viorel, 7 Aug. 2000. Used with permission.

13. Tom Kennedy, letter to author, 3 Feb. 1998.

14. Janzen, "Reno Block," 9.

15. Kennedy, letter to author, n.d.

16. Janzen, "Reno Block," 9.

17. Jim Larkin, quoted in Knox, *Korean War,* 472

18. Geer, *Reckless Pride,* 172–73.

19. Kreid, letter to author, 29 Aug. 1996.

20. Meid and Yingling, *Marine Operations in Korea,* 285–86.

21. Geer, *Reckless Pride,* 177.

22. 3d Battalion, 5th Marines, Command Diary, Mar. 1953, 7.

23. Quoted in Fugate, "Vegas, Reno and Carson."

24. Luther Hudson, letter to author, 24 Jan. 1997.

25. Chenoweth, *Three Rounds for Effect*

26. Ibid.

27. Meid and Yingling, *Marine Operations in Korea,* 293.

28. Chenoweth, letters to author, 8 May 1998.

29. Meid and Yingling, *Marine Operations in Korea,* 294. William Charette, from New York, remained in the Navy and retired as a Master Chief.
30. Chenoweth, *Three Rounds For Effect.*
31. Ibid.
32. Ibid.
33. Ibid.
34. Ibid.
35. Ibid.
36. 5th Marine Regiment, "Battle of the Cities," 5.
37. Hall, letter to Donald Knox, 20 Jan. 1986. Used with permission.
38. Ibid.
39. Kreid, letter to author, 29 Aug. 1996.
40. Meid and Yingling, *Marine Operations in Korea,* 298.
41. Ibid, 301–02.
42. Ibid.
43. Hall, letter to Donald Knox, 20 Jan. 1986. Used with permission.
44. Fugate, "Vegas, Reno and Carson."
45. Meid and Yingling, *Marine Operations in Korea,* 305.
46. Fugate, "Vegas, Reno and Carson."
47. Meid and Yingling, *Marine Operations in Korea,* 305.
48. Quoted in ibid., 308.
49. 1st Tank Battalion, Command Diary, Mar. 1953, 3.
50. Quoted in Ballenger, *Of Men and Machines,* 26.
51. Beaven, "Battle of Vegas."
52. Seabury, "Outposts Reno and Vegas Remembered."
53. 1st Marine Division, Command Diary, Mar. 1953, 3.

CHAPTER 9

1. Hall, letter to Donald Knox 20 January 1986. Used with permission.
2. Casserly, "Wounded Marine."
3. Ibid.
4. Russ, *Last Parallel,* 239.
5. Breur, *Shadow Warriors,* 222.
6. Kreid, letter to author. Used with permission.
7. Ibid.
8. Special Action Report, 1st Battalion, 7th Marines, Command Diary, 9 May 1953.
9. Kreid, letter to author, used with permission.
10. Saluzzi, *Red Blood,* 159.
11. Kreid, letter to author. Used with permission.
12. 1st Battalion, 7th Marines, Command Diary, Special Action Report, 9 May 1953, 2.

13. Richard Guidera, quoted in Byrne and Pendas, *Bloody George,* 27.
14. Jess Meado, quoted in Byrne and Pendas, *Bloody George,* 27.
15. Headquarters Battalion, Command Diary, Apr. 1953, Reconnaissance Company Patrol Report No. 99.
16. Meid and Yingling, *Marine Operations in Korea,* reported 32 British, 15 Turks, 6 Colombians, 5 Australians, 2 Canadians, 1 Greek, 1 South African, 1 Filipino, and 1 Netherlander, 317.
17. Hermes, *Truce Tent,* 415.
18. Meid and Yingling, *Marine Operations in Korea,* 316.
19. Ibid., 319
20. Marshall, *Pork Chop Hill,* 15.

CHAPTER 10

1. 1st Marine Division, Command Diary, May 1953, Appendix.
2. In later years and wars, Army combat uniforms used "subdued" insignia, black nonreflective rank symbols for wear on utility uniforms. During the early 1950s, however, subdued insignia did not exist, and officers wore their polished gold or silver dress insignia.
3. Robert E. Werckle, quoted in Byrne and Pendas, *Bloody George,* 28. Used with permission.
4. Harvey Dethloff, quoted in Byrne and Pendas, *Bloody George,* 29. Used with permission.
5. Kreid, letter to author, 14 May 1998.
6. March, letters home 16–25 May 1953. Used with permission.
7. Champlin, letter to author, n.d.
8. In modern South Korea, Hill 229 is Camp Bonifas, forward Headquarters of the United Nations Command, Security Battalion, Joint Security Area (UNCSBJSA).
9. Ballenger, *Of Men and Machines,* 121.
10. Lipper, letter home, 8 June 1953. Used with permission.
11. Command Report, 35th Infantry Regiment, U.S. Army, May 1953, 1.
12. Quoted in Ballenger, *Of Men and Machines,* 133.
13. During the Cold War of the 1950s, the bulk of the Army's M-46s remained in Europe, where they were available to engage the Soviets. Inferior M-4s and M-26s, plus a small number of M-46s, were relegated to Korea.
14. Montgomery, letter to author, 25 May 1998.
15. Ibid.
16. 1st Tank Battalion, Command Diary, May 1953, 2.
17. Montgomery, letter to author, 25 May 1998.
18. 1st Tank Battalion, Command Diary, May 1953, 3, 49.
19. Lipper, letter home, 8 June 1953.

20. Meid and Yingling, *Marine Operations in Korea,* 340–41.
21. Kreid, letter to author, 14 May 1998.
22. Ibid.

CHAPTER 11

1. Meid and Yingling, *Marine Operations in Korea,* 365.
2. 1st Tank Battalion, Command Diary, July 1953, 2.
3. Hall, letter to Donald Knox, 20 January 1986. Used with permission.
4. Kreid, letter to author, 2 Sept.1998. Used with permission.
5. Ibid.
6. Seabury, "For Three Weeks."
7. Schmidt, letter to Richard Dolan, 23 June 1992. Used with permission.
8. Thomas Parlin, quoted in Wilson and Strickbine, *Faces of War,* 421.
9. Meid and Yingling, *Marine Operations in Korea,* 370.
10. 1st Marine Division, Command Diary, July 1953. Associated Press, Press Release, 20 July 1953.
11. Saluzzi, *Red Blood,* 161.
12. March, letter home, 17 July 1953. Used with permission.
13. 1st Battalion, 7th Marines, Command Diary, July 1953, 6.
14. Saluzzi, *Red Blood,* 162.
15. 3d Battalion, 7th Marines, Command Diary, July 1953, 2.
16. Ibid., 5.
17. 1st Marine Division, Command Diary, July 1953. Associated Press, Press Release, 20 July 1953.
18. Seabury, "For Three Weeks."
19. Kreid, letter to author, 2 Sept., 1998.
20. Ibid.
21. Meid and Yingling, *Marine Operations in Korea,* 381.

CHAPTER 12

1. Timothy Tobin quoted in Byrne and Pendas, *Bloody George,* 31. Used with permission.
2. Harvey Dethloff, quoted in Byrne & Pendas, *Bloody George,* 34. Used with permission.
3. 1st Marine Regiment, Command Diary, Special Action Report, July 1953, 2.
4. Richard Champagne, quoted in Byrne and Pendas, *Bloody George,* 37. Used with permission.
5. Ibid., 34.
6. Ibid., 36.
7. Richard Johnson, quoted in Byrne & Pendas, *Bloody George,* 36. Used with permission.

8. Russ Church, quoted in Byrne and Pendas, *Bloody George,* 38. Used with permission.

9. Leland Snell, quoted in Byrne and Pendas, *Bloody George,* 38. Used with permission.

10. 1st Marine Regiment, Command Diary, Special Action Report, 3.

11. Leland Snell, quoted in Byrne and Pendas, *Bloody George,* 39. Used with permission.

12. 1st Marine Regiment, Command Diary, Special Action Report, 3.

13. James Everson Jr., quoted in Byrne and Pendas, *Bloody George,* 40. Used with permission.

14. Meid and Yingling, *Marine Operations in Korea,* 404.

15. Richard Johnson, quoted in Byrne and Pendas, *Bloody George,* 41. Used with permission. The reader might note that, in this account, Johnson was captured less than twelve hours before the Chinese signed the armistice ending hostilities. Legitimate questions would appear to be: Why was he interrogated further? Why was he kept and abused? Had he been Senator Johnson's son, would he have been treated differently or perhaps kept and used later as a political bargaining chip?

16. Saluzzi, *Red Blood,* 164.

17. 1st Marine Regiment, Command Diary, Special Action Report, 4.

18. Ibid., 5.

19. Champlin, letter to author, 24 Sept. 1998.

20. 1st Tank Battalion, Command Diary, July 1953, 2.

21. 3d Battalion, 7th Marines, Command Diary, Appendix IV, "Reports and Summaries, 1. Intelligence Reports," 14–15.

22. O'Neil, *Australia in Korean War.*

23. Broadhead, letter to author, 16 Mar. 2000. Used with Permission.

24. Gen. Sir John Wilton, letter to Robert O'Neil, 14 Sept.1980, quoted in O'Neil, *Australia in Korean War.*

25. Kreid, letter to author, 14 May 1998.

26. Robert Guertin, letter to author, 21 Feb. 1999.

27. 5th Marine Regiment, Command Diary, July 1953, 7.

28. Meid and Yingling, *Marine Operations in Korea,* 388.

29. Ibid., 391.

CHAPTER 13

1. Ballenger, *Outpost War,* chap. 12.

2. See *The Outpost War,* Chap. 6.

3. See *The Outpost War,* Chap. 9.

4. Ibid.

5. Howard Davenport, unpublished essay, 1983.

BIBLIOGRAPHY

Ballenger, Lee. "Of Men and Machines, Marines in Korea—1953," (unpublished memoir), 1992.

————, *The Outpost War: U.S. Marines in Korea, Vol. 1: 1952*. Dulles, Va.: Brassey's, 2000.

Beaven, William E. "The Battle of Vegas." *Leatherneck,* May 1973.

Berry, Henry. *Hey, Mac, Where Ya Been?* New York: St. Martin's Press, 1988.

Breur, William B. *Shadow Warriors: The Covert War in Korea*. New York: John Wiley, 1996.

Byrne, James, and G. Pendas Jr., eds. *Bloody George,* vol. 4 of *Western Front Korea, 1952–53.* George 3/1 Association, 1991.

Casserly, John. "Wounded Marine Describes Reds Brutal 'Treatment'." *Pacific Stars and Stripes* 9, no. 99 (10 April 1953).

Chenoweth, Theodore H. *Three Rounds for Effect.* Sonoma, Calif.: Boustrophedon Press, 1988.

Command Diaries and Special Action Reports, U.S. Marine Corps. National Archives. Viewing arranged by Marine Corps Historical Center, Washington Navy Yard, Washington, D.C.

  1st Marine Division, Command Diaries, January 1953 through July 1953.

  1st Marine Regiment, Command Diaries, January 1953 through July 1953.

  5th Marine Regiment, Command Diaries, January 1953 through July 1953.

  7th Marine Regiment, Command Diaries, January 1953 through July 1953.

  1st Battalion, 1st Marines, Command Diaries, January 1953 through July 1953

  2d Battalion, 1st Marines, Command Diaries, January 1953 through July 1953

3d Battalion, 1st Marines, Command Diaries, January 1953 through July 1953

1st Battalion, 5th Marines, Command Diaries, January 1953 through July 1953

2d Battalion, 5th Marines, Command Diaries, January 1953 through July 1953

3d Battalion, 5th Marines, Command Diaries, January 1953 through July 1953

1st Battalion, 7th Marines, Command Diaries, January 1953 through July 1953

2d Battalion, 7th Marines, Command Diaries, January 1953 through July 1953

3d Battalion, 7th Marines, Command Diaries, January 1953 through July 1953

1st Tank Battalion, Command Diaries, January 1953 through July 1953

Headquarters Battalion, 1st Marine Division, January 1953 through July 1953

Command Reports, 35th Infantry Regiment, U.S. Army, May 1953 through July 1953. National Archives, Suitland, Md.

Coggins, Lt. Col. Thomas M. "Replacements Are Coming!" *Marine Corps Gazette,* June 1953.

Coleman, TSgt. James F. "Ungok." *Leatherneck,* July 1953.

Crosby, Madison. "Hill 31A—Ungok." *Guidon,* July 1995.

Fugate, MSgt Robert T. "Vegas, Reno and Carson." *Leatherneck,* July 1953.

Gannon, R. A. *The Laughter and the Tears.* Kearney, Nebr.: Morris Publishing, 1997.

Gartz, MSgt. Spence R. "Staging Regiment." *Leatherneck,* January 1953.

Geer, Lt. Col. Andrew. *Reckless, Pride of the Marines.* New York: E. P. Dutton, 1955.

Heinl, Col. Robert Debs, Jr. *Dictionary of Military and Naval Quotations.* Annapolis: Naval Institute Press, 1966.

Hermes, Walter G. *Truce Tent and Fighting Front.* Washington, D.C.: Office of the Chief of Military History, U.S. Army, 1988.

Hicks, Lt. Col. Norman W. "U.S. Marine Operations in Korea 1952–1953 with Special Emphasis on Outpost Warfare," Master's Thesis, University of Maryland, 1962.

Janzen, William H. The Reno Block. Draft, unpublished monograph, n.d.

Keene, R. R. "A Thaw in the Freeze." *Leatherneck,* April 1993.

Knox, Donald, *The Korean War, Uncertain Victory.* New York: Harcourt, Brace, Jovanovich, 1988.

Marshall, S. L. A. *World War I.* Boston: Houghton Mifflin, 1964.

———. *Pork Chop Hill.* Nashville:Battery Press, 1986.

Matthias, Howard. *The Korean War: Reflections of a Young Combat Platoon Leader.* Tallahassee: Father and Son Publishing, 1995.

McKenney, Lt. Col. Tom C. (Ret.), "Recognition Delayed—Okinawa, 1945." *Military,* March 2000, 22–34.

Meid, Lt. Col. Pat and Maj. James M. Yingling. *Operations in West Korea,* vol. 5, *Marine Operations in Korea 1950–1953.* Washington, D.C.: Historical Division, Headquarters, U.S. Marine Corps, 1972.

Murphy, Edward F. *Korean War Heroes.* Novato, Calif.: Presidio Press, 1992.

O'Neil, Robert. *Australia in the Korean War, 1950–53.* Quoted in *Korea Remembered, Anthology,* Maurice Pears and Fred Kirkland, comps. Isle of Capri, Queensland, Australia: Wancliff Pty Ltd., 1996, chap. 37. Available on the Internet at http://www.ffasfs.com.au/korearemembered.htm.

Riddle, Cpl. Steve. "Depot Bids Farewell to an American Hero." *Chevron,* Nov. 6, 1998.

Russ, Martin. *The Last Parallel: A Marine's War Journal.* New York: Rinehart & Company, 1957.

Saluzzi, Joseph A. *Red Blood . . . Purple Hearts, the Marines in the Korean War.* Owings Mills, Md: Watermark Press, 1989.

Seabury, Roy. "Outposts Reno & Vegas Remembered." *Old Breed News,* February 1995.

———, "For Three Weeks We Held the Western Front." *Graybeards,* September 1993.

Williamson, Col. John I. *Dearest Buckie, A Marine's Korean War Memoir.* Austin, Tex: R. J. Speights, 1989.

Wilson, Arthur W., and Norman L. Strickbine, *Korean Vignettes; Faces of War.* Portland, Ore.: Artwork Publications, 1996.

Wood, Capt. Ralph C. "Pickel Meadows." *Marine Corps Gazette,* October 1952.

INTERVIEWS AND LETTERS

Barret, Barney B., Louisiana

Broadhead, George, Califorinia

Bruce, Cpl. Bev, Illinois

Burrill, Pfc. Charles ("Chuck"), North Carolina
Champlin, S/Sgt. James, Michigan
Chenoweth, Theodore, California
Crosby, Cpl. Madison, Nevada
Davenport, Pfc. Howard, North Carolina
Ellis, Sgt. Jerry, Florida
Finn, Sgt. Robert, North Carolina
Gannon, Sgt. Robert, New Hampshire
Guidera, Richard T., Minnesota
Guertin, Cpl. Robert, Minnesota
Hall, Cpl. Robert A., New York
Hudson, Pfc. Luther, Missouri
Hunter, Capt. Clyde, California
Ingalls, 1st Lt. John ("Jack") F., Rhode Island
Janzen, Sgt. William H., California
Jervis, Sgt. Thomas, Rhode Island
Kennedy, Pfc. Tom, New York
Kreid, Sgt. Robert, Texas
Lipper, Sgt. Arthur III, California.
Little, G/Sgt. Jack, California
Luminello, Patrick, New York
MacDonnell, Dermott
March, Lt. Robert, Tennessee
McGuire, Sgt. Thomas P., New York
Meado, Jess E., Illinois
Miller, S/Sgt. Kenneth, New York
Montgomery, 1st Lt. Robert, Texas
O'Hagan, Sgt. John J., Illinois
Parlin, Sgt. Thomas C., Oregon
Rauh, Stan, California
Rogers, John, Georgia
Scholten, Cpl. L. L. ("Jack"), California
Walsh, Vincent, California

ACKNOWLEDGMENTS

As in any work of this magnitude, large numbers of people have contributed to its completion. Foremost are the Marines who fought the Outpost War in Korea. For the most part, their contributions are historically unsung and unacknowledged.

During my search for anecdotal material, I was able to contact a representative few. To them, I owe a special debt. This book could not have been written without their willingness to share memories, thoughts, and fears so that others can relate to those experiences. War leaves us all scarred, some more severely than others. For many, it requires courage to break open old wounds.

The men who fought in Korea have attitudes similar to those of the World War II generation. They remain proud of their service to their country during "their war" and stoically accept the fact that many people have forgotten what they did, if they ever knew in the first place. In this work, I attempt to open a few windows into that era and demonstrate that those men did indeed fight as hard as did the participants in other wars.

During my nine years of research, many people rendered extraordinary help and assistance. My wife, Marj, was always there with support, encouragement, and patience for the things that I ignored at home. The staff at the Marine Corps Historical Center in Washington, D.C., particularly archivist Fred Graboske and the active duty Marines who shuttled records from the National Archives, deserve recognition for their helpfulness and willingness.

Christine Weiss, my daughter and research assistant, helped to locate and copy material from the University of California, Los Angeles, Library, the National Archives, and the Marine Corps Historical Center. Jim Byrne, a veteran of the Chosin Reservoir and historian for the George 3/1 Association, read each chapter and the manuscript as a whole. An expert grammarian, he edited the work and shared his advice, arguments, and support. His contribution is particularly appreciated, and we became friends during the process.

My thanks also go to the people at Brassey's, particularly to Don McKeon, who believed that my manuscript was important enough to publish and worked with me to get it to the publication stage. I know that Don Jacobs and Julie Wrinn also worked particularly hard to edit my work. I have learned that it takes a lot of hard work to publish a book. The author is but a single small gear who must mesh with a great many others to produce an acceptable publication.

I am particularly grateful to Jay Karamales, the cartographer who worked with me on the maps. The endpaper maps were particularly difficult because he had to put them together from my original research maps on topographical sheets. The MLR and outposts are located precisely according to the original tactical overlays. Grid coordinates were taken from Command Diaries of the time.

Researching this work has been an especially gratifying personal privilege. In the process of gathering material, I have met hundreds of Marines. We have exchanged correspondence, talked on the telephone, met for lunch, and visited in one another's homes. Our families have become acquainted, and I am proud to say that many have become close friends. Amon those who deserve special acknowledgment are Chuck Burrill and Howard Davenport, the "Combat Lou" of Recon, who have become particularly fast friends and supporters; Bob Kried, the history buff from Texas; Arthur Lipper III, who shared his letters; Ted Chenoweth, my favorite professor and map reader; Bill Janzen, from Reno Block, "J.J." O'Hagan, literally a lifesaver on Combat Outpost (COP)-2; and Vern Sylvester, my former platoon leader in tanks. So many, many others called, wrote, encouraged, and contributed to the point that I was overwhelmed. They confirmed that, in fact as well as in motto, Marines do remain "Always Faithful."

There is a spiritual acknowledgment that must also be made. When I began this research, I had little in the way of religious beliefs; I was perhaps an agnostic or, at best, a spiritual neutral. After hearing and absorbing the experiences of these Marines and reflecting on my own small exposure to combat, however, I came to believe that survival could not be the accident that it seemed. For whatever purpose, Divine intervention had spared us to live, marry, produce children and grandchildren, and share experiences.

There was the Marine who, alone and under a severe barrage of incoming fire, felt an unknown hand push him to the bottom of a trench.

Moments later, fire exploded all around him, but his life was spared. And the sergeant, during his first assault under intense fire, clawed his way into the dirt and prayed for the courage to lead his men forward. His prayer was granted. Without fear, he rose and successfully led his men into battle.

Through a number of conversations with such Marines as these and many others, I was finally able to face my own beliefs and ultimately to accept Jesus Christ as my personal savior, a meaningful and totally unexpected outcome of this project.

INDEX

ABOUT THE AUTHOR

Lee Ballenger enlisted in the Marine Corps in 1951 at age seventeen. During his first year in the corps, he trained at Camp Pendleton, California, with the 3d Tank Battalion. On reaching his eighteenth year, he shipped out for Korea and arrived there in January 1953. After a brief period with the 1st Division Reconnaissance Company, he returned to tanks in time to participate in the Nevada Cities fighting at the end of March. Ballenger remained a tank crewman through the conclusion of fighting in Korea and then reenlisted for service at the U.S. Naval Base in Yokosuka, Japan, where he was a military policeman. He was discharged from the Marine Corps in 1957 as a sergeant.

After his discharge, Ballenger made his home in California, where he raised a family, followed a long career in law enforcement, and graduated from California State University, Los Angeles. In 1989, he retired from the Los Angeles County Sheriff's Department as a lieutenant. He resides in the Mojave Desert north of Los Angeles with his wife, Marj, a teacher.

In 1990 Lee Ballenger began to research and write a history of the Marines in Korea, 1952–53. The data grew so voluminous and the manuscript so large that he eventually split the work into two volumes. The first volume, *The Outpost War,* was published in July 2000 by Brassey's. This is the second volume of the series.